THE FOUNDATION CENTER'S

GUIDE TO

Winning Proposals

Sarah Collins, Editor

Acknowledgments

This guide reflects the contributions of many who participated in the project. I am grateful to Judi Margolin for her guidance in the planning and preparation of the book and her unwavering enthusiasm; to Margaret Morth for her unstinting assistance in all the stages of preparation; to Sara L. Engelhardt, Pattie Johnson, Nora Mandel, and Marilyn Hoyt for their invaluable work in helping to review the proposal submissions; to Alyson Tufts, Loren Renz, Claire Acher, Charlotte Dion, Anita Plotinsky, Pattie Johnson, Cynthia Glunt Bailie, Janet Camarena, Susan Shiroma, and JuWon Choi for their initial consultations; to Maureen Mackey, Rick Schoff, and Loretta Ferrari for constructive advice; and to Cheryl Loe and Christine Innamorato for their skill in designing the book. I'm also grateful to Marilyn Hoyt, Deputy Director for External Affairs at the New York Hall of Science, for her thought-provoking foreword.

—Sarah Collins

Library of Congress Cataloging-in-Publication Data

The Foundation Center's guide to winning proposals / Sarah Collins, editor.

      p. cm.

  ISBN 1-931923-47-7 (pbk. : alk. paper)

  1. Endowments—United States. 2. Research grants—United States. 3. Proposal writing for grants—United States—Case studies. I. Title: Guide to winning proposals. II. Collins, Sarah, date. III. Foundation Center.

  HV41.9.U5F67 2003

  658.15′224—dc22

                2003016616

ISBN 1-931923-47-7

Table of Contents

Foreword

One Fundraiser's Perspective

As long as human society has existed, there has very likely been fundraising. The sharing of resources, after all, is the best way to get something significant done for the common good. And this sharing always starts with asking.

Over the years I've kept a file of "earliest solicitations"—partly for fun, and partly for models and case statements that I might use in my own professional efforts. The earliest reference I've found comes from Lucius Annaeus Seneca. Born in 4 B.C., he wrote seven books on how to be a philanthropist. Here are a few of his pearls of wisdom:

"Give generously, but not indiscriminately. . . . Select carefully those worthy to receive your gifts. . . . Let judgment be used; for what is given in a haphazard and thoughtless manner will be prized by no one."

Perhaps most insightfully, Seneca recognized that every gift would not yield the hoped-for results. He urged donors to face reality, and not to be deterred by the fact that some benefactions will not fulfill their promise, and some will even fail.

After 1000 A.D., there was a long period of expansion in charitable activity, often related to the work of the world's great religions. The congregations and institutions of healing and learning developed vehicles for fundraising that we still use today. For example, the call for offerings during religious services has remained essentially unchanged over more than a millennium. Even when the language of fundraising is antique, its priorities resonate with our own. For instance, in 16th-century England, Sir Thomas Bodley established the great Bodleian Library and wrote, "A library needs a great store of friends; so go stir up other men's benevolence."

By the 19th century, charitable efforts expanded rapidly to include many educational and social service organizations. Booker T. Washington wrote in the 1880s, "I would say that I have but two rules for fund raising. First, always to do my whole duty regarding making our work known to individuals and organizations; and, second, not to worry about the results . . . In order to be successful in any kind of undertaking, I think the main thing is for one to grow to the point where he completely forgets himself; that is, to lose himself in a great cause."

Expansion of charitable institutions continued worldwide through the 20th century and into the new millennium. In 2001, the number of active foundations increased by more than 5,000, to nearly 62,000. According to *Giving USA*, in 2002 nonprofits raised $240.1 billion from foundations, corporations, and individuals. Based on estimates from the Foundation Center, foundations granted $30.3 billion of this support.

Such growth tells us that today, the generous individual may well institutionalize his or her giving by establishing a foundation—a structure that allows for support of particular donor values, provides capacity for maintaining giving through good times and bad, and can even provide the opportunity for giving beyond the length of an individual's lifespan.

Foundations are exceptional tools for turning vision and values into influential daily action. It is good news for our society that the rate of growth of foundation giving has far outstripped other sources of private philanthropic support for more than a decade.

Today, we find ourselves as fundraisers working to build relationships between our own charitable organizations and many foundations. Although our professional interactions with foundation staff and sometimes even foundation trustees is a productive part of this relationship, the proposal we send from our charity to the foundation will be the primary communication vehicle that generates funding. If we do our jobs well, funding based upon the mutual priorities of our charity and the foundation will continue long after we and the foundation staff with whom we work have moved on in our lives. This is the meaning of an institutional relationship.

How do we identify foundations that will be interested in our work? Fortunately, because of the federal government requirements for annual reporting, both our own charitable organizations and incorporated foundations are fairly transparent. In addition, some foundations state their priorities in written guidelines, annual reports, or on the Web. And, to speed our work, foundation activity is analyzed and presented in searchable formats by the Foundation Center.

With a wide assortment of print and electronic tools at our fingertips, we can identify which foundations are most likely to have priorities and giving patterns that make them good prospects for supporting the work of our organizations. Once we have our prospect list in hand, we are ready to prepare a proposal.

This act of proposing is most effectively done with a model to emulate—a successful example of succinct prose and budget information presented in a standard format that tells the story of need and our capacity to meet that need with the foundation's help.

The Best Proposal of All

It is a truism that the proposal most likely to bring us success in our next foundation solicitation is a version of the most recently funded proposal for the very same project sent to a similar foundation. So effective is this approach that we don't even think of it as a strategy. It's just our organization's "senior nutrition program proposal," the "music fellows proposal," or the "after-school club proposal." We should view these tried and true documents as "master proposals" written or rewritten most likely once every year, and revised very modestly when sent to each foundation prospect in order to address particular interests and requirements.

Each year the master proposal changes as the program itself is revised and improved. It provides both the basic text and core budget for each new proposal and the basis for final reports to our funders. It lowers our cost per dollar raised as we send it to one foundation after another with minimal revision. And it helps us present a consistent and substantial story of our work to our foundation partners and prospective funders.

But what about brand new programs? How do we craft a proposal to a foundation that is outside our normal field of operations and is really not familiar with our work? What if we are new to proposal writing? And what about those of us who have written proposals for years but would like to improve and learn from others' practices?

This book is a response to all these needs. It is a chance to study proposals that foundations have actually funded because they found them (and certainly the programs they describe) exemplary. And it provides models for those setting out to write a funding proposal for the first time.

How Important Is the Proposal Format?

Every field has its common ways of working, and proposal writing is no different. As foundations have formalized and professionalized their review practices, so we as fundraisers have developed common presentation formats that speed our work.

During the twelve years I worked as a grantmaker, I was always interested in how often an idiosyncratic proposal format signaled larger problems with a nonprofit applicant. The same poor work habits that yielded a lack of investigation into how proposals should be written would often be duplicated in a lack of networking with colleagues in the field. Such nonprofits might be planning to replicate the work of others without even realizing it, because they are isolated from colleagues. Or they might be inventing a response to a problem about which much is already known, and for which others have already determined the best ways to make an impact. In the worst instances, they might have assumed that no one was doing anything like the program they're describing, thus closing the door to becoming a mature, able organization with the capacity to learn from others and to convert that learning into enhanced service and even leadership in accomplishing their mission.

There is a standard format upon which to build an effective proposal. It is the format for a master proposal that you'll find in *The Foundation Center's Guide to Proposal Writing*. It can be used whenever prospective funders have not already set forth their own format or guidelines. You'll see in the sample proposals included in this book that a common presentation logic is usually at work, with components often arranged in this order:

- Proposal summary—brief information about the request, the need, the program responding to the need, and our charitable organization.
- Need statement—supported by facts and/or statistics.
- Objectives—succinct statement of what it is we intend to accomplish.
- Program description—critical details on the program that respond to the need identified, including what is to be done, for whom, by whom, and most important, how and when.
- Evaluation—specifics on how we and the funder will know how well we accomplished what we set out to do.
- Budget—a realistic portrayal in dollars and cents of what the program will cost, including both projected expenses and revenue.

Many, but not all, of the proposals in this book follow this general outline and include the component parts listed above, though not always called by the same names or in the same order. Flexibility is key, of course, when it comes to choosing the preferred way to "sell" our program to a prospective funder. And some funders require use of their own application forms, which may differ considerably from this outline.

Use of Sample Proposals

The proposals included here are not valuable because they represent great writing. Rather they represent strong program logic and crisp, readable communication, presented in a standard format to funders who ultimately responded favorably to them.

While we don't mean to suggest that any one of us will raise an extra dime for our charities by copying these proposals verbatim and sending them off to a long list of prospective foundations, we find samples helpful, nonetheless, in organizing our own thinking about how to write about the needs our organization perceives, and the ways we are responding to them.

When I am writing a funding proposal from scratch in a situation where I don't have a good in-house master proposal to build upon, I often think about the different ways a good model would help me to organize my thinking and save me time. It is for me and proposal writers like me that the Foundation Center has gathered together this compendium of sample proposals, not to copy but to emulate.

Mining the Work of Others

Right now, three of us at the New York Hall of Science are working on an $850,000 expansion proposal to be submitted to the Kresge Foundation. The Kresge staff represents the gold standard of proposal review in the area of capital funding, and its guidelines give us everything we need to know in order to make our case for funding.

Monies from many different sources are key to completing our project. Such diverse funding also provides a way for us to demonstrate the broad community support we are receiving. My colleagues at the Brooklyn Children's Museum have just completed a Kresge-funded expansion project. As part of their proposal submission I know that they also took advantage of the opportunity to demonstrate diverse funding streams. A copy of their successful proposal will help me think about how to tell this important part of our story. I won't hesitate to ask them for it.

With such a massive investment in expansion, we hope the Kresge Foundation program officer will be interested in our strategic plan. We have a wonderful 140-page plan, but we realize that the foundation staffer will not have the time to read it all. I remember seeing a one-page overview of a three-year proposal for program and facility staff expansion at the Summit (NJ) Area YMCA that a colleague of mine submitted a few years ago. (This proposal was so effective, in fact, that you'll find it included in Chapter Four in this book.) Reviewing the excellent work my colleagues did in articulating a multiyear, multiprogram expansion will help me tease out the key, interlocking components of the Hall of Science's plan in order to present it on a single page.

While I am at work on these two pre-proposal writing chores, one of my co-workers at the Hall of Science is busy making contacts to identify sample proposals that include sections on science and education program expansion.

The Proposal As a Fundraising Tool

By now it seems clear that others' proposals can serve as tools for helping us think about how we will tell the story of the need we've identified and our organization's response. At the same time, others' proposals can be helpful by providing sample timelines, spreadsheets, budgets, or different approaches to formatting, all of which we can use in our own writing.

But that's as far as it goes concerning the usefulness of proposals crafted by other writers. Someone else's proposal cannot really influence how we help a particular grantmaker to recognize our program as important enough to fund right now. Creating this sense of urgency and importance is our job with every master proposal we write. It is our challenge to gather data and real-life anecdotes that clearly illustrate the need our charity has identified. And it is our job, if the opportunity arises, to sit down with the project director and her staff to elicit all the details needed for a thorough and comprehensive presentation of our organization's plans.

If we find that we cannot write several paragraphs or pages (in the case of a full-scale proposal) articulating the need and our programmatic response, then the problem is likely not one of writing, but one of clear thinking about what our organization does, and why. Problems of weak program focus often emerge during proposal writing. This is a much bigger concern than proposal writing. It relates directly to our ability to achieve our missions.

Proposal writing—and reading proposals written by others—makes us more effective fundraisers and contributes to better-run organizations. By demanding a proposal submission that requires our careful thought about why we do what we do, what the costs per service are, and how we evaluate our outcomes, foundations force us to continuously refine our efforts. Take a look at the proposals in this book with this perspective in mind. See how focused they are in linking need to program in a responsive way, while projecting costs that will appear reasonable to the thoughtful grants decision maker.

Budgets Are Important Too

Grantmakers who have participated in interviews for the first three editions of *The Foundation Center's Guide to Proposal Writing* make one important point over and over. Budgets receive a careful reading, and they are often the first part of the proposal a decision maker looks at. But fundraisers all too often compose them as an afterthought.

If the budget describes our program in a numerical fashion, then it is critical that it tell the same story as our proposal's prose. The proposals in this book provide an opportunity to check out the ways in which this parallel presentation—in numbers, and in program description—looks when it is done well.

A Collaborative Approach Is Best

In this brief foreword I've talked about how I often ask colleagues to share successful proposal samples with me. No one needs to tell you that fundraising is highly competitive and that foundations receive many more proposals than they can possibly fund. Given these realities, it might seem an odd sort of request to make of a colleague. But think again: Because the information on foundations is so very accessible and because it is a rare foundation, indeed, that chooses to dedicate its entire annual support to just one charity, we can relax in the knowledge that sharing our successful proposals with each other will only help make the process better for all. In other words, being generous in this way won't cost our organization a single grant dollar! So, ask your colleagues for model proposals and freely offer to share those with which you've achieved success. Just as in this book, you can remove the bits that invade the privacy of your organization or staff, and still have a fine sample to pass along to a colleague.

Good luck with proposals that succeed in the future!

Marilyn Hoyt
Deputy Director for External Affairs
New York Hall of Science
September 2003

Introduction

Why issue this guide? In assisting the Foundation Center's library users, we receive one request repeatedly: "Where can I find sample proposals?" While crafting the proposal is an essential step in the grantseeking process, almost everyone approaches this task with trepidation, probably in part because most new fundraisers rarely have the chance to see an actual proposal that has been funded. Some fundraisers aspire to write the perfect proposal. There's no such thing. However, excellent proposals are drafted every day by experienced fundraisers as well as new grantseekers. This book provides many samples that you can learn from, by sharing a number of outstanding proposals that were funded by the grantmakers who agreed to share them with us.

Many people worked to bring this book to fruition. Beginning in 2002, the Foundation Center approached grantmakers, asking them to share proposals that they thought were excellent, and that they had funded. We sought to collect a variety of types of proposals, ranging from simple letters of inquiry or basic support requests to complex multiyear special project requests. We aimed to include proposals submitted to large national or international foundations as well as small, locally oriented ones. The grantmaking community responded graciously to our call for proposals. From the dozens of submissions we received, we selected 20 full proposals and four letters of inquiry for inclusion in *The Foundation Center's Guide to Winning Proposals*. To the extent possible, we have reprinted the full proposals in their original form. We also asked each funder who ultimately responded favorably to provide brief commentary about the strengths and weaknesses of each proposal. And the grantmakers we talked to were very candid in their assessments. You will find the proposals in this guide to be as varied as the grantmakers who funded them.

What does it take to write a successful proposal? It takes thorough knowledge of your organization and its program, a concise writing style, attention to detail, common sense, empathy for the reader, and perhaps most importantly, evident passion for the project to be funded. The commitment and enthusiasm that are demonstrated in the proposal are major factors in getting the project funded.

Though proposals take many forms, most have certain elements presented in a standardized way. The variety of proposals in this book proves that different writers can succeed by customizing their proposals once they've mastered the basic techniques. One can think of the grant proposal as a recipe: in order to achieve the desired result, all the ingredients must be included. If something's left out, the final product won't be quite right.

Nancy Wiltsek, Executive Director of the Pottruck Family Foundation, states, "For us, the proposal is just the beginning of the conversation." Grants decision makers study the proposal with keen interest for what it reveals about the need for the project, the staff, and the budget, but rarely will they make a determination on a grant request merely on the basis of the proposal itself. The proposal is just a tool—a handy vehicle for communicating to the grantmaker all the information he or she needs to make a decision.

The new proposal writer has many resources to call upon, including *The Foundation Center's Guide to Proposal Writing*, by Jane Geever. In that book, the basic elements of the master proposal are explained. *The Guide to Winning Proposals* may be viewed as a companion piece that compliments *The Foundation Center's Guide to Proposal Writing*. A number of regional associations of grantmakers have designed common application forms, and these documents, available through the Foundation Center's Web site (www.fdncenter.org), are useful tools for learning how groups of funders expect requests to be presented, in what format and sequence. Refer also to the Selected Resources on Proposal Development at the end of this guide for other excellent tools on the topic.

While this book is designed to offer examples that will help improve one's proposal writing skills, each successful proposal we've included is very specific to the project and/or organization it describes. The first part of the book is comprised of eight chapters that feature a particular type of proposal or type of support request. Each chapter is organized alphabetically by the name of the organization that submitted the proposal. We've also included two additional chapters: one that presents cover letters, and another that displays proposal budgets. When asked to do so by the nonprofit organization or the funder, we removed or masked confidential or personal information, replacing those details with this image: XXXXX. Since it isn't practical to include every single appendix and/or attachment submitted with each proposal, we've been selective, and in some cases, have simply listed the attachments that accompanied the proposal.

The Foundation Center is highly indebted to the grantmakers and nonprofit organizations represented in this book for their generosity in sharing these proposals. We consider them to be pioneers in their willingness to participate in this project.

Sarah Collins
Manager of Bibliographic Services
The Foundation Center
October 2003

List of Contributors

The following grantmakers participated in the preparation of this book by generously contributing the proposals that they admired. Some submitted multiple proposals for our consideration. In addition, they graciously took the time to provide thoughtful and perceptive commentary on the proposals. We are very grateful for their collaboration on this project.

Grantmakers

Karen Topakian, Executive Director
Agape Foundation
San Francisco, CA

Nina B. Mogilnik, Senior Program Officer
Altman Foundation
New York, NY

Laura H. Gilbertson, Director
William Bingham Foundation
Rocky River, OH

Lara Galinsky, Vice President, Strategy
Echoing Green
New York, NY

Charles H. McTier, President
Lettie Pate Evans Foundation, Inc.
Robert W. Woodruff Foundation, Inc.
Atlanta, GA

Judy C. Walruff, Ph.D., Former Senior Program Officer and Director of Grants Management
Flinn Foundation
Phoenix, AZ

Lani Wilkeson, Secretary and Senior Program Officer
Frist Foundation
Nashville, TN

Allison McGee Johnson, Senior Communications Manager
Rick Jung, Senior Program Officer
Gill Foundation
Denver, CO

Nancy Kami, Executive Director
Lisa and Douglas Goldman Fund
San Francisco, CA

Dorothy Fleisher, Program Director
W.M. Keck Foundation
Los Angeles, CA

Penelope McPhee, Vice President and Chief Program Officer
The John S. and James L. Knight Foundation
Miami, FL

Sandra M. Ambrozy, Senior Program Officer
Kresge Foundation
Troy, MI

Michael Feller, Senior Vice President
J. P. Morgan Chase Foundation
New York, NY

Elan D. Garonzik, Program Officer
Charles Stewart Mott Foundation
Flint, MI

Maria Mottola, Executive Director
New York Foundation
New York, NY

Dick Matgen, Program Officer
Srija Srinivasan, Program Officer
Peninsula Community Foundation
San Mateo, CA

Nancy Wiltsek, MNA, Executive Director
Pottruck Family Foundation
San Francisco, CA

Kristin A. Pauly, Managing Director
Prince Charitable Trusts
Washington, DC

We also wish to thank the following nonprofit organizations and consultants for graciously allowing us to share their successful proposals:

Nonprofit Organizations

Pennee Bender, Associate Director
American Social History Productions, Inc.
New York, NY

Miyoko Sakashita, Founder and Program Director
Bay Area Regional Exchange and Development
Berkeley, CA

Rev. Jeff Carr, Executive Director
Bresee Foundation
Los Angeles, CA

Randy Parent, Executive Director
California Alumni Association
Berkeley, CA

Mark J. Holleran, Chief Executive Officer
Central Arizona Shelter Services, Inc.
Phoenix, AZ

Amy Brown, Director of Program Planning
Community Food Resource Center, Inc.
New York, NY

Jody Mahoney, Development Director
CompuMentor
San Francisco, CA

Dr. Deanna B. Marcum, President
Council on Library and Information Resources
Washington, DC

Sister Diane Donoghue, Executive Director
Esperanza Community Housing Corporation
Los Angeles, CA

Matthew Lee, Esq., Executive Director
Fair Finance Watch
Bronx, NY

Toni Blackman, Artistic Director/Founder
Freestyle Union
Washington, DC

Marc V. Buro, President
Lake Drive Foundation for Deaf and Hard of Hearing Children
Mountain Lakes, NJ

Paul Kaine, Executive Director
Nashville Ballet
Nashville, TN

Joseph Interrante, Ph.D., Executive Director
Nashville CARES
Nashville, TN

Jack Doyle, Executive Director
New Settlement Apartments
Bronx, NY

Alan J. Friedman, Ph.D., Director
Marilyn Hoyt, Deputy Director for External Affairs
New York Hall of Science
Queens, NY

Joanna Micek, Development Associate
New Yorkers for Parks
New York, NY

Kathleen F. Teodoro, Former Executive Director
NPower Michigan
Detroit, MI

Robert F. Wooler, Executive Director
Rhode Island Youth Guidance Center
Pawtucket, RI

Caroline Fisher, Executive Director
Karen Miller Wood, Director of Development
San Francisco Court Appointed Special Advocate Program
San Francisco, CA

Jen Collins
San Francisco Reclaim May Day
San Francisco, CA

Timothy G. Weidman, President and Chief Executive Officer
Summit Area YMCA
Summit, NJ

Tina Bartolome, Co-Director
Underground Railroad
Oakland, CA

Jane A. Lefferdink, Executive Director
United Cerebral Palsy Association of Santa Clara/San Mateo Counties
Mountain View, CA

John R. Curtis, Jr., President
Virginia Museum of Fine Arts Foundation
Richmond, VA

Tanya Neiman, Director
Volunteer Legal Services Program of the Bar Association of San Francisco
San Francisco, CA

Andrew Smiles, Chief Financial Officer
VolunteerMatch
San Francisco, CA

Linda Thieben, Director, Fund Development
Westside Children's Center
Culver City, CA

Consultants

Caroline Harris
Development Consultant
Gardiner, NY

Paulette Long
Senior Consultant
Not-For-Profit Grant Writers
New York, NY

Lynn Rothstein, Ph.D.
Former Executive Vice President
Echoing Green
New York, NY

1

Special Project: Single-Year

The proposals in this chapter are requests for funding of special projects. These grants support discrete projects within the organization. These projects are for new programs or new aspects of ongoing programs that the organization needs funding to initiate or continue. The proposals in this chapter all cover a one-year period. Special project support covers a wide variety of grant projects, from program development to short-term projects, to education initiatives, to technology enhancements for the organization.

Special project support is attractive to foundations for a number of reasons. Often the ideas presented are new (at least to the organization planning to implement them or to the audience that will benefit) or innovative. And since the projects are "special," they typically are time delimited, with fixed start and end dates, making it relatively easy for the funder to disengage at some point in the future.

The eight proposals in this chapter include requests ranging from $1,500 to $125,000, and are all for single-year funding. Other than that, they vary tremendously, since each special project is unique.

Bay Area Regional Exchange and Development (BREAD) of Berkeley, California, applied to the Agape Foundation for support in the amount of $1,500 for its Local Currency Project. This program offered an innovative exchange of time and labor for goods or services. Its aim is to retain economic power within the community.

CompuMentor in San Francisco, California, submitted a proposal for $50,000 to the Peninsula Community Foundation for funding the Bay Area Services Initiative to supply technology services that would benefit 20 small organizations in nearby communities. This technical assistance project involved computer installation as well as training.

Nashville CARES in Nashville, Tennessee, requested a grant from the Gill Foundation for $15,000 that would support two projects, RainbowEDGE and Brothers United. Both of these projects were HIV-prevention education programs for gay and bisexual men.

New Settlement Apartments, Bronx, New York, sought funding in the amount of $50,000 from the New York Foundation for support of a community revitalization project focused on parent organization and education reform in a local community school district. The strategic approach adopted by New Settlement Apartments was cited as a model program by both academic and community-based institutions.

New York Hall of Science in Queens, New York, requested $125,000 from the Altman Foundation for the Early Childhood Science Initiative, a plan to create a model program for science education for the youngest museum visitors. The project was a collaboration with the Brooklyn Children's Museum.

New Yorkers for Parks applied to the New York Foundation for a $45,000 grant to pay the salary of a community organizer, a new staff position. This individual's mandate would be to create and advocate for an agenda to enhance several neglected neighborhood parks in the city.

Rhode Island Youth Guidance Center in Pawtucket, Rhode Island, sent a proposal to the William Bingham Foundation seeking $25,000 to expand a pilot project in family mediation. The program assisted adolescents and their parents with counseling, prevention programs, and school-based services.

Underground Railroad of Oakland, California, asked the Agape Foundation for a $1,500 grant to support a community mural project entitled Know Justice, Know Peace. The project was designed to involve local young people in painting the mural, and it was intended to remain as a permanent installation outside the Youth Empowerment Center.

A Proposal From

Bay Area Regional Exchange and Development (BREAD)

Berkeley, California

To

Agape Foundation
San Francisco, California

Requested amount: $1,500; **Amount received:** $1,500

Funder's comments:

"At the Agape Foundation, we ask each grantseeker to complete a cover sheet that includes not only contact information, but also their organization's mission and the purpose of the grant. All of the components were present in the proposal, and the description of their educational and organizing program, and their organizational history, were the most well-developed sections. This proposal was a joy to read in both form and content. It was easy on the eye, didn't use jargon, and made its points clearly and simply. The budget was presented in a clear and concise manner.

"The strongest feature of the application is the quality of the writing. The proposal read beautifully and sparked the reader's interest by elegantly presenting this creative project. The attachments were useful; they included copies of their newsletter and a few news clips about the organization. The news articles highlighted the value of the currency for real people.

"Our board of trustees always returns to the grantees with questions regardless of the quality of the proposal. At least two board members as well as the staff review each proposal. After a board member reviews a proposal s/he completes a brief questionnaire for use in the evaluation process, and this includes any questions they might have for the grantee. These questions were generated by the board review: What is the diversity, age, and class of the staff? How do you define middle- and low-income? The only way to improve this proposal would be to include the grant amount and purpose in the cover letter."

—*Karen Topakian, Executive Director, Agape Foundation*

Notes:

The complete proposal included the following attachments: organization newsletter and news clippings.

Proposal written and submitted to the funder by Miyoko Sakashita, Founder and Program Director.

AGAPE FOUNDATION BOARD OF TRUSTEES GRANTS
FALL 2001

Grant applicant, please type or print clearly.

Name of organization project: **BREAD** *Local Currency*

Mission/Focus of organization and year of founding:
Bay Area Regional Exchange and Development (BREAD) encourages proactive solutions to community needs left unmet by the global economy. BREAD provides education and tools to promote ecologically sustainable, community-based economics. As a grassroots organization, BREAD promotes self-reliance and builds connections for a healthy community.

Founded in 1997.

Purpose of grant:
For support of BREAD's work educating and organizing for economic justice and providing local currency as a tool for change that work toward building an ecologically sustainable local economy.

Organization budget: $ 24,500

Project budget: $ 8,000

Grant amount requested:$ 1,500

Contact person with name, address, telephone number, e-mail address and website:
Miyoko Sakashita, Founder and Program Director
or Dina Mackin, Project Director
PO Box 3973, Berkeley, CA 94703 (*Visit:* 1920 Martin Luther King Jr. Way, Berkeley)
Phone: 510-644-0376   *Email:* miyoko@breadhours.org   *Web:* www.BREADHOURS.org

---

To be filled out by Agape (Do not write below this line.)
Granting history with Agape:

Comments:
____Budget too large ___Location ___Organization 5+years old

1st review by:_____ Accept_____ Reject___

___Other comments. If reject, why:

2nd review by:_____ Accept_____ Reject___

___Other comments. If reject, why:

July 23, 2001

Karen Topakian
Agape Foundation
1095 Market Street, Suite 304
San Francisco, CA ; 94103

Dear Ms. Topakian,

Bay Area Regional Exchange and Development (BREAD) is a community-based organization that aims to empower Bay Area residents to assuage economic injustice. BREAD operates a local currency system for the Bay Area. Local currencies are powerful tools for economic change because they force money and wealth to stay within the region—revitalizing the local economy.

In a healthy economy, all members of the community are able to meet their needs in a sustainable manner. The dominant modern economy based on globalization and monoculture has created mass unemployment, environmental destruction, and the disruption of long-standing cultural practices. BREAD seeks to address this problem through public education, organizing, and sustainable community development based on local self-reliance and community-building.

We're printing our own money called BREAD HOURS! Our membership consists of 500 individuals, locally-owned businesses, and community organizations. These local residents use BREAD Hours to exchange goods and services, such as carpentry, computer assistance, legal help, yard work, arts & crafts, plumbing, childcare, tutoring, and nearly anything else you can imagine. By hiring our neighbors we are building community and self-reliance. Local currency creates jobs and provides a way to learn and improve skills. BREAD is a unique organizing tool that brings together Bay Area residents in a proactive campaign against economic injustice.

BREAD local currency is valued in HOURS and it is backed by labor and trust. By denominating our money in hours we celebrate and value everyone's labor equally. When you exchange BREAD, your work is more meaningful because it also benefits the whole community. One of BREAD's guiding principles is that everyone in the community is valuable and has skills that benefit the community — even people who are usually ignored by the centralized economy.

Moreover, BREAD local currency is completely controlled by the community, decisions about circulation, distribution, etc. are made cooperatively by those that participate in the program. The Bay Area is an ethnically and economically diverse region, BREAD's membership represents a cross-section of the community. Our globalized economic system makes civic participation nearly impossible. For individuals and communities to have influence in political and economic arenas, we need small-scale models where people know and care about one another.

While dollars seep out of our community, BREAD HOURS stay home and continue to build wealth, trust, and self-reliance within our region. BREAD strives to bridge gap between what we *earn* and what we *need* to exist financially. I am grateful for the opportunity to introduce you to our work and I hope that you will find BREAD's local currency project to be within the scope of your granting program. Thank you for taking the time to review our enclosed proposal.

Most Sincerely,

Miyoko Sakashita
Founder & Program Director, BREAD
miyoko@breadhours.org

PLEASE NOTE our new phone number and office:

510-644-0376 • 1920 Martin Luther King Jr. Way, Berkeley

BERKELEY REGION EXCHANGE AND DEVELOPMENT · P.O. BOX 3973 · BERKELEY, CA 94703

BREAD LOCAL CURRENCY PROJECT

Mission Statement

Bay Area Regional Exchange and Development (BREAD) encourages proactive solutions to community needs left unmet by the global economy. BREAD provides education and tools to promote ecologically sustainable, community-based economics. As a grassroots organization, BREAD promotes self-reliance and builds connections for a healthy community.

BREAD's Philosophy of Social Change

Economic globalization is one of the greatest threats to biological and cultural diversity. There is a need for a nonviolent, proactive approach that counters the impacts of globalization. We need to foster bold regional economies that are accountable to the environment and allow for local culture to flourish. A healthy sustainable economy is one that benefits the entire community (both human and non-human). A local economy should preserve both ecological and cultural diversity and integrity. We envision a society that celebrates economic justice where people participate in the decisions that affect their lives. BREAD strives to establish an alternative model to the global economy.

Description of Project

We're printing our own money in the Bay Area called BREAD HOURS!

How it Works...

BREAD is a local paper money, in denominations of HOURS (valued at $12 federal currency). We publish a quarterly directory, *BREAD Rising,* of goods and services that are available in exchange for local currency. The directory also has informative articles on issues of economics, community, and sustainability. Members keep the newsletter close at hand so they remember to hire their neighbors and reinvest in their community. BREAD organizes the community from the grassroots through education and participation in our local currency system.

Local currency provides the community with a tool for social change — putting our community in control of the local economy.

Why not just use dollars?

Since 1 HOUR of BREAD = $12, we're raising the hourly wage, this benefits workers, and businesses too. BREAD reminds us that wealth comes from labor, and that everyone deserves fair pay. With better hourly income, people are better able to afford locally-made goods, locally-grown food and other local services. That means more local people can start businesses, or simply trade skills and services that they like to do.

We meet new people while trading locally, and expand a friendlier economy. BREAD is money with a boundary around it, staying here forever, not going overseas to exploit workers of other countries, or cause ecological harm. The dollar binds us to a finance system that could damage our local area. The dollar is constantly depreciating in value, while local money is always 60 minutes.

Local money is a good organizing tool, a great way to raise awareness about the necessity of local trade and community reinvestment. BREAD is not providing services to clients, but rather it is a grassroots initiative that engages people in creating their own local economy and community. Local currency builds community. Trading in BREAD is FUN!:

Goals
BREAD's overall goals are:

To demonstrate a model for alternative economics that promotes localization, justice, democracy, and ecological sustainability. We strive to build a foundation for a local economy that benefits the community. BREAD's long-term goal is to create a sustainable local economy—an economy based in place. We envision a regional economic system that functions in harmony with the environment and empowers those who have traditionally been disenfranchised. In collaboration with other non-profit organizations we hope to plant roots for a sustainable Bay Area.

To educate the public, locally and nationally, about the social and environmental impacts of the present economic model. Our economy, based on an assumption of unlimited growth and consumption, is at odds with the natural world and it encourages worker exploitation. Moreover, it functions in a way that drains resources and wealth from poor and ethnic neighborhoods. There's a need for a shift toward a place-based economy that provides all people with meaningful work and the preserves the ecology of the region. Integral to creating a healthy local economy is building a community that is well-informed on issues of economic justice and alternatives. BREAD aims to encourage people to take action and become engaged in critical campaigns and projects.

To provide inspiration, information and assistance to other towns that wish to experiment with economic justice efforts such as local currency projects. Other groups that are working to cultivate alternative economies may need support and assistance from BREAD. We hope to act as a clearinghouse, helping other communities with creative grassroots initiatives while respecting the different solutions that may arise in a world of many cultures and varying ecosystems.

BREAD's Education and Organizing Program

BREAD is seeking funds for general support or our community education and organizing program. The goals of this project are to broaden the diversity of our organization, give people information and tools that will empower them to take action, and to engage people in the local currency program to strengthen and revitalize our local economy. BREAD will develop workshops on economic justice and the global economy.

BREAD has already begun to develop a workshop curriculum on economic issues and alternatives. The workshop is intended to be participatory and educational. It aims to engage people in their communities to take action and become involved in community efforts to assuage economic injustices. This workshop debuted in late April at the Annual Skillshare Conference in Berkeley. We already have arranged to present the workshop at few other conferences and meetings. However, we still want to develop a comprehensive plan to hold the workshop in more diverse forums, including: church groups, schools, community centers, and so on. As a grassroots organization that relies heavily on volunteers we would like to develop the workshop into a curriculum and train volunteers/organizers to hold workshops in their own neighborhoods. By training community volunteers to hold the workshops we hope to provide them with leadership skills. This program will require volunteer management, training sessions, and producing a kit of materials for each of the "organizers."

A grant from the Agape Foundation could pay for the production and publication of the workshop kits for organizers. A grant would also boost our capacity to manage volunteers. Moving our organizing project from its curriculum stage to providing us with tools to begin organizing in Bay Area neighborhoods.

Request

BREAD would like to request $1,500 from the Agape Foundation in support of our work educating and organizing for economic justice and providing local currency as a tool for change that work toward building an ecologically sustainable local economy.

Project History

While there are many organizations that have campaigns to expose the injustices of our economic system, there are few that have proactive models for an alternative economic system. BREAD is among the most successful local currency systems in the United States. BREAD is in a unique position to organize the community around these issues because we can offer an alternative to the unjust economic model. Local residents can become directly involved in a program that attempts to reinvent community economics.

BREAD launched its local currency project in 1997 to contribute to the movement against economic globalization. It began with 25 members that began exchanging goods and services. In the last four years the local currency project has grown to have 500 members. The BREAD local currency project has grown and been nurtured for the last five years by a volunteer organizing committee. In 1999, we coordinated a local food program that included building organic gardens for low-income families. BREAD has led a successful education program about globalization and economic justice. This program included a local, national, and international media advocacy campaign and numerous public speaking engagements.

Specific achievements in 2000 include: hosted two major events (a barter fair and a winter craft sale); rewarded BREAD grants to community organizations (see grantee list); added several new businesses to our roster; presented at various conferences such as Bioneers; featured in local and international media (*Bay Area Business Woman, KPFA, Nikkei* "Japan's *Wall Street Journal*", etc.); published *BREAD Rising*; consulted other local currency organizations (Kuriyama, Japan; Edmonton, Canada; Mendocino, CA); and maintained our membership program.

BREAD's members represent a cross-section of the general Bay Area residents. BREAD's program is focused in the San Francisco Bay Area. Economically, most participants are in the low and middle-income range and we have representation from a diversity of ethnic backgrounds. As our program matures we want local currency to fill the gap between the income people *earn* in dollars and what they *need* to exist financially, in our area. BREAD is a social justice organization that encourages members of all ages, ethnicities, gender, and sexual orientation. Moreover, we want to cultivate diversity in our staff, constituency, and advisory board.

BREAD is a grassroots organization that is open and democratic. Major policy decisions are made by the members at bi-monthly Council Meetings. Decisions are made by consensus. BREAD has a staff of five that work collectively. One is half-time and the others are dedicated volunteers.

BREAD is a project of the International Society for Ecology and Culture (ISEC). ISEC works with communities around the world strengthening cultural self-respect and community, local and regional economies, while also encouraging sustainable development approaches. ISEC is a non-profit organization with 501 (c) 3 tax-exemption status from the Internal Revenue Service. BREAD and ISEC share an office in downtown Berkeley, California.

Fundraising Plan and Sources

BREAD has implemented a broad range of fundraising strategies (grant seeking, direct mail, house parties, events, and personal solicitations). BREAD's primary goal in development is to sustain and build the capacity of BREAD by increasing donations, income, and grants. BREAD will apply for at least ten grants per year.

BREAD's membership fees are a long-sustaining source of income. However, low-income members may arrange work trades in lieu of membership fees. We will continue our annual direct mail fundraising plea to continue to build our donor base. We have a plan to increase advertising income from our newsletter. Two BREAD events per year will all act as small benefits for the organization.

BREAD will, of course, continue to use local currency whenever possible. And organizational expenditures of BREAD HOURS will remain within the policy of no more than 25% over and above that issued to members. Moreover, the old adage says that "a penny saved is a penny earned." BREAD is improving its infrastructure so that we can build our capacity to work with more volunteers and interns.

We will plan ways of integrating new fundraising strategies into our development program. Avenues that we intend to explore include: planned giving, workplace giving, selling publications and t-shirts, consulting services to other local currency groups, seeking no-cost training and organizational management support, etc.

In general, BREAD's program is outside of the scope of many traditional funding sources.

Major Funding Sources (2000 & 2001):	*Foundations with applications pending*
East Bay Community Foundation (donor directed) $8,000	Foundation for Deep Ecology
Foundation for Deep Ecology...................$3,000	Common Counsel Foundation
Foundation de Sauve $5,000	CS Fund
Center for Community Futures....................$500	Tides Foundation
	Cottonwood Foundation

Advisory Board

Jerry Mander, International Forum on Globalization
Jerry Mander is the president of the IFG, an alliance of 60 organizations in 20 countries providing public education and campaigns on global economic issues. He is also the program director for the Foundation for Deep Ecology, and is a senior fellow at Public Media Center, a non-profit advertising company working only for environmental and social causes. His books include *Four Arguments for the Elimination of Television* (1977), *In the Absence of the Sacred* (1991), and *The Case Against the Global Economy And For a Turn Toward the Local,* co-edited with Edward Goldsmith (1996). He holds a graduate degree (MS) from Columbia University's Business School in international economics.

Helena Norberg-Hodge, International Society for Ecology and Culture
Helena Norberg-Hodge is a leading analyst of the impact of the global economy on diverse cultures around the world. She is founder and director of ISEC, which runs "resistance and renewal" programs on four continents aimed at strengthening cultural self-respect and community, local and regional economies, while also encouraging resistance to the global consumer culture. She is the winner of the Right Livelihood award—also known as the alternative Nobel prize—for her 20 years of devotion in Ladakh (also known as little Tibet), where ISEC has worked with local people to find alternatives to conventional development based on the region's ecological and cultural foundations. She is the author of numerous articles and books including the international classic, *Ancient Futures: Learning from Ladakh*, which together with an award-winning film based on the book, has been translated into over 30 languages.

Weyland Southon, KPFA Radio
Weyland Southon co-directs the apprenticeship program at KPFA Radio. KPFA's Apprenticeship Program teaches radio production and engineering to people (especially youth) from many cultural, social, political and ethnic backgrounds. The program is intended to remedy discrimination and create equality for those who have been under represented in media. He is the producer of the radio show, Seven Generations. He has also worked as the Director for CSA West (Community Supported Agriculture) a project of the Community Alliance for Family Farmers.

Patrick Archie, Urban Seed
Patrick Archie is the founder of Urban SEED. A program that is providing employment, job training, and family nutrition through its gardens for homeless and low-income residents of the former Alameda Naval Air Station. Urban SEED empowers urban communities by helping to build the capacity and provide resources for community based re-development that is economically viable, ecologically sound, and helps communities to meet the needs of all of their members.

Timothy Huet, Center for Democratic Solutions
Tim Huet is an attorney providing legal and consulting services to worker cooperatives through the non-profit Center for Democratic Solutions. The Center for Democratic Solutions is a nonprofit corporation providing technical support and educational services to worker cooperatives, with a focus on northern California. He is also the Personnel Liaison for the 140 worker-owners of Rainbow Grocery Cooperative and a member on the support staff of the Association of Arizmendi Cooperatives, a chain of cooperative bakeries.

BREAD Grant Program

BREAD aims to promote economic justice, ecological sustainability, community building, food security and diversity. Unlike the centralized economic system, BREAD aims to build a healthy local economy that nourishes community and nature. For this reason BREAD allocates a portion of local currency as grants to community groups. BREAD grant decisions are made at Council Meetings that are open to all members. In general, BREAD supports groups and individuals that directly benefit the local community. While we may grant to a broad range of projects, we would like to focus on the following priorities: economic empowerment and justice; ecological agriculture and community food security; resistance and dissent; housing and health; self-reliance and community economics (built to nature's scale); ecology and biological diversity; cultural, ethnic, and economic diversity.

The Ecology Center, Berkeley, 1997

The Ecology Center coordinates Berkeley City's curbside recycling program and farmers' markets. They also have a bookstore and library. BREAD was granted to reward volunteers for their help remodeling the Ecology Center.

Alliance for Democracy, Berkeley, 1997

The Alliance for Democracy helps progressive groups in the Bay Area network. They used the grant to rent a venue for an information fair on progressive issues.

New Village Public Charter School, Oakland, 1998

New Village Public Charter School is an elementary school that strives to give children a balanced education by involving students, parents and teachers in curriculum development. This grant was given to the school to pay for group facilitation consultations.

New Village Journal, Berkeley, 1998

The New Village Journal is a new publication by Architects, Designers and Planners for Social Responsibility. It is a magazine that focuses on sustainability and ecologically sound planning. Grant awarded to help ADPSR hire BREAD members to help with editing and other administrative work.

Berkeley Earth Day, Berkeley, 1999

Berkeley Earth Day is the annual celebration of Earth Day at Civic Center Park in Berkeley. It consists of a parade, music and entertainment, farmers' market, information, crafts, and food booths. BREAD grant was given to Earth Day volunteers. BREAD also was given a booth at the event.

Sustainable Agriculture and Nutrition Education, Albany, 1999 & 2000

The SANE farm is a student and volunteer operated farm on nearly an acre of land in Albany. They grow organic produce for homeless soup kitchens, like Food Not Bombs, and local schools. SANE teaches sustainable agriculture classes. Grant was awarded to SANE to help them hire carpenters, gardeners, grant writers and other labor.

Peralta Hacienda After-school Program, Fruitvale, 2000

The Peralta hacienda After-school Program serves youth though a bicycle program that trains youth to build, repair and safely ride bikes. The program also maintains a garden and nursery to teach youth about ecology and agriculture. Other projects include art, history, and creek restoration. BREAD's grant was used to put a new roof on the free community bike shop.

City Slicker Farm, West Oakland, 2000

The City Slicker Farm aims to provide the residents of the neighborhood with affordable, ecologically-grown produce (and hire some of them to work on the farm too). The farm was awarded a grant to hire labor to clear and develop the land, the first step of this important community food security project.

Rose Street House of Music, Berkeley, 2001

Rose Street House of Music is a completely volunteer-run house concert and workshop space. Their grassroots musical community center features women singers and songwriters. A BREAD grant will assist their concert series this year.

Destiny Arts Center, Oakland, 2001

Destiny Arts Center is a youth organization that incorporates arts education and violence prevention for youth ages 3-18. Participants build confidence, leadership skills, and self-esteem through dance, martial arts, theater, outdoor education, and more. The programs teach young people to become violence prevention/arts educators and community activists with skills to promote peaceful solutions to violence. A BREAD grant will provide general support to the center.

Fiscal Year 2000

Staff

Administrative Coordinator (1/4)	XXXXX
Outreach Coordinator (1/4)	XXXXX
Development Director (1/2)	XXXXX
Other Staff (4 volunteers)	In Kind
Payroll Taxes	500

Total 8,000

Office Expenses

Phone	100
PO Box	50
Web & Email	200
Postage	150
Copies	300

Total 800

Newsletter & Outreach Materials

Printing	7,000
Postage	300
Currency	1,000

Total 8,300

Events

Location	300
Publicity	50
Food & Entertainment	50

Total 400

Development

Direct Mail	2,500
Benefits	0
Consultation	0
Staff Training	0

Total 2,500

Total Expenses **$20,000**

Assets

Grants	3,000
Memberships	1,500
Donations	3,000
Ad Sales	100
Earned Interest	400
Balance from Previous Year	25,000

Total Assets $33,000

Projected Budget Fiscal Year 2001

Staff

Administrative Coordinator (XXXXX%)..........................XXXXX

Other Staff (4 volunteers) ....In Kind

Total...XXXXX

Office Expenses

Rent... 1,200

Phone 100

PO Box 50

Web & Email.. 200

Postage... 150

Copies 300

Total.. 2,000

Newsletter & Outreach Materials

Printing 7,000

Currency 1,000

Total.. 8,000

Events

Location.. Free

Publicity... Barter

Food & Entertainment.. Barter

Total.. 0

Development

Direct Mail... 2,500

Benefits 0

Consultation..Pro bono

Staff Training ....In Kind

Total.. 2,500

Total Expenses.. $24,500

A Proposal From
CompuMentor
San Francisco, California

To
Peninsula Community Foundation
San Mateo, California

Requested amount: $50,000; **Amount received:** $50,000

Funder's comments:

"The Peninsula Community Foundation (PCF) requires a letter of inquiry before the proposal, so PCF staff was aware of the general intent of the project before it actually received the proposal. That said, the cover letter was a good synopsis of the amount of funding requested, how it would impact PCF's funding area, and a general description of the project. CompuMentor provided all the information requested by our guidelines. The anticipated outcomes were clear and measurable, including one outcome that will measure client satisfaction. In addition, CompuMentor was careful to demonstrate how the grant would impact clients in our geographic funding area, even though the project encompasses a much wider area. But, CompuMentor was careful not to include a lot of extraneous information.

"The proposal's strongest feature is that it followed PCF's guidelines to the letter. It answered questions in the order they were asked so the information flowed and made the foundation program officer's work much easier. It made a convincing case for its project and facilitated the program officer's due diligence. PCF found the needs assessment included in part 3 of the proposal compelling.

"Because of our commitment to strengthening nonprofits' infrastructure and our awareness that funding for technology is often difficult, CompuMentor's project seems well suited to address a real need in the nonprofit community. The writing style is good, although that is not usually a significant concern on the part of our foundation staff. I typically request a simple project budget; this budget was exactly what I expected, and the same is true of the agency budget. The attachments were clear and easy to understand and read."

—*Dick Matgen, Program Officer, Peninsula Community Foundation*

Notes:

The complete proposal included the following attachments: project timeline, project budget, agency operating budget, list of other sources of support, audited financial statements, Form 990, and list of current board members with their affiliations.

Proposal written by Valeria Perez-Ferreiro, Grantwriter, and Bennett Grassano, Associate Development Director; edited by Jody Mahoney, Development Director; and submitted to the funder by Jody Mahoney and Mark Liu, Program Director, Consulting Services.

COMPU MENTOR

March 6, 2002

Mr. Richard Matgen
Program Officer
Peninsula Community Foundation
1700 South El Camino Real, Suite 300
San Mateo, CA 94402

Dear Dick,

We respectfully submit a request for $50,000 to help fund our Bay Area Services initiative, which will assist 20 small non-profits in San Mateo and Northern Santa Clara Counties in planning and implementing information technology systems that will enhance their capacity to serve their clients and to report on outcomes.

CompuMentor's Bay Area Services initiative will address the Peninsula's gap in technology implementation consulting services by providing Network Installation, Scheduled Support, Database Planning, Database Implementation, and Implementation Support Services, including basic technical planning, mentor matching, and technology information and referral services through our TechSoup/Bay Area program. The services, collaborations, and synergies created will benefit not only the 20 direct-service recipients, but will also have an impact the local non-profit sector, and other service providers

We appreciate the Peninsula Community Foundation's ongoing support for CompuMentor and look forward to our continued collaboration. Thank you for your time and consideration.

Sincerely,

Jody Mahoney
Development Director

Mark Liu, Ph.D.
Program Director

435 BRANNAN STREET SUITE 100 SAN FRANCISCO, CA 94107 TEL: 415 512 7784 FAX: 415 512 9629
E-MAIL: realperson@compumentor.org www.compumentor.org www.techsoup.org

Special Project: Single-Year 15

CompuMentor Proposal to the Peninsula Community Foundation
Bay Area Services Initiative

1. <u>Proposal Summary</u>

CompuMentor respectfully requests $50,000 to provide a suite of technical support services known as the Bay Area Services initiative, enabling 20 small non-profit organizations (ranging in size from $100,000-$1,000,000) in San Mateo and Northern Santa Clara Counties to effectively use technology as a tool in program management and evaluation. The program timeline is April 1, 2002 through March 31, 2003.

Most non-profits struggle with a variety of technical needs. Database planning and development is the most crucial of these needs, because it is central to a non-profit's ability to track and report on client outcomes. It is also the most challenging, due to a shortage of high quality, low cost technical support services available to non-profit organizations in the Bay Area.

CompuMentor's Bay Area Services initiative will address the unmet technical needs of selected non-profits by providing services in Network Installation, Scheduled Support, Database Planning, Database Implementation, and Implementation Support Services, including basic technical planning, mentor matching, and technology information and referral services through our TechSoup/Bay Area program.

2. <u>Organization</u>

CompuMentor is a San Francisco-based non-profit founded and incorporated in 1987 to act as a bridge to the information age for schools and organizations serving low-income communities. During its fourteen-year history, CompuMentor has updated itself multiple times. While we have always maintained our core mission to assist non-profits and community based organizations use technology to better accomplish their mission, the programs and services we have provided in support of our mission have changed over this period.

In our early days, we matched volunteers (mentors) with non-profits needing technical assistance. We then added our software program in which new, but unneeded, software was re-distributed to non-profits and schools. We then turned to circuit riding, technology planning, and other forms of consulting, in which we provide direct assistance to non-profit agencies. Finally, our newest major program is TechSoup, a non-profit technology website, where we help non-profits everywhere access technology-oriented information and resources. Our 2001-2002 annual budget is $5.1 million.

During its life span, CompuMentor has served over 2,000 non-profits with hands-on services; distributed discounted software to over 6,000 organizations; and provided over 165,000 online information and referral sessions to non-profits via TechSoup, our technology portal program.

3. <u>Project Description</u>

The Bay Area is one of the largest non-profit hubs in the United States. There are 7,138 non-profits in San Mateo and Santa Clara counties alone (See Attachment 1). A study commissioned by the Packard Foundation, *First Map: Exploring the Market for Consulting Services in the Bay Area,* found that most consulting services were in the area of computers and technology. Eighty percent of non-profits hired consulting help, but those with smaller budgets were less able to afford it. Computer consulting was the most difficult type of help to find and was, therefore, the area with the

3/6/02   Page 1

**CompuMentor Proposal to the Peninsula Community Foundation
Bay Area Services Initiative**

highest unmet demand. The high cost of consulting was identified as the primary reason for not contracting services.

CompuMentor's research indicates that most non-profits struggle with technology needs ranging from everyday network and PC support, to database planning and development. Moreover, non-profits are so busy on mission-related tasks that they often allocate too little time and attention to coherent planning, development and support of computer systems. As a result most have computer systems that are piecemeal, including a collection of donated and purchased software and equipment, obtained one-by-one as needed. This in turn limits their ability to use technology as a management tool.

Technology is a cornerstone of effective non-profit management. Databases, networks, and Internet connectivity are essential to program evaluation, client management, donor-constituent relations, fundraising, as well as advocacy and research-activities that inform and ensure continuous program improvement. CompuMentor proposes to help small non-profits with limited resources plan and implement effective uses of technology, so as to improve their capacity to deliver and track effective services. CompuMentor will accomplish this goal by providing partially subsidized technology and implementation consulting services and by providing information on best practices and referral to high quality consultants through TechSoup/Bay Area, a non-profit information technology portal.

Through the establishment of the Bay Area Services initiative, CompuMentor intends to bring implementation consulting and support services to scale, to provide technology planning consulting services to those small non-profits that lack an adequate technology plan, and to help non-profits gain access to low-cost, high quality technology consultants. The services we provide will allow non-profit organizations to get the office systems, databases, local area networks, and Internet connectivity they need at sustainable and affordable cost from CompuMentor and other reputable service providers.

CompuMentor proposes to address the unmet technology needs of small non-profits through the following suite of services:

Network and Infrastructure consulting, through which CompuMentor will:
- Manage the Implementation of the Project
- Set up LANs, gateways, routers, Internet access, firewalls, DSL, printers.
- Set up e-mail services, print services, file servers, backup, security, WANs, remote access, Virtual Planing Networks
- Install and upgrade PCs and Macs
- Provide training for the accidental techie
- Provide limited amounts of post-installation support
- Focus on Windows and Macintosh networks and systems.

We will expect the agencies with which we consult to have a current technology plan. If they do not have one, we will ask them to use our Technology Planning services.

Database Planning and Consulting
CompuMentor will offer small non-profits database planning consulting at affordable rates. The process will encompass technology assessment; database needs discovery; and database plan development. CompuMentor will empower non-profits to take ownership of the planning process,

3/6/02 Page 2

**CompuMentor Proposal to the Peninsula Community Foundation
Bay Area Services Initiative**

increasing their capacity to communicate their database needs to vendors, foundations, board members and other stakeholders.

We will focus on client management databases and fundraising databases, the most commonly requested databases by our clients. Consultation is expected to require from 5-10 days, with the average being 5 days. We plan to discount the service up to 60% from market rate.

Database Implementation Consulting

After we help develop an organization's database plan, they may decide that a custom-built database is the best answer for them. CompuMentor will offer a Database Implementation Consulting service to help them:

- Manage the implementation project
- Select database tools
- Develop a data dictionary from the Database Plan
- Develop an interface prototype
- Implement the database, scripts, reports, and screens
- Document the design usage and maintenance of the database
- Convert existing data
- Install the database
- Train users of the database
- Establish maintenance procedures for the database

The scope of database implementation projects is variable, with an average project lasting 20 days.

Scheduled Support Consulting

One of the greatest unmet needs among Bay Area non-profits is low-cost maintenance and support. CompuMentor plans to provide: (1) preventative and corrective support covering network and infrastructure items; and (2) special arrangements which allow for emergency fixes. We also plan to identify and use a toll for remote diagnosis and repair of Windows-based systems that will allow our Scheduled Support staff to accomplish much of their work remotely.

Clients will need to designate a computer "savvy" person who will be the primary contact, and agree to maintain a technology asset inventory.

Technology Planning Consulting

CompuMentor will provide agencies with budgets under $1,000,000 with technology planning consulting services if they lack an adequate technology plan. Indeed, a consequence of doing implementation work without an adequate technology plan is that the work may be incorrectly specified, unsupported by other needed changes, unmanageable, or unsupportable. In order to assist these organizations, our staff people will:

- visit the non-profit to assess its technology resources and needs;
- make recommendations based on budget and capacity;
- write a comprehensive technology plan outlining priorities, costs, and resources.

Technology plans are heavily subsidized. CompuMentor typically charges a client $500 for a plan that costs $2,500.00.

CompuMentor Proposal to the Peninsula Community Foundation
Bay Area Services Initiative

Volunteer Mentoring

CompuMentor matches individual non-profits with volunteer mentors who help them with discrete technology problems, ranging from de-bugging single computer to fixing a network problem; these mentoring matches may last up to three months. Mentors are also available free of charge through thrice-yearly service days, which are one-day events focusing on training and software installation.

TechSoup Bay Area

TechSoup/BayArea will address the difficulties local non-profits have in finding and selecting qualified service providers by providing information and referrals through its web portal focusing on Bay Area resources. TechSoup/Bay Area will provide a single point of entry through which individuals in non-profit organizations can find the discounted equipment, software, services, and quality consultants. The portal includes a customer-rating feature that allows non-profits to comment on the quality of service for the various technical assistance providers as well as message board that will allow clients to exchange messages with each other. The site also highlights best practices in the area of technology. We will train their clients how to increase their own self-sufficiency by using the resources on TechSoup/BayArea.

4. Geographic Area of Service

CompuMentor will launch its Bay Area Services initiative in approximately 20 small non-profits from Daly City to Mountainview, CA. The number of nonprofits served will depend on the services needed—for example, database implementation is a more difficult task than system administration activities.

CompuMentor has an established presence in the area served by the Peninsula Community Foundation, having worked with nonprofits in San Mateo and Santa Clara Counties since its inception. CompuMentor has worked with 341 non-profits in San Mateo County and with 481 in Santa Clara, matching them with volunteer mentors. CompuMentor also has an ongoing presence in the community through its biweekly print newsletter, Connect, through a biweekly electronic newsletter, ByTheCup, and through TechSoup.

5. Outcomes

CompuMentor will identify 20 small ($100,000-$1,000,000) non-profit clients in San Mateo and Northern Santa Clara Counties, in need of at least one of the technical services outlined above. Some of the non-profits may have already received other gateway CompuMentor services, such as Mentor Matching or Technology Planning Services, prior to requesting implementation consulting services.

Identification will occur a variety of ways: specific requests for our services; referral through other partners such as technical support organizations, foundations; referral from Peninsula Community Foundation; and contacts made during the official Spring 2002 rollout of the Bay Area Services Initiative. Recruitment will be ongoing during the duration of the grant. Service delivery will be provided between April 1, 2002 and March 31, 2003. Evaluation will be conducted between December 2002 and March 31, 2003.

CompuMentor Proposal to the Peninsula Community Foundation
Bay Area Services Initiative

- CompuMentor will provide implementation consulting services to 20 small non-profits in San Mateo and Northern Santa Clara Counties.

- 15 of the clients will be new clients as a result of the above outreach, and five will be existing or prior clients whom CompuMentor has previously assisted.

- CompuMentor will provide at least 5 clients with database planning and implementation services (at an average length of 20 hours per project). These clients will demonstrate an increase in the ability to track evaluation criteria, outcomes, demographic data, and other elements important to the agency.

- Six clients served will receive Network and Infrastructure Consulting. Each project will last 20 hours on average.

- Five clients will receive ongoing Scheduled Support Consulting (at an average of 5 hours a month per client) during the course of the grant.

- CompuMentor will help at least 5 clients develop a Technology Plan prior to providing implementation consulting services. All clients will have access to mentor-matching services as needed.

- 15 clients will report a satisfaction rate of average or above with the services received though this grant.

6. Evaluation and Assessment

Our evaluation plan is two-pronged. At the onset of implementation, we will administer a survey to measure customer knowledge of technical support and the services that will be provided. At the conclusion of each consulting engagement, CompuMentor will provide a questionnaire designed to measure our service delivery processes in order to continuously improve the quality of our services.

Upon completion of individual projects, we will ask customers to complete a customer satisfaction survey. The survey will ask questions about satisfaction with the project and probe interest in other service areas. We expect that 75% of customers will rate our service delivery as satisfactory or better. CompuMentor will also track and report on the number of hours spent on each project.

Our evaluation plan also includes a long-range summative component that will help determine whether the services delivered actually improved our clients' capacity to effectively use technology. CompuMentor will administer a customer feedback survey in December 2002. Through this survey we will capture short-term outcomes such as gains in technical knowledge, increase in technical skills, etc. However, CompuMentor is interested in assessing our longer-range outcomes, particular our ability to impact an agency's core work. To this end, CompuMentor will hire an evaluator who will assess the long-range impact of the project. It is our plan to have at least preliminary results available by the end of February, 2003, for inclusion in our final report to the Peninsula Community Foundation.

CompuMentor Proposal to the Peninsula Community Foundation
Bay Area Services Initiative

7. Agency and Staff Qualifications

Since its inception, CompuMentor has provided hands-on work with the non-profit organizations to help them develop their computer systems. Over the last 14 years, CompuMentor has developed a suite of non-profit computer consulting services that include technology planning consulting for small and midsize organizations and consulting for larger scale technology projects. Through this project we intend to use our experience and track record to help non-profits shepherd their technology plans through to implementation. To accomplish this goal we will leverage the expertise of our staff and that of our partner organization, NPower, a national implementation planning technical assistance provider.

CompuMentor now has 57 staff members. It is an unusual staff and worthy of note. We have dedicated young people with superb computer skills who come to us from digital divide 'peace corps' type projects like TeamTech and from universities across the country. We also have seasoned staff people who have decided to move from the private to the non-profit sector.

Phil Ferrante-Roseberry, our executive director, came to us from Amdahl and PG&E where he was an information systems engineer. Dr. Mark Liu, Program Director, will spearhead this program effort. He holds computer science degrees from MIT and UC Berkeley, and came to us from the Java development team at Sun Microsystems. A full listing of our remarkable staff can be found at <http://www.compumentor.org/about/staff.html>.

Daniel Ben-Horin founded CompuMentor in 1987 and serves as the organization's president. He holds a degree from the University of Chicago and spent his early career as a journalist. He has reported for the New York Times, co-founded the New Times in Phoenix, directed Media Alliance in San Francisco, and was an early leader in the 1st online community at The Well.

8. Collaboration

While there are a large number of non-profit-oriented technical assistance providers in the Bay Area, none of them provides a full spectrum of services. Moreover, some individual agencies have very narrow foci, focusing on very specific missions or localities. CompuMentor itself currently provides the broadest spectrum of technology specific services in the Bay Area, including San Mateo and Northern Santa Clara Counties.

There is a significant shortage of providers of Implementation Consulting and Maintenance Support. For instance, one of the few providers of implementation consulting services for non-profits, the Management Center, recently discontinued their practice in this area. The shortage in implementation services becomes all the more acute because good resources are now available for technology planning. Thus, Bay Area organizations find themselves with well-planned implementation projects, but have difficulty finding inexpensive, non-profit-attuned implementers. Part of the current demand for technology consulting is met by high-priced, for-profit consultants and consulting companies. Small non-profits, however, can scarcely afford these services.

Through a partnership with Seattle-based NPower, a national technical assistance provider in the area of technology implementation, and as the Bay Area NPower affiliate, CompuMentor has developed a suite of services that addresses the lack of quality, low cost implementation consulting and support

**CompuMentor Proposal to the Peninsula Community Foundation
Bay Area Services Initiative**

services in the Bay Area. Tapping into NPower's existing expertise will allow us to quickly and inexpensively create an ancillary set of implementation consulting services that will link with CompuMentor's existing Technology Planning consulting practice. This collaboration will allow us to serve a greater number of non-profits sooner than we would have been able to on our own. Discussions are also under way to collaborate with other technical assistance providers, such as Compass Point, the Management Center, and Wired for Good.

The Bay Area Services initiative will be highly collaborative, building synergies that will benefit non-profits beyond those receiving direct services, technical assistance providers, and consultants. Through TechSoup/Bay Area, CompuMentor provide a forum for non-profits to share best practices and resources. Indeed, CompuMentor will disseminate its consulting methodologies through this medium. Finally, TechSoup/Bay Area's information and referral component will enhance the non-profit sector's capacity to access low-cost and high-quality technology consulting services.

CompuMentor Proposal to the Peninsula Community Foundation
Bay Area Services Initiative

9. Project Timeline

	Year 1: Qtr 1	Year 1: Qtr 2	Year 1: Qtr 3	Year 1: Qtr 4
Staffing	• Hire Consulting Manager • Create new department • (See other hires below)	• (See other hires below)	• (See other hires below)	• (See other hires below)
Infrastructure		• install client management system		• Begin evaluation of first year
Service Days	• Hold Virus Vaccination Day/South Bay	• Hold 2nd Service Day		• Hold 3rd Service Day
TechSoup/ BayArea	• Obtain additional funding for TechSoup/BayArea • Hire TechSoup/BayArea Coordinator • Build TechSoup/BayArea	• Launch initial TechSoup/BayArea	• Fill out content of TechSoup/BayArea	• Hold technical assistance providers meeting
Technology Planning	• Transfer Technology Planning Staff • Update methodology for larger clients • Roll-out extended service		• Hire Technology Planning consultant	
Network & Infrastructure Implementation	• Hire network consultant • Design service • Pilot service	• Complete pilot • Evaluate pilot and revise service	• Roll-out service	• Hire network consultant
Scheduled Support		• Hire Support consultant • Pilot service	• Complete pilot • Evaluate pilot and revise service	• Roll-out service
Database Planning	• Complete pilot • Hire Database consultant • Evaluate pilot and revise service	• Roll-out service		
Database Implementation		• Design service • Pilot service	• Complete pilot • Evaluate pilot and revise service	• Roll-out service

	Year 2	Year 3	Year 4
Staffing	• Hire 2nd consulting manager • Hire 3 consultants	• Hire 2 consultants	• Hire consultant
Infrastructure	• Set up testing lab	• Open Silicon Valley Office	
Consulting	• Grow consulting to 175 projects and 10,700 hours	• Grow consulting to 200 projects and 13,300 hours	• Grow consulting to 235 projects and 15,600 hours
Service Days	• Hold 3 Service Days	• Hold 3 Service Days	• Hold 3 Service Days
TechSoup/BayArea	• Hold technical assistance providers meeting	• Hold technical assistance providers meeting	• Hold technical assistance providers meeting

**CompuMentor Proposal to the Peninsula Community Foundation
Bay Area Services Initiative**

10. Sustainability

CompuMentor plans to fund the Bay Area Services effort through a combination of philanthropic support and fees from consulting services. The Bay Area services initiative will derive a substantial portion of its income from fee-for-service consulting. In the first year of the project 32% of revenues will be derived from consulting. That percentage will increase to 75% by year 4.

In order to offer consulting services at reduced rates, CompuMentor must also obtain philanthropic support. Microsoft has committed $250,000 in matching funds for 4 years. The Soda Foundation and Stulsaft Foundation are also current supporters. Other foundations that have been approached include the Packard Foundation, Haas Jr. Fund, and East Bay Community Foundation. Current and prospective corporate donors include Wells Fargo Bank, Symantec, Schwab, and Compaq.

CompuMentor Proposal to the Peninsula Community Foundation
Bay Area Services Initiative

ATTACHMENT A: Bay Area Services Initiative Project Budget for FY 2001-2002

Income

Client Fees	210,000	
Foundation Grants		
Peninsula Community Foundation	50,000	
Haas Foundation	10,000	
NPower	50,000	
Total Income		**$320,000**

Personnel		
Salaries	234,163	
Fringe Benefits	46,833	
Subtotal Personnel		**$280,996**

Expenses

Accounting	500	
Advertising	1,000	
Bad Debt		
Bank Fees		
Client Equipment Purchases		
Dues, Fees and Subscriptions		
Education and Training	8,000	
Equipment		
Insurance	2,155	
Interest		
Legal		
Licenses & Permits		
Meals & Entertainment		
Outside Services	5,000	
Office Supplies	5,540	
Payroll Tax	9,315	
Postage		
Printing	4,000	
Rent		
Repairs		
Taxes		
Telecommunications	2,400	
Travel and Lodging	5,000	
Utilities		
Subtotal Expenses		**$42,910**
Total Expenses		**$323,906**

**CompuMentor Proposal to the Peninsula Community Foundation
Bay Area Services Initiative**

ATTACHMENT B: Agency Fiscal Year 2001-2002 Budget

Income

Service Derived Income

Client Supported Services	$1,168,200
Foundation Supported Services	$915,000
Product Distribution Fees	$2,550,000
Total Service Derived Income	$4,633,200

Donations

Sponsorships	$230,000
Grants	$1,627,000
Individual Donations	$5,000
Total Donations	$1,862,000
Total Income	$6,495,200

Expenses

Accounting	$4,600
Advertising & Public Relations	$2,000
Bad Debt	$1,000
Bank Fees	$36,100
Client Equipment Purchases	$19,000
Dues, Fees & Subscriptions	$24,200
Education & Training	$39,020
Employee Benefits	$277,833
Equipment	$58,250
Equipment Leasing & Rental	$5,000
Insurance	$53,374
Interest Expense	$100
Legal	$53,000
Licenses and Permits	$500
Meals & Entertainment	$ 25,660
Office Supplies	$44,690
Outside Services	$857,500
Payroll Tax	$214,045
Personnel Expenses	$23,000
Postage	$101,950
Printing	$65,700
Rent Expense	$171,120
Repairs & Maintenance	$15,000

**CompuMentor Proposal to the Peninsula Community Foundation
Bay Area Services Initiative**

Salaries	$2,835,031
Taxes	$1,000
Telecommunications	$73,600
Travel and Lodging	$106,120
Utilities	$32,000
Total Expenses	**$5,140,393**
Net Profit/(Loss)	$1,354,807
Increase to Fixed Assets	$93,000
Increase to Grants Receivable	($248,470)
Increase to Cash Reserves	$1,510,277

**CompuMentor Proposal to the Peninsula Community Foundation
Bay Area Services Initiative**

ATTACHMENT C: Other Sources of Support

Year 1 Income Analysis			
Source	**Service Area**	**Amount**	**Status**
Income			
Client Fees		$ 284,100	
Local Foundation and Corporate Support			
Wells Fargo Bank	Mentor Service Days	$ 15,000	Committed
Symantec, Schwab, Compaq	Mentor Service Days	$ 55,000	In discussion
San Francisco Foundation	Systems Administration (Workforce development)	$ 25,000	Committed
Miranda Lux Fdtn, Sun Microsystems, Inc., The Ahmanson Fdtn, Vodafone, Levi Strauss	Systems Administration (Workforce development)	$ 65,000	In discussion
Grants for the Arts	Technology Planning	$ 25,000	Committed
Valley Fdtn, Fleischaker Fdtn, Zellerbach Fdtn, Bank of America, Yih Fdtn, Soda Fdtn, Arillaga Fdtn, Stulsaft Fdtn	Technology Planning	$ 50,000	In discussion
San Francisco Fdtn, East Bay Community Fdtn, Community Fdtn of Silicon Valley, Peninsula Community Fdtn, other previous funders	Technology Planning	$ 35,000	Re-submissions planned
Cal Endowment, SF Fdtn, Haas Jr. Fund	TechSoup/BayArea	$ 60,000	In discussion
Packard Foundation	General Support	$ 15,000	Proposal submitted (Amount is 15% of total)
Total Local Foundation and Corporate Support		$ 345,000	
Npower/Microsoft Support		$ 250,000	
Total Income		$ 879,100	
Total Program Expenses		$ 878,562	

A Proposal From
Nashville CARES
Nashville, Tennessee

To
Gill Foundation
Denver, Colorado

Requested amount: $15,000; **Amount received:** $15,000

Funder's comments:

"This was a really good grant request: clear, concise, and simple. Nashville CARES showed they understood their community and were able to express their knowledge in clear terms. They were not afraid to show us their internal picture—and they provided all requested materials. We were particularly impressed with their financials; they were understandable and gave us everything we needed to fully understand their financial position as well as their support base.

"We strongly value organizations willing to show us the complete picture—deficits (if you have them) and all. The financials show who you are; your willingness to share the details allows us to better assist in making the right decision. The cover sheet allows us to readily see that the proposal is complete, and we can refer to specific sections more quickly as we do our work reviewing the request.

"There is just the right amount of information in the history and purpose section. We do not need to know what has happened every year since the founding of the organization—just a general historical perspective. On the other hand, the recent accomplishments section could have been stronger. They might have led off with the fact that the program they are applying for had won a local award in their community, rather than leaving that important item for the end of the paragraph. The project summary appropriately focused on Nashville CARES' prevention programs, not other aspects of the organization's work.

"The need and purpose section is a wonderful lead-in to the actual grant request: clear, simple, easy to understand, *and* compelling. The description of project activities is marvelous! It clearly lets our program officer know what the goals are—not just in numbers of people, but also by an indication of the diverse community being served, as well as the outcomes of the programs. This section gets a gold star!

"We don't need a research report from applicants, because our program officers are already familiar with the areas they are reviewing. The use of footnoted references was not necessary. If we don't know the latest things happening in a funding area, we'll ask about this in a site interview.

"The outcomes section is simple, verifiable, and measurable. This gives us something to work from in any future requests for repeat funding as we assess the organization's progress in meeting their objectives. Nashville CARES didn't promise more than they could do, and they gave us a realistic depiction.

"The staff list is important to us, and this one provides a good amount of information. We liked the fact that the list focused on the program staff and volunteers actually working on this particular project.

"The expenses component of this program budget is very clear. The math is correct (yes, we do check). It clearly indicates that the request fits within our guidelines. The income side of the budget (Program Funding) could have been improved by initially doing the math for us (but, yes, it all adds up)."

—*Rick Jung, Senior Program Officer, Gill Foundation*

Notes:

The proposal was written using the Gill Foundation format and guidelines. The complete proposal included the following attachments: organization's budget, project budget, newspaper clippings, most recent audited financial statement, description of fundraising activities, list of other donors, IRS tax-exempt letter, list of board members, "Computer Privileges and Responsibilities" statement, and "Policies of Non-Discrimination and Inclusion."

Proposal written by Joseph Interrante, Ph.D., Executive Director and submitted to the funder by Doug Hoekstra, Grants Specialist.

nashville
CARES!

May 22, 2001

Ms. Katherine Pease
Executive Director
The Gill Foundation
2215 Market Street, Suite 205
Denver CO 80205

Dear Ms. Pease:

Nashville CARES respectfully requests your consideration of a grant in the amount of $15,000, to support our RainbowEDGE and Brothers United HIV prevention education programs for gay and bisexual men. These are the only HIV prevention programs designed, respectively, by and for gay/bisexual men and gay/bisexual men of color in Middle Tennessee.

Nashville CARES is Middle Tennessee's leading nonprofit community based AIDS service organization, and the year 2000 commemorates our fifteenth year of continuous service. Our mission is to promote and participate in a comprehensive and compassionate response to HIV disease through community education for increased understanding and prevention of HIV transmission, advocacy for responsible public policy, and services that improve the quality of life for people living with HIV disease and their families.

A copy of our proposal, along with requested attachments, is enclosed. If you need further information, please feel free to contact our Executive Director, Joseph Interrante, or me at 615-259-4866. I can be reached via e-mail at dhoekstra@nashvillecares.org. On behalf of the clients, volunteers, Board, and staff of Nashville CARES, I thank you for your consideration.

Sincerely,

Doug Hoekstra
Grants Specialist

209 tenth avenue, south • cummins station • suite 160 • nashville, tennessee 37203 • v.615.259.4866 • f.615.259.4849

community AIDS resources, education, and services since 1985 • http://www.nashvillecares.org

GILL FOUNDATION – 4/25/01

Cover Page including:

Applicant Organization Name: Nashville CARES

Name of Person Submitting Proposal: Doug Hoekstra, Grants Specialist

Lead Contact and Title of Organization: Joseph Interrante, Ph.D., Executive Director

Organization Address, Phone, Fax, and E-mail: 209 Tenth Avenue South
Cummins Station, Suite 160
Nashville, TN 37203

615-259-4866 (phone)
615-259-4849 (fax)

dhoekstra@nashvillecares.org
www.nashvillecares.org

Dollar Amount Requested: $15,000.

Total Operating Budget: $2,629,871.

Total Project Budget: $132,611.

TABLE OF CONTENTS

Narrative

Outcomes and Evaluation

Statement of Challenges / Weaknesses

Description of Key Staff

Board of Directors

Community Leader Contacts

Letters of Collaborative Intent

Testimonials, Articles

Financial Information

Copy of IRS Determination Letter

Policy Statements re: Software Piracy and Non-discrimination

1. Brief Narrative on Purpose and History of Organization and Project, including Mission Statement, Recent Accomplishments, Need to be Addressed, and Summary of Project.

History and Purpose of Organization –

Nashville CARES is Middle Tennessee's leading nonprofit community based AIDS service organization (ASO). **CARES' mission is to promote and participate in a comprehensive and compassionate response to HIV/AIDS through community education for increased understanding and prevention of HIV transmission, advocacy for responsible public policy, and services that improve the quality of life for people with HIV/AIDS and their families.**

Like most ASOs nationwide, CARES was founded in 1985 by a group of HIV-infected and HIV-affected volunteers who recognized the need for community education about this emerging epidemic and for social services to help those living with HIV/AIDS survive with independence and dignity. CARES has addressed the challenges of HIV/AIDS without interruption since that time, expanding and diversifying its services and programs to meet the growing and changing configurations of the regional epidemic. Today, on an annual basis, CARES provides or brokers a full range of direct services to 1,300 men, women and children with HIV disease and their families and educates more than 50,000 adults and youth who live in the thirteen-county region surrounding and including metropolitan Nashville.

Client Services include individual and group counseling, case management, housing and financial assistance, a food pantry and home meals delivery, volunteer-provided practical support with daily tasks, outpatient substance abuse treatment, transportation, dental assistance, insurance continuation, nutrition and treatment education, and social activities. Education Services include awareness education; targeted prevention programs for African Americans, alcohol and drug using populations, the incarcerated, gay/bisexual men, women, and youth; agency and workplace training; and materials distribution. All services and programs are provided free of charge.

Recent Agency Accomplishments –

CARES is recognized locally and nationally as a mission-focused and accountable agency. Since 1996, three CARES programs (CARE Teams respite support, CARE-a-van Cuisine meals delivery, and Brothers United prevention education for gay/bisexual men of color) have been finalists for the prestigious *Frist Foundation Awards of Achievement*. The awards honor local nonprofits for innovative program development and management, creative coordination of staff-volunteer partnerships, and cost-effective production of mission-focused results. For nine consecutive years, an agency volunteer has been a finalist for Nashville's *Mary Catharine Strobel Volunteer of the Year Award*. This year, Brothers United won the award for volunteer group.

Nationally, Sista2Sista, our prevention education program for African American women, has been studied by the *Centers for Disease Control and Prevention (CDC)* as a "reputationally strong" program serving communities of color. The coordinator for Brothers United serves as a CDC consultant on program development for African American men.

Nashville CARES participates in a variety of inter-agency initiatives designed to maximize the potential of the non-profit sector. These include a unique "back office" collaboration among seven local agencies to share information systems, human resource management, and marketing. CARES is also currently conducting joint strategic planning with the local HIV medical clinic.

Project Summary–

Support from the Gill Foundation is requested for **RainbowEDGE** and **Brothers United**, CARES' HIV prevention education programs for gay and bisexual men. CARES has been providing education to the GLBT community since 1985, expanding and revising its prevention strategies as the community's patterns of risk taking and barriers to sustained prevention have changed.

RainbowEDGE targets men in the institutional gay community. Men in this community today face the challenge of sustaining or adopting behavioral changes at a time when the epidemic seems to have lost its sense of urgency. Since 1996, Brothers United has targeted African American gay/bisexual men who socialize in a subculture largely separate from the organized gay community of RainbowEDGE. The challenge for these men is to adopt and/or sustain behaviors to protect their lives when no community, gay or African American, publicly tells these men that their lives are worth preserving. Thus, for distinct reasons, both programs treat HIV as a community survival issue and offer opportunities to explore risk reduction as part of a personal sexual identity.

RainbowEDGE and Brothers United each use a variety of peer-based strategies to keep HIV issues visible in their respective communities, to connect HIV prevention to issues of gay/bisexual identity and health needs and, as a result, to build community-level support for continued HIV prevention efforts. These strategies include face-to-face individual counseling, internet-based education, workshops, discussion groups, and annual retreats. Trained volunteers conduct broad outreach activities at clubs and community events, which serve to recruit participants for individual and group interventions held throughout the year. Individual and group activities provide opportunities for gay/bisexual men to explore their reasons for taking risks and develop strategies for managing those risks more effectively. They also allow gay/bisexual men to link HIV prevention to other gay health needs. Since African-American gay/bisexual men have historically been excluded from the institutional gay community, Brothers United creates its own, alternative venues for African American men to explore and affirm their identities as gay/bisexual men of color and to explore and embrace HIV prevention as a health/survival issue for themselves.

These are the only HIV prevention programs designed by and for gay/bisexual men and gay/bisexual men of color in Middle Tennessee. During the project year, the programs will reach 6,853 gay/bisexual men, of whom 1,900 will be African American.

Need and Rationale for the Project -

Metropolitan Nashville/Davidson County has the second highest incidence of HIV in Tennessee. The local health department reported more than 450 new HIV infections in the last year. Of these newly infected individuals, 45% were African American, 51% were Caucasian and 4% were Hispanic or other ethnicities; 78% were men; 29% were under age 30, 65% were age 30-49, and 6% were over age 50. Although the local health department does not publicly report contributing risk factors, the state department of health identifies unsafe homosexual behavior as the primary risk factor for HIV infection in Tennessee as a whole and Middle Tennessee specifically, accounting for 40% of recent infections. This is twice as high as any other reported risk behavior. Gay/bisexual men, especially but not only younger men and African American men, remain significantly and disproportionately affected by HIV disease.

Perceived changes in the epidemic (new treatments resulting in fewer deaths and fewer visibly frail gay men)) have fueled a rise in new HIV infections among gay/bisexual men in Nashville as they have nationwide. This creates a new set of challenges for HIV prevention programs: to recognize and understand the attitudes, experiences and needs--what Fishbein would call the "cognitive structures"-- that inform risk taking by gay/bisexual men in 2001.

Drawing upon the studies of risk taking by HIV-negative gay/bisexual men offered by Odets, Rofes, and Stokes and Peterson, Brothers United and RainbowEDGE both give men opportunities to explore the deep psychic needs that drive risk taking. Both programs connect risk reduction to an affirmation of these men's specific sexual, and for Brothers United, racial identities. Both provide specific information about how risk can vary with HIV status, sexual practice, and sexual role. Following the Diffusion of Innovations Theory (Rogers), which describes the way new ideas and practices are shared over time among members of a "social system" of marginalized individuals, both programs anticipate communication of their HIV prevention messages beyond the immediate participants in education activities. The latter is especially true for Brothers United, whose dual marginality as gay/bisexual men of color serves as a prototype for the kind of group Rogers describes.

Description of Project Activities -

As peer-based programs, Brothers United and RainbowEDGE recruit and train volunteers continuously. Volunteers meet regularly throughout the year for continuing education and program planning. Along with the program coordinators, they conduct most of the education activities for their respective gay/bisexual target populations.

These activities include monthly outreach in three different community environments: at established commercial venues (bars), at community events (such as Pride and the Miss Gay TN pageant), and at alternative social spaces sponsored by the programs (such as a Bingo Brunch and "SIMBE" Socials). Brothers United also conducts street outreach at different "cruising sites" within the city. All outreach activities include distribution of condoms and/or safer sex kits of other prevention materials. Outreach will have contact with 5,000 men (770 of them African American.)

Program coordinators also host bimonthly discussion forums and bimonthly film nights where gay/bisexual men can explore HIV in the context of other gay identity issues. Often focusing on specific topics (like dating or spirituality), the forums generate discussions about HIV prevention and risk-taking. These will reach 260 men (120 African American).

These outreach, discussion and social activities serve an additional purpose of recruiting participants for more intensive and ongoing group and individual prevention activities. These in turn provide gay/bisexual men opportunities to explore in depth their reasons for risk taking and to develop strategies for managing those risks more effectively. These include prevention workshops, a monthly book discussion club, a monthly "Talk Safe" series, and retreats for each program. These intensive group activities will reach 435 men (320 African American).

Individual prevention activities include face-to-face counseling sessions by the program coordinators with 98 men (60 African American). They also include education by both programs to men in Internet chat rooms. RainbowEDGE and Brothers United have each been providing internet education for three years and have established program presences among local gay/bisexual men. Chat room anonymity and users' online pseudonymity make possible very frank discussions about risk behavior and risk reduction. Internet education will reach 360 men (130 African American).

Finally, both programs publish bimonthly newsletters which contain detailed information on HIV prevention as well as information on upcoming program activities. The newsletters will reach 700 men (500 African American).

REFERENCES:

Bandura, A. (1977). *Social Learning Theory*. Englewood Cliffs, NJ: Prentice Hall

Fishbein, M. (1980). "A Theory of Reasoned Action: Some applications," in Howe and Page, eds., *Nebraska Symposium on Motivation*. Lincoln, NE: University of Nebraska press.

Odets, W. (1995*). In the Shadow of the Epidemic: Being HIV Negative in the Sage of AIDS*. Durham NC: Duke University Press.

Rofes, E. (1996). *Reviving the Tribe: Regenerating Gay Men's Sexuality and Culture in the Ongoing Epidemic*. Harrington Park Press: New York.

Rogers, E.M. (1995). *Diffusion of Innovations (4ᵗʰ ed.)*. New York: Free Press.

Stokes, J.P. and Peterson, J.L. (1998). "Homophobia, self-esteem, and risk for HIV among African American men who have sex with men," *AIDS Education and Prevention*, 10(3), 278-292.

2. Project Outcomes with Timeline and Plan to Monitor and Evaluate your Success

Group Activities (both one-time and ongoing) use a pre-test/post-test evaluation to measure impact. Impact is evaluated in three areas: knowledge, attitude, and behavior. These evaluations also help us to measure baseline knowledge and to identify any non-standard information and/or motivation found among participants. **Individual Activities (face-to-face and internet)** conclude with participants confirming a "plan of action" which addresses the specific prevention needs of the participant. **Outreach Activities** measure program recognition and contacts' use of prevention information and materials through verbal questions and answers recorded by outreach volunteers.

Evaluation is conducted in an ongoing way along with the activities themselves. The program coordinators compile output and outcome data monthly and send it to the Education Director for analysis. Results are discussed and used for program modifications as needed.

The following outcomes are expected.

RainbowEDGE:
1. **Outreach** will result in (a) a 25% increase in program name recognition, (b) a 15% increase in contact with media materials, (c) a 15% increase in contact with outreach workers (d) a 15% increase in HIV testing, and (e) a 10% increase in condom use.
2. One-time **discussion forums** will result in (a) a 25% increase in knowledge, (b) a 15% increase in commitment to risk reduction, and (c) a 10% decrease in reported practice of unprotected anal intercourse.
3. Ongoing **Group programs** will result in (a) a 25% increase in knowledge, (b) a 20% increase in commitment to risk reduction, and (c) a 20% increase in perceived ability to negotiate safer sex, and (d) a 15% decrease in unsafe sexual behavior.
4. **Individual education** will result in (a) a 10% increase in program recognition, (b) a 15% increase in contact with program materials, (c) a 25% increase in risk reduction knowledge, (d) a 25% increase in reported commitment to condom use during anal intercourse, and (e) a 35% decrease in unprotected anal intercourse

Brothers United:
1. **Outreach** will result in (a) a 15% increase in program name recognition, (b) a 15% increase in contact with media materials, (c) a 15% increase in contact with outreach workers, (d) a 10% increase in HIV testing, and (e) a 10% increase in condom use.
2. One-time **discussion forums** will result in (a) a 15% increase in knowledge, (b) a 15% increase in commitment to risk reduction, and (c) a 10% increase in use of stated negotiation skills.
3. Ongoing **Group programs** will result in (a) a 15% increase in knowledge, (b) a 20% increase in perceived ability to negotiate safer sex, and (d) a 10% decrease in reported unsafe sexual behavior.
4. **Individual education** will result in (a) a 15% increase in program recognition, (b) a 15% increase in contact with program materials, (c) a 15% increase in contact with outreach workers, (d) a 10% increase in HIV testing, and (e) a 10% increase in condom use.

3. **Key Staff and/or Volunteers and list of Board of Directors and their Affiliations.**

Patrick Luther, MHS, Director of Education, was hired in January of 2000. Mr. Luther came to CARES with ten years of HIV program development and direct education experience. Most recently, Luther managed HIV training and education for a nine county consortium of substance abuse treatment facilities in upstate New York. His responsibilities include staff supervision and overall program planning, coordination, and evaluation.

Kevin Lawson, HIV Education Coordinator, is a Caucasian gay man hired in 1996 to develop RainbowEDGE. He has helped design and shape the program, providing community outreach, safer sex workshops/retreats, monthly group meetings, and the creation of innovative materials and public campaigns for gay/bisexual men.

Dwayne Jenkins, HIV Education Coordinator, is an African American gay man who was a founding member of Brothers United before being hired in 1996 as coordinator. He is a member of the state Tennessee Community Planning Group and is a Southeast Regional Technical Assistance Consultant with the Centers for Disease Control and Prevention for programs targeting African American gay/bisexual men.

A list of **Board of Directors** is attached.

4. **Letters of intent from other organizations with whom you propose to collaborate and whose partnership is important for your program's success**

Not applicable.

5. **Three community leaders not directly affiliated with your organization whom we may contact, including name, title, organizational or business affiliation, and phone number**

Jim Vaillancourt, Executive Director
Center for Nonprofit Management
44A Vantage Way
Nashville, TN 37228
615-259-0100

Ellen Lehman, President
Community Foundation of MiddleTN
210 23rd Avenue North
Nashville, TN 37203
615-321-4939

Peter Bird, Senior Program Officer, *or* Lani Wilkerson, Program Officer
The Frist Foundation
3319 West End Avenue
Nashville, TN 37203
615-292-3868

6. **Statement reflecting your greatest weakness or weaknesses, both programmatically and structurally.**

Technology
1. Hardware: Growth in staff and growth in use of our internal network for internal office communications and operations led recently to upgrading of our office network. We were able to do this with donations of software from Citrix International and Microsoft, along with an investment from our working capital in a new server. However, this in turn created a need for more hardware to link all staff to the network so that it can be used fully. In addition, many of our case managers and educators are outwardly deployed and therefore need portable technology for the electronic transfer of data.

2. Data Management: Program expansion and the complete introduction of outcome management to all programs has significantly increased the amount of data being generated by programs. This is especially true in our Education Department. We are currently collaborating with six other local nonprofits to develop a shared ASP/internet data management system to address this need.

3. Our budget size (approaching $3 million, with half of it in federal grants) and our needs for restricted fund management have outgrown our current (Peachtree) accounting software. We need to investigate an upgrade.

4. All of the above has created the need for personnel dedicated to managing and maintaining the network. This need is compounded by the tremendous variety among our staff in their computer skills (and comfort), creating a need for ongoing training and trouble shooting.

With regard to all of the above, the agency this year recruited two new Board members with background and expertise in information technology. They form the nucleus of a new ITS committee to help plan and evaluate our systems and needs.

Human Resources

1. Improved survival rates among our clients combined with continuing new infections has significantly increased the number of clients served by the agency. This has created extremely high caseloads of about 130 : 1 for our case managers. We need to hire more case managers to maintain the quality of our services.

2. CARES has kept overhead low throughout the agency by not investing in support staff. While a certain amount of this need is met through technology, some clerical/administrative staff are needed to manage daily operations in departments.

3. We have a very effective volunteer corps of about 500 individuals, but that department is managed by one single staff. Additional staff to help coordinate volunteers could free the Director to plan strategically with other departments to make better use of volunteers to address various program needs such as those outlined here.

4. In an era of increasing public apathy, public misunderstanding, and media disinterest, it would be invaluable to have a staff person dedicated to focusing attention on our cause by creating press releases, maintaining relationships with reporters and editors, and once again putting AIDS back in the forefront of community awareness. Currently, communications is the shared responsibility of the Executive Director and the Development Director. This means that communications work is often inconsistent. A paid communications specialist would assist significantly.

7. **Secondary sources providing alternative perspectives of your organization, for example newspaper articles written about you, testimonials, thank you letters, etc.**

Deb Runyon article
Joe Interrante article in Nashville Medical news
Joe Interrante op-ed piece in the Tennessean
Strobel article in City Paper

8. **Financial information including: organizational budget; event or project budget (if applicable); most recent year-end financial statements (audited if available); and description of fundraising activities outlining categories of revenue (i.e., major donors, corporate donors, etc.); and list of other corporate and foundation donors.**

Attachments enclosed.

9. Copy of your IRS © (3) determination letter. We do not fund private foundations individuals or other entities not considered public charities under sections 509(a)(1), 509(a)(2) or 509(a)(3) of the IRS Tax Code

Enclosed.

10. Special notice to 501(c)(3) organizations involved in lobbying activities; include copy of your 501(h) election form.

Not applicable.

11. Special notice to local chapters of national organizations: include an overview of how your local organization and national office will work together.

Not applicable.

Additional Requirements

1. A copy of an official policy from your organization stating that your organization does not pirate software.

Enclosed.

2. A copy of an official non-discrimination policy for your organization including sexual orientation.

Enclosed.

BUDGET:

	Brothers United	RainbowEDGE	TOTAL
PERSONNEL			**$77,076.**

Note: Detail removed for publication. Includes 2 full-time Program Coordinators and 20% time of Education Director, plus 19% taxes and benefits.

	Brothers United	RainbowEDGE	TOTAL
NONPERSONNEL	**20,126.**	**23,353.**	**43,479.**
Travel/Mileage (@ $.25/mile)	1,521.	652.	2,173.
Supplies	2,421.	3,321.	5,742.
Prevention Materials	2,550.	9,500.	12,050.
Printing	1,409.	2,139.	3,548.
Postage	1,100.	100.	1,200.
Telecommunications	915.	915.	1,830.
Meeting/Workshop/Retreat Refreshments	1,804.	650.	2,454.
Retreat Space Rental	2,130.	100.	2,230
Conference/Training	1,500.	1,200.	2,700.
Occupancy	3,628.	3,628.	7,256.
Insurance	157.	157.	314.
Equipment Maintenance	991.	991.	1,982.
PROGRAM SUBTOTAL	59,377.	61,178.	120,555.
Administrative Support and Grants Management (10%)	5,938.	6,118.	12,056.
TOTAL EXPENSES	**$65,315.**	**$67,296.**	**$132,611.**

PROGRAM FUNDING:

TN Department of Health HIV Prevention Grant (awarded)	$60,966.
Community Foundation/Middle TN Grant (in application)	3,300.
Retreat Participant Registration Fees	3,200.
General Fund (Direct Contributions and Special Events Revenue)	50,145.
Request to Gill Foundation	**$15,000.**

These programs (like all agency services and programs) are funded annually from a variety of sources, including government, corporate and foundation grants. The Nashville CARES General Fund flexibly makes up the difference between grants and program costs (especially when a grant is awarded at a lower than projected amount).

2001 Board of Directors

Officers

James R. Kelley, President *(2nd term ends 2002)*
> Partner, Neal and Harwell, PLC
> Board of Directors, Richland West End Avenue Neighborhood Association

Iris Buhl, Vice President *(1st term ends 2002)*
> Chair, Metro Charitable Solicitations Board
> Advisory Committee, Fund for Administrative Collaboration, CFMT

Cecelia L. Mynatt, Secretary *(1st term ends 2002)*
> Associate Executive Director, Center for Nonprofit Management
> Board of Directors, Comprehensive Care Center

D. Trigg James, Treasurer *(2nd term ends 2003)*

Steve W. Sirls, Immediate Past President *(2nd term ends 2001)*
> Owner, Steve Sirls Landscape Gardening
> Commissioner, Metropolitan Nashville Arts Commission

At-Large Members

Peggy Andrews *(1st term ends 2001)*
> Steering Committee, Ryan White Community AIDS Partnership

Fletcher Foster *(2nd term ends 2002)*
> Vice President Marketing, Capitol Records
> Board of Directors, Gilda's Club

Elizabeth Fox *(1st term ends 2002)*
> Owner, Corporate Solutions, Inc.
> Board President, Residential Services Inc.

Timothy Gistover *(2nd term ends 2003)*
> Person Living with HIV/AIDS
> Volunteer, Meharry Medical School OSCI Programs and First Response Center

Jon H. Glassmeyer *(1st term ends 2003)*
> Board of Directors, Artrageous Inc.
> Board President, Nashville Children's Theatre

Michael Gold, MD *(2nd term ends 2003)*
> Private Practice, Gold Skin Care Center
> Board President, Jewish Family Service

Jack Isenhour *(1st term ends 2001)*
> Writer/Television Producer
> Advisory Council, Artrageous and 1997 Artrageous CoChair

Rabbi Kenneth Kanter *(1st term ends 2003)*
> Congregation Micah
> Board President, Covenant Association

Adrienne Taylor Latham *(1st term ends 2003)*
> Associate Dean, Student Affairs, Fisk University
> Middle TN Workforce Investment Board, Nashville Career Advancement Center

Rick Murphy *(1st term ends 2002)*
> Principal, Bryan, Pendleton, Swats, and McAllister
> Member, Development Committee, Historic Rugby, Inc.

Johnny Ray Mutina *(1st term ends 2001)*
> Senior Sales Representative, Osram Sylvania
> Advisory Committee, H. Franklin Brooks Fund, CFMT

Harrell Odom, II, MD *(2nd term ends 2001)*
        Physician, Mid-State Cardiology Consultants
        Vice Chief of Internal Medicine, Baptist Hospital
Steven Oliver, DDS. M. Med. Sc. *(2nd term ends 2001)*
        Private Practice, Designing Smiles
        Member, Education Committee, Nashville Chamber of Commerce
Francis H. Phillips *(1st term ends 2002)*
        Community Volunteer
Kathy Plourde *(1st term ends 2001)*
        Owner, Metron Services
        Board of Directors, Good News International
Joe B. Rowland *(1st term ends 2003)*
        Vice President, Investments, Paine Webber
        Board of Directors, Artrageous Inc.
Scott Smith *(1st term ends 2003)*
        Founder and CTO, Medibuy
        President and CEO, Regional Airways
Very Reverend Kenneth Swanson *(2nd term ends 2003)*
        Dean and Rector, Christ Church Cathedral
        Executive Board, Covenant Association
Carrie Ferguson Weir *(1st term ends 2003)*
        Features Reporter, *The Tennessean*
Robin Bicket White *(1st term ends 2002)*
        Associate, Mendes and Gonzales, PLLC
        Community Outreach Committee, Young Lawyers Division, Nashville Bar Association
Jim Williams *(1st term ends 2001)*
        Horse Trainer
        Creator, CARES Classic Horse Show
James P. Wilson, MD *(2nd term ends 2003)*
        Assistant Medical Director, Subacute Care Unit, Vanderbilt University Medical Center
        Finance Committee, Diocese of Nashville
Vicki Yates *(2nd term ends 2001)*
        Anchorperson, WTVF NewsChannel 5
        Member, Nashville Association of Black Journalists

Kim Patterson, Intern
        National Account Executive, FISI Madison Financial
        Nashville Humane Association, Cause for Paws
Joseph Interrante, Ph.D., Executive Director
        Person Living with HIV
        Board of Directors, AIDS Action Council (Washington DC)
        Community Investments Committee, United Way of Metropolitan Nashville

Nashville CARES
Computer Privileges and Responsibilities

This policy applies to the use of all Nashville CARES computer and network resources as well as computers and peripheral equipment administered by CARES. Computer privileges may be granted to staff, volunteers, interns and clients with the understanding that the resources will be used for agency purposes. Incidental personal use may also be appropriate, so long as it does not interfere with regular agency operations.

Users are responsible for the correct and sufficient use of tools to ensure the security of information stored on their computers and accessible over the network. This includes, but is not limited to, the following precautions:

- Computer/internet accounts, passwords and other types of authorization assigned to users should not be shared with others. The only exception is that the Director of Finance & Administration will keep all user passwords on file.
- The user should be aware of computer viruses and other destructive programs, and take steps to avoid being a victim or unwitting distributor of viruses.
- The user should be aware that some CARES computing resources, including e-mail and internet access, may not necessarily be secure or private and may be monitored.
- Agency business should be conducted to the extent possible using software that has been selected and authorized by the agency. Other compatible software may be used for agency business and should be "registered" with the Director of Finance & Administration, but will not be supported/maintained/upgraded by the agency.

CARES computer resources should be used in a manner that protects the use privileges and property rights of others. Users must therefore:

- Abide by all local, state and federal laws, including copyright laws.
- Abide by applicable software license agreements.
- Use only accounts, access codes or network ID numbers assigned to them.
- Access only those files or data which they are authorized to use.
- Refrain from using agency computer resources to visit "adult sites" and/or downloading sexually-explicit pictures. An exception is Education staff with the prior approval of the Director of Education when such activity would be only for appropriate educational research/outreach.

Users are expected to cooperate so that all users may make maximum use of computer resources in a shared environment. Users are expected to:

- Refrain from unnecessary use of interactive network/internet utilities.
- Refrain from using sounds or playing music at levels that might be disruptive to others.
- Refrain from playing games except during breaks. The agency reserves the right to remove games from particular computers if necessary.
- Regularly backup data on their computers that could not be easily replaced.
- Refrain from using computer resources in ways that harass or impede the activities of others.

Violations of this policy may be grounds for discipline as outlined in your Personnel Policies. In addition, Tennessee and federal laws provide for civil and criminal penalties for violations of the law by means of computer use. Examples of unlawful actions include defamatory remarks, destruction or theft of data belonging to CARES or to others, unauthorized copying of copyrighted material, and the transportation of obscene materials across state lines.

Approved by Board of Directors
April 18, 2001

A Proposal From

New Settlement Apartments

Bronx, New York

To

New York Foundation

New York, New York

Requested amount: $50,000; Amount received: $50,000

Funder's comments:

"This proposal told a story and that made it easy to understand. It illustrated a process by which a local social service organization came to realize that it needed to work collaboratively with other local organizations to tackle a 'macro' problem—public school reform. It laid out in an honest and thoughtful way the limitations of its initial approach to the problem and proposed a new idea. We knew the work of the organization (having funded them before).

"In writing the proposal, they had a hard job to do. They had to describe the work of the large social service provider (New Settlement Apartments), an academic institution (New York University), the collaborative partners, and the component of parent involvement. They had to do it in a way that each piece made sense and the role of each player was clear. It's a challenge and they did that well.

"The work was also a continuation of work already begun, and they were able to place the reader in context. The budget did not contain much detail, as the funding request was for staff only. Underlining is distracting and has the effect of encouraging the reader to read less, not more. If a proposal is good, you want to read every word because there's nothing superfluous. It's concise and the words are chosen with care. Perhaps a bit less detail on New Settlement's history and accomplishments would have made it an even better proposal.

"Attachments included a longer report on parent organizing for school reform in New York City and that was enormously helpful because it fleshed out the story further. Now, because we are already a funder of many of these school reform efforts, I was anxious to read this particular report but I am not sure others would have read it. Still, I think it was important because it made a case for why this model of parent organizing was a critical model to test. It also lent the proposal an air of credibility because it was written by an academic institution and described the effort in the broader context of school reform."

—*Maria Mottola, Executive Director, New York Foundation*

Notes:

The proposal was written using the New York/New Jersey Area Common Application Form. The complete proposal included the following attachments: financial statements, list of board members, IRS tax exempt letter, photographs, and various printed materials. The report *A Case Study: Community Organizing for School Improvement in the South Bronx,* published by the Institute for Education & Social Policy of New York University, was subsequently submitted to the funder. Salaries of specific individuals in the budget have been deleted to ensure confidentiality.

Proposal developed by Jack Doyle, Executive Director, Megan Nolan, CSW, then Lead Community Organizer for the Parent Action Committee, and Janet Greenberg, Ph.D., Program and Fund Development Consultant; written by Janet Greenberg and submitted to the funder by Jack Doyle.

NEW SETTLEMENT APARTMENTS' COMMUNITY ORGANIZING PROJECT

PROPOSAL TO THE NEW YORK FOUNDATION

APPLICATION COVER SHEET

Date of application: March 31, 2000

Legal name of organization to which grant would be paid:
The Crenulated Company, Limited, dba New Settlement Apartments

Purpose of Grant: To support a community organizing project to improve the quality of education in the public schools of Community School District 9, with specific emphasis on Community Elementary Schools 64 and 58 in the southwest Bronx neighborhood of New Settlement Apartments in 2000, and expanding to include additional schools in the district in 2001. The project builds on the work of the Parent Action Committee of New Settlement Apartments, an organized nucleus of 220 neighborhood parents which has grown in size and matured through experience since it formed in late 1996.

Address of organization: New Settlement Apartments, 1512 Townsend Ave., Bronx, NY 10452

Telephone: 718-716-8000, ext.123   **Fax**: 718-294-4085

Executive Director: Jack Doyle

Contact Person and Title: Jack Doyle, Executive Director

Is organization an IRS 501 (c) 3: Yes

Grant request: $50,000

Request is for **project support**

Total organizational operating budget (for current year): $ 6,671,086*

Total budget for Community Services (for current year): $1,690,725

Dates covered by this budget: January 1, 2000-December 31, 2000

Total project budget: $248,747 (one year)

Dates covered by project budget: 12 months of funding is requested, beginning April 1, 2000. Budget presents 2 fiscal years, CY 2000 and CY 2001.

Project name: Parent Action Committee Community Organizing Project

**NEW SETTLEMENT APARTMENTS' COMMUNITY ORGANIZING PROJECT
PROPOSAL TO THE NEW YORK FOUNDATION
March 31, 2000**

I.   PROPOSAL SUMMARY

Ours is a parent and community organizing project, now in its fourth year of existence, focused on improving the quality of education for children and youth in the southwest Bronx public schools of Community School District 9—in the immediate and long term. Our organizing objectives and strategies for the next year extend the Parent Organizing Committee's previous efforts in several new directions: they are meant to deepen our focus on individual, failing schools while also expanding our ability to move this notorious District as a whole toward positive change. We will maintain our bottom-up approach to community organizing, with parents driving the agenda and leading the campaign, and we will continue building the internal capacity of both parents and staff. We will attempt to implement systematic, independent evaluation of the most unresponsive schools, through a Community School Review —beginning with CES 64, where lasting change has been elusive, despite many victories in the past four years. We will work with a wider coalition of diverse community-based organizations that share our goal of revitalizing the southwest Bronx step-by-step, school-by-school, and block-by-block. And we will attempt to forge a ground-breaking alliance between PAC parents and school teachers—by working in individual schools and with the UFT citywide leadership.

We are now a group 220 parents strong, with a core leadership of 50, and growing steadily. We are in close contact with networks and organizations with similar goals across the Bronx, New York City and State, and continue to benefit from the expert assistance of the NYU Institute for Education and Social Policy. Our successful campaign in 1998 to remove a failing principal at CES 64 called attention to the low reading and math scores at the school, at an historic moment when the education community was focused on "persistent educational failure" of the public schools. The Pyrrhic victory we achieved through that change in school leadership has heightened our understanding of the profound nature of the problems in the school and the intractability of district leadership. Our current campaign is similarly positioned to take advantage of the education community's newest focus on "performance standards" and the UFT's concern that teachers are, indeed, not prepared to teach to the new standards being set for our children.

New Settlement seeks New York Foundation funding for 2000-01 to offset the costs of expanded staffing and institutional support for this rapidly-growing organizing effort —which continues to be the very highest priority of parents in our area; is the cornerstone of New Settlement's broader community organizing agenda; and has been identified as a unique model of community organizing by researchers and other CBOs.

II.   NARRATIVE
A.   Background
A.1.   History and mission of New Settlement Apartments

New Settlement Apartments is a non-profit housing development of nearly 900 families, 30% of whom are formerly homeless, 99% of whom are Latino or Black. It is located in an underserved area of the southwest Bronx and has a nine-year track record of active commitment to neighborhood revitalization and community development—including educational excellence at community schools. An integral part of the progressive housing philosophy embraced by New Settlement is that "*housing is not just bricks and mortar*." Thus, our mission is not only to rebuild and maintain a sizeable portion of the housing stock in this impoverished neighborhood, but also to support the rebuilding of the social capital of this community.

Because favorable financing for New Settlement Apartments was negotiated during the pre-development, we are able to devote approximately 10.4% of rental income (nearly $580,000 in 2000) toward

New Settlement Apartments' Community Organizing Project
Proposal to the New York Foundation
March 31, 2000 / Page 2

Community Services—the community development, advocacy, organizing and education agenda. The remaining 89.1% is used to maintain and operate the buildings to the highest standards. Our extensive year-round community services and educational programs are structured in direct response to the interests of several thousand adults and youth who live in this chronically-underserved area. Programs serving over 2,000 people each year are staffed by paid professionals and dedicated volunteers, and delivered in beautifully-maintained, accessible community space in our residential buildings

A.2.   Need addressed by New Settlement Apartments and population served

The southwest Bronx neighborhoods of Concourse/Highbridge, Morrisania and University Heights, which surround New Settlement Apartments, comprise a geographic corridor of neglect of national notoriety. Our neighborhood youth are at very high risk of dropping out of high school, teen pregnancy, and entering the juvenile/criminal justice system, especially as a result of gang activity. The culture of failure is dominant, and is instilled early on in the underperforming schools of _Community School District 9_ [1] : In January 2000, at least 90% of all children at our local elementary school, CES 64, received "Promotion in Doubt" letters (according to best estimates of our Parent Action Committee, which has registered a formal request for the official figures from the District). District-wide, fewer than 28% of all elementary school students currently read or do math at grade level. Despite years of Title 1 funding, still fewer than _20%_ of students at CES 64 are able to read at grade level, and only 13.3% of students can do math at grade level—a new low for this school. At CES 58, 27.7% currently do math at grade level—also a decrease from last year. The three high schools that serve this community, Taft, Roosevelt and Walton, all have very poor on-time graduate rates and very high drop-out rates, compared with other schools in the Bronx and citywide. At these three schools, only 25%-37% of students graduated on time in each of the past several years; about 45% were "behind grade," and the rest dropped out. Like CSD 9, _Community Districts 3, 4 and 5_ are among the poorest and most underserved areas of New York City by every standard of measurement [2] : In CD 3, nearly 50% of all household incomes are below $10,000. Over 80% of all children in these districts are born into poor families, outranking all but two community districts (also nearby in the Bronx) in NYC. Concourse/ Highbridge has the highest percentage (89.8%) of infants receiving WIC of the entire city. In the elementary schools of District 9, nearly 100% of students are currently eligible for free breakfasts and lunches. And the quality of housing stock, with the notable exception of nonprofit housing developments like New Settlement, is among the poorest in the city: families pay an average of 50% of their income in rent; rates of crowding, eviction and homelessness and lead paint levels are among the very highest in NYC. Residents of the area are almost entirely Black and Latina/o, with very high rates of limited English proficiency among Latinos. Among City Council Districts, our Community District 4 ranks 45th of 51 in the low number of high school graduates, and only 6% of adults in this area are college graduates (compared to 72% of all adults over age 25 on Manhattan's Upper West Side).

---

1. Data on individual schools and on Community District 9 overall are from the 1998-99 Annual School Reports, published by the NYC Board of Education in March 2000. Data comparing the schools and district to others in NYC are culled from _The New York Times_ overview of all schools and districts (Sunday, March 12 and 19, 2000), based on Board of Ed. reports.

2. Data are from _Keeping Track of New York City's Children : A Citizens' Committee for Children Status Report, 1999_, which uses most recent government data to rank the city's 59 community districts and 32 community school districts, and _City of Contrasts: 51 New York City Council Districts: A Report of the City Project and Community Studies of New York, Inc./Infoshare_ (February 1998).

New Settlement Apartments' Community Organizing Project
Proposal to the New York Foundation
March 31, 2000 / Page 3

A.3. Current programs and accomplishments

New Settlement Community Services currently offers a wide range of social services and ongoing educational and recreational programs to nearly 2,000 children, youth, adults and seniors annually. All programs are filled to capacity and staff conduct extensive community outreach — on the street, in schools and community gathering spots to inform people of new opportunities.

Regular programs for adults currently include orientations to introduce unemployed mothers to effective job training programs; on-site Board of Education Adult Basic Education, GED and English for Speakers of Other Languages (ESOL) classes; and a resource center for parents of children with special needs. In the area of youth development, our priority is to meet the pressing need to reach many more children and young people through enhanced, year-round programs of high quality which, as a matrix, build broad-based literacy skills not adequately supported in local public schools; open windows and doors to career and educational opportunities too often beyond the reach of residents of this neighborhood; and focus the creative energies of alienated, low-income youth of color through community service, leadership development, and youth organizing.

Over a dozen positive youth programs are designed to engage participants in fun and educational activities which improve their academic skills, build awareness of self and community and support overall healthy development. Literacy skill development is infused into all program components— beginning in our *Multicultural After-school Programs* (held at NSA for 75 neighborhood children, ages 8-11, and at CES 64 for 320 students, grade K-6). Three of our fastest-growing teen programs are the *College Access Center* whose goal is to broaden awareness of, and focus options for, careers and post-secondary education for youth, aged 12-21; *Rocking the Boat*, a boat-building experience in which teens construct sea-worthy wooden boats in the 19th century style, with workshops and field trips that focus on the environmental, historical and cultural context of the Hudson and Harlem River Valleys in which they live; and *The Bronx Helpers*, a cornerstone of New Settlement's *youth organizing* and *community service* agenda, which has received recognition from the Bronx Borough President and the NY Yankees for teen members' service work.

A brief summary of our recent accomplishments demonstrates, above all, New Settlement's comprehensive commitment —as a housing and community development organization—to revitalize our neighborhood, beginning with the housing stock and the streets, including health and social services, and targeting youth development and the public schools in particular.

In the past year, we acquired the only remaining abandoned apartment building still owned by the City in this neighborhood and are now undertaking its renovation to yield apartments for 26 families and street-level space for our new College Access Center. We are particularly proud of the exponential growth of services to support positive development of children and youth, including the opening, in February 2000, of a new *after-school program for 320 children, grades K-6, on the premises of C.E.S. 64* (the same school which has been the focus of our parent organizing project), providing comprehensive youth development programs every school day of the year, with support from The After School Corporation. After two years of piloting our *College Access Center,* it is now professionally staffed and offering a full range of services to middle- and high-school youth and their parents. Its focus of keeping youth on track academically through high school, so that they have post-secondary educational and career *options*, is a key aspect of New Settlement's commitment to strengthening the educational pipeline in this neighborhood. Response from parents and teens has been very enthusiastic. And we continue to sponsor *community arts projects* that engage adults, youth and professional artists to create public beautification projects: in 2000, in collaboration with City Arts, we will create two major murals— decorating the entire playground-side wall of CES 64 (running the length of the playground up 16'), and the street-side

New Settlement Apartments' Community Organizing Project
Proposal to the New York Foundation
March 31, 2000 / Page 6

reading scores, but also by creating the space for parents to participate in their children's education; (B) *Building Our Internal Capacity*: To continue building the capacity of the parents and community members to analyze power dynamics, claim their rights to quality education for their children, and organize for social change, while also building the capacity of the PAC staff (which has grown to keep pace with the membership) to facilitate the organizing work of the Committee; and (C) *Holding the District and Central Board Accountable*: To expand our outreach efforts, through partnering with many area-based organizations serving parents and children in CSD 9, so that a large, critical mass of allied groups and individual parents—together— can draw the entire City's attention to the persistent educational failure of this school district.

The Need: Community School District 9 has long been one of the most consistently underperforming districts in NYC—plagued by leadership problems and some of the lowest reading scores and highest dropout rates in the City. CES 64 and 58, the two neighborhood schools targeted thus far by the Committee, are still among the very worst-performing schools in this notorious school district—by every standard of measurement. Yet, with total enrollment of over 1,750 children in grades K-6, they are attended by the majority of elementary-school-aged children in the immediate neighborhood. In January 2000, nearly 100 percent of PAC members' children received "Promotion in Doubt" letters, with no orientation yet provided for parents to school or district plans for teacher training to implement the new standards. (A PAC member reported that, in her child's 4th grade class at CES 58, 28 of 30 students were told yesterday that they will be "left behind" in June.) Since 1996, the Committee has established itself as a force to be reckoned with at 64, 58, and within District 9, but too many of our victories remain Pyrrhic. We are after nothing less than the transformation of the entire culture of failure in District 9 into an educational environment of achievement—with respectful communications between parents and officials, and high expectations of students taught by well-prepared teachers.

B.2.   Population that will be served and how population will benefit from the project

In the immediate term (2000-01), the people directly served will be (a) parents and children enrolled at CES 64, 58 and one or two additional schools, yet to be selected; (b) all parents, teachers and community members who participate in the organizing campaign and put the skills and resources they gather to work in their own schools and neighborhoods across CSD 9; (c) parent organizing groups across the city, state and country who ask to know more about our model, and who use it to fashion their own efforts; and (d) CBOs committed to family services of all sorts, who agree to work with us in a broad-based organizing effort. Over the longer term, we hope that our model of bottom-up parent organizing might be of use to many more parent- and community-organizing groups across the city and country.

Snapshot of PAC membership, which has grown and become more diverse over the past year: Our member roster increased from 165 in 1999 to nearly 220 in early 2000, as a result of stepped-up outreach. Members are 55% Latina/o and 45% Black, from a growing number of countries of origin, a balance more reflective of the schools than in the past. The group includes *fathers* as well as mothers and members have children in C.E.S. 64, 58 *and* other neighborhood schools. Increased participation by Latinas/os is the positive result of our persistent bilingual translation of all reports, minutes and flyers; alternating primary languages at meetings, and simultaneous interpretation at all meetings. (The lack of translation of key Bd. of Ed. and District documents or interpretation into Spanish at official meetings is one focus of our current District campaign.) Many more of the "core" of parents who attend Monday evening meetings are working for pay outside the home, yet still make time to participate regularly. (At least 30% of the parents have been called to work through W.E.P.) A core of about 50 parents comprises the base of membership, and receive PAC meeting minutes mailed weekly; about 100 attend various larger events on a fairly regular basis; and about 120 more attend occasionally. All 220 receive our

New Settlement Apartments' Community Organizing Project
Proposal to the New York Foundation
March 31, 2000 / Page 7

calendar, mailed monthly. Our goal is to increase the membership to at least 400 by the end of 2000, and double it again, to at least 800 by the end of 2001.

B.3.   Strategies we will employ to implement the project

Project Objectives in 2000-01 include: (1) Keeping the focus on CES 64 through a comprehensive campaign designed to confront the profound, intractable problems there. (2) Expanding the campaign at CES 58 and maintaining our focus on positive, comprehensive change. (3) Extending the school-focused campaign to include one or two additional schools, using the successful models of a comprehensive, school-based campaign we are developing through experience at 64 and 58. (4) Building the capacity of parents and community members to organize toward education reform, and to make a difference both in the immediate term and at the systemic level. (5) Strengthening the capacity of the (rapidly expanding) PAC staff to support all facets of the Committee's work, partnering with parents in the most creative ways possible. (6) Expanding the PAC's relationships with diverse organizations and coalitions in CSD 9 and in Community Districts 3, 4, and 5, which encompass CSD 9, who all share a commitment to enhancing the quality of life for their constituencies. (7) Reorganizing our outreach campaign with the goal of doubling each year the total number of members, and expanding the diversity of parents (by native language, blocks of neighborhoods, country of origin, and gender) to be representative of the students of CSD 9. (8) Sharpening our focus on CSD 9 and the Central Board, so that the sum total of our community-building efforts is concentrated on holding those in positions of power accountable for significant and visible improvement in the education of our children *now*.

The organizing strategies underway extend our efforts in several new directions: they are meant to deepen our focus on individual schools while also expanding our ability to move the District as a whole toward positive change, (a) by working from "inside" and "outside" the education system simultaneously; (b) by strengthening the leadership of the Committee while also reaching out to communities of parents who have not so far been involved; and (c) by making common cause with *teachers*, with *groups and coalitions experienced in community organizing*, as well as CBOs committed to neighborhood revitalization. Using these methods, we will extend our organizing model and build a critical mass that can draw media attention and influence decision-makers through large public actions. **At CES 64**, we will implement a new *platform for action* which calls for (a) the systematic evaluation of the school by outside experts (through an independent Community School Review, facilitated by the NYU Institute for Education and Social Policy); (b) sustained support for teacher training (to meet the new student performance standards); (c) respect for parents and children; (d) significant improvement in reading/math scores; (e) elimination of school disorganization, and (f) ensuring children's safety at school. We will build an alliance between parents and teachers in the school *and* with the UFT in NYC, around the staff development needed to train teachers to reach the new standards. And we will update the PAC's first action research report, *Persistent Educational Failure and the Case for New Leadership for Community Elementary School 64* (May 1998), presented to the Central Board of Education and District 9 officials, to show the improvements and lack thereof over the past two to three years. **At CES 58**, parents have identified four areas of PAC focus this year: (a) lack of communication with parents, and lack of teacher training to meet the new academic standards, (b) the lack of curriculum in physical education, music and art, (c) the safety of the children in school and on the buses, and (d) low math and reading scores and the high number of children whose promotion is in doubt. **And at the District level**, we have declared a "State of Emergency," based on the latest data released by the Bd. of Ed.. We will advocate that a complete and independent evaluation be made of CES 64 (for starters), to replace the PASS system of evaluation conducted by teachers and staff inside the system and school. Our goal is to set the stage for independent "audits" of each of our targeted schools, and eventually, to set a new standard for Board of Ed.-mandated audits in this district.

New Settlement Apartments' Community Organizing Project
Proposal to the New York Foundation
March 31, 2000 / Page 8

B.4.   Proposed staffing pattern for the project, and names and titles of people who will direct it

The staffing plan for 2000-2001 is designed to support the continued growth of the Committee's membership and of its major campaigns. *As in 1999, the PAC will continue to be staffed by* (a) <u>Andrea Case</u>, Community Organizer, whose time is dedicated 100% to this project; (b) <u>Megan Nolan</u>, CSW, NSA Program Associate for Community Development, who dedicates 33% of her time, as Committee staff trainer and supervisor and as senior coordinator of the planning and implementation of all PAC activities; (c) <u>Cynthia Cummings</u> and <u>Nilda Louisa</u>, two Parent Organizers (75% each); (d) <u>Rebecca Ferrer</u>, Program Assistant (75%); (e) a <u>graduate student intern</u> (50% during school year) specialized in community organizing, from the Hunter School of Social Work; and (f) <u>Antonio Torres</u>, Parent Organizing Intern (40%). <u>Eric Zachary, DSW</u>, of the NYU Institute for Education and Social Policy, will continue to provide *pro bono* technical assistance through research, data analysis, group training and by participating in a monthly meeting of the strategic planning team of the PAC. <u>Maria Santana</u>, Coordinator of the NSA Multicultural Afterschool and Summer Programs, will continue to provide essential liaison to parents of children in those programs. <u>Katty Fernandez</u>, coordinator of our new afterschool program for 320 children on the premises of CES 64, will be an important link to parents who are not yet familiar with New Settlement or the PAC. <u>A core of 50 parent members</u> who comprise the leadership of the PAC organizing efforts will expand their volunteer outreach and coordination work. And <u>Jack Doyle</u>, Director of New Settlement, will continue to oversee the development and staffing of the project, and ensure smooth coordination with all other aspects of the organization's strategic agenda. *New staff positions in 2000 include*: (a) a 2nd full-time, experienced <u>Community Organizer</u> who is Latina/o (interviewing is underway now) and (b) a 3rd <u>Parent Organizer</u> (75%), to be hired later this year. In addition, <u>Michael Fabricant</u>, Professor of Social Work at Hunter College, will continue consulting with PAC staff on staff coordination and professional development, *pro bono*, as part of a broader NSA-based research project on community building begun in 1999.

B.5.   Ways in which the project contributes to the overall mission of New Settlement Apartments

The neighborhood revitalization of the surrounding material, social and economic environment— which New Settlement has spearheaded in the eight-square-block area of its 14 buildings—is crucial to positioning this community organizing campaign for success in the immediate and longer term. Just as New Settlement has raised the bar in its neighborhood since 1990 on standards for clean, safe streets and well-maintained, affordable housing, we have also built a sense of shared community through diverse educational programs, services and organizing initiatives (which include reforming the public schools and providing opportunities for youth where too few have existed). As a result, we have also gained the trust of young people and adults now finding a collective voice to claim their rights to a healthy environment in which to live, study, grow and work. With each community-building initiative, we confirm our commitment to supporting the positive development of people of all ages in this neighborhood—as healthy individuals and productive community members who understand their rights and believe in their own capacity to make progressive social change now and in the future. Ultimately, this neighborhood is only as good as its schools, and the children's future is only as good as the education they get in this community. Thus, by combining a commitment to community development with a commitment to community organizing around the persistent educational failure of the schools, New Settlement plays a crucial—and altogether appropriate— role consistent with the clear interpretation of its mission.

C.   Evaluation plan

The PAC parents and staff will continue to engage in ongoing, participatory project evaluation—focused on the process of the group's work, as well as on the impact the work has on the members, the New Settlement environment, specific schools we have targeted, and the education system we are focused on

New Settlement Apartments' Community Organizing Project
Proposal to the New York Foundation
March 31, 2000 / Page 9

changing. We keep very good records of all meetings held, through written agendas developed in advance and minutes now taken by a rotating team of parents. Files are kept of all correspondence with officials and all agendas of public meetings in which we participate. Photos are taken of public actions; testimony presented at public meetings of the District and conference presentations to other CBOs are archived. These documents–especially weekly meeting minutes–are used as the basis of a monthly meeting now held by a core leadership team of the PAC, composed of five PAC members, three staff and Eric Zachary, who leads a discussion where progress is assessed and a strategic plan for the next month is worked out. (The monthly strategic plan is then presented to the general membership for its consideration.) We also have a growing "database" of information gathered from parents recording and cataloging their specific concerns about the schools' failure to meet the needs of the children (on standardized, user-friendly forms we have developed), and about their recent experiences advocating on behalf of their own children with teachers and principals. Project staff meet weekly with Megan Nolan, CSW, for ongoing strategic training and staff development. They also meet monthly with Michael Fabricant, Professor of Social Work at Hunter College, for ongoing training. With the support of the NYU Institute for Education and Social Policy, we have now collected detailed data on the academic performance of CES 64 over 4-year period, and began in 1999 to do the same for CES 58, within the context of CSD 9 and all elementary schools in NYC and State. We continually reconsider our strategic plan as a group of parents and staff, and share successes and challenges with like-minded organizations and researchers interested in understanding our model and how it might be adapted to other environments. For technical assistance in maintaining our ongoing project assessment, by which we will continue to measure our progress toward goals through both process and outcomes, we depend on the expert assistance of staff of the Community Involvement Project at NYU's Institute, who are skilled in the evaluation of numerous community organizing projects. They are currently completing a case study of the PAC, which may provide a new base for the comparative data that could result from this project over time. Above all, the primary goal of our evaluation plan is gather information which can be used immediately and over the longer term to improve and refine our agenda and our strategies for accomplishing it. On a monthly basis, we are now asked to consult with NYC-based organizations about our organizing model, and we have made several presentations to university researchers and graduate students about our work thus far in 2000. Researchers from NYU, Hunter College, Brooklyn College and Harvard University are now writing about our work, as an exemplar, from various angles. We hope that the information we gather and analyze will continue to be of use to others engaged in education reform and broader community organizing efforts across the city and the country.

New Settlement Apartments
Parent Action Committee Community Organizing Project
Projected Expense Budget/Calender Years 2000 and 2001
(Jan. 1, 2000 - Dec. 3, 2001)

	2000 Budget	2001 Budget	Request to New York Foundation for 2000
Personnel			
Two Community Organizers (100 %)			
Program Assoc. for Community Dvlpmnt. (33 %)			
Three Parent Organizers/Part Time (75%)			
Administrative Asst./Part Time (75%)			
Benefits			
Subtotal Personnel	$ 179,554	$ 184,942	$ 39,670
Other than Personnel Services			
Equipment & Supplies			
Office Equipment	$ 750	-	-
Simultaneous Translation Equipment	$ 900	-	-
Computers & Peripherals	$ 1,500	-	-
Portable P.A. Systems	$ 800	-	-
Subtotal Equipment	$ 3,950	0	0
Meetings & Conference			
Space Rental	$ 400	$ 400	-
Meals	$ 7,000	$ 9,500	$ 750
Travel	$ 1,600	$ 2,400	$ 600
Child Care	$ 6,600	$ 9,000	$ 1,000
Guest Trainers	$ 500	$ 500	-
Conference/Retreats	$ 3,500	$ 5,500	$ 715
Other Meeting Expenses	$ 400	$ 800	-
Subtotal Mtgs. & Conf.	$ 20,000	$ 28,100	$ 3,065
Publications, Printing & Duplication	$ 4,800	$ 6,200	-
Translation to Spanish	-	-	-
Monthly Newsletter	-	-	-
Meeting Agendas & training materials	-	-	-
Fliers and information materials	-	-	-
Subtotal Publications, Printing & Dup.	$ 4,800	6200	0
Other Supplies & Expenses			
Telephone & Internet Services	$ 1,250	$ 1,250	-
Postage and office supplies	$ 1,000	$ 1,400	-
Arts supplies for placards; film; etc.	$ 400	$ 600	-
Publications	$ 200	$ 200	-
Advertising	$ 450	$ 900	-
Miscellaneous expenses	$ 1,000	$ 1,000	-
Subtotal Other Supplies & Expenses	$ 4,300	$ 5,350	0
Total Direct Expenses	$ 212,604	$ 224,592	$ 42,735
Indirect Expenses	$ 36,143	$ 38,181	$ 7,265
Grand Total Expenses	$ 248,747	$ 262,773	$ 50,000

A Proposal From
New York Hall of Science
Queens, New York

To
Altman Foundation
New York, New York

Requested amount: $125,000; **Amount received:** $125,000

Funder's comments:

"We do accept the New York/New Jersey Area Common Application form, but it was not used in this case. However, all the required components were included and were well described. The cover letter, for example, provided a brief but specific articulation of the overall objectives of the Early Childhood Science Initiative.

"At ten pages, the proposal was longer than we typically prefer (we ask that proposals not exceed five pages), but the way the proposal was laid out—including clearly marked sections on the Early Childhood Science Initiative, Need, Learning Goals, Experiences and Activities, and Collaboration with the Brooklyn Children's Museum, among others—as well as the use of subheadings and bullets in certain sections, made the proposal very readable and interesting. All of the information was relevant, and served to answer any questions I might have had. These factors compensated for the length, though in general, given the volume of material program staff has to read, briefer is still better.

"I thought the statement of need was excellent. In a single page, the author cited numerous research studies pointing to the percentage of young children enrolled in preschool programs, the need for youngsters to be science literate, the ability of very young children to engage in critical thinking, and the wide disparities in enrollment in preschool programs between children from low-income and high-income families.

"The overall presentation was very strong, and the link made between the statement of need and the details of the proposed initiative was especially noteworthy. The section entitled 'Collaboration with the Brooklyn Children's Museum' was especially well done, and of particular interest to Altman since we had encouraged the two institutions to work together to share expertise and knowledge in order to enhance their individual and collective efforts.

"The writing style and presentation were excellent and should serve as an example to others on how to construct a proposal that program staff would want to read. The writers were able to articulate clearly the goals and objectives of the proposed initiative, support the arguments with data, and give evidence as to how the success of the initiative would be measured. Visually, the proposal was well laid out and very readable, using bold headings, subheadings, and bullets to break up the material and allow the reader to zero in on discrete sections.

"The budget has a great deal of detail, but could have been clearer in terms of presentation. One can figure it out, but it takes a bit of going over to be sure the numbers add up, and to match funds already raised with the articulated need, especially since the initiative we were being asked to support is part of a much larger Early Childhood Science program involving capital construction.

"All the attachments we require were included, and were therefore relevant and helpful. In the future, I would hope that it might be possible for them to do as good a job in a submission of fewer pages, and I would add that it would have been extra helpful to have some articulation of expectations of outcomes and sustainability beyond the single year of the grant. But that having been said, I think this proposal is very strong."

—*Nina B. Mogilnik, Senior Program Officer, Altman Foundation*

Notes:
The complete proposal included the following attachments: project budget, current year operating budget, list of board members, IRS tax-exempt letter, summary of support for current year, summary of funding sources for the proposed project, current museum newsletter featuring program for which funding was requested, and newspaper clips and brochures related to the proposed project.

Proposal written by Terry Billie, Grants Officer, New York Hall of Science; Preeti Gupta, Director of Education, New York Hall of Science; and Paul Pearson, Vice President of Programs, Brooklyn Children's Museum; submitted to the funder by Alan J. Friedman, Ph.D., Director, New York Hall of Science.

Alan J. Friedman, Ph.D.
Director

3 January, 2002

Ms. Jane B. O'Connell
President
Altman Foundation
521 Fifth Avenue, 35th Floor
New York, NY 10017

Dear Ms. O'Connell:

On behalf of the Board of Trustees of the New York Hall of Science, we are writing to request a grant of $125,000 from the Altman Foundation. We are requesting support from the Altman Foundation toward the **Early Childhood Science Initiative**; specifically, we are requesting funding to prototype and test new programs for our youngest visitors, and to begin an exchange of expertise with the Brooklyn Children's Museum. Together, these will improve our ability to serve the fastest growing segment of our constituency, family audiences with young children.

The Hall is located in what the New York Times called the "epicenter of immigration" to the region and to the country. In our closest school district, District 24, over 100 languages are spoken in the students' homes. It is our mission to assure that *all* the young people, families, and teachers of this region have access to high-quality science learning experiences. Therefore we are working to engage culturally diverse communities with a wide range of educational backgrounds.

We are grateful for your consideration of this proposal, and for the initiative that your staff has taken to foster new collaborations. You and Nina will be glad to hear that the planning for this collaborative program has already led to joint activities between the Hall and the Brooklyn Children's Museum.

Have a wonderful new year, and please do feel free to call me (718) 699-0005 x 316 or Eric Siegel at x 317 if we can provide further information.

Sincerely,

Alan J. Friedman

New York Hall of Science 47-01 111th Street, Queens, NY 11368-2950 ✳ 718.699.0005 ✳ Fax 718.699.1341 ✳ www.nyscience.org

The Early Childhood Science Initiative
At
The New York Hall of Science

A Proposal to the Altman Foundation

January, 2002

Ivan G. Seidenberg, Chairman
Dr. Alan J. Friedman, Director

New York Hall of Science 47-01 111th Street, Queens, NY 11368-2950 ✳ 718.699.0005 ✳ Fax 718.699.1341 ✳ www.nyscience.org

REQUEST

The New York Hall of Science is requesting $125,000 from the Altman Foundation toward the Early Childhood Science Initiative. These funds will be applied to increasing our capacity to serve families with young children and preschool groups. Specifically, we are requesting $100,000 toward prototyping and testing of new programs for young visitors and $25,000 toward a collaboration with the Brooklyn Children Museum.

NEW YORK HALL OF SCIENCE EARLY CHILDHOOD SCIENCE INITIATIVE

The New York Hall of Science is undertaking major expansion of our early childhood science education programming for visitors under eight years old and their parents, guardians, and teachers. We are doing this for two principal reasons. First, there is a growing body of knowledge that age-appropriate, hands-on science learning is effective for younger children than had previously been considered. Second, like most informal science institutions, we are finding that our visitors increasingly include families with younger children.

The goals of the Early Childhood Science Initiative are:

- To offer innovative ways to stimulate curiosity among children from infancy through six years old, their parents/caregivers, and teachers
- To encourage sharing of ideas and enthusiasm among children, their parents/caregivers, and teachers

The Early Childhood Science Initiative will include four components:

1) *The Curiosity Center,* a new, indoor 2,000 square foot early childhood exhibition and program space within our new expansion.
2) A new 10,000 square foot outdoor preschool science playground and the adaptation of our current 30,000 square foot *Science Playground* for visitors from 1-6 years old.
3) Programs to support parent/child learning activities that will take advantage of these new facilities and strengthen our services to young audiences and their families.
4) Professional development programs for early elementary teachers in our new Harcourt Teacher Leadership Center.

The $3,000,000 bricks and mortar cost of this project are either in hand or anticipated from public and private sources. Toward program and exhibition costs we have raised $400,000 of the remaining $1,000,000. A list of funders is attached.

- Page 1 -

NYHALL OF SCIENCE

NEED

In February 1998 the American Association for the Advancement of Science convened a forum on Early Childhood Science, Mathematics, and Technology Education. The impetus for the forum was three-fold:

1) Increasing numbers of children are enrolled in some type of preschool program (from 50-69% depending on the state)
2) Widespread agreement exists on the need for students to be science literate if they are to succeed in today's rapidly changing world, yet few preschool programs address science, mathematics, and technology.
3) New technologies and research suggest new approaches to early childhood learning.

Recent research (Elkind, D. (1998) *Educating Young Children in math, science, and technology*, AAAS, Washington, DC) challenges earlier beliefs that science is too "formal, abstract, and theoretical" for the youngest learners and their teachers. Until recently, science had principally been taught through teacher-led activities such as labs and lectures. These settings are not effective for younger children, who learn most effectively in child-centered experiences and activities. This mismatch reinforced the notion that science would be inappropriate for preschool and early elementary settings. It is critical that young children have access to developmentally appropriate experiences and environments to encourage effective science learning. That is a central goal of the Hall's major investment in early childhood learning.

The highlight of the 2001 American Association for the Advancement of Science meeting in San Francisco was the elegant and provocative work of Alison Gopnik of UC Berkeley. Her research demonstrates that younger children are more capable of the kind of critical thinking that underlies science inquiry than is accounted for in the Piagetian model. ("*The Scientist in the Crib: What Early Learning Tells Us About the Mind*" published by Perennial Harper Collins, 2000)

Educational inequality for early childhood programming reflects income inequality. In the preschool arena, "only 45% of three- to five-year-olds from low income families are enrolled in early childhood programs, compared with 71% from their high-income counterparts." (Day, B., and Yarbrough, T. [1998] *The state of early childhood programs in America*, AAAS, Washington, DC). Longitudinal research conducted by the Canadian Institute for Advanced Research (http://204.101.252.85/aeceo/articles/RaisingChildren/findings.htm) suggests that high-quality early childhood experiences have a significant impact on long-term neurological development of the child and also such factors as life expectancy, mental health, and employment success.

- Page 2 -

Providing high quality science education experiences for *all* New Yorkers is central to the Hall of Science's mission. Because we are located in a low income community with the greatest ethnic diversity in the nation, we offer ready access to underserved families, preschool centers, and schools. The Hall's current offerings for families and groups with young children have proven tremendously successful. There is clearly a demand among families and schools for rich, stimulating, and creative science learning for young children. Our Early Childhood Science Initiative will extend the reach of our offerings to these groups to a critical age.

LEARNING GOALS

Based upon research that we have conducted with other informal learning centers a critical measure of success is the ability to accommodate the tremendously diverse developmental stages that range from toddlers through early elementary school students. As one advisor told us: *the difference between three-year-olds and six-year-olds is greater than the difference between six-year-olds and adults.*

One common approach is to create segregated spaces to support the learning styles of each different group. The approach that we plan to take is to create exhibitions and experiences that are flexible enough to accommodate a wide range of developmental stages in learning and exploration.

Another major goal of the Early Childhood Science Initiative is to engage parents in two equally important ways. First, the spaces and programs will encourage informal parent interaction with their children; second, parents will be provided with a wealth of information on their child's developmental stages and how what the children are doing reflects these developmental stages. This information will be delivered principally through direct contact with trained instructors and Educators, supported electronically via web pages, and in printed material.

EXPERIENCES AND ACTIVITIES

We have compiled an outline of experience criteria and sample experiences for the different age ranges in the *Curiosity Center* based upon research into informal early childhood learning spaces conducted by Jeff Kennedy Associates. We have also prototyped many activities in our current preschool space. Activities may address developmental needs of different age groups, and we will not necessarily organize the exhibitions around the age groups outlined below, but might instead organize around common themes.

- Page 3 -

NY HALL OF SCIENCE

Infants & Toddlers

Early childhood spaces should provide sensory stimulation and opportunities for safe gross motor activity and self discovery; experiences that offer control over the environment; opportunities for gross motor activity; a sense of object permanence; satisfaction for short attention spans. Possible elements for inclusion in infant/toddler area:

- crawl-through and walk-through spaces with varying wall and floor textures, soft surfaces, high contrast colors
- peek-a-boo windows; mirrored, reflective surfaces
- flaps to lift, doors to open; cranks, curtains, drawers
- practice walking on ramps, negotiating doorways, tunnels
- things suspended from the ceiling
- places to hide things
- seating for adults in proximity to exhibits/experiences to encourage interaction

Three Year Olds

The spaces should provide opportunities for self expression and imaginative play; small motor skill practice; sorting; assembling a whole from its parts; tactile experiences; physical manipulation of objects. Possible elements for inclusion in one or more clusters of exhibits for three-year-olds include:

- lacing
- manipulating tools and utensils
- sand and/or water play
- balls and ramps
- dumping and filling
- constructing/deconstructing

4-5 Year Olds

The spaces should provide opportunities for cooperative play; following multi-step directions; exploration of action/reaction mechanisms; questioning why: high energy play; investigation of natural world. Possible elements for inclusion in one or more clusters of exhibits for 4-5 year olds include:

- speaking tubes
- gears
- magnets
- balls and ramps
- gravity wall
- sand play

- Page 4 -

- climbing structure

Six to Eight Year Olds
The spaces should provide opportunities for formation of complex thoughts and understanding of complex situations; group play; problem solving and question answering; reading; physical coordination. Possible elements for inclusion in one or more clusters of exhibits for six to eight year olds include:

- ball chase
- stream or bubble play
- easy-view microscopes
- construction zone, bridge building, earthquake table
- magnet challenge
- trading post or swap shop

Parents and Caregivers
Parent and Caregiver programming will stress that the work of childhood is play, and young children are natural scientists. Parents will learn that different types of exploration are appropriate at different ages, and trying to engage a child in developmentally-inappropriate learning can be frustrating for both the parent and the child.

PROGRAMS

In all of the Hall's surveys and formal evaluations, our visitors express a strong preference for face-to-face contact with knowledgeable Explainers and instructors. This is a core strength of the Hall, and we will build that strength into the Early Childhood Science Initiative. Our current preschool space is only open when there is a trained instructor or Explainer present.

A full-time, experienced early childhood science educator will be hired to provide specific training for our Explainers, and to coordinate the goals and activities of the Initiative. While this is an expensive way of running a program, our research has consistently documented its value for both the visitors and the Explainers. For visitors, face-to-face learning provides contact with knowledgeable and diverse role models, with ethnic and social backgrounds that mirror our constituency's. For Explainers, gathering experience in early childhood education offers a new set of skills and exposure to new career alternatives.

Families, Students, and Teachers Working Together. In order to assure that the Hall's $4,000,000 investment reaches the early childhood audience, we will develop and test programs with young children, their caregivers/parents, and their teachers. By

- Page 5 -

prototyping age-appropriate activities we will assure that we design interactive exhibitions that are effective in meeting the learning goals outlined above.

This prototyping will involve creating rough mockups of environments and exhibition elements for specific age groups in our current preschool space or on the Science Playground. We will then invite target age groups for these exhibits, interview them (where appropriate) and observe their interaction with the exhibits. After they have interacted in the space for about a half hour, we will interview them again. We will do this with young children playing by themselves, and with their teachers, guardians, caregivers, or parents.

We will work with this same process to develop take-home *Curiosity Kits* for parents to work with their children at home, and for teachers to work with early childhood classrooms.

Teacher Professional Development. Through a new program at the Hall, the Harcourt Teacher Leadership Center, teachers will participate in a long-term residency developing programs, exhibitions, and working with families. To support professional development for early childhood teachers, we have developed a partnership with PS 499, the Queens College Math, Science, and Technology school. This is a magnet school located on the Queens College campus that began three years ago with two pre-k classrooms, and is now extended into the second grade.

We will extend the reach of the program into the classroom through a collaboration between our Explainers, college age students who are trained and employed by the Hall of Science to conduct hands-on science learning, and classroom teachers. These Explainers will spend twenty days in the classroom with each selected early childhood teachers from PS 499 to support the teacher in implementing inquiry-based science in the classroom. As an ancillary benefit, the Explainer will also get strong classroom training.

Explainer Training. Explainers are high-school and college participants in the Science Career Ladder, a hierarchy of paid training and job experiences that the Hall offers to a diverse group of 100 young people each year. Each year, Explainers participate in 150 hours of peer and instructor led skills development. These training programs might focus upon a content area, a demonstration, or an exhibition. Through the Early Childhood Science Initiative, we will add training modules on reaching younger visitors in school and family groups.

- Page 6 -

COLLABORATION WITH THE BROOKLYN CHILDREN'S MUSEUM

While the Hall of Science has extensive experience in content-rich learning for young people, families. and teachers, we have only recently begun to focus in earnest upon our youngest visitors. Though we do have active and successful programs for early childhood learning, we are planning to expand this area. Therefore, we are glad to collaborate with our colleagues at the Brooklyn Children's Museum (BCM) to complement the Hall's expertise. Specifically, with the timely and welcome encouragement of the Altman Foundation, we have been planning three collaborative programs, as well as an assessment of our work:

- *Sharing of staff knowledge and experience*

  Symposium. We will plan a two-day symposium to be held at each partner organization, six months apart, which will include a guest speaker or a panel discussion by experts in the field of early childhood learning; exhibition demonstrations, science content training, and teacher development programs for the education and floor staff of each organization; and a roundtable discussion in which each organization shares how they conduct community outreach and marketing efforts. Explainers, Educators, Public Program, Marketing, and Development staff from each organization will attend the symposium.

  Staff Exchange. We will conduct a small staff exchange focusing on the interns or floor staff of each organization. Ten Explainers from each organization will work a select number of hours at the partner institution over a period of six months. These high school and college-aged students will experience a valuable opportunity to learn how other organizations conduct their operations. Hall of Science Instructors and Explainers will train BCM Explainers in science content and on the exhibitions, and will share techniques and talents as to how each organization interacts with preschool children and families with older siblings. BCM will share information on how they conduct and coordinate their outreach programs, and train the Hall's Explainers on their **Totally Tots** exhibit, among other exhibitions.

- *Creation of Family Guide*

  Family Guide – We will develop educational materials that families can use to help them plan their trip to the BCM and to the Hall of Science. **Family Guides** will include a brief description of each exhibit that is suitable for early childhood learning, accompanied by hands-on activities to be completed at home. In this way, families can make the most of their visit to the museum, and "re-live" the science experience by completing the hands-on activities together at home.

Each at-home activity will correlate with a specific exhibition area, for example the guide will show parents how to do simple experiments with their children with rainbows, mirrors and eyedroppers, which are content areas connected with the *Seeing the Light* exhibit. The Guide will include exhibits and at-home activities from both the NYHOS and BCM.

In addition to the exhibition and activity areas, there will be background and history of the Hall of Science and the Brooklyn Children's Museum, as well as a section explaining our shared approach to early childhood learning. These guides will be developed and tested by local parents (participants in focus groups already established at both institutions), and will be distributed at family or parent workshops at both sites.

- *Develop Family and Parent Workshops*

When a family arrives at the Hall or at BCM with a two year old, a six year old, and a ten year old, they encounter a difficult challenge: how to engage each of these young people, at their vastly different developmental stages. As this is a challenge common to our institutions (and, we have discovered, at many other informal learning institutions), we propose to develop a workshop for families with children of different ages. Current workshops at the Hall involving parents and children include tours, guided activities that can be replicated at home, printed materials, and a video guide about parent involvement in family science learning. We will start with this format as a basis for family workshops. Again, we will engage parents in developing and prototyping these programs.

- *Assessment of Programming*

We propose to create a succinct and staff-driven evaluation process to test the success of these and future programming. We have several objectives for this process:

- To increase our shared knowledge of families with early learners;
- To engage families and professionals to help us create and implement programs and activities that are most meaningful to them;
- To increase the capacity of our staff to analyze programs, "read" audience, and sharpen and direct programs toward positive outcomes for visitors;
- To create and incorporate simple tools for assessment into each early learner program;
- To share findings with each other and to the field.

- Page 8 -

The assessment tools we create through the workshop will be used to answer several key questions:

- What outcomes do parents and teachers desire through participation in our early learning programs?
- What activities will help prepare our youngest visitors for engaging content and for success during their first organized school-based experiences?
- What activities will help young parents gain the skills and habits they will need to support their children's learning now and in the years ahead?

We will engage an evaluation consultant (we are currently considering Selinda and Associates of Chicago, noted specialists in program assessment) to conduct a two-day intensive joint staff-training workshop focusing on early childhood program development and assessment. The workshops will take place on consecutive days in late August 2002. The first day activities will introduce museum educators from BCM and Hall of Science to best practice methods and tools of program assessment in three parts:

- Methods that help us understand specific audience needs and capabilities relevant to our shared educational goals (front-end evaluation);
- Assessment tools that help educators shape developing programs to effectively engage visitors with content and learning standards for early childhood (formative evaluation);
- Tools that can help us determine how well our finished programs meet their expected outcomes (summative evaluation).

During the second day, our early childhood educators will work with the consultant to design three sets of assessment tools specific to our needs based on the proven models introduced on the first day. The tools will be developed with particular attention to our shared learning goals.

The initial workshops will offer a chance for staff to come together around a common goal and share existing experience and ideas as well as engage in a joint creative process that will yield useful products. The assessment process itself promotes opportunities for positive family, school, and community connections through focused audience interviews, parent and teacher forums, visitor surveys and direct observation and tracking of program performance (several of the tools that are likely to result from the workshop). Developing and administering these tools and sharing findings over the next two years will offer each institution the advantages of a broader and deeper data base from which to draw more accurate conclusions and achieve insight about audience and effectiveness of program activities.

- Page 9 -

Ongoing assessment is a powerful method of ensuring that the programs we deliver are continually relevant for our visitors and create optimum conditions for learning in each of our environments. At the end of this assessment period, we intend to present the results of this collaboration at the New York City Museum Educators Roundtable conference, the Northeast Informal Educator's Network, and publish an article on the collaboration in education newsletters, magazines, and journals that reach New York and the surrounding states.

CONCLUSION

The New York Hall of Science is in the midst of a $68,000,000 expansion that will enable us to reach more visitors and extend the highest quality science learning to *all* New Yorkers. As the family audience is one of the key priorities for this expansion, and as our surveys demonstrate that families are coming with very young children, we are committed to strengthening our work with our youngest visitors. Three million dollars will be invested in new indoor and outdoor facilities to meet this goal. We are requesting $125,000 from the Altman Foundation to develop programs and exhibitions that will make these facilities come alive for young children, their families, and their teachers.

By collaborating with the Brooklyn Children's Museum, we will be sharing institutional strengths. Clearly, BCM is a national leader in early childhood informal learning and in developing programs that are engaging and relevant for a diverse community. The Hall of Science brings its own well-documented strengths to this collaboration. We are grateful to the Altman Foundation for encouraging this collaboration and for your consideration of this proposal. We hope that you will join us in this important work.

- Page 10 -

Early Childhood Science Initiative
New York Hall of Science
Proposal to the Altman Foundation
Four Year Costs Combined
3 January, 2002

Capital Construction Costs	Total	Calendar 2002	notes
Preschool Science Playground	$2,300,000	$250,000	*design*
The Curiosity Center	$400,000	$200,000	*50% construction*
30% of Harcourt Teacher Leadership Ctr	$300,000	$150,000	*50% construction*
Total Capital Construction Costs	**$3,000,000**	**$600,000**	

Program Costs

	Total	Calendar 2002	notes
Exhibitions	$400,000	$60,000	*prototypes*
Personnel	$240,000	$60,000	*education/public prog*
Design and Evaluation	$120,000	$35,000	
Professional Development	$80,000	$20,000	
Program and Capital Administration	$110,000	$35,000	
Materials, Supplies, Printing, Meetings	$50,000	$15,000	
Total Program Costs	**$1,000,000**	**$225,000**	
Total Expenses	**$4,000,000**	**$825,000**	

Brooklyn Children's Museum/NY Hall of Science Collaboration

	Total	Calendar 2002
Meetings/Travel	$5,000	$5,000.00
Printing	$15,000	$15,000.00
Explainer Time	$5,000	$5,000.00
Total Collaboration Budget	**$25,000**	**$25,000**

Current Funding @ 2 January, 2002

Capital	Total	Calendar 2002	
Harcourt General Foundation	$300,000	$ 150,000	
Curiousity Center	$400,000	$ 200,000	
Preschool Science Playground	$250,000	$ 250,000	*(design funds in hand*
Total Capital Funding	**$950,000**	**$600,000**	*construction in 2003)*

Program	Total	Calendar 2002
Chevron Foundation	$250,000	$ 75,000
Rockefeller Brothers Foundation	$150,000	$ 50,000
Total Operating Funding	**$400,000**	**$ 125,000**

New York Hall of Science 47-01 111th Street, Queens, NY 11368-2950 ✳ 718.699.0005 ✳ Fax 718.699.1341 ✳ www.nyscience.org

NEW YORK HALL OF SCIENCE
Fiscal Year 2002 and 2003 Operating Budget
DRAFT

Support and Revenue	FY 2002	FY 2003
Contributions	916,850	990,198
Appropriations City of New York	1,878,652	2,028,944
Earned Income	2,706,854	2,923,402
Net Assets Released from Restrictions:		
Grants Continuing	2,641,300	2,852,604
New Grants, Current Program	1,070,687	1,156,341
New Grants, Expansion	572,893	718,724
Total Support and Revenue	**9,787,236**	**10,670,213**

Expenses		
Administration and Business Office	1,339,068	1,446,193
Admissions	158,999	171,718
Biology	838,688	905,783
Program Planning & Development	1,138,548	1,229,631
Education	1,608,794	1,737,497
Exhibits Maintenance	327,192	353,367
Facilities, Security and Parking	1,082,121	1,168,690
Marketing and Communications	1,086,147	1,173,038
Public Programs	983,796	1,062,499
Special Projects	844,184	911,718
Gift Shop	351,495	379,614
Total Expenses	**9,759,032**	**10,539,748**

Please note: This is NOT an approved Budget for FY 2003. The Board will approve the Hall's FY 2003 Budget at the September 2002 meeting.

New York Hall of Science 47-01 111th Street, Queens, NY 11368-2950 ✱ 718.699.0005 ✱ Fax 718.699.1341 ✱ www.nyscience.org

(Over)

A Proposal From
New Yorkers for Parks
(formerly The Parks Council)
New York, New York

To
New York Foundation
New York, New York

Requested amount: $45,000 **Amount received:** $45,000

Funder's comments:

"What struck me most about this proposal is that it's written with a great deal of confidence. In other words, the writer makes a case as though you'd be left behind to some extent if you didn't decide to support this effort to improve parks. Unlike some other issues, improving parks is not a hard sell. We all have some idea of what a good park looks like and what a neglected park looks like. If you fund in cities, you know why they are important. This proposal uses statistics and budget numbers to take the argument beyond the reader's initial (somewhat superficial) response—'Yes, parks are good. We need good parks!'—and articulates why. In other words, it's not just a subjective argument but an objective one that can be backed up with good statistics. Especially compelling in this case were the stats that compared public and private spending for parks, the private spending on New York City's Bryant, Central, and Prospect Parks, and the reduction in the numbers of recreational staff. The cover letter helped to set the tone. The first paragraph said right up front what the funds were to be used for. The cover letter acted as a proposal summary in this case.

"However, the proposal could have used more of a need statement, and less about goals and objectives. I'm not a big fan of bullets and outlines. I prefer a more narrative proposal. In this case it worked well because the logic of how the work was to be implemented made sense. It could have been written out in a narrative form just as easily, though. This budget was very, very confusing and may have worked fine as an internal document but did not work well for someone trying to get a picture of what the work would cost. Where is the project in that list? Which column? How do the columns relate to one another? The budget should have a way of showing why the money is needed and what it will pay for. This format is an example of what might work internally that makes no sense to an outsider.

"The Parks Council had amazing attachments that were very illustrative and helped make the case. They included interesting and graphic reports that had additional statistics. They included photographs that compared conditions in the three premier New

York City parks (Bryant, Central, and Prospect) with photos of neglected neighborhood parks. They were very stark and made a good case for the need for advocacy.

"The site visit, in this case, sealed it. The confidence that came across in the proposal was apparent in the staff people I met. A common problem I see is that program people and development staff are not always on the same wavelength. You can read a compelling, well-written proposal and then, when you go on a site visit, you find that the people actually doing the work are less than enthusiastic or have not been consulted on the proposed scope of work at all. This was a case where there was very little, if any, division between the development staff person and the program staff. The development person functioned as a 'cheerleader' for the program and really let the work speak for itself."

Maria Mottola, Executive Director, New York Foundation

Notes:

The complete proposal included the following attachments: organizational budget, staff biographies, list of board members and affiliations, illustrations, and graphic representations. As of January 2002, the organization's name is New Yorkers for Parks.

Proposal developed by Juliet Page, then Development Director; Mike Caserta, then Public Policy Director; Michael Klein, then Deputy Director; and Elizabeth Cooke, then Executive Director; written by Juliet Page and submitted to the funder by Elizabeth Cooke.

The Parks Council
The Urban Center
457 Madison Avenue
New York, NY 10022

August 7, 2000

Ms. Madeline Lee
Ms. Maria Mottolla
New York Foundation
350 Fifth Avenue, Rm. 2901
New York, NY 10118-2996

Dear Maddie and Maria,

Thank you for inviting the Parks Council to submit a full proposal for our work to restore maintenance and recreation programs in parks throughout the five boroughs. We are asking the New York Foundation to provide a grant of $45,000 that will fund the salary and fringe benefits of a community organizer who will manage our work with community-based organizations in underserved areas of New York City.

The Parks Council's 2000 strategic plan sets forth several practical program initiatives that we are confident will lead public officials to plan and implement a more equitable distribution of basic maintenance funds, staff and other resources in park land throughout the City.

As you know, there are several not-for-profit park groups that are able to manage the responsibility of restoring, maintaining and programming a local park. However, most New York City parks are not adequately maintained. Total funding for parks has declined by over 30 percent in the last ten years and funding for public recreation programs is down by 60 percent. Most communities are struggling with the challenge of replacing the reduced City funding for the New York City Department of Parks and Recreation.

To achieve our objectives, the Parks Council is working with park constituent groups and producing profiles of open space conditions and needs in every City Council District. Our constituent groups include non-profit providers of athletic, recreation and education programs, school personnel, housing and civic groups, environmental and business leaders, as well as dozens of friends-of-parks and greening groups.

Park stakeholders have not forged a common vision and agenda of how reinvestment in parks can achieve broad common goals. And, there has not yet been an effective effort to link the needs of middle-income communities (traditionally the communities with the most political clout) with those of low-income communities. We have received a very enthusiastic response to our proposals from constituent groups. In fact, they are pressing us to increase our staff and move quickly. The only speed bump is the need to obtain funding commitments to launch and sustain a three to five year effort.

Why support this effort now? Term limits take effect beginning with the 2001 fall elections, and will result in an unprecedented change in city government. In January of 2002, New York will have a new Mayor, Comptroller, Public Advocate and at least 36 new City Council members, quite possibly more. Many non-profit organizations will assist in training candidates for the transition in leadership. The Parks Council's role is to ensure that every community's needs related to parks, public open space and public recreation programs are understood and promoted during the campaign period and transition process. It is also the role of the Parks Council to ensure that park issues are included in the agendas of other influential organizations, in addition to traditional park advocates and politicians.

Support from the New York Foundation for a community organizer will make it possible for us to nurture, educate and activate representatives from the City's neighborhoods that do not have viable park advocate groups and are particularly underserved. For example, we will work in the following neighborhoods: Washington Heights, Manhattan; Hunts Point, Bronx; Park Hill, Staten Island; South Jamaica, Queens; and East New York, Brooklyn.

Your grant will ensure that there are community leaders speaking for these local needs in our citywide effort.

I know the New York Foundation prides itself on making grants that truly make a difference. This fall, equipping the Parks Council with an organizer to coalesce grassroots support for equitable parks maintenance is a smart grant, which will leverage long-term funding for all parks. An organizer on staff at the Parks Council will make it possible to rally support for parks programming when and where it matters most.

As always, the Parks Council and I are a resource to the Foundation. Please feel free to call me directly with questions about this proposal and the 2001 campaign, or anyone else on staff whom you think might be helpful.

Warm regards,

Elizabeth A. Cooke
Executive Director

Recreational Opportunities for the Youngest New Yorkers

The overriding goal of the Parks Council for 2000-2002 is to restore public commitment to equitable recreational opportunities for the youngest New Yorkers.

In the last ten years, public-private partnerships in parks have achieved astounding successes. Indeed, New York's Central Park, once emblematic of urban decay, is now the City's jewel with more daily visitors than ever imagined. Private funding for parks in New York City has climbed more than 100 percent since 1989. Over the same period of time, however, *public* funding for parks has decreased to such an extent that total parks funding is down by 30 percent. Endured by New Yorkers throughout the boroughs, the decline in public spending on parks is without precedent. Although there are 26,907 additional acres of parkland citywide, private funds go almost exclusively to only three parks: Central Park (843 acres), Bryant Park (8 acres) and Prospect Park (526 acres). And it is the youngest New Yorkers who are suffering. The need for recreation facilities has grown with social changes but public funding has been reduced drastically since 1989. For example, over the past 15 years, the Parks Department has reduced staffing of its recreation programs from 2,000 to 400 people.

Simply stated, although a small portion of City parks benefit from generous private funding, it does not provide recreational opportunities for the overwhelming majority of New Yorkers.

The critical value of play, recreation and sports opportunities has long been recognized as essential to the healthy development of New York's youngest citizens. But—with a 60% decrease (since 1989) in public funding for recreation alone—New Yorkers have unwittingly wavered in their support for the very programs, facilities and parks that aid in the development of their children and contribute to the City's attractiveness as a place for families to live. (See Attachment A for *Play, Recreation & Sports: A Celebration*, an analysis of the impact of recreational opportunities.)

Young people in all five boroughs currently find themselves without adequate recreation facilities near where they live in which to play, without sufficient programming to channel their energies and their intellect, and without the natural environments needed to connect them to the earth. All children need positive, healthy alternatives to the gangs, drugs and violent activity prevalent on the streets, and to the social isolation that is sometimes the product of modern technology use.

From every corner of the City and every economic and cultural background, parents are becoming more aware and concerned about the lack of recreational opportunities available to their children.

Advocacy for Parks and Recreation

With term limit laws beginning to take effect, an unprecedented number of incumbents cannot run for reelection in Fall 2001. The Parks Council effort will entail meeting with every Mayoral, Comptroller, Public Advocate and City Council candidate to educate him or her on the positive impact of investing in public parks. In each Council District, the Parks Council will address the district's unique public space needs. The Parks Council anticipates that there will be more than 100 candidates for the 36 open City Council seats and aims to work with local constituents to educate every one of these candidates. Although spending is not the only, or the best, measure of services, these briefings will include a budget analysis outlining the impact of various parks spending plans, including cost barriers to the creation and maintenance of public recreation facilities. And because of the Parks Council's unique programmatic combination of watchdogging and demonstration projects, the briefings will include "lessons learned" from direct service in neighborhood parks.

To produce a larger public investment in parks and recreation, the Parks Council will increase public awareness and build concerned constituencies in support of its mission.

Throughout the advocacy campaign, the Parks Council will continue to collaborate with the New York City Audubon Society, the Children's Environmental Research Group of the City University of New York and hundreds of community and environmental organizations to document conditions that threaten the City's open spaces. The Council will also develop public policy recommendations to provide city officials with a better understanding of the scope and gravity of longtime underfunding of parks. The documentation process will involve and educate a broader constituency, and the findings will be used to build support for maintenance and management solutions.

Programmatic Goals and Objectives

I. To undertake a proactive advocacy agenda

The Parks Council will make funding for parks a high-priority issue in the 2001 city elections. Integral to an effective advocacy campaign is the expansion of the circle of park advocates to include all stakeholders in a strengthened Department of Parks and Recreation. The Parks Council advocacy goals are as follows:

A. Increase substantially New York City's fiscal commitment to the Department of Parks and Recreation such that it is one percent of the City's annual operating budget to provide New York City with a model parks system, including:
   1. A recreation worker in every playground.
   2. Skilled gardeners, horticulturists and arborists in every borough.
   3. Fixed post staffing to provide a visible security presence.
   4. An appropriate presence of park rangers.

B. Restore specifically recreation funding to the Department of Parks and Recreation and thereby ensure accessible recreational programming on public parkland for every young New Yorker.

C. Promote excellence in the design of parks and open spaces through the provision of pro bono landscape design.

D. Using academic research, increase public understanding of the benefits of parks for a healthy community; specifically:
   1. Demonstrate and disseminate information about the economic impact of parks on business development and housing property values.
   2. Demonstrate and disseminate information about the psychological and physical health benefits of urban parks.

E. Analyze and influence the City's multi-year capital planning process to rebuild existing parks and create new parks.
   1. Reclaim public access to New York City's waterfront.
   2. Revitalize the City's flagship parks in all boroughs.
   3. Enhance parks and recreation facilities, especially in low-income communities.

Strategy for Advocacy

Understanding the scope and challenges of this advocacy effort, the Parks Council will:

Documentation, Research and Analysis

1) Research and document park conditions in each City Council District and identify needs of specific parks. For districts with a low ratio of parkland to population, identify and include community initiatives to develop potential sites for new public open space.

2) Produce a District Profile for every City Council District that includes demographic data on population density, age, education and other indicators of service needs. Interview major service providers and identify priority needs of households and youth in each District.

3) Provide Professional Budget Analysis of the City operating budget, the capital budget and the Parks Department budget, on both the revenue and expenditure sides. Generate credible budget recommendations that allocate adequate city support for parks. Analysis may require hiring a consultant to demonstrate how the city could increase support for Parks to one percent of its operating budget and still maintain a balanced budget. Expenditure analysis will include reviewing the cost of maintenance per square acre of Central Park, Battery Park City and major state parks; review of existing guidelines for the management of natural areas and ballfields; and a review of budgets of other municipalities. Guidelines will be developed for staffing and maintenance budgets for different types of park uses.

4) Document public programs provided in public parks in counties surrounding New York City that compete to attract corporate headquarters and jobs; estimate cost per 1,000 residents.

5) Research the experiences of other municipalities, and identify practices they have used to increase <u>public</u> support for parks and public recreation programs.
6) Continue to participate in citywide "Green" Mapping initiative.
7) Interview and enlist advice from those who have led successful advocacy campaigns to change public policy or priorities.

Public Education and Constituency Building

1) Share District Profiles with local organizations and park constituents and work with them to develop their own statements of need and expectations for each City Council District.
2) Build collaborative agreements and press events with major environmental, environmental justice, labor, educational, health, criminal justice and social service organizations.
3) Identify how park and recreation goals 'cross-over' to their platforms.
4) Build collaborative platforms and press events with community-based development and housing groups; assist them in integrating park and recreation needs into their agendas.
5) Assist community-based organizations in conducting voter registration drives and get-out-the-vote efforts.
6) Initiate public policy discussions and forums between public policy experts, officials, media representatives, park funders and constituents to broaden common understanding of identified needs. Examples of Public policy issues that warrant discussion:
   - Should private donations of time and money augment or replace public support.
   - Are there <u>any</u> fixed responsibilities of city government regarding park maintenance, operations and programs? If so, what are they? If not, Should private funds be solicited for every category of park maintenance, program and capital expenses?
   - Should the same funding policies apply to all parks in all communities?
   - Should Parks and Recreation continue to be a City Mayoral agency?
   - To what extent should non-government organizations be encouraged to assume management and funding responsibility for an increasing number of public parks and recreation programs?

Communications

1) Publish findings and positions on a Web page and in a weekly blast-fax/newsletter.
2) Promote positions and findings to media sources; get stories of local interest covered in daily and community outlets; develop stronger relationships with reporters.
3) Prepare and place Op-Ed articles. Pitch feature articles.
4) Ask editors of major daily and community newspapers to endorse campaign goals; meet with editors to brief them and solicit support.
5) Provide a guest column, or special articles for newsletters of partner organizations.
6) Create a public service advertising campaign.

Advocacy

1) Arrange meetings with every candidate for Mayor, Comptroller, Public Advocate and City Council to solicit support and inform them of our position on parks.
2) Meet with the chiefs of staff, and committee staff, of current City Council members. They will have greater influence when newly elected officials are installed.
3) Provide supportive candidates with position papers and suggested language for their own speeches and position papers.
4) Get park and recreation issues included in major political debates and public interviews.
5) Invite supportive candidates to appear at public events.
6) Publicize position statements made by candidates in newsletters and on Web page.
7) Create campaign slogans, palm cards and buttons.
8) Encourage board members and members to donate contributions to candidates that support park and recreation funding restoration.
9) Prepare short 'elevator-ride' or 'cocktail party' scripts in support of park and recreation goals. Train influential supporters to deliver them. Print main points on a palm card.

After 2001 Fall elections

1) Congratulate all newly elected officials.
2) Reiterate desired objectives.
3) Track and publish voting records and other actions of candidates, after they assume office in January of 2002
4) Monitor progress toward attaining goals.

Trustee and Staff Commitment to 2000-2002 Plan of Action

A board of 40 accomplished trustees and 12 professional staff lead the Parks Council. Recent recruitment efforts attracted several skilled public policy and parks management staff members. Trustees, staff and Urban Conservation Corps members are drawn from all boroughs, possess a range of professional expertise, and have access to decision makers who can support the organization's agenda and to those who can secure financial support. In addition, board and staff represent varied ethnic, social and cultural backgrounds (see Attachments B and C for staff biographies and a board list).

Beginning last summer with 27 external interviews representing voices from all five boroughs—ranging from the Parks Commissioner to the grassroots advocates we assist—the Parks Council completed its current strategic plan in February 2000. The findings, including both Parks Council strengths and weaknesses, have invigorated the board and staff's commitment to promoting *all parks for all New Yorkers*.

THE PARKS COUNCIL
PROJECTED REVENUES AND PROPOSED EXPENDITURES
BUDGET FOR May 01, 2000 -to- April 30, 2001

ACCOUNT & PROGRAM CATEGORIES	Actual Year-End 04/30/2000		2000 -- 2001		
			Repeated Programs	Additional Programs	TOTALS
REVENUE:-					
BENEFITS:-					
Annual Award Dinner	288,958.00		310,000.00	0.00	310,000.00
CORPORATIONS:-				0.00	0.00
General Operating	15,800.00		10,000.00	0.00	10,000.00
Program Grant			20,000.00	0.00	20,000.00
FOUNDATIONS:-				0.00	0.00
General Operating	217,785.00		198,000.00	0.00	198,000.00
Program Grant	472,635.00		221,300.00	546,500.00	767,800.00
INDIVIDUAL GIFTS	167,295.00		190,000.00	387,500.00	577,500.00
MEMBERSHIP	90,951.00		100,000.00	0.00	100,000.00
GOVERNMENT	319,694.00		283,495.00	74,500.00	357,995.00
OTHER:-	9,950.00		12,000.00	0.00	12,000.00
TOTAL REVENUE :-->	$1,583,068.00		$1,344,795.00	$1,008,500.00	$2,353,295.00
EXPENDITURES:-					
ADMINISTRATION:-					
Administration	345,000.00		325,000.00	0.00	325,000.00
Development	85,000.00		133,500.00	0.00	133,500.00
Finance	100,900.00		98,000.00	0.00	98,000.00
Annual Awards Dinner				0.00	0.00
ADVOCACY:-				0.00	
General Advocacy	110,000.00		150,800.00	0.00	150,800.00
NYC Elections 2001 Campaign				270,000.00	270,000.00
Recreation Initiative	42,500.00			235,500.00	235,500.00
Floating Swimming Pool	13,000.00			25,000.00	25,000.00
Park Design Excellence	30,000.00			25,000.00	25,000.00
RESEARCH, ANALYSIS & COMMUNICATION:-				0.00	
Communications General			25,000.00	0.00	25,000.00
Open space & Publications	12,000.00		8,000.00	4,000.00	12,000.00
Parks Council Web Site	10,000.00		50,000.00		50,000.00
Benchmarks & Sunshine Zoning	50,000.00			42,000.00	42,000.00
Protecting Parks & Natr'l Areas Inst.				50,000.00	50,000.00
DIRECT SERVICES:-				0.00	
Direct Services General	233,190.00		196,000.00	0.00	196,000.00
AmeriCorps	275,000.00		283,495.00	72,300.00	355,795.00
Summer UCC	232,000.00		75,000.00	75,700.00	150,700.00
Designated Park Improvement P	125,000.00			50,000.00	50,000.00
'(Eib's/R.Wilken's)				0.00	
School Gardens	9,600.00			34,500.00	34,500.00
Success Gardens	5,300.00			20,000.00	20,000.00
Grand Ferry Park	7,700.00			40,000.00	40,000.00
Betsy B. Rogers & Wein Funds	1,500.00			64,500.00	64,500.00
TOTAL EXPENDITURES:-->	$1,687,690.00		$1,344,795.00	$1,008,500.00	$2,353,295.00
REV's Over(Under) EXP's :--->	-$104,622.00		$0.00	$0.00	$0.00

A Proposal From

Rhode Island Youth Guidance Center
Pawtucket, Rhode Island

To

The William Bingham Foundation
Rocky River, Ohio

Requested amount: $25,000; **Amount received**: $25,000

Funder's comments:

"Because many of the proposals The William Bingham Foundation receives are from organizations in other states, I usually am not able to visit the organization, although our trustees visit organizations in their communities. The best proposals are the ones that enable me to visualize the program, and the proposal from Rhode Island Youth Guidance Center is an excellent example. It did a great job of describing who, what, when, where, why, and how. On the first read-through of a grant proposal I jot down the things I wonder about in the margins, such as: How did the program originate? What will happen to the participants? Which staff members will carry out the activities? How will the board decide whether or not to continue this program? What does that word (any word not used in standard conversation) mean?

"All of these questions were answered during the reading of the Rhode Island Youth Guidance Center's proposal. The best thing about it is that it reads like a description of an internal plan, and not something written with a prospective funder in mind, and thus covered all of the things I normally wonder about. Instead of puffed-up adjectives trying to convince us that this will be a terrific program, it contained facts, which speak for themselves."

—Laura Gilbertson, Director, The William Bingham Foundation

Notes:
The complete proposal included the following attachments: list of board members, most recent audited financial statements, current and projected agency budgets, and IRS tax-exempt letter.

Proposal written and submitted to the funder by Robert F. Wooler, Executive Director; case scenarios by Rebecca Minard, Program Director.

RHODE ISLAND
YOUTH GUIDANCE CENTER

A Gateway Healthcare Provider

82 Pond Street
Pawtucket, RI 02860
Telephone: (401) 725-0450
Facsimile: (401) 725-0452
TT/TTY Relay Service
(800) 745-5555

March 15, 2001

Laura H. Gilbertson, Director
The William Bingham Foundation
20325 Center Ridge Rd.   Suite 629
Rocky River, OH 44116

Dear Laura:

On behalf of the Board of Directors of the Rhode Island Youth Guidance Center and the staff of the agency's growing Mediation program, I am pleased to have the opportunity to submit the enclosed proposal for consideration by The William Bingham Foundation for a grant in the amount of $25,000. With this grant, Rhode Island Youth Guidance will be able to expand its current pilot venture in Family Mediation to serve more families in Rhode Island in the upcoming 2001-02 program year. The lessons which have been learned from our experience thus far shows us that mediation is a refreshing and productive alternative for parents and their adolescent children because it is rooted in the present, focused on the future, concrete, and user-friendly. Given the project's careful development during the past year by our excellent co-coordinators, Becky Minard and Kim White, the foundation has been laid for expanded activity as we take the project to scale in the Providence metro area, encompassing the cities of Providence, Pawtucket, and Central Falls.

In addition to the requested twelve copies of the proposal, budget, and program information, we include our IRS determination letter, FY2000 audited financial statements, FY2002 projected budget, agency strategic plan, and Board of Directors list. Please feel free to contact me at (401) 725-0450 ext. 127 with any questions you may have during the review process. Thank you for your time and consideration. I look forward to speaking with you in the near future.

Sincerely,

Robert F. Wooler
Executive Director

Enclosures

A UNITED WAY AGENCY

Family Mediation Program

Cover Summary

March 15, 2001

1. Legal Name of Organization, Address, and Name of Executive Director:

   Rhode Island Youth Guidance Center
   82 Pond Street
   Pawtucket, RI 02860

   Robert F. Wooler, Executive Director

2. RI Youth Guidance Center is a 501 (c) (3) non-profit organization.

3. Contact Person and Title: Robert F. Wooler, Executive Director

4. Phone: (401) 725-0450 x 127   Fax: (401) 722-4806   e-mail: mcwooler@aol.com

5. Amount Requested: $25,000

6. Type of Request: Project Support

7. Organization's Mission:

   The Rhode Island Youth Guidance Center fosters the healthy development of children and youth through school-based and school-linked services.

8. Proposal Summary:

   The Youth Guidance Center is proposing to expand its current efforts in Family Mediation to work with a projected 100 families in greater Providence in the 2001-02 program year, using mediation as a problem-solving tool to work with adolescents and their parents. Through an expanded outreach and marketing program, the agency will attract referrals from schools, the police, community agencies, churches, and families themselves. Through regular follow-up and outcomes assessment activity with families, the project will help to increase family communication, restore healthy functioning, and reduce need for further external intervention.

9. Target Population and Communities:

      Parents and adolescents primarily from the cities of Pawtucket, Central Falls, and Providence, RI.

10. Total Number of Board Members: 12   Total Number of Volunteers: 17

      Nature and Extent of Board Involvement and Giving:

      Number of Board Members who
- Attend monthly meetings: 8
- Participate on the annual auction event committee: 5
- Serve as program advisors/ambassadors: 3
- Serve on the Executive Committee: 4
- Serve on the Gateway Healthcare Board of Directors: 2
- Give financially to the agency annually: 12

11. Total Number of Staff: Full-time: 35   Part-time: 15

12. Total Annual Organizational Budget: $1,743,000   Fiscal Year-end: 6/30/01
                            $1,720,000   6/30/02

13. Period this grant will cover: 7/1/01 – 6/30/02

14. United Way affiliate: Yes

15. The William Bingham Foundation has previously supported the Conflict Resolution Model Schools program at the Rhode Island Youth Guidance Center:
      1996-97: $24,400
      1997-98: $12,000

Rhode Island Youth Guidance Center
Family Mediation Program

Executive Summary

The Rhode Island Youth Guidance Center, a statewide leader in the provision of counseling, prevention, and school-based services, is combining its strong background in mediation programming with the success of its current pilot programs in Victim-Offender Mediation and Family Mediation to propose the establishment of an expanded multi-community program in Family Mediation. The program would serve as a resource in metropolitan Providence and northern Rhode Island for the growing number of families who are seeking an efficient, flexible, user-friendly resource to help them work their way through the upheavals associated with adolescent children. Referrals to the Family Mediation Program would be made by the RI Family Court, local Juvenile Hearing Boards, the police, schools, state and local agencies, and by families themselves in response to outreach about the program through dissemination of program materials, face-to-face contact by program coordinators, and publicity through the media.

Over the course of a year beginning in July, 2001 the Family Mediation Program proposes to serve 100 families who will meet at the Youth Guidance Center offices or other convenient local sites with a mediation coordinator and co-mediator to explore the dimensions of family conflict, determine areas of compromise and agreement, and fashion a written agreement based on these understandings. Over the course of the next six months, follow-up through telephone contact and additional mediation sessions will occur to help family members adjust to new roles, strengthen their relationships, and reinforce or modify the agreements as circumstances dictate. Successfully implemented, it is anticipated that the project will achieve the following goals during the period between July 1, 2001 and June 30, 2002:

- Families will find that communication between family members is easier.
- Families will experience less conflict and a higher degree of family functioning.
- Families will experience less need for continuing involvement with external services.

The design for the program is based on the program model which has worked well for the agency's current pilot efforts in statewide Victim-Offender Mediation with the RI Family Court and with Family Mediation in the city of Central Falls which is supported by a mini-grant through the RI Division of Substance Abuse. With continued success in mediation work with families and continued flexibility in how juvenile justice and child welfare funds are programmed in the future, it is expected that the program will be well supported by alternative revenue streams and core funding support following the conclusion of the proposed program which will solidly establish the Family Mediation program model based on the pilot and this proposed "growing to scale" effort in the coming year.

Toward an overall budget of $35,000 to serve 100 families over the course of the year, the Rhode Island Youth Guidance Center is requesting a grant of $25,000 from the William Bingham Foundation.

1

Family Mediation Program

Background on the Organization and the Project

The Rhode Island Youth Guidance Center offers a full spectrum of counseling services and prevention programs to children, youth, and their families. Based in Pawtucket, the agency offers programs that are school-based and school-linked throughout the Blackstone Valley, Greater Providence, and the region. Having developed a continuum of care that helps children succeed in school and community life, the Youth Guidance Center pursues a mission that has kept it in the forefront of social services and behavioral healthcare in Rhode Island and the region since 1916. By partnering with educators and pioneering innovative approaches to school-based care, the Center takes natural advantage of the places where a community goes to learn, to grow, and to translate those gains into a richer community and family life. Finally, by offering a range of programming that embraces children, youth, and parents at every point on the age spectrum, Rhode Island Youth Guidance Center offers young people and their families many opportunities for help and support through its constant presence in schools and classrooms, after-school programs, clinics and community centers, and family homes.

The Youth Guidance Center offers a range of counseling and therapeutic after-school services to children and families in Rhode Island's distressed urban core: Pawtucket, Central Falls, and Providence. These clinical programs are complemented and extended by a range of prevention and skill-building programs which include:

- Social and Emotional Learning Programs, including social skills development, conflict resolution, violence prevention, and mediation.
- Youth Development and Teen Leadership programs, including the SPIRIT Education Program, peer education, service learning projects, comprehensive after-school programming, and school-to-career support.
- Early Childhood outreach through Parents As Teachers, helping young children get a healthy start in life.

Together, the programs and services of the Rhode Island Youth Guidance Center reach over 7,000 people each year and form a strong school-based and school-linked continuum of services that can follow children and families, whatever their level of need, from infancy to adulthood.

The agency blends 40 separate funding sources in an annual budget of $1.7 million, just over half of which are municipal funds from the school systems with which the agency has contracts. Services are delivered by a diverse professional staff of 50: social workers, psychologists, educators, counselors, and youth workers. To meet the changing needs of the cities we serve, the staff is increasingly diverse, with 25% being Latino, Cape Verdean, or African-American. The agency is led by Robert Wooler, an Executive Director with over 25 years of experience in child, youth, and school-based services, the last ten of which have been with Rhode Island Youth Guidance. Through our 12 member Board of Directors and support from our Gateway Healthcare partners, the agency receives the broad governance and management support it needs to succeed with those it serves. Gateway Healthcare is a large behavioral healthcare organization that encompasses two community mental health centers, a substance abuse treatment agency, and RI Youth Guidance. Its state-of-the-art management services support combined agency budgets of $42 million annually, 700 employees, and over 33,000 clients in Rhode Island. Rhode Island Youth Guidance receives accounting/auditing services, employee benefits, technology support, and commercial insurance through our association with Gateway.

Mediation Programming at Rhode Island Youth Guidance

The agency has a strong background in mediation programming. Mediation has been a continuous thread in our prevention and problem-solving efforts with youth and families throughout the 1990s. Our school-based mediation efforts were started by a Carlisle Foundation grant in 1990 that established peer mediation in the Pawtucket Junior High Schools. Our involvement in each of the junior highs has been substantial throughout the decade, with full-time counseling and prevention staff in all three schools. The agency's support of the mediation programs in the schools has been constant as well, as annual peer mediation training and regular follow-up assistance have supported over 200 mediations annually at each of these schools. In addition to the Pawtucket junior highs, the agency has regularly trained and supported peer mediation programs at Shea and Tolman High Schools and St. Raphael Academy in Pawtucket and Central Falls Junior-Senior High School. This year, peer mediation

2

programming expanded to the Times2 Academy charter school in Providence. At Goff Junior High, the peer mediation program is supported by a full-time conflict resolution specialist on the staff of the Youth Guidance Center who started at the school in 1996 through support from the William Bingham Foundation for a Conflict Resolution Model Schools project from 1996 to 1998. The Model Schools program contained an evaluation component which demonstrated the effectiveness of full-year intensive programming at schools as compared to shorter-duration, less-intensive interventions. Based on the strength of this experience and the power of this service model, the Youth Guidance Center has developed a new school-based program using full-time behavior specialists who incorporate the conflict resolution/problem-solving orientation with short term counseling, consultation, and crisis intervention. This popular and successful program now operates in six local middle and high schools.

Between 1993 and 1996, the Youth Guidance Center carried on an active dialogue with the RI Family Court, the local Juvenile Hearing Boards, the Attorney General's office, the Ocean State Center for Law and Citizen Education, and the Rhode Island Anti-Drug Coalition on developing more resources for mediation to serve the growing youth population seen by the courts for whom mediation represents a positive alternative to court or other diversion programs. In 1998 this dialogue bore fruit as the agency has extended its mediation expertise into the Rhode Island community on a statewide basis through an innovative pilot program in Victim-Offender Mediation which we conduct through referrals from the Rhode Island Family Court. This program is based on a restorative justice orientation which empowers the victim to be active in arranging solutions and reparations and moves the offender toward active accountability in making reparation for criminal behavior. With the community acting as the facilitator in this process, victims and offenders are brought together to mediate solutions. The court targets cases which are good candidates for resolution through mediation and refers them to mediation coordinators at the Youth Guidance Center who arrange for a mediation at a convenient, community-based site. Over a three year period dating from March, 1998, the program has completed over 90 mediations on a variety of property and personal matters. Agreement has been reached in 100% of the cases mediated, and an excellent working relationship has been established with the Family Court. In one compelling case, a group of teens slashed the tires of the vehicles of several adults at a bowling center. The opportunity to bring the victims and offenders face to face was an incredibly powerful experience, allowing the offenders to hear and know the pain and anger of the victims, while the victims were brought to a greater understanding of the randomness and senselessness of some juvenile behavior. The financial restitution and community service meted out in the agreement was an appropriate resolution to the incident.

<u>Community Needs and Challenges that the Family Mediation Program will Address</u>

The Victim-Offender Mediation project sets the stage for this proposal for the Family Mediation Program, for the majority of the referrals to our Victim-Offender project have been referrals for family mediation with adolescent issues as the focus. Typically, these cases have come to the attention of the Family Court through "wayward" petitions filed by families seeking the assistance of the court in regaining the upper hand in parenting. Mediators at Rhode Island Youth Guidance are seeing adolescents in single parent or blended families that have reached the breaking point because of the control issues that have been stirred up by adolescent acting out behaviors. The agency's work in schools throughout Pawtucket and Central Falls where candidates for family mediation have been identified in great numbers by school personnel, coupled with the steady stream of calls the agency receives requesting assistance and support with adolescent parenting issues, supports the notion that the market for family mediation services here in greater Providence and northern Rhode Island is quite significant. Over the course of the past year, our school-based clinicians have documented over 100 cases of adolescent-parent conflict that are appropriate for mediation, and 70 requests for adolescent parenting support have been received by the agency from local parents. This documented need has helped the agency pilot a small Family Mediation pilot program with the Central Falls police department, and mediation and follow-up assistance with thirteen referred cases over the past six months have proceeded well. An appended page offers details on two types of mediation cases which are typical of the families served in the pilot project to date.

Other factors at work in highlighting the need for mediation are the changing nature of mental health treatment and the rapid diversification of the population in urban Rhode Island. Until very recent times, family counseling was a more universally accepted approach to addressing the upheaval in families associated with adolescence. The managed care revolution and the changes in the delivery of behavioral healthcare both nationally and locally have contributed to a situation where there are diminished resources for youth and family counseling and the types of problems authorized for treatment are more narrowly defined by insurers and managed care companies. It is estimated that a full 60% of the mental health providers in urban Rhode Island that were available to families just three years ago are no longer involved in outpatient work due to changes in the marketplace, credentialing, and declining rates of reimbursement. This has restricted the geographic availability of counseling services statewide, with corresponding effects regarding the times that services are available to families as well. The managed care industry's bias toward more serious mental health problems has tended to screen out less critical family struggles, often pushing these problems into the realm of private pay and therefore out of the economic reach of many families. While piloting this mediation model with Family Court and Central Falls referrals, we found that nearly all of the cases required either two mediation sessions or mediation and a follow-up meeting to reinforce or adjust the mediation agreement, a feature that counseling in a strict managed care environment would rarely offer. Finally, the immigration of many Latino, Cape Verdean, African-American, and Southeast Asian families into Rhode Island in recent years has changed the consumer mix dramatically in the cities of Pawtucket, Central Falls, and Providence where the percentage of minority families now exceeds 40%, up from just 11% in 1990. Within the immigrant community, there exists a general cultural bias against mental health services, and Rhode Island offers very few credentialed clinicians who are bi-lingual and bi-cultural. Moreover, the traditions of many cultures favor the dynamics of mediation over those of counseling for a variety of reasons. Mediation has proven to be particularly successful with African-American, Latino, and Asian populations around the country because it avoids the stigma of mental health counseling and judicial proceedings and is more culturally-sensitive in that it offers access to a process where mediators can be of the same racial/ethnic background as the disputants.

Project Description: The Family Mediation Model of Service

The discussion above highlights many of the reasons why a mediation model is often more effective with families in the 1990s: streamlined, efficient, concrete, future-oriented problem-solving which is almost always successful in the course of one or two meetings, flexibility to meet family needs at mutually convenient times and places, culturally friendly services delivered by mediators from the same backgrounds, and a foundation in conflict theory which is generally at the root of family power struggles with adolescents. The theoretical base for the mediator role is rooted in the reality of conflict, whereas a family systems approach is a more common basis for social work practice. The differences between the two are striking in the conflict orientation focuses on individuals and takes a practical, solution-focused approach, while family systems sees individuals only in the context of the family and takes a long-term approach to working with process, family dynamics, and treating problems as symptoms of family dysfunction. The recognition of the inherent conflict between systems or people provides the context for the mediator role. An important factor in mediation is getting participants to recognize that each has something the other party needs and that the best way to get one's needs met is to decide what others need and exchange behaviors. Teenagers and parents have been able to do this successfully in mediation because of the presence of a neutral third party even when they have not been able to listen and communicate with each other in everyday life. In this way, mediation provides tools to find agreeable solutions between parties with unequal bases of power, such as parents and adolescents.

Mediation has another important advantage as well. It can be thought of as an intervention with empowering qualities because to the extent it keeps resolution on the community level and as close to home as possible, the greater the power that is retained by the family and the less that is relinquished to outside authorities like the court system. The final inherent advantage of community-based family mediation is the potential for resolving the conflict at the earliest possible stage, before serious damage may be done to the family. Mediation concerning problematic adolescent behavior, for example, will be far less effective if it occurs after the adolescent has run away from home and or has become involved in delinquent behavior and more trauma is inflicted on the family system. The Family Mediation Program at the Rhode Island Youth Guidance Center has been effectively piloted over the past three years with referrals from the RI Family Court and the Central Falls police, and, having recently trained a talented and diverse group of mediators, the time seems appropriate for expanding the program to more families and more communities. The mechanics of the mediation program work as follows:

4

1. Referrals are made to the Mediation Program co-coordinators at the Youth Guidance Center who obtain basic information about the background of the case and the nature of the dispute, contact the parties, obtain agreement to mediate, and arrange for the mediation to take place at a mutually convenient time and place. Youth Guidance has been able to utilize a variety of community-based agencies, libraries, and other meeting places to host mediations at sites close to families so as to maximize comfort and familiarity. To reduce barriers for families, mediation is offered on a no fee basis at the Youth Guidance Center.

2. The mediation session is conducted by one of the co-coordinators who gathered the facts on the case and arranged for the mediation and a partner from program's pool of mediators, including staff members of the Youth Guidance Center and community residents who have been trained in family mediation by our mediation coordinators over a 20 hour period of time. To accommodate the linguistic diversity of the community, mediations may be conducted in Spanish and Cape Verdean Creole. Through a series of joint sessions and individual sessions, the disputing parties work with the mediators to discover similarities and differences in family member's views and concerns, focus on actions each member has suggested as possible and positive changes, transmit new information, concerns, and solution options from one party to another, and specify areas of agreement. After a process in which the parties have discussed areas of compromise with the mediators, the mediators have shared information with each party, and the parties have reached specific points of agreement, the final agreement is written. Sometimes this mediation process can be completed in two to three hours, but most often family members find it beneficial to break the mediation into two sessions to reach an agreement that both parents and teens can live by.

3. Follow-up is a key element in family mediation cases, as our experience has shown that agreements are more workable and durable in family mediation cases when the parties involved return to a follow-up session to review and reinforce the terms of the agreement, modify or re-negotiate the provisions of the agreement, or obtain support and reassurance as they attempt to navigate the choppy waters of adolescence with the agreement as their map. Family feedback to program coordinators regarding the value and utility of the Family Mediation process has been very positive, suggesting the potential of an expanded, specialized program in Family Mediation being offered in multiple communities, perhaps statewide, in the near future.

Program Goals, Objectives, Activities, and Timetable

The overall goals of the Family Mediation Program at Rhode Island Youth Guidance are to provide families from Pawtucket, Central Falls, and Providence with an appropriate and effective tool for managing conflict with adolescents and to establish the program as a resource for families on an ongoing basis. Objectives related to these overall goals in the year beginning July 1, 2001 and ending June 30, 2002 are as follows:

1. To conduct outreach about the program through local schools, police departments, Juvenile Hearing Boards, state and local agencies, churches, and the media to acquaint potential referral sources with the program and encourage referrals of appropriate families. [July, 2001 – December, 2001]
   - Prepare and distribute a program brochure to all appropriate referral sources, following up key resources with a meeting to cultivate working relationships and referrals of mediation-appropriate families.
   - Cultivate press coverage and media attention for the program to generate wider visibility and cultivate self-referrals from families.

2. To offer Family Mediation services to a projected 100 families over the course of the year, reaching agreement successfully in at least 90% of the cases. [July, 2001 – June, 2002]
   - Receive and process referrals expeditiously, scheduling 90% of referrals for mediation within two weeks.
   - Conduct mediation sessions at a variety of convenient, community-based locations throughout the state, concluding 90% of them with written agreements.

3. To provide appropriate follow-up on mediation cases, offering additional sessions to families as needed. [July, 2001 – June, 2002]

- Provide telephone follow-up to families within two weeks of the mediation to monitor progress and success, offering support and guidance as needed. Continue scheduled phone follow-up at the intervals of two months and six months.
- Schedule needed follow-up sessions as necessary to reinforce or modify provisions of the agreement.

4. To conduct evaluation of mediation activities by assessing both family satisfaction with the process and the outcome of the mediation for the family. [July, 2001 – June, 2002]
   - Families will complete a satisfaction/feedback survey at the conclusion of mediation.
   - Outcomes will be tracked by families and coordinators through ongoing longitudinal contact at two weeks, two months, and six months to assess impact in terms of school, family, and community functioning. Longer-term follow-up may be appropriate for families with whom a particularly close or intensive working relationship develops, but this practice would not be practical or appropriate with all families.

Program Staffing

The staff of the Mediation program at the Youth Guidance Center have strong professional credentials and extensive experience in the mediation field:

- The program is co-coordinated by Rebecca Minard and Kim White. Ms. Minard, who joined the agency in 1998, is an attorney and a social worker with several years of experience in community-based mediation in Rhode Island. Ms. White, who began her work with RIYG in 1997, is a conflict resolution and behavior specialist with an extensive background child welfare who has experience with mediation in both school and community settings. Both coordinators are experienced mediators and trainers who are members of the National Institute of Dispute Resolution and the Victim-Offender Mediation Association and attend ongoing professional trainings.

Co-mediators are drawn from a group with varied professional backgrounds including youth work, social work, education, and the ministry. Effective co-mediators are a key to the program's success, as their quality, reliability, and commitment translates naturally into a smoother mediation process and a more realistic, practical agreement.

Program Outcomes, Results, and Evaluation

Successfully implemented, the Family Mediation Program expects to achieve the following results in 2001-02:

1. In at least 70% of the 100 cases handled, the level of family conflict will be decreased and the level of family functioning will be increased as documented in follow-up contact that is conducted after the mediation sessions.

2. In at least 80% of the mediation cases, families will report a sense of satisfaction with the process and will indicate they felt more empowered, communicated better, and felt more in control of the outcome than they might have through an alternative proceeding such as the courts or counseling.

3. In at least 80% of the cases, families will report that they feel more knowledgeable and effective as parents of adolescents due to the information and support received through the mediation and follow-up process.

4. In at least 70% of the cases handled, the need for further intervention through the courts, mental health, or child welfare systems will not occur within the year.

These outcomes will be tracked by the program co-coordinators through an exit survey administered at the conclusion of the mediation and through follow-up contact with families that is scheduled at regular intervals over the course of the program year to monitor the effectiveness of the agreement, offer follow-up assistance as needed, and obtain information on levels of family and community functioning, the extent of further intervention by outside systems, and parents' self-perceptions as to parenting knowledge and effectiveness.

6

Documentation of program impact will be maintained by the coordinators in case files throughout the program year and will be summarized in a final report on the program in August, 2002. The report will contain a comprehensive overview of the program model and its experiences throughout the year as well as an analysis of the outcomes achieved, providing a useful model for program replication in other settings. Longer term, we see the Family Mediation model as one with great potential for statewide replicability. As it expands, we envision partnering with and training coordinators and mediators at several other regional host organizations to give the program an appropriate local flavor. In this scenario, RI Youth Guidance would be the mediation provider in the Providence metropolitan area, and a provider of training and technical assistance to mediation partners statewide.

Program Budget and Future Support Plan

Program Co-coordinators (2) @ 10 hrs/wk each x $24/hr x 50 wk........... $ 24,000

Co-mediators @ $70 per mediation x 100 mediations........................ 7,000

Clerical support/administrative assistance: 10 hrs/mo. x $15/hr x 12 months: 1,800

Total Personnel   32,800

Supplies, Materials, and Communications
Program brochures, support materials, and office supplies................. 1,200

Telephone... 1,000

TOTAL EXPENSES $35,000

To support this budget and the delivery of mediation services to 100 families, the Rhode Island Youth Guidance Center commits $3,500 of its United Way of Southeastern New England annual allocation and its legislative grant through the Department of Children, Youth, and Families of $6,500 for fiscal year 2002. To fully fund our effort to bring this promising pilot to a larger scale, the agency is requesting a grant of $25,000 from the William Bingham Foundation.

To fund the Family Mediation Program on an ongoing basis in the future, Rhode Island Youth Guidance is committed to supporting over half of the program's annual budget through recurring core operating support comprised of the following elements:
- $6,500 through an annual legislative grant from the RI Dept. of Children, Youth, and Families.
- $8,500, representing approximately 5% of the agency's annual allocation from the United Way of Southeastern New England.
- $5,000 from an annual grant received by the agency from the John R. McCune Charitable Trust.

The $15,000 balance in will be secured from among several sources, including juvenile justice funds from the RI Justice Commission, the RI Family Court, and federal comprehensive strategy juvenile justice funds administered by local municipalities. Other potential sources include continuing prevention grant support from the RI Division of Substance Abuse and grant, fee-for-service funding from the RI Dept. of Children, Youth, and Families, and support through our collaborative activity with the new school-based truancy courts which are being started in Rhode Island's core cities.

Appendix

Family Mediation Program Case Scenarios

<u>Mediation #1</u>

A mother of an adolescent boy called the mediation program as a result of a referral from the Rhode Island Family Court. Her son had gone through the diversionary program for first time offenders due to his arrest for the possession of marijuana. She indicated to the juvenile intake worker that she was having difficulties with her son, and wished for some help.

At the initial session, it became evident that "David" had not been provided with a stable home environment by his mother, "Susan". She had given him to her grandmother to raise for several years when he was entering adolescence, soon after her divorce from his father. She then became involved in an abusive relationship, and allowed her son to move back in with her during the course of this relationship. Recently, David and Susan moved out of the home of the abusive boyfriend, and at the time of the first mediation session were living in temporary quarters.

The mediation was initiated because of the mother's concern with her son's lack of communication with her. She said that she felt that he did not approve of her, and did not feel close to her. While David was not particularly talkative, he did indicate that he was not angry with his mother, but felt quite independent as a result of his upbringing. In this context, she seemed receptive to this information, and decided to be a little less aggressive in getting him to confide in her, but let him know that she would be there for him, and would try to provide a stable home for him. They agreed to eat together as often as possible, and to try to do some projects together. David said that he would always let her know where he was. All of this was written into a contract.

At the second session three weeks later, the Susan appeared much more relaxed. She reported that David and she ate together almost every night, and that David called regularly when he was out to let her know where he was and when he would be getting home. She said he would even call just to say hello. They had found a new place to live, and both were very pleased with their new surroundings. David had begun bringing his friends over, allowing his mother to get to know them.

Susan seemed pleased with the results of the mediation. As with all of the families we see, we will be tracking them over the course of the next six months to evaluate the long-term benefits of the program.

<u>Mediation #2</u>

Two boys, their father and their stepmother were referred to the program by the vice-principal of the older child's high school. The stepmother was the one who was seeking intervention.

The first session with this family lasted four and a half hours. There was a great deal of bitterness and mistrust on everyone's part. All members of the family seemed to be seeking some structure that would provide some objective standards for each others' behavior. The contract addressed issues of school attendance, household chores, and the appropriate discipline for various infractions. The length of the mediation was primarily the result of the parents'

Case Scenarios, continued

need to "vent"; it seemed apparent that they felt that the behavior of these two boys went beyond any normal adolescent testing of limits.

The second session was also quite lengthy. The parents felt that the contract had not been adhered to, and the boys felt that the lack of trust exhibited by their father and stepmother was not based on fact, and they felt humiliated by the constant checking up on them. What became evident at this second mediation was that this family currently lacks the basic trust and honesty that is necessary for the give and take that defines mediation. While the fact that there are "step" issues involved does not preclude mediation, there is too much anger and mistrust for constructive negotiation.

The hours spent with this family were not wasted. The parents agreed that the issues were appropriate for family therapy and agreed to follow through on the referrals that we would seek for them. It was evident from our sessions with them that they boys are verbal, articulate, and willing to share their concerns with persons outside the family. All involved were aware that they needed some help with the complex issues that were raised and clarified through the mediation sessions. We have made referrals for them, and will follow up to insure that they are getting services.

Mediation #3

The Family Mediation Program recently received a referral from a local high school vice-principal. A senior, "Nicole", had spoken with the administrator about her recent difficulties with her mother. Her mother had asked her to leave the home because of conflicts they were having over behavior and responsibilities in the home. As a result of Nicole leaving the home and staying at the homes of various friends, her attendance and grades had begun to slip.

The first mediation session lasted about three hours. Present were Nicole, her mother, an aunt, and the two mediators. The aunt attended at the request of both mother and daughter, because the aunt had been acting as an informal mediator and was hoping that her role could be more informed and constructive as a result of being witness to the mediation. Mother and daughter reached an agreement by the end of the session. The agreement contained a "reunification plan" that contained a specific date within the next week for Nicole to move back in and contained obligations for both parties to fulfill. These obligations included an agreement that mom would help Nicole find a new therapist and that Nicole would use therapy to address her anger in an effort to contain some of the explosive rage that had permeated their communications. The contract also contained agreements on the part of Nicole to advise her mother of her schedule. They also agreed to treat each other with respect and to spend every other Friday night doing something together.

The second mediation took place one month later. The mother and daughter had reunited, and life at home was going much more smoothly. The agreement was amended to include some further issues that had not been priorities at the first mediation.

The evaluations filled out by the parties indicated that they were very satisfied and pleased with the process. Nicole's evaluation indicated that she felt differently in a positive way about her mother as a result of the mediation sessions. In response to the question, "Did you feel you were given the opportunity to share your concerns?", Nicole responded, "Yes, very much so." We will be contacting this family over the next six months to evaluate the long-term effectiveness of the mediation process with this family.

A Proposal From

Underground Railroad
Oakland, California

To

Agape Foundation
San Francisco, California

Requested amount: $1,500; **Amount received:** $1,500

Funder's comments:

"At the Agape Foundation, we ask each grantseeker to complete a cover sheet that includes not only contact information, but also their organization's mission and the purpose of the grant. All of the proposal components were present. The organization's philosophy of social change was well developed and well written. Social change was obviously a core value of the organization. Since Agape only funds nonviolent social change, this section is a crucial component of the proposal.

"Underground Railroad provided the requested information in the length and level of detail required. The strongest feature of the proposal is the methodical and concise presentation. The group's dedication, passion, and commitment shine throughout. The proposal also articulates clear, realistic, and measurable goals. I found the writing to be free of jargon, but I did grow a bit weary of the use of bolding, bullets, and underlining. The budget was presented clearly and completely.

"The attachments were helpful; in this case Underground Railroad included several news clips reviewing or announcing their cultural events. Since they were seeking a grant for a mural project, the reviews illustrated their ability to organize successful events.

"Our board of trustees always returns to the grantees with questions, regardless of the quality of the proposal. At least two board members as well as the staff review each proposal. After a board member reviews a proposal s/he completes a brief questionnaire for use in the evaluation process, and this includes any questions they might have for the grantee. These questions were generated by the board review: What is your organizational analysis of nonviolence? Will this be reflected in the mural content? Do you have previous mural experience? Are you working with any other group with this experience? How will you recruit for this project? The proposal could have been improved by including the names of other organizations with which they are collaborating, and by less frequent use of the bold function."

—*Karen Topakian, Executive Director, Agape Foundation*

Notes:

The complete proposal included the following attachments: project budget, fundraising plan, news clippings, 2000 and 2001 organizational budgets, and flyer.

Proposal written and submitted to the funder by Tina Bartolome, Co-Director.

**AGAPE FOUNDATION BOARD OF TRUSTEES GRANTS
ART, COMMUNITY AND SOCIAL CHANGE
SPRING 2001**

Grant applicant, please type or print clearly.

Name of organization project: UNDERGROUND RAILROAD

Mission/Focus of organization and year of founding: 1997.
Underground Railroad enables urban youth to work for systemic social change through the creation & promotion of art and culture.

Purpose of grant: To support the KNOW JUSTICE, KNOW PEACE MURAL PROJECT, an 8 week mural project that will enable West Oakland youth to visually articulate their realities and visions of peace and justice.

Organization budget: $67,051   Project budget: $ 2675
Grant amount requested: $ 1,500

Contact person with name, address, telephone number, e-mail address and website if available:
TINA BARTOLOME, CO-DIRECTOR
1357 5TH STREET
OAKLAND, CA 94607
#510.451.5466 ex 313
URCYouthec.org

To be filled out by Agape (Do not write below this line.)
Granting history with Agape:

No granting history

Comments:
____Budget too large ____Location____Organization 5+years old

1st review by:_____Accept ____Reject_____

____Other comments - If reject, why:

2nd review by:_____Accept ____Reject_____

____Other comments If reject, why:

Underground Railroad Proposal to Agape Foundation

PROJECT REQUEST

Underground Railroad (UR) is proud to request $1500 to support the **Know Justice, Know Peace Mural Project. Know Justice, Know Peace** is an eight week mural project that will enable West Oakland youth to visually articulate their realities and visions of peace and justice. UR's commitment to genuinely "put down roots" in West Oakland's neighborhood requires offering tangible opportunities for dialogue, creative expression and action that inspire and develop unity around relevant issues. This project marks the first of many opportunities to engage in meaningful social change work and community building with the young residents of the neighborhood in which Underground Railroad's new and first office is located.

Know Justice, Know Peace will be created at the Youth Empowerment Center, where Underground Railroad's office is housed in West Oakland. The mural-making process will be facilitated by a lead artist and produced by eight to ten young people from West Oakland. The finished mural will first be honored at a neighborhood cultural gathering and permanently displayed outside the Youth Empowerment Center.

GOALS

Know Justice, Know Peace aims to:

- Provide art-based community-building skills to young, low-income youth of color living in West Oakland;
- Impart technical training for socially responsible mural-making;
- Result in a large-scale mural that can also function as an educational tool;
- Foster dialogue and awareness around themes of peace and justice within a historical and current, neighborhood and global, race, class and gender framework.

ORGANIZATION DESCRIPTION AND HERSTORY

Underground Railroad (UR) enables urban youth to work for systemic social change through the creation and promotion of art and culture. Through cultural organizing, productions and public education, UR develops leadership in young artists to popularize their visions of freedom and social transformation. This activity works within the broader nexus of grassroots activities in low-income communities and communities of color, to provide the cultural vision of a changed world that inspires, educates, and builds strong movements for social, political and economic justice.

In 1997, five Bay Area youth of color came together to form Underground Railroad. Committed to economic self-determination, we financed productions out-of-pocket and passionately volunteered our efforts, homes and minimal resources towards manifesting our vision. We soon gained a reputation for producing low-budget model "edutainment" events that were respectful, life-affirming, informative and safe for large numbers of diverse youth to attend. The profits from each event fueled the fire for future productions, which increasingly raised levels of artist collaboration, analysis of community issues and grassroots participation. Since 1997, Underground Railroad has grown from a small collective led by women of color to a membership organization where up and coming young cultural workers in the visual, performing and media arts, can become involved in activism. It has also grown from an independent, collective entity into a project fiscally sponsored by the Youth Empowerment Center (YEC), a new umbrella non-profit that supports youth organizing, training and cultural production. As part of YEC, Underground Railroad will play a much more significant role in integrating the use of art and culture for social change into all elements of the youth movement.

Some of Underground Railroad's major accomplishments include: Producing eleven (11) multi-media events highlighting various community issues and themes; providing murals, banners and performance art to accompany direct actions, conferences and rallies; producing and distributing an all-female artist hip-hop recording against Proposition 21; designing a yearly inspirational calendar organizer featuring works from local artists; educating and coordinating dozens of young, local artists to perform pieces about the growing prison industry and training the staff & members of youth groups in elements of cultural organizing.

UNDERGROUND RAILROAD'S PHILOSOPHY OF SOCIAL CHANGE

Over the past three years, UR has developed five core beliefs, which guide our practice.

1. Revolution is not only won by numbers, but by visionaries, and if artists aren't visionaries, then we have no business doing what we do. -*Cherrie Moraga, Chicana writer*

Big corporations have plenty of visionaries working hard and getting paid to win the public over with images, words and music promoting corrupt, oppressive values and ideas. As conscious progressive artists, we must be visionaries in exposing the lies and expressing convictions for a world that is just. If our communities are starved for positive and self-determined representations of our cultures that offer upliftment and meaning amidst everyday survival, then we aim to create culture and art that feeds people's desire for change.

2. No one is free as long as others are oppressed.

We respect and value people's different histories and experiences with oppression. We believe that only solidarity amongst all of us with our collective creativity and knowledge will create true and lasting social change. We don't prioritize race, gender, sexual orientation, or any other form of oppression over another. Rather, we strive to understand and articulate the intersections between them, using the dynamic mediums of art and dialogue. Building a widely diverse community of artists allows us constant opportunity to engage in solidarity work on a wide arrange of issues to actively express this belief.

3. Faith is the substance of things wished for, the evidence of things unseen. -James Baldwin

Whether it's faith in God, Allah, Buddha or faith in the people, we understand that this work requires faith. It is a powerful foundation for guiding us towards the world we want, but can't yet see. Underground Railroad creates space for the expression and reflection of faith so that we, as individuals and as communities, have a solid and powerful source of strength to manifest social change work.

4. Culture is a natural resource of our communities, not to be misused by corporations for profit.

More and more, corporations are replacing the practice of culture with the purchase of culture. The money made off these products too often does not go back to the communities they came from. Rather than exerting all of our efforts towards holding corporations accountable, UR practices economic self-help through selling cultural products that raise consciousness and sustain social change work in our communities.

5. Culture is a weapon. –*Amilcar Cabral, movement leader in Guinea-Bissau*

Our communities face daily attacks on the streets, in the classroom, on the job and from the media. Our communities also fight back. Creating and living a culture of liberation is crucial in showing our communities that we don't have to accept a world based upon exploitation and oppression, that there is a more decent and humane society to be created. Whether it's painting a mural that creates dialogue on the affects of gentrification within a targeted neighborhood or putting out a CD compilation about reproductive rights, we see culture as an effective weapon to educate, unify and inspire our communities to action.

OUR STRATEGY: MOVEMENT BUILDING WITH "CULTURE AS A WEAPON"

Underground Railroad is firmly committed to developing the next generation of artist-activists who will be strong leaders in their communities. Our programmatic work seeks to build a synergy between culture, identity and new media, providing the most up-to-date tools for youth to express ideas and involve themselves in grassroots organizing for justice.

•ORGANIZATIONAL DEVELOPMENT
Our main goal for the coming year is to carry out a successful capacity-building drive to support a substantial membership base of youth and young adults from the Bay Area. This growth will continue to prioritize the recruitment and development of young women of color.

Objectives
- Hire two (2) part-time staff;
- Rent and maintain office space with other Youth Empowerment Center projects
- Provide stipends for art educators and youth interns

PROGRAM AREAS
•CULTURAL ORGANIZING. Through building our membership base of artists and collaborative partnerships with other youth organizations and coalitions, we develop tactics that use art and culture to inspire youth to action and widely disseminate messages to support ongoing campaigns of resistance.

GOALS- To grow our membership base and creatively collaborate with other youth organizations around community issues.

Objectives
- Recruit fifty (50) new members by the end of 2001 by going to local events and holding open membership meetings;
- Produce at least five (5) multi-media events to rally youth around a current political issue they can get involved in, either by joining the Underground Railroad or another endorsed youth organization;
- Formalize collaborative relationships with two (2) local mass-based youth organizations; and
- Develop literature & posters for street promotion & recruitment.

•CULTURAL PRODUCTION. Through the creation of cultural products for sale and/or exhibition, we: promote specific messages to educate on a particular issue, counter negative media representations of youth, women and people of color, reach far beyond our immediate communities, feature local artists, build community in the creation process and provide an alternative funding source to sustain our work. The popularity and response to our creations has brought national attention in print and radio to the issue of youth criminalization and the power of art and culture within movements for social change.

GOALS-To increase the number and volume of quality products sold as a tool of recruitment and consciousness-raising.

Objectives
- Enable membership to successfully produce, market and distribute at least three (3) cultural products with staff assistance;
- Develop and execute a strategic distribution plan; and
- Feature the artistry of young women of color in at least 2 of the 3 products.

•SKILLS TRAINING & POLITICAL EDUCATION. Underground Railroad invests organizational resources into preparing young cultural workers to be skilled, educated, and expressive leaders in their communities. We provide a **comprehensive and participatory political education** program that has the following elements:

1. The development of a race, class and gender analysis;
2. Comprehensive study of cultural workers in social change movements throughout history;
3. The basic elements of organizing; and
4. An examination of local and global issues

The second component of leadership development focuses on the **practical application of art and cultural production.** From graphic design and music production to creative direct action/events planning, skills workshops ensure the delivery of quality productions that educate and inspire action. All UR members participate in a thorough orientation process that includes; regular attendance at general membership gatherings, a series of four (4) introductory workshops called "Infinity Lessons" and the collective production of a cultural event around a chosen theme. Members and staff carry out trainings and workshops in community and school settings. Curriculum is also developed for upcoming productions or projects with specific themes or issues.

GOALS-To increase the amount of workshops, educational projects and trainings for membership and in the community and to document our curriculum.

>   **Objectives**
>   •Facilitate at least two (2) educational art projects for West Oakland youth;
>   •Hold monthly "Infinity Lessons" for all members;
>   •Train ten (10) new members to facilitate;
>   •Deliver workshops in at least fifteen (15) school classrooms;
>   •Deliver workshops in at least eight (8) local young women's organizations and after school programs;
>   •Recruit forty (40) potential new members from outside workshops and projects;
>   •Develop a curriculum manual.

DEMOGRAPHICS, DECISION MAKING & STRUCTURE

Underground Railroad defines its constituency as urban youth of color. **Urban youth of color play a leading role in developing mass culture, but remain politically marginalized and socially stigmatized, even as our styles, ideas, and images are sold globally.** We are developing a new generation of young artists and cultural workers who will lead their communities toward justice. We uphold an affirmative action policy to ensure that staff, members and the advisory board are majority people of color, women, working class, youth and young adult and highly representative of GLBT people. Our current goal is to actively recruit more high school age youth into membership.

Currently, UR's membership breakdown is as follows: 22 members total, 8 Asian American, 6 Latino/as, 6 African Americans, 2 Jewish Americans, 14 women, 8 men, 8 ages 15-21, 14 ages 22-26, 9 GLBT identified.

Since we are fiscally sponsored by the Youth Empowerment Center the **board of directors** is not active in the day to day activities of the organization. Their responsibility is to make sure that Undeground Railroad meets legal and fiscal requirements. The two part-time staff are **Co-director positions.** The first Co-director position is responsible for day to day administrative tasks, grantwriting, and preparing the agendas and materials for membership meetings. The second Co-director position is responsible for maintaining the logistical and organizational needs of the membership, implementing and carrying out membership decisions. The responsibilities of **core members** are to propose projects, actively participate in projects and decision making, set agendas for meetings, coordinate political education and artistic skills trainings of the membership, help direct the political vision of the group and pay regular dues. The responsibilities of **general members** are to propose projects, actively participate in projects, political education sessions and decision making, give input on agendas and pay regular dues. The membership generally relies on a mix of consensus and 2/3 voting majority for making programmatic and structural decisions. The board, staff and membership come from the communities with which we work.

•KEY PEOPLE
STAFF
Tina Bartolome, 25, is a founding core member, Co-director of Underground Railroad and has been highly active in its day to day functions and growth since 1997. Born and raised in San Francisco to working class immigrant parents from the Philippines and Switzerland, she has been politically active since high school in various Bay Area youth organizations for social justice. She currently serves as a board member of the Women's Building and works part-time as the Coordinator of Youth Power, an after school program for Mission youth. Her skills are in the area of youth leadership development, political education curriculum and facilitation, event production, strategic planning, office administration and fiction writing.

Omana Imani, 24, is also a founding core member and Co-director of the Underground Railroad, highly active in its day to day functions and growth since 1997. A Bay Area native and proud mother of a five year old, Omana comes from a working class East Indian and White background. She has been politically active since high school, coordinating various youth programs and taking leadership in cultural organizations. She also works part-time as an Organizer for Youth Force Coalition, made up 35 membership organizations committed to social justice. Her skills are in the area of youth leadership development, networking, event production, facilitation, administration and singing.

VOLUNTEER
Stefan Goldstone, 26, has been an active core member of Underground Railroad since Fall 2000. A San Francisco native, Jewish American and accomplished hiphop DJ, Stefan's turntable talents have been a regular fixture and blessing at almost every Bay Area youth movement function in the past two years, from cultural events and benefits to protests, rallies and high school walkouts. He currently works full-time as the Coordinator of Mentor Court, an educational program for young adults on probation. His skills are in the areas of fundraising, event production, mentoring, membership development and workshops on cultural resistance and hiphop history.

BOARD OF DIRECTORS
Since we are fiscally sponsored by the Youth Empowerment Center, the board of directors is not active in the day to day activities of the organization. Their responsibility is to make sure that Underground Railroad meets legal and fiscal requirements. The board consists of the following individuals: **Adam Gold,** Executive Director for **Youth Empowerment Center, Harmony Goldberg**, Executive Director for **School of Unity & Liberation, Anthony "Van" Jones**, Executive Director for **Ella Baker Center for Human Rights, Lateefah Simon**, Executive Director for **Center for Young Women's Development** and **Cindy Weisner**, Lead Organizer for **People Organized to Win Employment Rights**.
We are currently creating an **advisory board** that will be composed of representatives from our constituency and allies. Although the advisory board will have no direct decision making power, they will be called upon by staff and membership for regular input and support.

Appendix

I. Project Budget
II. Fundraising Plan 2001
III. Organizational Budget 2001
IV. Organizational Budget 2000
V. Raber, Erin. "Hip Hop Her", <u>Curve Magazine</u>, p 18, Vol 10#5, 8/00
VI. "Freedom of Art", <u>Blu Magazine: Women in Struggle</u>, Issue #7 Vol 2 Spring 2000
VII. Arnold, Eric. "Her Mighty Presence", <u>East Bay Express</u>, 9/1/99
VIII. Event flyer, 5th Annual International Women's Day-Volando con Nueva Vida, March 5, 1999

Underground Railroad
Know Justice, Know Peace Mural Project Budget
January 1, 2001-December 31, 2001

Personnel
Lead Artist Fee-$100 x 8 weeks   800

Materials   950
Paint, drop cloth, panels, snap line, paints, brushes, etc.

Food   400
$50 x 8 weeks

Outreach   50
Posters, Flyers

Documentation   100
Film, Video, curriculum

Symbolic Honorarium for Youth Artists   200
Sketch books, colored pencils
                                              Subtotal: 2500

Overhead
Insurance, fees, bookkeeping, accounting   175
                                              Total: **2675**

FUNDRAISING INFORMATION

Note on Financial Statements*: Since our fiscal sponsor, YEC, is less than a year old, we will not have financial statements available until 2001.

FUNDRAISING PLAN JANUARY 1, 2001-DECEMBER 31, 2001

Our fundraising strategy includes raising revenue from events, products, membership dues, fees for service and inkind support. However, currently our revenue from sales alone is not enough to support our programmatic goals and the building of organizational infrastructure. June of 2000 marks our first time receiving fiscal sponsorship. We are now also seeking money from foundations to accommodate the hiring of staff and to build the infrastructure of the organization. Below is a percentage breakdown of sources we plan on funding our work with from January through December 2001:

Grants-57% Events-14% Products-11% Membership Dues-6% Fees for Service 3% Inkind-8%

Ultimately, our goal is to diversify our funding to reflect the following percentages:
Grants-30% Products-25% Events-20% Membership Dues-10% Fees for Service-10%Inkind-5%

Grants	Status	Amount
Active Element Foundation	received	$ 2,000
Serpent Source Foundation	received	$ 1,000
Surdna Foundation*	received	$ 7,500
Levi Strauss Foundation*	received	$ 3,000
Third Wave Foundation	received	$ 5,000
Hazen Foundation*	committed	$ 2,500
Peace Development Fund	committed	$ 8,500
Marta Drury	committed	
Threshold Foundation	pending	$20,000
Vanguard Foundation	pending	$10,000
Tides Foundation	pending	$10,000

(*collaborative grants with Youth Empowerment Support Center)

Events $10,000
We will produce 5 multimedia cultural events featuring young local
artists and highlighting various political themes and issues.

Products $ 8,000
We will design, produce and market three products for sale
such as: calendar organizers, t-shirts and CDs.

Membership Dues $ 4,325
We will increase our membership to 50 members by the end of
2001.

Fees for Service $ 2,300
We intend to charge for consultation, managing and training services
when appropriate.

Inkind Support $ 5,000
We will continue to rely on donations in the form of sound equipment, Volunteer

Underground Railroad
Organizational Budget
January 1, 2001-December 31, 2001

EXPENSES		AMOUNT	REVENUE	AMOUNT
Personnel			Foundation Grants	40,000
2 Co-directors PT		XXXXX	Events	10,000
Fringe benefits		XXXXX	Products for sale	8,000
	Subtotal:	27,600	Membership Dues	4,325
Consultants			Fees for services	2,300
Project Intern		XXXXX	In-kind support	5,000
Art educators		XXXXX	**Total Revenue:**	69,625
	Subtotal:	3,000	**Balance:**	2,574
Other Services				
Rent		3,000		
Utilities		600		
Telephone		840		
Printing		1,500		
	Subtotal:	7,440		
Office equipment				
Computer		1,000		
Printer		220		
Scanner		150		
	Subtotal:	1,370		
Office Supplies				
Postage		500		
General		600		
Photocopies		1,000		
	Subtotal:	2,100		
Programs				
Space		2,500		
Equipment		2,400		
Artist stipends		5,000		
Audio/Visual technicians		2,000		
Art supplies		1,800		
Production		3,500		
Marketing		1,500		
Distribution		1,500		
Documentation		500		
Travel		1,000		
	Subtotal:	21,242		
Overhead				
Insurance, fees, bookeeping, accounting		4,299		
	Total Expenses:	67,051		

Underground Railroad
Organizational Budget
January 1, 2000-December 31, 2000

EXPENSES			REVENUE		
Personnel			Grants received		3,000
5 Core members of collective PT		volunteer	Events		1,500
	Subtotal:	-	Products for sale		2,000
Other Services			Fees for services		250
Rental meeting space		1,200	Individual donations		300
Telephone and Internet		790	Residual from 1999		2,800
Printing		600	Inkind support		2,500
Childcare		100		Total Revenue:	12,350
Training		150		Balance:	(30)
Post Office Box		180			
	Subtotal:	3,020			
Office equipment					
Computer		1,000			
Printer		215			
Scanner		200			
Supplies/materials		225			
	Subtotal:	1,640			
Programs					
Event space		2,000			
Equipment		1,150			
Artist stipends		1,100			
Audio/Visual technicians		200			
Art supplies		250			
Production		1,700			
Marketing		600			
Documentation		120			
Travel		150			
Event supplies		250			
	Subtotal:	7,520			
Donations					
Emil Gru Wiig Fund		100			
Akil Francisco Dream Fund		100			
	Subtotal:	200			
	Total Expenses:	12,380			

2

Special Project: Multiyear

The proposals in this chapter are requests for special project support spanning more than one year. Because of the longer time frame involved, devising a multiyear proposal requires careful program planning, since the grantseeking organization is required to look further into the future to define the parameters of the project. This planning may hinge on several variables and can be subject to change as the initiative progresses. Funders understand that unexpected events can alter the fine points of a project, but they will expect that the proposal demonstrate clarity of objectives and methods. Creation of a timeline can help both nonprofit and funder visualize the intended progress of the program.

Establishing and presenting fiscal details—anticipated expenses and revenues for several years—can be accomplished in various ways. For example, the budget component of the Council on Library and Information Resources proposal for the Digital Leadership Institute used a five-year format.

Of the two proposals in this chapter, one grant request was for $30,000 and the other was for well over a million dollars, demonstrating that multiyear grants can be relatively small or quite large, depending on the nature of the project.

The California Alumni Association in Berkeley, California, submitted a request for $30,000 to the Lisa and Douglas Goldman Fund for support over three years for a new endeavor, the Achievement Award Program. The program was developed to identify excellent students who needed financial support in order to attend college, and then to provide monetary and mentoring support once the students were enrolled.

The Council on Library and Information Resources in Washington, D.C., approached the Robert W. Woodruff Foundation for more than $1,300,000 to establish and support the Digital Leadership Institute over five years. The plan for the Institute was to provide a comprehensive training program for information and library professionals, who subsequently would be prepared to assume leadership roles in the management of digital information and communication technology.

A Proposal From
California Alumni Association
Berkeley, California

To
Lisa and Douglas Goldman Fund
San Francisco, California

Requested amount: $30,000; **Amount received:** $30,000

Funder's comments:

"This proposal was very well crafted, clear, and concisely written. The first paragraph provides a summary of the project and the amount of funding requested. The background information provided about the California Alumni Association succinctly highlights its purpose, history, and relationship to the university. The project description provides relevant research and statistical information to support the proposal without giving unnecessary details. Current and future plans for funding the program are clearly outlined, and the different funding streams that support the overall program are explained. The proposal has a strong conclusion that reminds the reader of the personal impact the program has on students.

"This proposal was complete, with all supporting materials provided in one packet. They anticipated questions by providing notes to the project budget to clarify specific expenses. I appreciated the fact that all the budget information (notes and actual budget) were included on one separate page, since this made it easier to present in the board docket."

Nancy Kami, Executive Director, Lisa and Douglas Goldman Fund

Notes:
The complete proposal included the following attachments: list of the Honorary Committee of the Achievement Award, list of staff, list of recent grants, references, and financial statement. One budget page is included here.

Proposal written by Laura Garcia, Annual Programs Director; submitted to the funder by Jim Burk, then Executive Director, and Carolyn Burwell, Director of Development.

California Alumni
A S S O C I A T I O N

April 27, 2001

Ms. Nancy Kami
Executive Director
Lisa and Douglas Goldman Fund
One Daniel Burnham Court
Suite 330C
San Francisco, CA 94109-5460

Dear Ms. Kami,

It is with pleasure that we submit to the Lisa and Douglas Goldman Fund the attached proposal requesting $30,000 for the program component of our newly established scholarship program, The Achievement Award Program. The Achievement Award Program was created for two reasons: to maintain Cal's accessibility by providing much-needed financial assistance to students, and to provide a network of support once the students are on campus. We partnered with the University-sponsored outreach programs to better identify those students who are academically prepared to come to Cal, but simply lack the funds.

The applicants we interview, and those who are ultimately selected to receive the award, are *amazing*. As we listen to the challenges they face and the obstacles they overcome daily, and witness their sheer determination, we are reminded again and again why it is so important for us to ensure that these talented young scholars are given the financial means to pursue and the academic support to achieve their educational goals. Theirs is a diversity of thought, talent, and experience that *is* the essence of UC Berkeley.

Lisa and Doug Goldman have always been so generous and supportive of our Alumni Leadership Scholarship, while in the process showing a tremendous amount of confidence in the California Alumni Association. Their gifts have made a significant impact on the lives of many Alumni Scholars. We are grateful for their confidence, and hope they appreciate the importance of our newest endeavor, The Achievement Award Program.

Once again, thank you for your consideration. Please call me with any questions you may have.

Sincerely,

Jim Burk '62, MBA '63
(888) CAL-ALUM

Proposal for The Achievement Award Program
Submitted by The California Alumni Association
Friday, April 27, 2001

List of Attachments

Attachment One………..Staff, Recent Grants, References
Attachment Two………Financial Statement

Achievement Award

Honorary Committee

President Richard C. Atkinson

Chancellor Robert M. Berdahl

Kevin M. Johnson '87

Brett Kanazawa '89

Irene Miura '60

Vice Chancellor Genaro Padilla

John W. Rosston '42

Richard L. Russell, Jr. '78

Carl J. Stoney, Jr. '67

Alfredo Terrazas '74

Chang-Lin Tien, NEC Distinguished Professor of Engineering

Katharine S. Wallace '48

The Achievement Award Program

The California Alumni Association's Achievement Award Program was created to tackle two concurrent problems facing the University of California, Berkeley: maintaining access to one of the country's premier public universities, and providing effective retention services that support the students through graduation. We are asking the Lisa and Douglas Goldman Fund for a gift of $30,000 over a three-year period to support the programmatic components of our Achievement Award Scholarship Program.

The California Alumni Association

The California Alumni Association (CAA) was organized in 1872 to "serve the alumni and together with the alumni, to advance the interests and promote the welfare of the University of California, Berkeley."
The Association is one of the few independent alumni associations in the country, and has remained formally separate from UC Berkeley.

Today, the California Alumni Association has over 92,000 members, and is one of the largest dues paying alumni associations in the world. Our first scholarship program, The Alumni Leadership Scholarship, was established to reward students who show leadership on campus and in the community. The first thirteen award recipients in 1934 each received a $180.00 scholarship. This past fall, after successfully completing an $11 million dollar campaign to raise funds for The Alumni Leadership Scholarship, we awarded over 1,000 scholarships for approximately $1,200 each.

Recent Accomplishments
With the generosity of our donors, the commitment of our alumni, the never-ending stamina of our students and volunteers, and the support of our friends, here are a few of our more recent successes.

- Camp Oski, which was purchased in 1998 and is adjacent to the Lair of the Golden Bear in the Sierra Nevada mountain range, is booked for the entire 2001 season.
- A 21% increase in memberships in the last seven years.
- The collaboration with University Relations staff to create and produce Homecoming and Parents Weekend began four years ago, and has drawn several thousand alumni and friends back to campus who have contributed over $6 million in class gifts to the campus.

The Achievement Award Program

The Achievement Award Program (TAAP) began in 1998 as a direct result of a request from Chancellor Robert Berdahl. He asked the California Alumni Association, as an independent 501 (c) (3) with a successful history of scholarship program development, to help with his endeavor to maintain access to Cal. While designing The Achievement Award Program, we had three goals in mind:

1. To partner with University-sponsored outreach programs[1] in order to identify students with financial need, who have shown initiative despite tremendous hardship.
2. To provide the financial resources so that they can afford to attend Cal.
3. To create a "family of support" for these students once here.

Outreach
The Achievement Award Program is integrally connected to the University-sponsored outreach programs that promote higher education and provide the information and skills needed to excel in school and to gain admission to college. By linking eligibility for a scholarship to these programs, we are endorsing the University's outreach efforts, and providing a pipeline of support for these high-achieving

---

[1] University-sponsored outreach programs include MESA (Math, Engineering, Science Achievement), Puente Project, EAOP (Early Academic Outreach Program) and the programs of the Berkeley Pledge.

students. It is worth noting that of our first two-cohorts 50% of the award recipients come from families in which neither parent holds a high-school diploma, and 99% of the award recipients come from families in which neither parent holds a university degree.

Maintaining Access
Increasingly, with the numerous outreach and college preparatory programs available to youths, there are large numbers of low-income students graduating high-school who are academically prepared to enter college, but are unable to enroll or maintain enrollment due to tremendous financial barriers. The average family income of the current TAAP scholars is just over $22,000, while the current cost of attaining a Cal education, if one lives in the University residence halls, is $15,642.

In February 2001, the U.S Advisory Committee on Student Financial Assistance[2] published a report entitled, *Access Denied: Restoring the Nation's Commitment to Equal Educational Opportunity*. The Advisory Committee found that while 60% of jobs available today require some college, "only 6% of students with the lowest socioeconomic status (SES) earn a bachelor's degree compared to 40% with the highest SES."

The committee found that our federal, state, and institutional policy makers are working at an unprecedented rate to provide students with better academic preparedness through early outreach programs, are simplifying the financial aid application process, and are providing better and earlier information about financial aid. However, they have not accounted for the excessive unmet need that will skyrocket as a consequence of their outreach efforts. The Achievement Award Program is our effort to help remedy this situation.

In addition to outright grants from the University, the state, and the U.S. government, TAAP scholars receive up to $5,700 per year, depending on individual need, to replace the work study and loan component of their financial aid package. Next year an additional $1,200 per student is required to cover the personal and academic advising, and the array of support programs and services aimed at helping these scholars achieve success.

Retention Services
Once the scholars receive their award, we immediately orient them to the network of support services aimed at helping them be successful throughout their stay at Cal, and in their adult lives.

The desired results stemming from these services reflect a combination of current youth development and student retention theory. Student development seeks to "articulate and pursue desirable outcomes for youth, including attributes such as confidence, character, connection, and competence in a number of areas: civic and social, cultural, physical and emotional health, intellectual curiosity and learning, and employability."[3] Successful student retention is "the ability of a student to become integrated into institutional life…. Institutions therefore plan activities around this notion to attempt to integrate or 'fit' students socially and academically into the institution…. The greater the congruence between the student's values, goals, and attitudes and those of the college, the more likely that the student will persist at the college."[4]

The grant we are requesting from the Lisa and Douglas Goldman Fund will be used to support the services that form the Achievement Award's student development and retention program. Listed on the next page are the goals and strategies for this program.

---

[2] Created by Congress to advise the Secretary of Education and Congress on higher education and student aid policy, and to make recommendations that improve access.
[3] For a general overview of youth development programs, visit http//:www.etr.org/recapp/theories/youthdev/index2.htm
[4] Seidman, A. (1989). "Recruitment begins with retention: Retention begins with recruitment." Colleague. State University of New York, 40-45.

Goal	Strategies	Method of Measurement	Expenses
Reach 100% UCB graduation rate. Reach 80% graduation rate within two years for Jr. Transfers and within four years for Freshmen.	Provide staff to answer questions and refer students to appropriate campus resources, including health services, tutors and academic advisors; require regular meetings. Organize faculty workshops to increase student comfort-ness with professors. Organize academic-related workshops (e.g., study skills, research skills, time management). Establish a strong student-to-campus relationship. Organize activities for the scholars, donors and alumni volunteers (e.g., Welcome Reception, "Fall Feast", Graduation Celebration). Involve students in the TAAP selection process upon graduation.	Track academic progress and graduation year for each scholar. Conduct scholar self-assessment about their interest and likelihood to contribute to Cal as alumni at their time of graduation. Track scholars after they graduate and conduct an annual survey to assess their involvement in Cal.	Staff Presentation materials Cost by Fiscal Yr. FY2002 - $25,000 FY2003 - $26,125 FY2004 - $27,300
Develop and strengthen "real-world" skills to better prepare students for life after college.	Organize annual orientation retreat, which includes team building and leadership development. Support the Achievement Council, a student-run organization of recipients whose mission is to support each other and to return to their communities to encourage others to attend college, especially Cal. Implement the Achievement Council Outreach Program, while training scholars to be mentors and tutors. Implement the Achievement Council Overnight Stay Program to host newly admitted students. Provide conference opportunities for Achievement Council officers. Provide leadership opportunities for each cohort of TAAP students. Assure each scholar has an alumni mentor and student mentor. Participate and/or volunteer in alumni-centered CAA and University events and programs (e.g., Charter Banquet, Homecoming, Cal Day) Involve students in donor-related activities	Evaluate scholars' needs at entry and again at the beginning of each school year, tracking our effectiveness of meeting those needs. Conduct scholar self-assessment about their own skill development annually and at the time of graduation. Track student-donor and student-alumni contact while on campus.	Staffing Retreat space rental and food Meeting expenses Social and community service project expenses Campus visit costs (Outreach Program) Classroom, teaching and training materials (Outreach Program) National or Regional Student Leadership Conference registration, hotel and transportation for 4 officers. Cost by Fiscal Yr. FY2002 - $27,500 FY2003 - $28,800 FY2004 - $30,150

Because this is a new program, it is still a work-in-progress. The first cohort of 15 students came to Cal in 1999. From them we learned the extent of their needs, and how we should begin to modify the program to meet those needs. In 2000 we added 23 students to the group, and we will welcome 25 more in the fall of 2001. From these students we will begin to truly test the efficiency of the services we provide. We have learned from the current TAAP students that their basic problem solving and leadership skills are not as developed as in other UCB freshmen. Our mission is to provide a comprehensive program that can reach and serve a large number of students. Because we have partnered with well-respected outreach programs, and have allowed the program to evolve with the needs of the students, we have thus far been successful in carrying out our mission. The funds we are requesting from the Lisa and Douglas Goldman Fund will help us to continue this tradition of success.

Future Funding

Later this fall, the California Alumni Association will launch a three to five year endowment campaign to secure long-term funding for the program. The 'working goal' for this campaign is to increase the endowment from the current $3 million to $10 million. This will provide permanent financial and programmatic funding for 50 students. Concurrently, we will continue our separate annual campaign to ensure a steady yearly flow of income into the program. This money will be used to offset programmatic costs. We are also beginning to look to foundations such as the Lisa and Douglas Goldman Foundation to fund programmatic aspects of the program.

Conclusion

This June we will celebrate the achievements of our first two TAAP graduates, Jamika Lopez and Leon Lozano. Because they represent the first group of award recipients, or the "Founding Fifteen" as they like to call themselves, they occupy a very special place in all of our hearts. As they said goodbye to our board members this past March, it became apparent to everyone in the room why we have been working so hard to secure long-term funding for this program.

> *"What is the Achievement Award? For one thing, it is money. In this world money is power: to be without it is to be without options and to be without opportunities. I feel that I have been given the opportunity of a lifetime, and that I now have options in life. The Achievement Award [also] provides access to resources and networks. If ever a need or question arose, without hesitation I approached my Achievement Award family...at the Alumni House. My access to such assistance, resources and networks has helped me to become accepted by the top graduate film programs in the nation." ~Leon Lozano '01*

No student should be forced to turn down an invitation to attend Cal simply because he or she lacks sufficient funds. More importantly, the support we provide these students should not end with the mere awarding of money. As recognized by the Advisory Committee on Student Financial Aid, "the impact of independent federal, state, and institutional initiatives and programs can be greatly enhanced through effective partnerships that ensure that low-income students are financially AND academically supported throughout the entire education pipeline."

We at the California Alumni Association have stepped up to this challenge through The Achievement Award Program. For this we are proud. We hope that you, too, will recognize the importance of maintaining access to Cal, and will support The Achievement Award Program.

Attachment One

Names and Qualifications of Project Staff

<u>Cindy M. Leung</u>
Cindy Leung has served as the Director of Student Services at the California Alumni Association for over four years. She manages the Student Services Department, which primarily develops and implements scholarship, mentorship, internship and leadership development programs, events and services for incoming and current UC Berkeley students. She played an integral role in creating The Achievement Award Program. She created the selection process for the program and continues to participate in the management of selecting scholars. Recently, she led a taskforce in the creation of a program policy manual to ensure continuity in the program. Her interest in K-16 educational access developed while overseeing a $14 million federal and state JOBS program at the Human Resources Department in New York City. In 1997, she received her Masters in Public Affairs from the Lyndon B. Johnson School of Public Affairs at University of Texas at Austin with a focus on social welfare and educational access. She held an internship at the University of California Office of the President in 1996 where she supported the systemwide objectives of the Outreach Taskforce and the Early Academic Outreach Program. She helped develop and implement the first UC Systemwide Outreach Conference, which brought together high school and college students, parents, K-12 teachers and administrators, California policymakers, and faculty and administrators from all nine UC campuses.

<u>Elizabeth Ramirez</u>
Ms. Ramirez is the Program Manager for The Achievement Award Program. Prior to serving as Program Manager, she was employed by the California Alumni Association as the program assistant for The Achievement Award Program. Her responsibilities include advising all Achievement Award Scholars, coordinating the selection process, and coordinating all program workshops, activities, and events. Ms. Ramirez works closely with the Board of Director's Achievement Award Policy Committee, the individuals who set the policies for and oversee the program. She has extensive experience organizing events, facilitating meetings, and working with, mentoring and counseling students.

Recent and Pending Grants

<u>Current Foundation funders:</u>

Harris Family Foundation	$22,400 June 2000
	$32,000 May 2001

<u>Verbal pledge of support from:</u>

XXXXX Fund (to be listed anonymously)	$32,000 expected in October 2001

<u>Outstanding proposal:</u>

Regnar and Beverly Paulsen Foundation	$25,000 submitted February 2001

<u>Proposals to be submitted this fall:</u>

Wayne and Gladys Valley Foundation	$96,000 to be requested
Bank of America Foundation	$2,500 to be requested

References

<u>Nora Sandoval</u> – Student Group Advisor, Office of Student Life, University of California, Berkeley (510) 643-5010. As the Program Manager during TAAP's first two years, Nora was instrumental in helping to conceptualize, create and implement much of the program portion of The Achievement Award Program. Her current position works in conjunction with the campus retention programs.

<u>Richard W. Black</u> - Assistant Vice Chancellor of Admissions and Enrollments and Director of Financial Aid, University of California, Berkeley (510) 642-7117. Dr. Black has administered the financial aid for our Alumni Leadership Scholarship for 15 years and for The Achievement Award Program for three years. Additionally, he was actively involved with CAA in creating The Achievement Award Program.

<u>Eugene Garcia</u> – Dean of the Graduate School of Education, University of California, Berkeley (510) 643-6644. Dean Garcia understands the pedagogy and importance of retention programs on campus and, therefore, acts as an advisor to the program.

Notes on the financial pages that follow:

The Income Statement reflects the year-to-date actual and the year-to-date budget as of February 2001, our most recent report. The annual budget for each program is also shown on the far right.

Revenues:
Fundraising revenue for scholarships is not reflected on CAA's books because the funds are held by the University of California, Berkeley Foundation and the Regents. This year, as of April 15th, we have raised $677,880 for the Alumni Leadership Scholarship and $286,000 for the Achievement Award Program, primarily through direct mail. It is our expectation that the funding for the Achievement Award Program will significantly increase as our official campaign begins. As of March 28, 2001, our endowments for the Alumni Scholarship are valued at $31,915,000 and for the Achievement Award, $3,631,000.

Expenses:
Lair of the Golden Bear
The report shows the expenses for the Lair of the Golden Bear are significantly over budget. Last year, as the budget was being developed, CAA had just hired a new director for the Lair who was not yet familiar with the operation. He, therefore, created a more modest budget than was required. Additionally, CAA was in the middle of a conversion to new accounting software last summer when most of the Lair expenses were incurred. As a result, financial reports that would assist the new director in managing expenses could not be produced in a timely manner.
Achievement Award
The Achievement Award Program expenses are included in the expenses for Student Services. Below is the proposed budget for TAAP for 2001-02.

Salaries	
Program Director (100%) and part time Assistant	XXXXX
Outreach Program Partnership Development	3,500
Marketing	1,500
Application Process	5,000
Selection & Yield Process	3,000
Student Support Services	4,150
Achievement Council	2,000
Program Events	4,500
Achievement Council Outreach Program	1,000
TOTAL Expenses (projected)	$ 74,954.00

A Proposal From

Council on Library and Information Resources

Washington, D.C.

To

Robert W. Woodruff Foundation, Inc.

Atlanta, Georgia

Requested amount: $1,388,665; **Amount received:** $1.2 million over four years

Funder's comments:

"As is our preference, the foundation had received a brief letter of introduction describing the project before this proposal was submitted. This introductory process enables the foundation to have a general idea of the nature of the project, and an early indication of whether it fits within the foundation's grant guidelines could be given prior to submission of the proposal. The CLIR project did fit within our giving interests at that point in time, and the organization was invited to submit a full proposal.

"The foundation does not require that proposals be presented on an application form. It is requested that the proposal be in letter form and that it be concise. The art of the proposal's presentation and the manner in which an organization describes and expresses itself is important in our evaluation of the proposal.

"The executive summary of the CLIR proposal is well done. Overall, the various components of the proposal are well-balanced, and the need statement is compelling. The description of goals, objectives, and methods is complete. The description of collaborative relationships is persuasive. The lack of jargon is helpful and appreciated, as we prefer plain, concise English and forthrightness. Points are well developed but not exhaustive.

"The budget presentation is first-rate. It is helpful to include a budget narrative, but it does not need to be exhaustive.

"This proposal established a dialogue between the foundation and the grantseeker. The foundation does not depend solely on the written word when considering a proposal. Dialogue is important in a project such as this, particularly because this is not an organization with which we had previously worked. When working with organizations with which we are familiar, much of what appears in the formal proposal has been discussed previously with the organization's leadership, a pattern which is more characteristic of our grantmaking than the grant made to a first-time donee.

"Details about the project's administration and staffing had been included in an earlier submission by the organization. This proposal demonstrates that the organization had thoroughly considered the sustainability of the project after the period of the grant, and that was another convincing aspect of the proposal. The absence of such a program and its compelling value influenced the foundation's decision to provide support."

Charles H. McTier, President, Robert W. Woodruff Foundation, Inc.

Notes:

The complete proposal included the following attachments: list of board members of the Council on Library and Information Resources, a press release for the book, *The Mirage of Continuity,* brochure, program statement and governance document of the Digital Leadership Institute, a copy of *Into the Future,* and accompanying educational materials. The Digital Leadership Institute is now named the Frye Leadership Institute.

Proposal developed, written and submitted by Dr. Deanna B. Marcum, President, Council on Library and Information Resources.

PROPOSAL

for a

DIGITAL LEADERSHIP INSTITUTE (DLI)

from

THE COUNCIL ON LIBRARY AND INFORMATION RESOURCES (CLIR)

to

THE ROBERT W. WOODRUFF FOUNDATION

SUMMARY

The Council on Library and Information Resources (CLIR) requests $1,388,665 from the Robert W. Woodruff Foundation in partial support of a Digital Leadership Institute over a five-year period. The purpose of the Institute is to effect fundamental change in the way universities manage their information resources in the new digital era. In letters that accompanied the original proposal, library and information-technology directors attest to the urgent need felt on university campuses to manage information resources more effectively. They believe that this Institute will be critically important for instilling new methods and practices and for creating a new information culture.

As more and more information has become available in electronic format, formerly distinct organizational responsibilities on university campuses have overlapped and blurred. At the same time, the instructional and scholarly uses of technology have changed pedagogical and research methodologies. Thus, digital information and communications technologies are shaping new relationships among librarians, their information technology counterparts, and faculty members.

The mission of the Institute will be to provide continuing-education opportunities for individuals who currently hold, or will one day assume, positions that make them responsible for transforming the management of scholarly information in the higher-education community. Over the course of the next decade, the Institute will train a cadre of some 600 professionals-- most likely to be in mid-career and drawn from library and administrative staffs, computer centers, and faculties--who can preside over this transformation on the nation's campuses and comprehend its far-reaching implications for the way universities allocate their financial resources and fulfill their educational mission.

We anticipate that the Institute should have an initial life of 10 years, during which it will enroll 50 to 70 individuals a year. Participants will undergo a training experience that begins with a two-week seminar on the Emory University campus, proceeds through a subsequent year-long practicum on the home campus or in some other setting appropriate to the goals of the individual, and concludes with a summary session that reunites the participants to discuss and evaluate what they have learned. The program of the Institute will equip these future leaders with a sophisticated understanding of the characteristics of digital technology and its radical effects on traditional academic management.

No one organization can be expected to fund a project of this magnitude, no matter now needed the Institute is. We are turning to a diverse group for financial support, chief among them, the Woodruff Foundation. CLIR is investing a substantial portion of its own funds in the project because its Board considers this an activity of highest priority. The Board of EDUCAUSE (an organization newly created by the merger of EDUCOM and CAUSE, the two principal associations that represent educational computing) voted in August 1998 to contribute

2

$50,000 per year to the Institute, either in the form of tuition support for EDUCAUSE members or through cash payments. The Andrew W. Mellon Foundation has agreed to support the participation of international librarians and information technologists by contributing $30,000 per year for that purpose. Emory University, the host for the Institute, in recognition of the benefits that will accrue to the institution, has agreed in principle to contribute $10,000 per year in general support. The Library of Congress, in recognition of the importance of this Institute, has offered to divert funds that are being used internally for professional development to support the Digital Leadership Institute. Specific agreements with all of these and with other institutions will be concluded over the next few months.

This Institute meets a need that many universities are only beginning to recognize. It is important that the Institute have enough financial support to assure a strong program for the first few years. After consulting widely with librarians, information technologists, provosts, and faculty who are now in the new business of managing and distributing information resources, we are confident that the Institute will be sustained through tuition paid by sponsoring universities.

Introduction

Since the beginning of the digital revolution, libraries and universities have been using the technology to devise more effective means of storing, providing access to, and disseminating information in their local communities and of creating a capacity for the collaborative development of information resources. Libraries and archives are now seeing the large-scale introduction of materials in digital format, and they face the prospect of adding to their print collections an ever-increasing volume of electronic materials. Although they have made progress, the process has been difficult. The quickening pace of digitization--of both content and services--lends a new urgency to addressing the problems it has introduced.

The shortage of talented individuals to fill leadership positions on campuses is among the most significant of these problems. In addition to having the requisite intellectual skills, the persons qualified for these positions would understand (1) the characteristics of the technology and what is required to avoid obsolescence and to establish the necessary standards of accuracy, control, and access; and (2) the institutional culture on American campuses and how it accommodates decision-making and change.

Traditional library-school education does not produce individuals with these qualifications, in part because the curriculum is conservative, and because the intent is not to prepare graduates for leadership roles in large numbers. Moreover, to be fair, the emergent issues cannot simply be "taught." The problems have to be defined and the solutions sought by a new generation of information managers even as they assume roles of practical leadership within their institutions. For all these reasons, the Council on Library and Information Resources is seeking another approach to identifying and training skilled managers.

To develop leadership skills on the nation's campuses adequate to the demands of the electronic age, CLIR proposes to establish and manage at Emory University a **Digital**

3

Leadership Institute (DLI). The mission of the Institute will be to provide continuing education opportunities for individuals who currently hold, or will one day assume, positions that make them responsible for transforming the management of scholarly information in the higher-education community. These individuals are likely to be in mid-career and to come from libraries, administrative staffs, computer centers and information-technology divisions, and faculties.

The Institute should have an initial life of 10 years, during which it will enroll 50 to 70 individuals a year. These individuals will undergo a training experience that begins with an intensive two-week seminar on the Emory campus, proceeds through a subsequent year-long practicum experience on the home campus or in some other setting appropriate to the goals of each individual, and concludes with a summary session that reunites the participants to discuss and evaluate what they have learned. The effect over a decade will be to create a critical mass of skilled agents of change. The program of the Institute will equip these future leaders with a sophisticated understanding of the characteristics of digital technology and its radical effects on traditional academic management. They will learn to plan and manage processes of digital transformation in support of higher education.

Background to the Digital Leadership Institute (DLI)

As more and more information has become available in electronic format, formerly distinct organizational responsibilities on university campuses have overlapped and blurred. At the same time, the instructional and scholarly uses of technology have changed pedagogical and research methodologies. Thus, digital information and communications technologies are shaping new relationships among librarians, their information-technology counterparts, and faculty members.

Information-resources management varies widely from institution to institution. In some settings, the university librarian has become the principal officer coordinating the information functions on campus. In others, however, the librarian continues to operate in a restricted role as manager of library materials and staff, while an "information technology director" or "computer czar" is responsible for the technical infrastructure.

Digital technology will force us to devise integrated systems of information resources, and the effective management of these systems will change the organization and management of institutions of higher education. Because electronic information resources are not site-dependent, financial formulas based on the characteristics of print-on-paper technology are no longer useful. Similarly, intellectual-property rights, developed for print materials, must be redefined for electronic information transfer.

Because the technology evolves at a pace that makes obsolescence inevitable and routine, those charged with the acquisition and care of collections must not allow technological change to outrun their capacity for progressive adaptation. The digitized component of libraries and archives must be held to the same standards of accuracy, control, and accessibility as patrons have come to expect of the print component.

But the process of assuring orderly growth and continuing access in the electronic age

4

will involve more individuals on the nation's campuses than have been needed for the management of information heretofore. Decisions that affect the provision of information services to students and scholars will be made not just in libraries but in computer centers, and in the offices of university administrators who will have to decide how best to allocate an institution's resources, financial and otherwise, to the acquisition and maintenance of service technologies. The process must be informed and coordinated, and its complexity will require leadership of an increasingly sophisticated kind.

The operations of university libraries will soon be linked, literally, to all parts of the campus. Those who preside over the development of the new hybrid libraries--part print, part digital--must have knowledge and skills not demanded of them in the past, and become familiar with issues that have no precedent. Yet there are few opportunities for them to acquire this knowledge in an orderly fashion, or to hone their leadership skills in an atmosphere that is at once rigorous and sympathetic.

In September 1995, Emory and CLIR jointly sponsored a meeting in Atlanta that was attended by library directors, provosts, directors of information technology, library-school faculty members, and a library-school dean. (We might note that the collaboration between CLIR and Emory has another dimension: Emory's recently retired Provost, and now Chancellor, Dr. Billy Frye, currently serves on the Board of CLIR and was for a long period the Chairman of the Commission on Preservation and Access.) The purpose of the meeting was to consider the mix of skills and educational background necessary for successful management of 21st-century information services. In the digital era, when information is no longer site-specific and its transfer is instantaneous, universities cannot rely on their current compartmentalized procedures for drawing budgets and assigning responsibilities. The technology will break down the categories and force institutions to see themselves whole and to transform their operations if they are to cope with fundamental change.

CLIR and Emory commissioned a plan for a new "Institute" and invited CAUSE, the professional organization for managers of information technologies in higher education, to join the effort. (CAUSE, which has merged with EDUCOM, has run a very successful management institute for many years.) It soon became evident to all participants that, because of its substantial experience with leadership development programs, CLIR was the best organization to establish and manage the proposed Digital Leadership Institute, with support and assistance from Emory and CAUSE.

The Nature of the DLI

The Institute we are planning must be perceived as having both the form and the substance to attract individuals of the highest caliber. The quality of the Institute's faculty must be exceptional, and the educational experience different from any other available. The Institute is neither a management seminar nor a skills seminar; those exist already in sufficient number. Rather, it will focus on a new set of ways to think about problems of higher education, and it will help talented individuals understand how to effect fundamental change.

5

We propose the following goals and purposes for the DLI:

• To train, over the next decade, a critical mass of 600-700 "agents of change" and leaders of integrated information-resources management for our campuses (in practical terms, some 50-70 Institute participants each year), individuals with the skills to participate as partners in the articulation of broad university processes;

• To convey an understanding of digital technology and the effects it will have on traditional university management and operations;

• To give participants an appreciation of the historical, cultural, and technical roles of information-resource functions, and an understanding of how technology is changing those roles as they evolve in a digital context;

• To develop both a philosophical and a practical framework for introducing change into the management of forces shaping our universities.

We expect that it may be 10 years before the concerns the Institute is meant to address will be incorporated routinely into the administrative procedures of colleges and universities. We know that certain schools of library and information science are beginning to adapt their curricula to meet them. But those schools are meant to educate future generations of library staff, who will come in due course to positions of responsibility. The Institute is aimed specifically at individuals in a quite different stage of their careers, and with far more varied expertise. (If they once attended library school, the experience is well behind them.) They are in mid-career and hold positions of some importance on campuses, and they are unlikely candidates for enrolling in routine continuing-education classes. Such classes are likely to be populated by individuals with widely disparate motives for attendance--for example, the additional credits gained through a class may mean an increase in salary. A commitment to transformational change is not on the minds of these students.

The Institute is to be for a dedicated core of individuals whose motivation for attendance is directly tied to serving their institutions more knowledgeably and effectively. The atmosphere in the DLI should be very different from what prevails in standard continuing-education circumstances. In fact, the Institute is planned as a kind of living laboratory where problems facing academic institutions today can be considered by members of a class who, because of their professional experience, may have as much to contribute to the sessions as the instructors who are presiding over them. This differs fundamentally from the atmosphere in library-school courses, which are necessarily committed to research agendas at levels the Institute participants will have moved beyond. There should be a shared intellectual exhilaration to the atmosphere of the DLI that erases the line between teacher and student.

Participants in the DLI

The Institute will be geared toward those whose experience has brought them to the point of being in line to assume leadership positions. The ideal participants will come from the following categories:

6

- Mid-level library managers;

- Directors and associate directors of user services in libraries;

- Directors and associate directors of academic computing and telecommunications on campuses;

- Faculty members with an expressed interest in information-resources leadership.

There are several reasons for the focus on middle-level managers:

- The vast majority of librarians and technology specialists work in mid-level positions and deal daily with the nuts-and-bolts operations that are most affected by technological change.

- There currently exist opportunities for senior officers and library directors to develop leadership skills.

- We expect the schools of library and information science to design the educational preparation programs for newcomers to the profession, who may be leaders of digital libraries in the future.

Information-technology applications are likely to push the demand for specialized knowledge much farther down into the organizational structure of campuses, and it is important that the informed judgment of mid-level staff members be available to campus administrators who are responsible for policy decisions.

Individuals wishing to attend the Institute must apply in writing and include an essay on their professional interests and their expectations of the Institute. A letter of support from someone at the executive level of the institution--president, provost, vice president for academic affairs--will be an essential requirement for participation and must indicate specific support for the subsequent practicum component, which will entail a considerable financial contribution by each institution. To the extent possible, it would be useful to choose two individuals from different organizational units of a single campus to participate simultaneously in the Institute--someone from the library, for example, and someone from academic computing. Their combined strengths will better assist the transformation of operations on the campus.

Applications will be screened by a committee made up of CLIR staff, Emory staff, and members of an advisory group. The participants will be selected on the basis of their essays, information provided by references, and, in some cases, personal interviews. The selection committee will give special consideration to balancing the numbers of librarians, technologists, and faculty members. Throughout the process, the committee will be supportive of candidates from minority groups, who are underrepresented in the information-resources professions.

The Components of the DLI: Curriculum and Practicum

After the Emory/CLIR conference in 1995 endorsed the idea of an Institute, a small advisory group was appointed to develop a model curriculum. Brian Hawkins, now the president

7

of EDUCAUSE but at that time the Senior Vice President for Planning and Administration at Brown University, drafted a preliminary version, and it became the basis for intense discussion with many individuals. The revised curriculum, which was presented in the notebook accompanying the original proposal, is the outcome of long deliberations involving Mr. Hawkins, the advisory group, and representatives of Emory and CLIR.

The following considerations underlie the curriculum:

• The current needs in information-resources leadership will not be met by mastering a specific body of knowledge. The process will require a new way of thinking about issues confronting higher education.

• The presentations and discussions should favor practical applications over abstract philosophy. Though presentations might raise questions from a theoretical context, the real challenge, if the intent is transformation, will be to turn the theoretical considerations toward practical operations.

• The specific teaching methods, readings, and pedagogical models will be determined by faculty members.

• Discussion will provide the best opportunities for learning, and the curriculum includes ample time for small-group discussions, case studies, and models beyond the traditional lecture.

• While the coordinators and the faculty members are important, the most valuable resource in looking for "answers" will be the cohort of participants themselves.

• Presentations should be provocative and stimulate the group to challenge previous assumptions.

• The Institute cannot achieve everything. The director will have to set priorities on what will be most beneficial in the long run.

We realize that much time has passed since the initial formulation of the curriculum. A new committee of librarians, information technologists, and academic officers is being formed to revise the curriculum to respond to the rapid changes in the digital environment. The first meeting of the group is scheduled for early September.

It is important that the formal two-week educational experience identified as the curriculum not be taken for the whole of the Institute, for it is merely the first stage. Though we recognize that many individuals will choose to take part in the Institute based on their perceptions of the educational substance of the curricular component, the Institute is meant to be the sum of the seminar and the subsequent practicum experience. *Indeed, it is the practicum that distinguishes the DLI from other current efforts to provide training for the digital age.*

The year-long practicum--whether undertaken on an individual's home campus or elsewhere--must be flexible enough to meet the particular needs of each participant. (Applicants should identify at least the rudiments of the practical experience they consider both

8

desirable and manageable.) The Director of the Institute must negotiate the best possible practicum for each of the participants, and the experiences, dilemmas, challenges, and conclusions of the practicum projects should be the subject of inquiry, suggestion, and advice (normally through electronic means).

The practicum year will culminate in a three-day seminar at Emory, during which participants will discuss what they have learned. The seminar will provide an opportunity, against the background of the year's events, to compare experiences, to question received theory, and to affirm--or perhaps to counter--the advice of some of the speakers.

The Director of the DLI

The curriculum is still in outline form; its substance must be fleshed out, and the best-possible instructors enlisted. The advisory group has strongly recommended that a director be charged with advancing the project. So important is this project that Deanna Marcum, president of CLIR, will assume the responsibility and devote approximately half her time to directing the Institute, at least in the formative years. She has been a dean of a school of library and information science, in addition to nearly three decades of experience as a library manager, training specialist, and non-profit organization director. Dr. Marcum will be assisted by a consultant experienced with digital technology.

The director must give cohesion to the entire enterprise and oversee a diverse series of tasks, particularly at the start:

• Developing promotional materials that are persuasive about the program;

• Working with important figures in librarianship, higher education, and information technology to attract first-rate candidates to the Institute;

• Selecting the faculty for the first Institute;

• Making certain that the seminar sessions, as they are planned, focus on restructuring and on thinking about solutions outside the traditional functional boundaries.

• Identifying appropriate mentors for the participants.

Evaluation of the Institute

Evaluation of the Institute, especially in its first several years, is critical, for we are making large claims for it, and we must be confident that our assertions are correct. Our thinking on the evaluative process is still incomplete, but we propose at least the following:

• That evaluations of each major session of the seminar be conducted on the day of presentation.

• That there be a comprehensive evaluation at the end of the two-week seminar, perhaps mailed to the participants after they return home.

9

• That there be an evaluative component to the practicum year, and then another final retrospective evaluation for the participants a year after the original seminar.

• That we allow a period of several years before we judge how Institute participants have been able to effect change at their home institutions.

CLIR will make every effort--for example, through its publications program and Web site and through public reports at meetings of academic and professional associations--to share with others the progress of the cooperative experiment that is the DLI. It should be possible to issue accounts of the most interesting Institute discussions in summary form. And participants will be expected to report in writing on their home-campus practicum experiences. The reports can then be gathered and edited for wide distribution. The DLI curriculum will undergo revision in the light of what proves genuinely helpful and enlightening to participants.

The Timetable

When funding is available, we shall establish the exact dates for the seminar on the Emory campus (the first Institute will take place in the summer of 1999). Within approximately three months, we would hope to secure commitments from coordinators and faculty members for the first Institute. We shall make presentations to relevant organizations, such as EDUCAUSE, the Association of Research Libraries, and the Association of American Universities to recruit participants, and brochures will be designed, printed, and disseminated.

Continuing the Digital Leadership Institute

The Emory University Library is prepared to sponsor, through a Digital Leadership Center, annual conferences focused on the principal themes of the DLI--the development of leadership adequate to the task of managing scholarly information resources in the digital environment, and the transforming effects of digital technology on the traditional ways academic institutions support and organize information resources. The Library is also prepared to continue digital initiatives and projects to explore the many issues and concerns that surround the economics and organization of managing digital information resources.

The immediate challenge is to launch the project and to identify the most promising future leaders to take part. We have not calculated costs of the Institute beyond five years, a period we believe sufficient to allow us to evaluate the Institute and demonstrate its worth. Over time, we expect universities to underwrite the cost of staff participation. We have identified several organizations that are willing to share the risk of establishing the Institute because they are convinced that universities must find better ways to prepare information resource managers for quite different kinds of leadership roles.

The Council on Library and Information Resources relies entirely on support from private foundations to sustain its core staff and its various programs, there being no endowment funds. There is a long history of generous support from foundations for the work of CLIR's predecessor organizations, the Council on Library Resources (CLR) and the Commission on Preservation and Access (CPA). The Ford Foundation established the CLR in 1956 and singlehandedly sustained it for two decades. The Andrew W. Mellon Foundation has provided

10

continuous support since the 1970s for the Council on Library Resources, and for the Commission on Preservation and Access since its inception in the mid-1980s. This support has been both general and project specific, and it is fundamental to our operations today.

Other assistance has come from the Carnegie Corporation, the William and Flora Hewlett Foundation (10 years of assistance to the Commission on Preservation and Access), and the Kellogg Foundation (for work with public libraries). The Gladys Krieble Delmas Foundation and the H.W. Wilson Foundation have been helpful time and again for a range of initiatives.

Foundations that were exceptionally generous in the past, such as Ford and the Pew Charitable Trusts, whose resources would allow them to provide major assistance, have shifted their programmatic interests and have not been accepting requests on behalf of libraries and library-related activities. We continue to hope that these foundations may shift their focus toward interests that accord with the goals of CLIR, or that they will be persuaded by the argument we have tried to make that a project like the Digital Leadership Institute is not about libraries only but about the proper management of fundamental capacities at universities.

In addition to seeking substantial foundation support for the Institute, we shall explore a different pattern of sustaining it--through sponsorship arrangements. Sponsorship is currently working well for two other major CLIR initiatives. Our preservation efforts are supported by more than 100 university and college sponsors, and the Digital Library Federation encompasses 21 contributing research libraries (a number that is expected to grow). Sponsors make annual payments to these activities and receive certain defined benefits in return. The strongest argument for their participation is that they have a stake in what the projects are trying to accomplish: the work promises fundamental long-term institutional benefits.

Related Activities of CLIR

Several recent initiatives of CLIR have contributed to our strong belief in the need for this Institute. For the past several months, in collaboration with the Association of American Universities, we have been engaged in preparing for publication a monograph entitled *The Mirage of Continuity: Reconfiguring Academic Information Resources for the 21st Century*, edited by Brian Hawkins and Patricia Battin. It is a volume of essays that comes to grips with the profound, and indeed transforming, changes technology will effect in how the nation's university campuses provide information resources in the coming century. The monograph will be released on September 2, and we expect it to be a basic text for the Institute.

The Digital Library Federation, made up of 21 large research libraries, is committed to "bringing together, from across the nation and beyond, digitized materials that will be made accessible to students, scholars, and citizens everywhere." After nearly a year of formal operation, the Federation has produced a program statement and a governance document that will guide its development over the next few years. Central to the work of the Federation is an educational capacity that will produce leaders adequate to the challenges produced by digital technology. Background material describing the Federation is attached.

In the Preservation and Access Program, CLIR has actively sought to remind the educational community that the preservation of digital information is critical to the vitality of

11

scholarship. We produced a documentary film, *Into the Future,* for public television broadcast in January 1998. The film is now being translated into several languages for distribution to an international audience. In concert with the film, we produced several documents that amplify the message, and we include these for your information.

Through the International Program, we have consistently included education and training as a staple of the offerings. Although preservation is the focus for the International Program, we recognize that without leadership training, preservation programs have little chance of success in some of the developing countries. This program has been funded by The Andrew W. Mellon Foundation, so we were especially pleased when the Foundation agreed to support tuition costs of the Institute for some of the most promising librarians and technologists identified through the International Program.

Conclusion

CLIR has been interested in establishing the Digital Leadership Institute for the last few years. Emory University, especially as represented by Chancellor Billy Frye and University Librarian Joan Gotwals, has shown great interest in providing a home and moral support for this new approach to producing leaders for a challenging era in higher education. We have sought to gain support for the concept from a number of communities that stand to benefit from the Institute. We are most hopeful that the Woodruff Foundation will see fit to offer the financial support to turn the plan into a reality.

We appreciate your willingness to consider this proposal and look forward to hearing from you.

Attachments

Attachments sent with earlier submission include curriculum notebook, resume of Deanna Marcum, and letters of support from university librarians and information technologists.

Additional attachments include a list of members of the CLIR Board, a press release for the soon-to-be-released monograph *The Mirage of Continuity*, a DLF brochure to introduce the Federation, a program statement and governance document for DLF, a copy of *Into the Future,* and accompanying educational materials.

12

[Budget Notes]

Estimated Costs of the DLI

The amount needed to organize the Institute and conduct the first year's activities is $500,650, of which we are requesting $284,650 from the Robert W. Woodruff Foundation. We would want to provide for some rise in costs in subsequent years, as a reflection of modest (approximately 4%) inflationary increases in conference facility costs. The salary for the Director of the Institute has been reduced in subsequent years because we assume that the greatest concentration of effort will occur in the first year of the program. Emory University will supply conference space and housing for the participants and make arrangements for seminar equipment.

The categories of costs for which we are seeking support include the following:

• Institute Faculty and Staff Costs

The Institute cannot succeed without a director who is a person of some stature in the higher-education community and who oversees all phases of the enterprise. A technology expert is required to assure high-quality content. Sufficient support-staff time must also be available to handle the logistical support for the Institute.

• Operational Costs

    • Advertising Costs

The Institute must be publicized among academic administrators, information technologists, librarians, and faculty members. The publicity must be particularly skillful the first year, through such means as brochures and electronic postings.

    • Course Materials

Participants will receive a notebook of readings prior to the seminar and additional materials throughout its course.

    • Video Production

Some presentations can best be made visually. We have included an amount to accommodate video productions for at least two subjects of the Institute--the history of computing and the history of libraries.

13

Digital Leadership Institute
Five Year Budget

	Year 1	Year 2	Year 3	Year 4	Year 5	5-Year Total
Institute Faculty & Staff						
Director						
Salary	XXXXX	XXXXX	XXXXX	XXXXX	XXXXX	XXXXX
Benefits @ 25%	XXXXX	XXXXX	XXXXX	XXXXX	XXXXX	XXXXX
Support Staff						
Salary	XXXXX	XXXXX	XXXXX	XXXXX	XXXXX	XXXXX
Benefits @ 25%	XXXXX	XXXXX	XXXXX	XXXXX	XXXXX	XXXXX
Technology Consultant (XXXXX days @ XXXXX/day)	$25,000	$26,000	$27,040	$28,122	$29,246	$135,408
On-site Coordinators (2 @ XXXXX/day, XXXXX days)	$13,000	$13,520	$14,061	$14,623	$15,208	$70,412
Travel to Emory (2 @ $1,000)	$2,000	$2,080	$2,163	$2,250	$2,340	$10,833
Lodging and meals (2 @ $200/day, 13 days)	$5,200	$5,408	$5,624	$5,849	$6,083	$28,165
Faculty Presenters (XXXXX @ XXXXX/day)	$14,400	$14,976	$15,575	$16,198	$16,846	$77,995
Travel to Emory	$12,000	$12,480	$12,979	$13,498	$14,038	$64,996
Lodging and meals	$28,800	$29,952	$31,150	$32,396	$33,692	$155,990
*Participants						
Lodging and Meals (60 @ $200/day, 13 days)	$156,000	$162,240	$168,730	$175,479	$182,498	$844,946
Travel	$60,000	$62,400	$64,896	$67,492	$70,192	$324,979
Operational Costs						
Advertising	$10,000	$10,400	$10,816	$11,249	$11,699	$54,163
Course Materials ($300 x 60 participants)	$18,000	$18,720	$19,469	$20,248	$21,057	$97,494
Video Production	$10,000	$10,400	$10,816	$11,249	$11,699	$54,163
Telephone, Fax, and Network Charges	$5,000	$5,200	$5,408	$5,624	$5,849	$27,082
Contingency	$10,000	$10,000	$10,000	$10,000	$10,000	$50,000
Total	**$500,650**	**$504,276**	**$508,547**	**$513,489**	**$531,628**	**$2,558,590**
Amount Contributed by Other Sources	**$216,000**	**$224,640**	**$233,626**	**$242,971**	**$252,689**	**$1,169,926**
Amount Requested from the Woodruff Foundation	**$284,650**	**$279,636**	**$274,921**	**$270,518**	**$278,939**	**$1,388,665**

> *It should be noted that the annual costs shown above are not the full amount of what will be invested in the institute. The practicum will involve substantial costs for the home institutions.*
>
> *CLIR will contribute additional support staff, as needed, as well as administrative space and equipment.*

*   Institutions will be expected to cover the costs of their participants' travel to and from Atlanta. Other funders will provide the necessary dollars for participant lodging and meals.

3

Endowment

Endowments are bequests or gifts intended to be kept permanently and invested to provide income for continued support of an organization. Endowment grants, especially those for unrestricted support, are attractive to grantseekers, since the income can be used for programs, staff salaries, maintenance of buildings and equipment, or whatever the organization deems appropriate. And foundations that award this type of funding may appreciate the opportunity to ensure the long-term viability of organizations they care about. An endowment request may also be part of a larger capital campaign. Nonetheless, endowment funding is relatively rare, and fundraisers may find that such grants are difficult to secure. Yet, because they are a reliable source of ongoing income, development staff continue to devote time and effort to this component of a long-term fundraising strategy.

Generally, because of the nature of this type of investment by the funder, nonprofits will seek endowment funding from grantmakers who know their work well and have supported the organization in the past. It may still be wise, however, to provide as much background information in an endowment request as in other types of proposals. And as with other types of proposals, it is important to demonstrate that the donation of endowment funds will have a substantial and positive impact on the quality of the services offered by the agency.

The proposal in this chapter, submitted by the Virginia Museum of Fine Arts Foundation in Richmond, Virginia, to the Lettie Pate Evans Foundation, is an example of an endowment request—in this case, part of a larger capital campaign—to a funder that is already quite familiar with the work of the organization making the request. Often these kinds of requests are preceded by several conversations, and sometimes the organization is invited by a long-time donor to apply for endowment support.

A Proposal From
Virginia Museum of Fine Arts Foundation
Richmond, Virginia

To
Lettie Pate Evans Foundation, Inc.
Atlanta, Georgia

Requested amount: $500,000; **Amount received:** $500,000

Funder's comments:

"The Lettie Pate Evans Foundation has an ongoing relationship with the Virginia Museum of Fine Arts. Since prior knowledge and understanding of the museum preceded this particular proposal, the proposal spoke only to the purpose for which the grant was sought. An extensive explanation about the institutional mission of the museum and how it has developed over time was unnecessary.

"The proposal shows sensitivity to how much information was needed. The foundation was given sufficient but not excessive information. The writing style is straightforward, plain English, without jargon. Overall, the proposal is comprehensive without being exhaustive. Points are presented and explained in three or four sentences, which is sufficient to communicate the main ideas that needed to be understood.

"We were comfortable that all background information was provided in the proposal or was already in the foundation's files. We were not left with many unanswered questions, which is a hallmark of a well-prepared proposal. We would be pleased if all proposals were this well presented."

Charles H. McTier, President, Lettie Pate Evans Foundation, Inc.

Notes:
The complete proposal included the following attachments: capital campaign brochure and the 1993-1999 Stewardship Report of Special Exhibitions made possible by the Evans Exhibition Fund.
Proposal developed by members of the Virginia Museum of Fine Arts Foundation development staff with Anne Barriault, Editor for the Capital Campaign; submitted to the funder by Dr. Herbert A. Claiborne, Jr.

VIRGINIA MUSEUM OF FINE ARTS FOUNDATION

2800 GROVE AVENUE/RICHMOND, VIRGINIA 23221-2466/804-367-0805

August 30, 2000

Mr. Charles H. McTier
President
The Lettie Pate Evans Foundation, Inc.
50 Hurt Plaza, Suite 1200
Atlanta, GA   30303

Dear Pete,

You may remember that we spoke earlier about the possibility of the Lettie Pate Evans Foundation supporting the Virginia Museum of Fine Arts' capital campaign, which has yet to be publicly announced.

As a Director of the Virginia Museum of Fine Arts Foundation, I am writing with a special request. In December 1992, The Lettie Pate Evans Foundation gave a generous $500,000 gift to the museum for the purpose of creating the Evans Exhibition Fund. As of December 31, 1999, the market value of this fund had grown to $1,096,000. As we approach the eighth anniversary of the establishment of this endowment, I am writing to ask the Foundation to consider augmenting the corpus of the fund with a gift of $500,000.

Your gift would increase the value of the Evans endowment to $1.5 million. Moreover, in recognition of the immense support that the Evans Foundation has given the museum through the years, we propose to match that endowment. A match of $1.5 million, made from institutional reserves, would raise the value of the Evans Exhibition Fund to more than $3 million. At that level, the Fund would not only enable the museum to compete nationally and internationally for special loan exhibitions of the highest quality, but also to recognize the Evans Foundation on a regular basis as the generous sponsor.

We hope you will find this suggestion as appealing and exciting as we do. We have enclosed a 1993-1999 stewardship report of special exhibitions over seven years that have been made possible by the Evans Exhibition Fund. The report reflects the museum's original proposal to use the endowment to underwrite exhibitions of European, British, and American art, as well as Ancient Eastern and Western art, in deference to Mrs. Evans' personal taste.

We are also enclosing our campaign brochure, which presents an overview of the museum's future plans. If I can provide any further information, please do not hesitate to contact me. I look forward to hearing of the Foundation's decision. Thank you for considering our request.

Sincerely yours,

Herbert A. Claiborne, Jr.
Director, Virginia Museum of Fine Arts Foundation

A Proposal and Stewardship Report for
The Lettie Pate Evans Foundation

From
The Virginia Museum Of Fine Arts

Virginia Museum of Fine Arts
The Evans Exhibitions Fund and the Museum's Plans for the Future

The primary mission of the Virginia Museum of Fine Arts is to collect the art of world cultures and interpret it through exhibitions and programs. Our visitors most often cite two reasons for coming to the museum: the opportunity to experience the art, and the opportunity to teach their children about it in a relaxing and entertaining environment.

Since the establishment of the Evans Exhibition Fund, the museum has made significant strides in evaluating our audiences' needs and enhancing our welcoming atmosphere. Audiences tend to seek a balance between returning to view favorite objects in the permanent collections and wanting to see new and changing exhibitions, many of wide appeal that travel to Richmond from national and international venues.

To help us serve our increasing numbers of visitors and to accommodate our growing permanent collections and exhibitions schedules, the museum has launched a capital campaign. It is in its early stages and not yet publicly announced. A successful campaign promises funding for a new wing, with improved amenities for our audiences; dedicated galleries for large traveling exhibitions, so that our permanent collections galleries will not be disturbed; and expanded permanent collections galleries to display more of our works of art than our current space allows. We have recently received an endorsement from the governor and state legislature, and we have begun the search for an architectural firm.

An increased endowment for special exhibitions from the Evans Foundation would be considered a contribution to the campaign. Your gift would place us in a stronger position to host "upper tier" exhibitions and keep pace with their rising costs. In 1992, the average cost of a small-to-medium-sized loan exhibition ran between $50,000 and $100,000. Today, the cost of exhibitions now offered the museum--which have grown in size and

2

caliber as the museum itself has--ranges from approximately $250,000 to $400,000. The museum now realizes approximately $50,000 in annual revenues from the current Evans endowment. An additional gift of $500,000, together with the museum's contribution, would provide an estimated $200,000 annually. These funds would enable the museum to offer highly attractive exhibitions, while freeing other museum funds for accompanying lectures, teachers workshops, and youth and family programs, which have earned the museum its reputation as a major resource for art education across the Commonwealth.

Increasing the endowment in partnership with the museum would enable the Evans Foundation to become the sole sponsor of select exhibitions, and the museum will, of course, acknowledge your sponsorship in appropriate ways.

We want very much to recognize the Evans Foundation for its continuing support. One of our two central courtyards are now named in honor of Lettie Pate Whitehead Evans, in recognition of her devotion to the museum and in appreciation of forty years of ongoing support from the Evans bequest. The courtyard currently houses our recently acquired collection of English silver, given to us in 1997, and our collection of European tapestries, rotated for the purposes of conservation.

By helping our collections, gallery spaces, and endowments to continue to grow, we hope to build upon the high standards that our museum has come to represent among art institutions in the southern and mid-Atlantic regions. A renewed gift from your Foundation would greatly contribute toward that effort.

8/30/00

3

Stewardship Report to the Lettie Pate Evans Foundation
Evans Exhibitions Fund

From its Inception January 1, 1993 to December 31, 1999
Submitted by the Virginia Museum of Fine Arts Foundation

History of the Endowment

In December 1992, the Lettie Pate Evans Foundation awarded to the Virginia
Museum of Fine Arts a generous gift of $500,000 over five years for an endowment
to support exhibitions.

Management and Performance of the Fund

The Evans Exhibitions Fund endowment is accounted for separately, but is "pooled"
for investment purposes. The Virginia Museum of Fine Arts Foundation employs
multiple investment managers in accordance with an asset allocation plan developed
by the Finance Committee of the Board of Directors. The Committee has adopted
investment guidelines and objectives including a 5% spending plan based on a three-
year moving average of the fund's market value. For three years and five years, the
annualized returns were 18.6% and 18.0% respectively. As of December 31, 1999,
the market value of the endowment was $1,096,000.

Exhibition Support

The Evans Exhibitions Fund has supported seven exhibitions from *America Around
1900* in FY 1994 to *Splendors of Ancient Egypt*, which closed on November 28, 1999.
The Evans Exhibitions Fund will have expended $221,692 through the end of 1999.
Attendance at exhibitions for the reporting period is 306,878.

Current Revenues

At its current market value of more than $1 million, the Evans Exhibitions Fund is
providing the museum with about $50,000 annually. A full description of each

4

exhibition supported by the Evans Exhibitions Fund is attached, showing the amount of support and level of attendance.

8/30/00

5

Stewardship Report to the Lettie Pate Evans Foundation
The Evans Exhibitions Fund
Exhibition Support from 1994 through 1999

1999 *Splendors of Ancient Egypt*
Attendance 248,000   **$77,600**

The Virginia Museum of Fine Arts was the only East Coast venue for one of the largest exhibitions of ancient Egyptian treasures ever to visit the U.S. This show offered more than 200 masterpieces ranging from the Predynastic period around 3200 B. C., through the Old Kingdom age of the pyramids, to the 7th century A.D. Objects included gilded and painted mummy cases, alabaster and life-size limestone figures of pharaohs and noblemen, an 18-foot-long papyrus scroll from the Egyptian Book of the Dead, gold and lapis lazuli jewelry, wall carvings, and pottery. The exhibition was drawn from the world-renowned collection of Egyptian art at the Pelizaeus Museum in Hildesheim, Germany.

1998 *Gabriele Munter: The Years of Expressionism 1903-1920*
Attendance 7,138   **$12,400**

Gabriele Munter (1877-1962) was one of the leaders of the German Expressionist movement and one of the few women artists associated with it. Despite the quality and invention of her artwork, Munter's contributions to modern painting have often been overshadowed by those of her male colleagues, particularly Wassily Kandinsky, her mentor and companion. During the first decade of this century, Munter developed a distinctive style in which simplified form, bold color, and rich brushwork characterize her vibrant portraits, landscapes, and still lifes. As a founding member of the Expressionist artists' colony in Murnau in 1908, the New Munich Artist Association in 1909, and the Blue Rider group in 1911, she helped shape the art and ideas of Expressionism in the

6

years before World War I. Through 80 paintings, drawings, and prints, the exhibition explored Munter's work and the diversity of her key role in the artistic developments of this revolutionary period.

1997 *William Blake: Illustrations of the Book of Job*
Attendance 6,916   **$20,000**

In 1973, the museum purchased a complete set of engraved illustrations of *The Book of Job* (1825), the most important example of line engraving ever executed by the English visionary poet William Blake (1757-1827). Because these are fragile works on paper, they can be placed on view only for brief periods, such as this special exhibition. Some 60 drawings, watercolors, and engravings investigated the aesthetic and spiritual implications of Blake's *Book of Job*. Also on display were selections of watercolors on which the engravings were largely based, commissioned nearly 20 years prior to the engravings; the entire set of Blake's preliminary drawings for the engravings; and, for comparison, a selection from the "New Zealand" set of watercolors originally thought to be by Blake, but now accepted as copies after his work.

1997 *Adornment for Eternity: Chinese Jewelry Through the Ages*
Attendance 9,495   **$13,692**

This was the first major exhibition to trace the evolution of personal adornment from China's Shang period (ca. 1500-1050 B.C.) to the Ming dynasty (A.D. 1368-1644). During China's early history, jewelry and other objects of personal adornment served as symbols of status and rank. Later on, they were marks of beauty and wealth. Included in this elegant exhibition are earrings, garment and belt clasps, mirrors, combs, plaques, belt sets, hairpins, pendants, and diadems. All were exquisitely crafted from gold, silver, bronze, jade, and other sumptuous materials. Many of these objects were discovered in Chinese tombs, where they were intended to accompany the dead in the afterlife—as adornments for eternity.

7

1996-97 *Masterpieces in Little: Portrait Miniatures from the Collection of Her Majesty Queen Elizabeth II*
Attendance 6,807   **$33,000**

The art of miniature painting, or limning, came to the fore in England during the 16th and 17th centuries at the Tudor and Stuart courts. This selection of 75 miniatures represented the cultural elite and others at the courts of Elizabeth I, James I, and Charles I. The tradition continued through the 18th and 19th centuries and culminated in a portrait of Princess Victoria (the daughter of Queen Victoria) in a Turkish costume. "These works have rightly been called 'some of the great masterpieces of northern renaissance art.' Marked by a careful attention to detail and sometimes surprisingly complicated iconography, miniatures have a rare and sophisticated brilliance," according to Malcolm Cormack, the museum's Paul Mellon Curator and coordinator of the exhibition. "The British Royal Collection is understandably rich in such images, never before lent abroad. Major works by Hans Holbein the Younger, Francois Clouet, Nicholas Hilliard, and Isaac Oliver, as well as Samuel Cooper, Richard Cosway, and Sir W.C. Ross [were] featured in this stunning pictorial history of the British royal family."

1996 *Splendors of an Age: Italian Paintings from Burghley House*
Attendance 4,682   **$40,000**

Since members of England's Cecil family first began collecting in the late 1600s, the art at Burghley House has represented one of the first great English country-house collections of Italian Old Master paintings. This exhibition of 60 works highlighted the collecting efforts of two family members—John Cecil, 5th Earl of Exeter (1648-1700), and his great-grandson Brownlow, the 9th Earl (1725-1793). John traveled to all parts of Italy long before the Grand Tour became fashionable among the English upper classes. While there, he put together a collection of paintings by the Italian masters of his time, including Carlo Dolci, Luca Giordano, Mattia Preti, and Carlo Martha. The 9th Earl bought works by earlier Italian painters such as Jacopo Bassano and Paolo Veronese. The exhibition's combination of devotional images from the Counter-Reformation period, as well as scenes of mythical heroes and heroines, still lifes, and scenes of

8

everyday life, provided a fascinating overview of late Renaissance and Baroque subjects and styles.

1994-95 *America Around 1900: Impressionism, Realism, and Modern Life*
Attendance 23,840   **$ 25,000**

Important Impressionist and Realist paintings by such all-American favorites as Mary Cassatt, William Merritt Chase, Childe Hassam, John Singer Sargent, John Sloan, Robert Henri, and others revealed how artists reacted to massive social change in the turn-of-the-century America.

Total Attendance   306,878

Total Evans Exhibitions Fund Contributions $221,692

8/30/00

9

4

Building/Renovation

Grants in this category make possible the building, renovation, remodeling, or rehabilitation of property. Because these projects tend to be quite large in scope, no one funder typically takes on the entire cost of a construction project. Grants from several supporters often will be sought simultaneously. The amounts requested may vary in size, with certain funders taking a lead role. Some funders may pay for only particular aspects of the project, such as a playground or auditorium.

Depending on the funder's requirements, proposals for building/renovation may include specific and definitive plans, such as architects' renderings and specifications, engineers' reports, design schematics, and other technical documents, frequently handled as attachments.

As in other types of proposals, the need for the project is expressed in terms of the community members to be served, not just the benefit to the organization and its staff. The writer of a construction proposal succeeds by demonstrating how the new or renovated facility will enhance the programs that serve an audience that the funder cares about.

The proposal presented here from the Foundation Center to Prince Charitable Trusts combined a request for $3,000 in general support with $30,000 to fund the enhancement of the Center's Washington, D.C., office. This is an example of a fundraising strategy that can prove successful when a grantseeker wants to keep a funder as an annual donor, while still requesting a one-time gift. The proposed installation in this case included a library, training room, computer lab, and staff work areas.

The request from the Summit Area YMCA, Summit, New Jersey, was a proposal to the Kresge Foundation for a $400,000 challenge grant. The organization sought to increase its capacity to serve the community, and this grant request was for a portion of its overall capital campaign. The proposal is reprinted along with a response from the Kresge Foundation requesting additional information and the reply letter from the

Summit Area YMCA. For such a complex grant project, this type of back-and-forth communication between grantseeker and funder is to be expected.

A Proposal From
The Foundation Center–Washington, D.C.
Washington, D.C.

To
Prince Charitable Trusts
Washington, D.C.

Requested amount: $30,000; **Amount received:** $10,000

Funder's comments:

"The first criterion for a winning proposal is whether the purpose fits the organization's mission and values. In this case, the proposal to expand the Foundation Center offices was pretty much of a 'no-brainer.' The Foundation Center is an invaluable local resource for the nonprofit sector in general, and we feel privileged to have a branch in Washington, D.C. Moving and expanding the facility also made sense because of the major changes in information technology in the past 35 years. Finally, it was easy to understand why the Center needed more training and meeting space to support their role. Our organization had funded the Foundation Center in the past, so we were a likely candidate to assist with this project.

"That said, the proposal makes the case and provides the important information in a clear and precise manner. I appreciated the subheadings—it is easier to navigate through a proposal when the text is sensibly divided and the different sections are well labeled. The proposal consistently speaks to our interests—it describes how the new facility will support the function we care about most—being an essential resource for grantseekers.

"I like to have the request clearly stated in the first paragraph. The proposal uses the second paragraph to explain why this request is larger than usual and gives a legitimate reason. Our trustees are very skeptical of 'bracket creep' (a group asking for just a little bit more money each year), and find vague reasons annoying: 'due to increased demand for our services.'

"We prefer that grantseekers use the Washington Grantmaker's Common Grant Application, which was not done in this case. The Common Grant Application specifies a summary page, which is especially important, since we use this information to assist the grants manager in entering the proposal in our Gifts Data Base, and for preliminary staff review. Nevertheless, the proposal is well organized, which made it easy to move from section to section.

Building/Renovation

155

"As someone who reads many proposals, it is refreshing to have good, concise information without a lot of verbiage. This proposal strikes a good balance. It provides needed information but does not overwhelm the reader. More is not better.

"The timetable, total cost of the project, and other sources of support are critical information. We generally do not fund a proposal until we have this information."

Kristin A. Pauly, Managing Director, Prince Charitable Trusts

Notes:

The complete proposal included the following attachments: library expense budget, construction budget and narrative, floor plan, and IRS tax-exempt letter.

Proposal written by Alyson J. Tufts, Vice President for Development; submitted to the funder by Sara L. Engelhardt, President; and Anita Plotinsky, Director of the Foundation Center-Washington, D.C.

THE
FOUNDATION
CENTER

1001 CONNECTICUT AVENUE, NW
SUITE 938
WASHINGTON, DC 20036-5588
PHONE: 202-331-1401
FAX: 202-331-1739

May 8, 2000

Ms. Kristin A. Pauly
Senior Program Officer
Prince Charitable Trusts
816 Connecticut Avenue, N.W.
Washington, DC 20006

Dear Kristin:

We are grateful for your past support of the Foundation Center – Washington, D.C. As you may know, our Washington office has served the information needs of grantseekers and grantmakers in our nation's capital and the surrounding region since 1964. This year, when our current lease expires, we plan to build a state-of-the-art library and training center to better serve the needs of our audiences in the electronic age. I write now to request your increased support of $3,000 for our programs this year and ask that the Prince Charitable Trusts also consider making a special, one-time grant of $30,000 toward the cost of building this new facility.

On occasion, we ask our funders to provide special, concurrent grants to enable us to invest in our infrastructure and develop new capacities to serve the nonprofit community. The new library and its state-of-the-art technology will permit further growth in our educational and information services. We are pleased to announce that we have filled the position of director for the Foundation Center - Washington, D.C. Anita Plotinsky, who assumed this role on May 1, will lead the office through an exciting period, as we work to become a more effective communication bridge between grantmakers and grantseekers and a meeting ground for the area's philanthropic community.

Support for the Foundation Center – Washington, D.C.'s Programs and Services

For thirty-five years, the Foundation Center – Washington, D.C., has provided high-quality information services for grantseekers and grantmakers in the region. As documented by the positive and enthusiastic responses of our visitors, our library and programs are an essential resource for those seeking information on philanthropy.

Our traditional information services include providing top-quality reference assistance in the library, as well as by telephone, fax, and e-mail, and providing access to an array of resources on foundations and their grantmaking. Today, some of our library's most popular resources are electronic, including *FC Search: The Foundation Center's Database on CD-ROM*, IRS Forms 990-PF online for all 50,000 foundations, and the Center's site on the World Wide Web.

SERVING THE INFORMATION NEEDS OF GRANTSEEKERS AND GRANTMAKERS
HEADQUARTERS: NEW YORK CITY • OFFICES: ATLANTA / CLEVELAND / SAN FRANCISCO / WASHINGTON, DC

To help grantseekers develop their skills and use our resources effectively, the Foundation Center – Washington, D.C., provides a wide range of free educational programs. Our training includes weekly basic orientations to our library and instruction in the use of electronic resources.

We will also increase our collaboration and outreach efforts. Working with the Washington Regional Association of Grantmakers, the local Support Center, and others, we will create and present a variety of programs. Recent panel discussions have focused on funding for international programs, the environment, the disabled, and corporate funders. In addition, we will continue to serve as participants in the Congressional Research Service training programs for new congressional staff, and we will continue our annual complimentary offers of publications in our foundation research series and the *Foundation Directory* to members of Congress.

Your renewed and increased general support is essential to help us sustain our existing programs this year, while we are developing new resources and training programs and building a new facility.

New Washington, D.C., Facility

Our plans for the new Foundation Center – Washington, D.C., include a state-of-the-art library with adjacent training room, computer lab, and staff work areas, in a space that is larger than our current facility. The design of our new space will be flexible, allowing us to adapt it to the changing needs of our audiences. We plan to fully equip the space to support emerging technologies. We hope to begin construction in June in a building located close to the Metro.

The Library

Our D.C. library was built for an era when our resources were largely print and microform. Today we need larger, more flexible space to eliminate the crowded conditions for library visitors and staff, and we need more computer workstations to accommodate the growing demand for electronic resources and additional bookshelves for our expanding collection on foundations, fundraising, and nonprofit management. A new, technologically equipped library reference desk will give our librarians easy access to all the print and electronic resources they call upon to provide high-quality reference service.

FC Search has revolutionized the way grantseekers conduct their research. It allows users to select grantmaker and grant records according to multiple search criteria and provides direct hyperlinks to the Web sites of some 1,000 grantmakers. Currently, we have only five public-access computers in the library, and they are in almost continuous use during our hours of operation. We plan to install 20 public access terminals in our new library and computer lab. The design of our new space will allow us to add more public-access computers as demand increases in the future.

The Internet has quickly become a popular fundraising research tool, and the Center is in the forefront in organizing and delivering online information and educational services for grantseekers. We have the most comprehensive Web site devoted to philanthropy, including links to grantmakers' Web sites and many other nonprofit resources. In addition, we have created numerous services and

Ms. Kristin A. Pauly   May 8, 2000
Prince Charitable Trusts   Page 3

resources that are available only at our site, such as a "Foundation Finder" look-up tool, several online educational programs, the weekly *Philanthropy News Digest*, and a searchable database of *The Literature of the Nonprofit Sector*. As our online resources expand, and as more grantmakers post information about themselves on the Web, demand for Internet access in our library will continue to grow.

In 1998, we developed FC Cat, an online library catalog that permits visitors to quickly identify books, articles, and non-print resources such as CD-ROMs and audiovisual materials pertaining to their particular interests. FC Cat contains 18,000 entries, of which more than 60 percent contain descriptive abstracts. Library visitors are able to verify a particular author, title, or publisher; read an abstract; and print out their own customized bibliographies with call numbers. At least one computer terminal in our new library will provide access to FC Cat.

Over the years, the Foundation Center and its Washington, D.C., office have served a unique role by providing public access to all of the 990-PFs for foundations in the United States. In late 1998, the IRS began scanning 990-PFs onto CD-ROM instead of microfiche. Computers in our new library will allow visitors to view foundations' annual IRS tax returns in electronic format.

Computer Lab and Training Room

The Foundation Center's reputation for providing access to high-quality information resources is reinforced by our efforts to educate grantseekers in the effective use of these resources. In order to expand our educational programs in Washington, D.C., we are constructing a computer lab in the new library. The computer lab will allow Foundation Center – Washington, D.C., staff to offer hands-on computer-based training for grantseekers and grantmakers. When we are not conducting training sessions, library visitors will be able to use the computers in the lab for their research.

We are also constructing a training room that will be suitable for a variety of purposes. State-of-the-art multimedia equipment will facilitate professional presentations for our various audiences. The space will allow us to expand our programming efforts, convene meetings of local Cooperating Collections supervisors and Center staff from across the country, and offer meeting space to others in the nonprofit community.

Initially, our free educational programs will include: Grantseeking Basics, an orientation to the funding research process; Getting Started with *FC Search*, an introduction to the basics of searching our grantmaker and grants database on CD-ROM; CyberTour, an overview of the Center's Web site; and BiblioTour, an introduction to our online public access catalog and our searchable bibliographic database on the Internet. Other free programs will include: Introduction to Library Resources on Corporate Giving; Foundations Today; and Demystifying the 990-PF. Plans for new training programs include such topics as grantseeking basics for individuals, proposal writing basics, and foundation fundamentals. Once the new space is completed, we will introduce fee-based seminars including all-day basic and advanced training courses on *FC Search* and one on grantseeking on the Web.

With a separate computer lab and training room adjacent to the library, we will be able to increase the number and type of educational programs we offer, hold programs throughout the day, and expand our collaborative programming efforts.

Staff Work Areas

In our new space, we will construct modular workstations for our staff. New computer equipment for our professional and support staff will enhance the work environment and better enable staff to carry out their varying responsibilities, such as preparing programs, evaluating new resources for the library, serving members of our Associates program and our Friends of the Library program, preparing educational programs for the public, and keeping abreast of developments in the field.

Our relocation and expansion project will greatly benefit grantseekers and grantmakers by enabling us to make high-quality information resources and educational services available to all.

In support of our two requests, we are enclosing an expense budget for the Foundation Center – Washington, D.C., library, and for the facility relocation and expansion. We estimate that the total cost of this project will be $825,000, which will be offset by a landlord's workletter and the Center's own contribution to the project.

We are most appreciative of the support you have shown the Center. We will send you our 1999 Annual Report with audited financial statements shortly. Please let either of us know if we can provide additional materials or information in support of our two funding requests.

Sincerely,

Anita H. Plotinsky
Director, Foundation Center – Washington, D.C.

Sara L. Engelhardt
President, The Foundation Center

The Foundation Center		
Estimated Costs for the Construction and Furnishings of the Washington, D.C. Library and Training Annex		
2000		
Buildout of Space	$425,000	
Furniture	125,000	
Computer Equipment	90,000	
Professional Fees	60,000	
Audiovisual Equipment	40,000	
Security System	10,000	
Finishes, Signage and Artwork	25,000	
Evaluation	20,000	
Moving	5,000	
Contingency	25,000	
Total Budget	$825,000	
Landlord Contribution	$154,000	
Foundation Center Operating Funds	200,000	
Special Project Grant Support	471,000	
Total Estimated Project Costs	$825,000	

A Proposal From
Summit Area YMCA
Summit, New Jersey

To
The Kresge Foundation
Troy, Michigan

Requested amount: $400,000; **Amount received:** $400,000

Funder's comments:

"The Kresge Foundation is known for funding bricks and mortar projects. We believe, however, that a challenge grant toward an organization's capital project does more than just build a building. It presents an opportunity to build institutional capacity by helping an organization broaden and deepen its base of support from the private sector and by encouraging volunteer involvement in the fundraising effort and beyond.

"A proposal to our foundation is a comprehensive document describing the organization and its programs, project, and campaign. Grantseekers need to carefully plan in advance of their application to the foundation, since many important elements must be in place before submitting the proposal. Our guidelines are clearly outlined in printed materials and at our Web site.

"In proposals we review we expect to find evidence of financial stability, substantiation that demand for programs or services is stable or increasing, and an effective board, administrative, and program staff. These fundamentals were all demonstrated in the proposal from the Summit Area YMCA. The portrait of the community clearly described increasing ethnic and cultural diversity and changing needs that the organization sought to meet.

"The Summit Y had firm costs based on completed construction documents. The narrative description of the project was clear and straightforward, indicating how many people could be served by the various components of the enlarged facilities. As our guidelines stipulate, major collaborations were indicated in a separate section, as was the policy for maintaining the current physical plant.

"We require very specific plans regarding an organization's fundraising strategies. Though the Summit Y provided many details about the stages of their campaign, we did have several follow-up questions about that aspect of their application. Their response provided us with the necessary information about their strategy to approach the community to support the Y's capital campaign. Importantly, the Summit Y described how they planned to seek gifts from new donors and to increase the level of support from previous contributors. After the capital campaign is completed, this expanded donor base will help support the Y's future, ongoing, operating needs. Evidence that there is a capacity-building opportunity is a key competitive factor in our review. The documentation about this aspect of the Summit Y's efforts was crucial to our decision to award the grant."

Sandra M. Ambrozy, Senior Program Officer, The Kresge Foundation

Notes:
The complete proposal included the following attachments: list of board members, organizational overview, artist renderings and floor plans, campaign leadership and gifts to date, *pro forma* income and expense projections, current fundraising prospects, IRS tax-exempt letter, audited financial statement, long-term financing documentation, and regulatory approvals.
Proposal written and submitted to the funder by Timothy G. Weidman, President and Chief Executive Officer.

Investing
in our
Community
Campaign for the Summit Area YMCA

SUMMIT AREA YMCA
67 Maple Street
Summit, New Jersey 07901
Phone: (908) 273-3330
Fax: (908) 273-0258

April 3, 1996

Mr. John E. Marshall, III
President
The Kresge Foundation
3215 W. Big Beaver Road
PO Box 3151
Troy, Michigan 48007-3151

Dear John:

We appreciated the chance to meet with you in January regarding the Y's expansion project
and the associated capital campaign.

Since we met with you, the Board has looked again at the project and the campaign, and has
raised our campaign goal from the $4,000,000 we discussed in January to $4,500,000.

Two factors came into play in making this decision -- one relating to contributed income, and
the other relating to expenses. We received an unanticipated major gift which we did not
identify in our campaign feasibility study, we identified the immediate need for a project
manager, and the estimated costs of construction increased as a result of the architect's
advanced work.

The acquisition of our project manager is already benefiting the project. Opportunities for
cost savings are outweighing unanticipated cost increases, and we see that our project overall
is under control.

Enclosed please find our proposal to the Kresge Foundation for a $400,000 challenge grant.
We are seeking an 18 month challenge deadline following your decision in order to maximize
the capacity building your grant would provide us.

As of today, we are nearly to the $2,100,000 campaign mark. We will keep you informed
of our progress, and will make the $2,250,000 campaign halfway point by May 15th, your
spring application deadline.

Design schematics are now complete. I will forward them to you this month. Design
Development and Construction Documents will be complete in May. I will forward these to
you as they are completed.

Member:
United Way of Summit
New Providence
and Berkeley Heights

SUMMIT   MILLBURN   SHORT HILLS   BERKELEY HEIGHTS   GILLETTE   NEW PROVIDENCE   STIRLING   SPRINGFIELD

Our construction is due to begin a year from now, in the spring of 1997, with project completion scheduled for 1999.

I appreciated your offer to give us feedback as you review our proposal, and I look forward to working with you.

Roger Parsons and John Hill send their greetings.

Sincerely,

Timothy G. Weidman
Executive Director

P.S.   I have heard the good news of Kresge's award to the Metuchen YMCA. This is an excellent boost for their campaign, and the important work which will be possible with their expansion.

cc: Roger B. Parsons, President

enc.

The Kresge Foundation FACT SHEET

Name of organization: ___Summit Area YMCA_____ Date: _____

Contact Person/Title: ___Timothy G. Weidman_____ Telephone: __908-273-3330____

ORGANIZATIONAL INFORMATION

Year established ___1886___

ACCREDITATION/LICENSURE

Name of accrediting body, date of last accreditation review, and current status: __YMCA of the USA, April 95, Approved___

FINANCIAL DATA

CURRENT UNRESTRICTED FUNDS

Show budget projection for current Fiscal Year and actual data for 3 prior years
Omit 000's

	Income	Expense	Surplus or Deficit
FY 19 95 (est.)	$ 2,547	$ 2,534	$ 13
FY 19 94	$ 2,314	$ 2,312	$ 2
FY 19 93	$ 2,143	$ 2,139	$ 4
FY 19 92	$ 2,019	$ 2,014	$ 5

Attach explanation of any operating deficits and indicate how the deficits were covered.

Market value of endowment $_____
Date of valuation _____

IMPACT OF COMPLETED PROJECT ON OPERATING AND MAINTENANCE BUDGETS

Increases/(decreases) expected for

• Staff	$ 297,000
• Utilities	120,000
• Debt service	180,000
• Other occupancy	123,000
(identify) Total	$ 720,000

Increases to be met by revenue generated from

• New/increased program fees	$ 700,000
• Rental savings	
• Additional fund raising	50,000
• Endowment income	
• Other _____	
(identify) Total	$ 750,000

PROFILE OF PERSONS SERVED

Ethnic and Gender Representation

	% Minority	% Women
Board	14	25
Staff	36	63
Clients/Students/Attendance	20	52

Colleges/Universities

Enrollment	Full-time	Part-time	FTE
Fall 19___			
Fall 19___			
Fall 19___			

Attach explanation of any significant fluctuation in data shown.

Average freshman SAT or ACT scores _____
Student-to-faculty ratio _____
% Faculty with Ph.D. or terminal degrees _____

Health Care/Residential Care Organizations

_____/_____	_____	_____
no. of licensed beds/ no. of beds in use	% occupancy (of beds in use)	length of stay

Project will result in increase/decrease of _____ beds.
(circle one)   no.

Number of inpatient admissions
19___ _____ 19___ _____ 19___ _____

Number of outpatient visits
19___ _____ 19___ _____ 19___ _____

Charitable care (not contractual allowances)
19___ $_____ 19___ $_____ 19___ $_____

Patient Mix
Medicare _____% Medicaid _____% Ins./Private Pay _____%

All Other Organizations

Attendance	19__ _____	19__ _____	19__ _____
Members	19__ _____	19__ _____	19__ _____
Other*	19__ _____	19__ _____	19__ _____

*Identify _____

Please complete both sides of this FACT SHEET

PROJECT INFORMATION

PROJECT COSTS

Construction/renovation	$ 4,500,000
Equipment	85,000
Furnishings	15,000
Fees	35,000
Contingency	450,000
Fund raising expense	210,000
Interest expense	150,000
Other _Planning Board Approval_	50,000
(identify)	
Other _Architect & project mgr._	505,000
(identify)	
Project Cost	6,000,000
Endowment Goal	
(if applicable)	
TOTAL COST	A) $ 6,000,000

Project costs are based on what level of architectural plans:
(check one)

__x__	Conceptual
__X__	Schematic
__x__	Design Development
_____	Construction Documents

General construction contract was/will be signed: __2-97__
If multiple contracts are involved, provide schedule.   mo./yr.

Project timetable

When did/will work commence:	3-97	mo./yr.
What is the completion date:	9-98	mo./yr.
Building/land purchase agreement signed:	NA	mo./yr.
Equipment purchase agreement signed:	NA	mo./yr.

Date of receipt of regulatory approval

Zoning:	NA	mo./yr.
Certificate of Need:	NA	mo./yr.
Environmental Impact:	NA	mo./yr.
Other: _Planning Board_	9-95	mo./yr.
(identify)		

FUNDS AVAILABLE

Gifts and grants *formally pledged or paid*

Staff/Trustees	$ 240,790
Corporations	229,500
Individuals	1,536,207
Foundations	83,000

Fund raising for these leadership gifts began __9-94__
                                                                      mo./yr.

Government

Long-term financing
Bond issue	
Loan	1,500,000

Date of formal commitment of loan or actual sale of bond issue
__3-25-96__ ; maturity date _____
    mo./yr.   mo./yr.

Organization's funds

_____	
(identify)	
Bequests (paid or in probate)	
Other _____	
(identify)	
Other _____	
(identify)	
TOTAL AVAILABLE	B) $ 3,589,497
BALANCE REQUIRED	$ 2,410,503
(A minus B)	

Following the formal commitment of a Kresge challenge grant, the balance required will be raised by _____. This date will be the requested challenge deadline.   mo./yr.

18 months following commitment

Amount requested from The Kresge Foundation	$ 400,000

Please complete both sides of this FACT SHEET

Investing in our Community
Campaign for the Summit Area YMCA

SUMMIT AREA YMCA
67 Maple Street
Summit, New Jersey 07901
Phone: (908) 273-3330
Fax: (908) 273-0258

Proposal to

The Kresge Foundation

for

the Summit Area YMCA

April 2, 1996

Tim Weidman, Executive Director
Summit Area YMCA
67 Maple Street
Summit, NJ 07901
(908) 273-3330

Member.
United Way of Summit
New Providence
and Berkeley Heights

SUMMIT   MILLBURN   SHORT HILLS   BERKELEY HEIGHTS   GILLETTE   NEW PROVIDENCE   STIRLING   SPRINGFIELD

TABLE OF CONTENTS

NARRATIVE STATEMENT - ORGANIZATIONAL INFORMATION

EXECUTIVE SUMMARY

The Summit Area YMCA requests a challenge grant of $400,000 from The Kresge Foundation in support of its capital campaign, renovation and expansion. An 18 month period following the Kresge Foundation decision is requested to meet the challenge and complete the campaign total fundraising of $4,500,000. At this time, the campaign has raised nearly $2,100,000 in its first 18 months. By the Kresge Foundation spring deadline of May 15th we will have completed half of our goal, $2,250,000.

With these campaign monies plus an additional $1,500,000 in long-term financing, the Y will renovate 18,300 square feet and expand its downtown Summit facility by 24,969 square feet to a total facility of 61,796 square feet. The expanded facility will allow the Y to continue its service expansion in response to community needs, while eliminating turnaways for program registration, and long waits for core facilities and equipment.

Now, the Y is experiencing ever increasing turnaways and waiting lists as a result of the inadequacy of its downtown facilities. Outreach programs have absorbed growth for services which require no specialized equipment or space. However, essential child care, youth service, 7 day a week facilities for teens, young adults and families, and senior therapeutic programs, require additional specialized space.

Expansions in service to traditionally affluent members have yielded earned and contributed income adequate to support financial aid and program subsidies. However, the member base alone cannot carry the costs of the capital expansion which is now critically needed.

The Kresge Foundation, with a $400,000 challenge grant can provide the substance, the leverage, and the endorsement needed to complete this vital project.

BRIEF HISTORY OF THE ORGANIZATION AND DESCRIPTION OF SERVICES PROVIDED AND PERSONS SERVED

The Summit Area YMCA, founded in 1886, is located at 67 Maple Street in Summit. It serves the region of Summit, Gillette, Berkeley Heights, Millburn, New Providence, Short Hills, Springfield, and Stirling. The historic YMCA facility was built in 1912 and a pool was added in 1955. In 1974, squash and racquetball courts were added and a Y branch was opened. The facility underwent a $4,000,000 renovation in 1988/89. In 1993, a $100,000 first floor renovation was completed to expand the fitness center and redesign the reception area. This renovation was financed from operating surpluses. In 1995, the Y opened a satellite serving Berkeley Heights with child care, youth sports and a range of fitness services.

For more than a century, the Y has been the Summit area's largest multi-service provider. Over the past five years it has proactively initiated programs to reach out to the community across the broadest age, economic, racial and cultural demographics. This effort is meeting with great success. The Y currently has 8,500 members enrolled.[1] By contrast, in 1990, the member enrollment was 4,700. An additional 1,800 individuals participate in Y programs that do not require membership including the annual Y Corporate Games, after school tutoring, Friday night $1 basketball and swimming, Black Achievers, Model U.N.,

---

[1] Figures used throughout represent number of enrolled members as of February 29, 1996. Were numbers of uses presented, totals would be much higher. The Kresge Foundation files may show these higher "use" numbers reported for the Y's last campaign. Since that time, the Y has adopted a policy to report only member numbers, and Y-Ware software has been installed to provide the infrastructure needed to supply accurate counts.

2

Youth and Government, after school middle school drop-in gym program, teen adventure

trips, and senior citizen line dancing. The age make-up of the membership is:

12.6%	1 - 5 years old
23.0	6 - 11
7.1	12 - 17
17.4	18 - 29
32.4	30 - 54
3.9	55 - 64
3.6	65 +

Twenty percent of Y memberships are family and 49% of Y members are female.

Minorities as a percentage of our child care and day camp participants exceeds the

percentages in the overall regional population for African American and Hispanic youth.

The 300% increase in membership since 1988 provides solid earned and contributed

income base supporting the Y's core programs and community outreach. Currently Y

membership is growing at a rate of about 8% a year. This trend is reflective of the Y's

strong performance in delivering high quality, reasonably priced, and accessible services for

its regional constituency. The success of thoughtful Board policy making -- such as the

determination to avoid duplication of services with the YWCA and other local organizations,

and the high priority placed on recruiting high quality staff of various ages and ethnic

backgrounds[2] -- are also a part of this growth. The Y's tradition of service to families with

young children and senior citizens is playing directly into growing population segments.

---

[2] According to Jacke Harris, a recently retired consultant with the New York Management Resource Center offices of the YMCA of the USA, the Summit Area YMCA has the most ethnically diverse staff, with the most minority staff in management and management assisting positions of any Y in the region. The Metropolitan Region includes Newark and New York City.

3

In addition, the Y promotes broad community access to its services, reaching out beyond its membership through programs like Friday Night $1 basketball for teens and young adults and Corporate Games for 1,200 area employees. This access is provided by the Y through its own programs, such as after school, supervised drop-in gym for middle school youngsters, or the swimming program for disabled. Access is also provided through co-operative partnerships. Examples include a tutoring program for 4th, 5th, and 6th grade students in conjunction with Fountain Baptist Church, and aerobic exercise classes and square dances for disabled individuals in cooperation with Union County Parks Department. The Y is an active participant in the national Black Achiever's program, involving over 50 middle school students with minority mentors drawn from area industry and a school year schedule of activities ranging from college visits to video production.

A policy to respond proactively to the region's demographics drives this expansion. At first glance, Summit appears the stable, comfortable community it was laid out to be in the last century. It has diminished slightly in size between 1980 and 1990 as the trend toward later marriage and smaller families continues. Its population is dominated by families, young adults, active older adults whose families have grown, and senior citizens.

4

But Summit's internal demographic shifts over the last decade are significant. Each one

represents changing regional needs to which the Y is uniquely positioned to respond:

1) Census data reveals a 28.7% jump in pre-schoolers from 1980 to 1990.[3] This trend continues in the first half of the 1990's, putting increasing pressure on child care and enrichment resources for young children and their families. The number of students in the Summit School system is projected to increase by over 700 by the year 2,000.

2) A 33.5% drop in school age youth lead to reduced public school and recreation programming. The sudden rise in service demand as pre-schoolers reach school age has stressed schools and community organizations alike.

3) At the same time, the number of adults aged 45 to 64 dropped 11.6% as downsizing corporations transferred or eliminated management-level employees, and others moved out of town to smaller living quarters. Within this age group still living in town, more two-earner couples can be found than ever before. The net result is a significant loss in time available for community volunteer effort and care of elderly parents and grandchildren.

4) Reflecting advances in geriatric care, those 85 and older rose 13.6%.

5) Summit's income diversity is increasing. Young couples and families moving into Summit's most expensive homes have higher median incomes than the older couples they replace. Meanwhile, modestly-priced rental property continues to draw singles and families with lower incomes.

During this period, the region mirrored the larger New Jersey trends of increased

ethnic and cultural diversity.

1) Traditional white and black population segments dropped as those who moved away were replaced by other ethnic groups. (Non-Hispanic white dropped 9.9% and black dropped 7.8%) Even within these traditional populations, households identifying themselves as Jewish and Islamic increased, so that diversity increased. There are currently over 35 languages spoken in the homes of Summit students.

---

[3] Data for the Needs section was prepared by Vito Gallo, Executive Director, Summit Housing Authority, September 1994, utilizing 1990 Census and Housing Authority sources.

5

2)   The Asian population grew 135%. Ranging from young highly educated professionals to immigrant households of limited means, this group challenges the Summit region with its desires for amenities and needs for specialized services.

3)   The Hispanic population grew 57.7%, again presenting great diversity in household resources and resulting service needs.

4)   The total minority population in Summit grew from 10.8% in 1980 to 15.1% in 1990. The Summit Housing Authority reports that this trend continues.

5)   In five years, the Y has gone from awarding $60,000 to over $135,000 in annual financial assistance to individuals and families who wish to join and participate in Y membership and activities but can not afford them.

While Summit continues to be dominated by family households, fully half of them are married without children. Because of the presence of high quality housing stock for singles, 80% of Summit's non-family households are single, mostly young adults.

This data tells an explicit story of the need for high volume, highly specialized services for pre-schoolers and young families, young adults, minorities and aged seniors. Summit leadership is aware of this data. Area residents interviewed for the Y's 1994 Feasibility Study recognized that Summit's public and community service institutions must respond to this changing community profile. The Y was cited repeatedly as "one of the few community organizations well positioned to respond to the demographic changes taking place in Summit."[4] The diversity of age, economics, and ethnicity which come together was also noted in comments like, "It's the only place I can think of where all ages, all groups, come together around common interests."

_____

[4]   J.C. Geever, Inc., <u>Feasibility Study for the Summit Area</u>, New York, 1994

6

Among all of the other non-profit agencies in the Summit area, the YMCA is the only one with a comprehensive plan to respond to the increases in youth and minority populations.

Of immediate concern to the Y's Board is the way in which the data is being echoed every day at the Maple Street facility. Because the Y has high quality services for the growing populations of Summit -- families with pre-schoolers, young singles and couples, and aging seniors -- its membership has grown dramatically since the last renovation, up from 2,700 in 1988 to 8,500 this year. Community needs pressing the physical facility of the Y are leading to increasing turnaways:

1) Over 1,000 lap swimmers and families are not able to swim during the week because the only hours available to them fall during the workday.

2) Although water therapeutic program participants rate the program as "outstanding" and "filling the (regimen) my physician outlined for me,"[5] another 170 are turned away annually for lack of pool space.

3) 50 pre-school and after school program users are turned away each fall.

4) Up to 60 users wait for court space on open basketball gym nights -- a primary service for older youth and young adults.

5) 2,700 fitness center users seeking access to weights and cardiovascular equipment lead to waits and turnaways during peak use hours.

6) Space for high school and middle school-age youth drop-in programs is extremely limited due to space constraints. These programs must be greatly expanded to enhance the teen outreach efforts of the City of Summit and other youth serving agencies.

---

[5] J.C. Geever, Inc., *Feasibility Study for the Summit Area*, New York, 1994

7

DESCRIPTION OF MAJOR AFFILIATIONS WITH OTHER NONPROFIT ORGANIZATIONS

The Y is an active citizen of the Summit area's non-profit and civic community.

Collaborations with numerous agencies include:

City of Summit
Berkeley Heights Board of Education
Central Presbyterian Church
Chamber of Commerce
Christ Church
Fountain Baptist Church
Kent Place School
New Providence Board of Education
Overlook Hospital
Rotary
S.A.G.E.
Springfield Project
Summit Family Services
Summit First Night
Summit Municipal Alliance
Summit Recreation Department
Summit Board of Education
Summit Red Cross
TV-36
Union County Parks Department
United Way

In many instances, the Y provides space for non-profit programs and events such as Summit First Night, blood drives, clothing drives, meetings, and gym time. As the Y membership has grown, the Y's ability to provide space for other organizations has been diminished. The increased facilities will expand the Y's ability to respond to these needs.

8

The Y has been a pro-active non-profit colleague. Most recently, we were able to use our lease negotiations for satellite space in Berkeley Heights to arrange space for S.A.G.E., a local non-profit organization serving the elderly. S.A.G.E.'s survival had been endangered by its loss of leased space, and its inability to leverage reasonable rents on its low square footage requirements.

The Y also enjoys collegial support from the community. Most recently, Overlook Hospital signed a parking provision agreement with us -- a key element in our ability to obtain Planning Board approvals for our expansion. In Summit, where municipal parking is a severely stressed resource, Overlook has many options for the use of its excess parking spaces. The agreement on Overlook's part was a very generous act of support for our work.

The Y is also an active member of its own non-profit YMCA network. Executive Director, Tim Weidman, serves on the New York MRC Council, an elected Board of Managers. One of Mr. Weidman's duties on the Council was to conduct an evaluation of the New York MRC staff with the 55 YMCA's in the MRC service area. Mr. Weidman also serves on the Board of Directors of the local chapter of the National Association of Professional Directors, the YMCA professional society, and has represented the chapter at national conferences. The Summit Area YMCA also hosts many regional Y training events.

POLICY FOR MAINTAINING THE PRESENT PHYSICAL PLANT

In 1989, we initiated a Building Preservation Reserve Fund financed by joiners fees. The Fund currently stands at $500,000. Revenue is utilized annually for routine maintenance and the annual August "tear-down" where scheduled renovations are implemented.

9

A preventative maintenance schedule has been developed and implemented for the scheduled maintenance and replacement of all equipment and mechanical systems. The schedule extends to the year 2,025. Funding for this work will be provided by the Building Preservation Reserve Fund.

The Y's structure for managing facilities, finances and programs has been noted by the National Association of Professional Directors in presenting its Administrative Award of Excellence to the Summit Area YMCA in 1992 and 1995.

LISTING OF YOUR GOVERNING BOARD WITH PROFESSIONAL AFFILIATIONS

See appendix attached

NARRATIVE STATEMENT - PROJECT INFORMATION

DESCRIPTION OF THE PROJECT AND ITS EXPECTED IMPACT ON THE ORGANIZATION

Recognizing the long-term planning implications of these trends and needs identified in the Summit Region, in 1992 the Summit Area YMCA retained the New York-based Management Resource Center (MRC) to survey active and former members.

In 1993, the Biber Partnership, an architectural firm from Summit, was engaged to produce a Facilities Feasibility Study and Masterplan responding to the needs identified in the Management Resource Center survey. They utilized the MRC Study, programming interviews, and inputs from staff, members, Board, and the New Facility Committee -- a group of trustees, staff and community leaders.

The planning process revealed that to respond adequately to both community and member/user needs, the Summit Area YMCA needed to undertake a partial renovation of its current 36,927 square foot building in downtown Summit, and construct a 24,969 square foot

10

addition to the building. In addition, all current programs, including outreach sites, must be retained.

At this time, the scope of the project is defined. Construction is set to begin in the spring of 1997, with conclusion in 1999. The planned renovations and additional space are oriented toward programming which meets broadest community needs, both in terms of age, and demographics.

The project includes:

I.   New 6 lane, 25 yard swimming pool

The new competition pool will expand service to youth swim teams and lap swimmers. The pool will also be available for use by the facilities-pressed public schools who are now absorbing larger classes as each new grade moves up. The additional numbers which can be served are encouraging:

1)   1,000 additional lap swimmers and family groups currently locked out of weeknight swimming for lack of evening swim hours

2)   more than 400 children annually turned away from swim lessons and teams for lack of pool space

II. Current pool refitted for accessibility and dedicated to high temperature uses:

The existing pool will be dedicated to full-week, higher temperature water programs for infants and tots, as well as therapeutic uses for senior citizens and the handicapped. Based upon current user numbers and turnaways, we project services to an additional 170 seniors and individuals with disabilities or in physical therapy.

11

III. Fitness center facilities grow 100% to a total of 4,000 square feet

The fitness center with its trained support staff operating 7 days a week, is a linchpin of service to youth, adults of all ages, and seniors in therapeutic regimens. Because its services cross many of the demographic segments which are rapidly growing, it is the fastest growing use area at the Y. With doubled space the Y will be able to:

1) Meet peak hour demands during evenings and weekend hours

2) Meet the needs of seniors, both fit and those in therapeutic regimens

3) Earn increased revenues to support the costs of increased operations and community outreach services

IV. An 8,000 square foot gymnasium

The new gym facility will be dominated by basketball, youth sports, and volleyball. It is a high priority facility for area employees before work, during lunch hours and after work. Nights and weekend hours, it draws together a diverse group of young adults. Friday night $1 basketball ensures access by non-members and youth. The Feasibility Study revealed community awareness of and dependence on this facility as a "healthy outlet" for those who would "just hang around downtown" otherwise. With the new facility, service hours can be expanded.

1) For teens and young adults seven days a week, waits and turnaways will be eliminated during critical evening hours when Summit is lacking leisure and recreational outlets for this age group

2) Adults, including many who do not reside in Summit, but drop by before or after work will find waits eliminated

3) The Corporate Games can expand to include gym-based sports, increasing access by another 400

4) Youth sports, after school programs, child care and day camp programs can expand to serve 6,000 youth annually.

12

V.   Staffed Drop-in Babysitting Center

Support for the parents, grandparents, and caregivers of pre-schoolers is provided through staffed babysitting on weekdays. It will expand with the expanding facility, guaranteeing Y users the opportunity for personal participation and time to enjoy activities with their older children while their younger children are safely supervised.

VI.   3,200 square feet of handicapped accessible Multi-Purpose Space

This new space will greatly expand usable meeting and program space available 7 days a week, near public transportation, in downtown Summit. It responds not only to the peak hour space needs of the Y, but also to other community organizations engaged in meeting community needs. The Multi-Purpose Space will provide:

1)   25 - 50% expansion in the Y's peak hour after school and daycare programming

2)   social programs for seniors, in conjunction with the therapeutic pool and fitness center

3)   community organization conference use (The Chamber of Commerce, Red Cross, and United Way have already requested regularly scheduled use.)

4)   A family fun and fitness area allowing family members of all ages to play and work out together

VII. Infrastructure

The Y Masterplan recognizes the facilities, staff, and volunteer infrastructure that is necessary to support these expanded services to the broad Summit community.

1)   Locker rooms will be renovated and expanded, including private changing areas for mothers and fathers with infants. Areas for team use will be separated from those for general use, facilitating family and senior therapeutic participation, even during peak youth team programming hours.

2)   Wet and dry corridors will be handicapped accessible throughout, supporting those using the therapeutic pool as well as other facilities.

13

3) Plumbing and filter upgrades will reduce maintenance downtime, releasing hours for community and school scheduling of the competition pool.

4) An expanded membership office will support outreach to new users, continuing strong earned income trends which undergird the Y's capacity to maintain its facilities and underwrite financial aid for children and families.

5) Conference space in the administrative area which is currently utilized for overflow activities such as yoga classes, will be released for staff planning and evaluation, and meetings with parents and community leaders.

VIII.   Comparison of Service -- 1990, Current, After Expansion[6]

Facility/Program	1990	Current	Post-Expansion
Competition Pool	----	----	5,000
Gymnasium	2,300	3,400	5,200
Fitness Center	950	2,300	3,500
Weight Room	200	500	900
Babysitting	15 per day	40 per day	60 per day
After School	60 per day	105 per day	150 per day
Day Camps	125 per week	250 per week	350 per week
Corporate Games	----	1,200	1,600
Senior Programming	275	400	1,000
Multi-Purpose Space	2,200	2,700	4,500
Scholarships	215	450	700
Therapeutic Pool	2,800	4,400	3,000[7]

---

[6] Numbers used represent individuals served. Were numbers of uses presented, totals would be much higher.

[7] Programming of the therapeutic pool for senior citizens, the handicapped, and infants requires a reduction in density of use. Therefore, services provided by the therapeutic pool will decline

14

STATUS OF ARCHITECTURAL PLANS AND BASIS FOR COST ESTIMATES

The Y has contracted TORCON, a provider of construction services, as a project manager to represent the Y in overseeing the design development and the preparation of construction documents. TORCON is providing input for cost savings and alternative ways to solve design and construction concerns. They are also responsible for providing cost estimating as the project progresses. Estimates were provided upon the completion of the Schematics. They will be provided again at the completion of Design Development, and at several stages of the development of Construction Documents.

Currently Schematics are 100% complete. By April 15, 1996, the Design Development will be 75% complete and the Construction Documents will be 50% complete. By May 15, the completed Design and Construction documents along with the final cost estimates will be sent.

EFFECT OF COMPLETED PROJECT ON ORGANIZATION'S OVERALL BUDGET

The Y anticipates that the Bylaws, Board Committee, Financial Management, and Executive Management structure of the Y will absorb the impact of this expansion as they are currently configured. Staff will rise from 140 to 190 as the added square feet and their associated activities come on line. In order to ensure that unearned income projections are met without a distortion of program staff job descriptions, a development officer will be added in the fall of 1996.

Pro forma calculations of increased operating costs indicate a rise in budget from $2,112,100 (1995, actual) to $3,217,800 in 1999, the first year of expanded operation. (See

---

from current totals.

15

Pro forma Projection Detail in the appendix)[8] This includes additional staff, facilities, and administrative costs.

In producing pro forma projections, it was assumed that the new facility will open and be fully operational on January 1, 1999. Increased revenues were based upon the 1996 dollar. Increased revenues projected are a result of projected increases in enrollments and participation. Increases in fees are not a factor.

Membership growth is projected as the largest factor in increased revenues:

9%	1997
8	1998
25	1999
15	2000
10	2001
7	2002
7	2003
5	2004
5	2005
5	2006

Program revenue is also projected to increase:

Program	1st yr	2nd yr	Subsequent
Aquatic	30%	15%	5%
Child Care	15	10	5
Youth Sports	15	7	5

---

[8] <u>New Facility Operating Projections</u>, produced by Tim Weidman, Director of the Summit Area YMCA, for Board review, June, 1994.

16

Staff will increase as the facility comes on line:
(*5% increase in salaries projected for each year*)

2 full time cleaning ($8/hour)	$35,000
1 full time maintenance	30,000
2 professional staff	56,000
1 full time clerical ($9/hour)	19,000
Lifeguard staff (double current)	45,000
Swim instructors (increase by 75%)	20,000
Fitness Center (increase by 50%)	25,000
Fitness Class Instructors (increase by 50%)	22,000
Babysitting (increase by 50%)	15,000
After school care (increase by 25%)	20,000
Youth sports (increase by 30%)	10,000
Total staff increase	$297,000

Occupancy Projections were also produced:

Custodial supplies	60%	8,000
Repairs and maintenance	40	30,000
Contracted maintenance	100	10,000
Property/Liability insurance	100	45,000
Utilities	100	110,000
Water	100	10,000
Total Occupancy		$223,000

Once open, institutional impact will be monitored both internally and externally.

Checkpoints include:

1) Increase in usage, monitored in total and by user constituency

2) Elimination of turnaways in programs serving pre-school through age 12 youth, and the elderly

3) Reduction of waiting times during peak use hours

4) Increase in both the number and size of services and programs as existing waiting lists are filled and new members and users are attracted

5) Balance of operating costs versus increased income from user and membership fees

17

Annual, financial audits will continue to provide the staff, the Trustee Finance Committee and full Board with independent financial data.

MRC or a similar consultant will be retained again following the first year of operation to review user response.

MEETING THE AMERICANS WITH DISABILITIES ACT REQUIREMENTS

The Y is committed to accessibility as a primary feature of its facilities. A current therapeutic swimming program for seniors and individuals in physical therapy is oversubscribed. A major feature of the capital project is the conversion of the existing pool to therapeutic uses to provide for expansion of this program, as well as services to families with very young swimmers.

Biber Partnership, our architects, have included this priority in design from the most initial stages. Not only are gross features such as elevators and accessible restrooms included, but attention has been paid to floor surfaces through wet and dry areas, and the installation of a pool lift to ensure safety and accessibility for all.

NARRATIVE STATEMENT - FUND RAISING INFORMATION

FUND RAISING TRACK RECORD

In its first capital campaign, in the late 1980's, the Y raised $4,000,000. In 1992, it conducted another $250,000 drive to retire the mortgage. Currently, the Y is raising $90,000 through an annual campaign composed of direct mail appeals, the Corporate Roundtable, and an annual phone-a-thon.

18

FUND RAISING PLAN

To date we have conducted an "invisible" major gifts campaign. We began in the fall by assembling a Steering Committee composed of Y Board members and experienced volunteers from the last campaign. This Committee has met monthly since the beginning of the campaign. Each meeting, guests from the Board or community with particular insight into an aspect of the working agenda are invited to join for a specific task. The campaign was initiated in fall 1994 with a solicitation of Board and staff. Immediately following we recruited Honorary Chairpersons with their lead gifts ranging from $100,000 to $150,000. Honorary Chairpersons are:

1) Jon and Joanne Corzine
   Mr. Corzine is Chief Managing Partner, Goldman Sachs

2) Walter and Judy Shipley
   Mr. Shipley is CEO, Chase Bank

3) Douglas Watson
   Mr. Watson is CEO, CIBA

In early 1995, we assembled a group of Campaign Vice Chairs composed of Y Board members and "young leadership" from the community -- a group identified in our Feasibility Study as critical to campaign success. Vice Chairs join the campaign with gifts of $25,000 and commitments to solicit at least six major gifts. This group, and the Committee for the Campaign composed of lower dollar donors with solicitation commitments, are expanding throughout the campaign.

19

Over the first 18 months of the campaign we have solicited 119 gifts and pledges totalling $2,089,497. (See attachments listing campaign leadership and detail on gifts by category.) The status of our five largest gifts is:

$1,000,000	-	1 gift -	received
$250,000	-	2 gifts -	initial gifts totalling $150,000 have been received. Subsequent solicitation of these sources is invited.
$150,000	-	1 gift -	received
$125,000	-	1 gift -	received

Over the next six months we will continue the "invisible" campaign. Our goal in this period is to raise an additional $600,000. Priorities are set to:

1) Close major gifts where first solicitations have taken place ($200,000 - see Ask Master enclosed)

2) Produce intimate cultivation events to inform major gift prospects outside of the Y's circle about the campaign, and follow-up these events with face-to-face solicitation. Currently scheduled are:

- an individual gifts prospects event April 28 -hosted by Honorary Chairs

- downtown business gift prospects luncheon hosted by a Vice Chair

- "young leadership" gift/volunteer prospects event with the New York Giants produced by Steering Committee members

3) Continue face-to-face solicitation of major gift prospects who are also campaign volunteer prospects ($300,000 - see Prospect list $25,000 + enclosed)

4) Complete the first contact and proposal follow-up to 20 foundations who fund community services regionally ($75,000 funding projected within the six month period. Additional funding follows as fall meetings are held. -- See Foundation List enclosed)

20

5)   Model the Y's internal small gift fundraising (Gifts of $10,000 and less) via launch of the swim team campaign with its $100,000 goal. A $25,000 challenge gift is in place. We will gain 1 - 2 additional challenge gifts totalling $25,000 during this period so that the team can launch its small gifts campaign in the fall. ($25,000)

Following the Kresge Foundation decision, we will launch the public campaign. With a positive Kresge Foundation decision, the public announcement will be anchored by the Kresge grant, providing a prestigious outside imprimatur, and shaping the campaign close with its fixed demands to meet the $4,500,000 campaign goal within 18 months. The Kresge Foundation grant will be particularly helpful to reaching out to 5 constituencies:

1)   Major gift donors who are self-identified community leaders, but who are not close to the Y ($400,000)

2)   Capstone gifts from initial lead donors who identified their gifts as "first gifts" (One foundation, one Honorary Chair, one corporation - $300,000. Smaller capstones from Board, Steering Committee, Vice Chairs, and lead donors - $150,000)

3)   The Y's membership families rated at gifts of $10,000 and less ($250,000)

4)   Local community including small business, churches, and civic organizations at $10,000 and less ($50,000)

5)   Donors with corporate matching plans where we must compete to have the match designated to the Y ($50,000)

21

PROJECT BUDGET

Expense:

Additional 25 yard, 6 lane pool

Additional 8,000 sq. ft. gymnasium

New elevator for new pool and gym

Convert existing gymnasium to fitness center

Convert courts to weight room

Improve waiting areas in lobby

Convert fitness center to multi-purpose room

Create 2nd level in courts for child care

Renovate lower level locker rooms and create direct
wet and dry access corridors, parent/child areas

Renovate mezzanine of existing gym for cardiovascular equipment

Multi-purpose floor above existing pool (divisible 4,000 square feet)

Site work related to all of above

CONSTRUCTION	$4,500,000
EQUIPMENT AND FURNISHINGS	100,000
FEES	35,000
CONTINGENCY (10% of Construction)	$450,000
FUND RAISING AND MARKETING	210,000
INTEREST EXPENSE	150,000
PLANNING BOARD APPROVAL	50,000
ARCHITECT & PROJECT MANAGER	505,000
TOTAL PROJECT EXPENSES	**$6,000,000**

Income:

CAPITAL CAMPAIGN	$4,500,000
LOANS	$1,500,000
TOTAL PROJECT INCOME	**$6,000,000**

22

THE KRESGE FOUNDATION

July 10, 1996

Mr. Timothy G. Weidman
Executive Director
Summit Area YMCA
67 Maple Street
Summit, NJ 07901

Dear Mr. Weidman:

A preliminary review of your application has been completed and we find that additional information is needed. We ask that you respond to the following questions by July 29:

1. Please update the funds available for your project using the enclosed Fact Sheet and identify the three largest pledges in each category. Do you believe you are on track with your goal to raise an additional $600,000 by the end of September?

2. At the time of your appointment with John Marshall, the draft Fact Sheet showed $1,651,500 from individuals whereas $1,536,207 is now presented. Please reconcile. Also, additional discussion would be appreciated on how you have revised your fund raising plan to cover the $500,000 increase in your campaign goal. Your cover letter indicates that the decision was made, in part, due to the receipt of an "unanticipated major gift", but given that there has only been net progress of approximately $106,000 since your appointment, there is a significant amount of additional fund raising which must occur to cover the higher goal.

3. Please complete the enclosed Gift Chart Form and describe the status of any outstanding major gift prospect(s).

4. You indicate that the fund raising end date is 18 months from a Kresge decision. Please confirm that this would mean a challenge deadline of March 1, 1998, assuming a September decision from Kresge.

5. Will your campaign need to go "underground" during the United Way campaign? If so, what impact will this have on your activities?

6. Under the section on fund raising track record, you note that the Y raised $4 million in a previous capital effort and is currently raising $90,000 through an annual campaign. Please describe what "capacity-building" occurred during the previous capital campaign in terms of securing gifts from new donors and increasing contributions from current supporters. How does this increased capacity assist your current annual operating appeals? How do you envision that this present capital campaign will strengthen your organization's long-term ability to raise on-going contributed support from the community?

3215 W. Big Beaver Road P.O. Box 3151 Troy, Michigan 48007-3151 Fax 810-643-0588 Tel. 810-643-9630

Timothy Weidman
July 10, 1996
Page 2

7. Your narrative (page 15) indicates that a development officer will be hired in the fall, 1996. Do you currently have development staff? Will the new person be responsible for overseeing this campaign?

8. Please update your project costs on the Fact Sheet. Were the costs originally presented based on the $5 million or $5.2 million estimate? Please describe any modifications to the project scope since application which may have occurred to keep the project within budget. Is the project completion date in September, 1998 or in January, 1999?

9. Please confirm that you have secured long-term financing for your project. As you know, this commitment should have been in place at the time of application to Kresge. If the amount of financing differs from the $1.5 million shown on the original Fact Sheet, please reconcile (e.g., the Summit Bank document refers to a $2 million loan).

10. Please provide your 1996 budget on the Fact Sheet and forward your 1995 audit, when available.

11. You plan to meet the higher operating costs associated with the expanded facility primarily through additional income from new memberships. We understand that your membership is currently growing by 8% per year. Please elaborate on the assumptions which give you confidence that this growth will be sustained.

12. Please provide the membership and attendance information as marked on the Fact Sheet.

We appreciate your attention to our request for additional information. If you have any questions as you prepare your response, please do not hesitate to contact me.

Sincerely,

Sandra McAlister Ambrozy
Senior Program Officer

SMA:ckp
Enclosures

July 26, 1996

Ms. Sandra McAlister Ambrozy
Senior Program Officer
The Kresge Foundation
3215 West Big Beaver Road
PO Box 3151
Troy, Michigan   48007-3151

Dear Ms. Ambrozy:

Thank you for your counsel last week regarding our presentations of the long-term financing for our project. I appreciated the opportunity to talk with you about our financing plans.

Here is the response to your correspondence of July 10th:

1.   Funds Update and Fact Sheet

Enclosed please find the Fact Sheet you sent July 10th plus Exhibit A: a summary of the fact sheets which we have sent to date. We have met and surpassed our goal to raise an additional $600,000 by the end of the summer.

In our proposal dated April 2, 1996, our fund raising total was $2,098,497 and our goal was stated as raising an additional $600,000 over the next six months for a total of $2,689,497. We are currently at $2,819.967.

The excellent progress in individual and foundation giving we have experienced from April to the present is a direct result of the awareness of key donors and volunteer solicitors regarding Kresge's expectations for campaign progress during this period.

In a community populated by major donors and local foundations whose support is constantly sought for both local and national needs, it is clear that the Kresge Foundation's requirements and its potential for involvement in our project are meaningful to our volunteers and area donors.

It is encouraging to see this demonstration of the leverage which a Kresge challenge grant would offer the campaign.

2. As noted above, Exhibit A provides a summary of the Fact Sheets which we have submitted plus an update using the same categories for this month. As you can see, progress is consistent throughout this period.

The $500,000 increase in the campaign goal is related to two factors. We received an unanticipated major gift of $500,000 from Joe Fiaccone, a long-time Y member. At about the same time, we identified an immediate need for a project manger, and the estimated costs of construction increased as a result of the architect's advance work on construction documents.

We determined to utilize this extraordinary gift as the base for our confidence in increasing the campaign goal to meet these needs.

3. Enclosed please find the completed Gift Chart Form which you sent July 10th.

We are continuing with the major gifts strategy outlined in our April proposal. Updating our proposal, as of this month we are:

- Continuing to close major gifts where first solicitations have taken place

- Producing intimate cultivation events to inform major gift prospects outside of the Y's circle about the campaign, and follow-up these events with face-to-face solicitation.

  a. On April 28 our Honorary Chairs hosted a cultivation event for major gifts prospects

  b. "Young leadership" gift/volunteer prospects are being invited to an October event with the New York Giants produced by Steering Committee members.

- Completing the first contact and proposal follow-up to 20 foundations who fund community services regionally

In addition, as described in our proposal, we are modeling the Y's internal small gift fund raising (Gifts of $10,000 and less) via launch of the swim team campaign with its $100,000 goal. In April, a $25,000 challenge gift was in place. Since then we have met the first phase of the challenge via procurement of 3 additional challenge gifts totalling an additional $25,000. The team is currently recruiting solicitors and will launch a fall campaign to match this first $50,000 with a second $50,000 for a total of $100,000 in swim team support.

4. Assuming a September Kresge Foundation decision, we are prepared to reach the $4,500,000 total campaign goal by March 1, 1998.

5. Our campaign will not be required to go "underground" at any time. Prior to the campaign we sought and received an unconditional waiver for our capital fund raising on this project from the United Way.

6. Substantial capacity building occurred as a result of our $4,000,000 capital campaign in the late 1980's. During that period, the annual campaign raised $35,000.

   However, as the campaign ended, the expanded base of donors generated by the campaign became a solid base for expanded support. In addition to expanding the base of donors, that campaign also built capacity by changing the vision of trustees, staff and donors involved with the Y.

   The Y began to consistently see itself as an able, non-profit institution which should identify needs and move to address them. Donors, having participated in the capital campaign and having seen the Y begin to assertively address community issues beyond service to members, increased their sense of what the Y might appropriately request of them.

   Since the time of that first campaign, the annual fund has grown to $90,000. Membership has grown from 4,700 to 8,500 members. An additional 1,800 are served annually through community programming.

   The capacity building of the late 80's has been used to provide expanded and enhanced service to both members and the larger community in the 90's. Our primary facility is saturated. Despite our use of satellite spaces to expand programs which require only unspecialized space, we are experiencing persistent turn-aways in both youth and adult services.

   After two years of strategic planning, a marketing study, and a campaign feasibility study, we launched this capital campaign in the fall of 1994.

   We can already see the capacity building of this campaign as it continues. We have garnered our first $1,000,000 gift, our first $500,000 gift, and a new, energized level of young leadership who are serving as our campaign Vice Chairs.

   Board nomination is possible at a higher level. This is particularly noticeable when we recruit for diversity. Our women and minority nominees exhibit personal capacity and leadership access.

   Although our community outreach efforts in recent years have already made us a desirable partner in charitable, educational and local government committees and projects, the pace of our involvement is also increasing dramatically. Past and current Board members now routinely represent the Y in these efforts as the demand for time and involvement increases.

7. As you noted in your correspondence, we will be hiring our first development officer this fall.

   This will be our first development staff member. Currently our annual fund effort is produced utilizing a group of Y staff. Our capital campaign is managed by a fund raising consulting firm, J.C. Geever, Inc.

   When our development officer is in place, management of the capital campaign will move in-house and J.C. Geever will continue consulting to the campaign.

8. The costs originally presented were based upon a $5,000,000 architect's projection. An updated summary of the cost of construction estimate is included with this letter.

   Currently we have retained a construction manager to work with our architect through the final construction drawings and preparation of bid documents. Cost containment is resulting from this partnership.

   We will address changing the scope of the project, if a change is necessary, when we go through the bid process. We plan to go out to bid in late 1996.

   We anticipate an April 1997 construction start date and the project is expected to take 18 months for an October 1998 completion date.

9. Summit Bank has committed to a $2,000,000 line of credit to be converted to a mortgage upon the completion of construction.

   Currently we anticipate utilizing that line beginning in the summer of 1997. The actual start date and amount that we draw will be based upon:

   - Amount raised in the campaign

   - Start and completion of construction vs. timing on pledge collection

   - The actual construction bid amount

   - Any changes in the project scope to reduce the cost of construction

   The final mortgage will not be any more than $2,000,000 and we will strive to keep it as close to $1,500,000 as possible. Our operating projections indicate that a mortgage of between $1,500,000 and $2,000,000 could be supported out of earned revenue.

10. Enclosed please find our 1994 audited financial statement and our 1996

operating budget.

I will forward our 1995 audited financial statement when it is completed later this month.

11. The following is a history of the growth in membership revenue from 1988 to the 1996 budget. 1989 was the first year that the renovated YMCA was in operation.

YEAR	MEMBERSHIP REVENUE	PERCENT INCREASE FROM PREVIOUS YEAR
1988	$ 263,000	
1989	513,600	95.00%
1990	576,500	12.25
1991	641,750	11.30
1992	778,600	21.30
1993	882,200	13.30
1994	1,088,600	23.30
1995	1,231,914	13.20
1996	1,330,500	8.00

1989 represents the extremely positive response to the completion of the newly renovated facility.

1990-91 represents the baseline 11% - 13% median growth we are experiencing. This median is driven by our annual marketing and new program offerings, and also by the changing demographics of Summit which we discussed in the proposal you are reviewing.

In 1992 membership revenues popped up as we initiated a monthly payment plan which made our membership affordable to a broader public.

In 1993, we returned to our median growth, despite a fee increase.

In 1994, our membership grew again as we restructured membership to include the popular adult fitness program.

1995 represents another median growth year.

This year we project 8% growth based upon facility saturation. Six months into the fiscal year, this figure is holding.

This chart represents projected growth in membership revenue at the Summit facility. Our projections represent the following membership growth assumptions:

	PERCENT INCREASE FROM
YEAR	PREVIOUS YEAR
1999	25%
2000	15
2001	10
2002	7
2003	7
2004	5
2005	5

From 1999 to 2001 the projections are based upon several factors which include:

-   Prior experience

-   Experience of other YMCA's after opening new facilities

-   Surveys and independent market research

-   Pent up demand for facilities and programs demonstrated by the number of people who are turned away because there is not enough space

-   Census data research

In years 2002 through 2005, 5% - 7% projections represent the conservatism of our business plan. Fee increases are not projected, although a fee increase will be instituted early in the next century.

12.   Enclosed please find membership data submitted on the fact sheet. We do not track attendance.

Thank you for this opportunity to provide you with additional detail. Please let me know if there is anything else that would be helpful to you as you prepare for the September review.

Sincerely,

Timothy G. Weidman
Executive Director

cc: Roger Parsons, President of the Board of Trustees
encs.

The Kresge Foundation
Gift Charts

ORGANIZATION NAME: Summit Area YMCA

CAMPAIGN TITLE: Investing in our Community

CAMPAIGN GOAL: $ 4,500,000   DATE: July 26, 1996

SCALE OF GIFTS:

GIFT RANGE	DOLLAR GOAL $	DONORS NEEDED #	PROSPECTS IDENTIFIED #	GIFTS FORMALLY PLEDGED OR IN HAND #/$
1,000,000	1,000,000	1	1	1 / 1,000,000
500,000	500,000	1	1	1 / 500,000
100,000	1,075,000	6	9	3 / 375,000
50,000	482,000	9	22	6 / 332,650
25,000	339,000	12	56	5 / 131,000
10,000	660,000	64	124	25 / 283,789
5,000	290,000	55	73	22 / 112,700
1,000	143,000	138	400	41 / 71,950
smaller	11,000	110	400	41 / 12,877
TOTAL	$4,500,000	396	1086	145 /$2,819,966

N.B. Each gift level represents a range of gifts from that level up to the next level. The $400,000 Kresge Foundation request is included in the $100,000 gift range.

GIFTS BY SOURCE:

DONOR CATEGORY	DOLLAR GOAL $	PROSPECTS IDENTIFIED #	GIFTS FORMALLY PLEDGED OR IN HAND #/$
Trustees	225,000	36	29 / 197,820
Staff	30,000	54	54 / 45,462
Corporations	298,000	20	12 / 254,500
Individuals	3,124,000	268	43 / 2,179,185
Foundations	348,000	16	7 / 143,000
Kresge Fdn.	400,000	1	
Other *			
Other **			
Government	75,000	1	
Bequests			
TOTAL	$ 4,500,000	369	145 /$ 2,819,966

*   Other: _____
               (Identify Source)

**   Other: _____
               (Identify Source)

594

Project Information

Project Costs

Construction/renovation	$ 5,193,000
Equipment	85,000
Furnishings	15,000
Fees	25,000
Contingency 5%	259,700
Fund raising expense	210,000
Interest expense	150,000
Other (identify):	
Planning Board approval	50,000
Other (identify):	
Architect & Project Manger	505,000
Project Cost	6,492,700
Endowment Goal (if applicable)	0
Total Cost (A) $	6,492,700

Project costs are based on what level of architectural plans (check one)

Date was/will be completed (mo./yr.)

☐ Conceptual _____
☐ Schematic _____
☐ Design Development _____
☐ Construction Documents _____

General construction contract
was/will be signed: _____

If multiple contracts are involved, provide schedule for each component.

Project timetable   mo./yr.
When did/will work commence: _____
What is the completion date: _____
Building/land purchase
agreement signed: _____
Equipment purchase agreement signed: _____

Date of receipt of regulatory approval
Zoning: _____
Certificate of Need/Waiver: _____
Historic Preservation: _____
Environmental Impact: _____
Other (identify): _____ _____

Funds Available

Gifts and grants *formally pledged or paid:*

Staff/Trustees	$ 243,282
Corporations	_____
Individuals	_____
Foundations	143,000
Government	0

Long-term financing:
Bond Issue _____
Loan _____

Organization's funds (identify):
_____ _____

Bequests (paid or in probate) _____
Other (identify):
_____ _____

Other (identify):
_____ _____

Total Available	(B) $	_____
Balance Required	$	_____
(A minus B)		
Amount requested from		
The Kresge Foundation	$	400,000

▸ Fund raising for these
leadership gifts began _____
                                    mo./yr.

▸ Date of formal commitment of
loan or actual sale of bond issue _____

Maturity date _____

▸ Following the formal commitment of a Kresge
challenge grant, the balance required will be raised by
_____ (mo./yr.). This date will be the requested
challenge deadline.

Please complete both sides of this Fact Sheet

5

General/Operating Support

The proposals in this chapter are requests for general/operating support. Typically this type of support is defined as unrestricted grant funds that pay for operational expenses, such as staff salaries and benefits, rent, program costs, and utilities, among other kinds of expenses. This type of support is much sought after by nonprofit grantseekers because it has the fewest restrictions on the use of funds. Though many fundraisers consider it difficult to obtain grants for general/operating support, the most recent information in *FC Search: The Foundation Center's Database on CD-ROM* indicates that more than 14,500 foundations say that they give this type of grant.

The requests in the proposals replicated here range from $5,000 to $160,000. And one proposal ultimately resulted in a grant of $750,000 over three years. The challenge for proposal writers is to condense the description of an often complex roster of activities into a cogent document that makes the case for the overall value of the organization as opposed to a specific project or projects. Requests for general/operating support need to feature persuasive and informative explanations regarding the organization's essential benefit to the community it serves.

Lake Drive Foundation for Deaf and Hard of Hearing Children of Mountain Lakes, New Jersey, provides a full array of services to hearing impaired youngsters and their families throughout northern New Jersey. The organization used a common application form to request $5,000 in operational support from several foundations.

NPower Michigan, a new organization in Detroit, provides technical assistance in the form of technology training and consulting services to smaller nonprofits. NPower sought general support, $160,000 in each of two years, from the Charles Stewart Mott Foundation.

The San Francisco Court Appointed Special Advocate Program provides for the intervention and mentorship of volunteer youth advocates with high-risk abused and neglected client children. SFCASA sought $15,000 in general/operating funding from the Pottruck Family Foundation.

The mission of VolunteerMatch in San Francisco is to help people find suitable volunteer opportunities, and it achieves its goal through an interactive Web site. With this proposal, VolunteerMatch requested support from the John S. and James L. Knight Foundation.

A Proposal From

Lake Drive Foundation for Deaf and Hard of Hearing Children

Mountain Lakes, New Jersey

To

Four funders from New York and New Jersey

Requested amount: $5,000; **Amounts received:** Grants ranging between $2,500 and $10,000

Comments:

This proposal was written using the New York/New Jersey Area Common Application Form and was a general support request submitted to several funders. Four foundations responded with grants, ranging from $2,500 to $10,000. The writing is clear and crisp throughout, and the flow of the narrative is logical. There is a minimum of jargon or technical language, and in fact, the reader becomes educated about the issues by reading the proposal.

The various components of the request are well-balanced.

As it should, the summary provides all the basic arguments for the request in a distilled form, and lays the groundwork for the more detailed narrative that follows. The agency information section begins to build a compelling case for support, describing the inadequacy of public funding levels, details on the community served and the staff of the school, and a brief discussion of the school's philosophy. Other funders are mentioned at the beginning of this section. Sometimes proposal writers are concerned about whether, and how, to indicate that an organization is also receiving support from other funders; this proposal provides a good example of how to include this information in such a way as to create a positive sense of community.

The need statement stresses the importance of early and comprehensive intervention, providing data and research results about newborns and children. The proposal speaks frankly about the costs of treatment, and makes the case that total costs can be reduced by the earliest possible intervention by professionals. A lengthy paragraph places the reader in the midst of the work of the specialists at the school, describing the progressive steps of treatment. This need statement neatly avoids a classic trap: creating an atmosphere of such dire need that funders might be convinced the situation is hopeless. Indeed, this proposal paints a very hopeful outcome, assuming that grants are received to further the school's work.

The funding request indicates, once again, how grant monies will be used, but this time as enumerated program goals. The final paragraph of this section acts as a conclusion, emphasizing the need (note that some phrases are a bit emotional: "stretched almost beyond capacity," "work day and night"—this is the hallmark of a concluding statement) and it is persuasive.

Editor, The Foundation Center

Notes:

Commentary from the funders was not available. This proposal was written using the New York/New Jersey Area Common Application Form. The complete proposal included the following attachments: audited financial statement, operating expense budgets, list of supporters, status of proposals to other solicited sources of support, board of directors, IRS tax-exempt letter, one-page resumes of key personnel, and program evaluation documents.

Proposal written by Paulette Long, Senior Consultant, Not-For-Profit Grant Writers; submitted to the funders by Marc V. Buro, President, Lake Drive Foundation for Deaf and Hard of Hearing Children.

COMMON GRANT APPLICATION FORMAT
Cover Sheet

Date of application: _____February 20, 2001_____

Name of the organization to which grant would be paid. Please list exact legal name.

_____Lake Drive Foundation for Deaf and Hard of Hearing Children_____

Purpose of the grant (one sentence): Its purpose would be to provide general operating
support.__

Address of organization: P.O. Box 155, Mountain Lakes, New Jersey 07046_____

Telephone number: _____Voice/TTY: 973-299-0166_____Fax: 973-299-9405_____

Executive director: _____Marc V. Buro, President_____

Contact person and title (if not executive director): Same_____

Is your organization and IRS 501(c)(3) nor-for-profit? (yes or no):_____Yes_____

        If no, please explain: _____N/A_____

Grant request _____$5,000_____

Check one:

        General support: _____√_____
        Project support: _____

Total organization budget (for current year): _____$146,165_____

Dates covered by this budget (mo/day/year): _____September 1, 2000, to August 31, 2001

Total project budget (if requesting project support): $_____N/A_____

Dates covered by project budget (mo/day/year): _____N/A_____

Project name (if applicable): _____N/A_____

Common Grant Application Format

PROPOSAL SUMMARY: **Purpose of the agency; Why our agency is requesting this grant; What outcomes we hope to achieve; How we will spend the funds if a grant is made.**

> **Mission Statement:** *"The purpose of the Lake Drive Foundation for Deaf and Hard of Hearing Children is to seek funding to support the identification, evaluation, therapeutic intervention and education of hearing-impaired and communication-impaired children served by the Lake Drive School for Deaf and Hard of Hearing Children."*

The Lake Drive Foundation was established to support the programs of the Lake Drive School for Deaf and Hard of Hearing Children; with a special emphasis on the school's Early Intervention Program. The school is dedicated to educating children with hearing loss, so that they can attain the communication skills and academic competency that will allow them to have a full array of life choices upon graduation from high school. The Lake Drive School serves approximately 280 students from birth through high school graduation, from nearly 100 communities across the northern half of New Jersey, and also operates an itinerant-services program serving 25 additional students in their home communities.

The students and families the school serves include a large number of children from inner-city areas and children from homes where English is not the primary language. About one-third of the students have serious additional disabilities that affect their ability to learn—such as impaired vision, problems in gross and fine-motor coordination, perceptual difficulties and specific learning disabilities. Meeting the needs of these children and their families requires a comprehensive network of services provided by professionals from many disciplines, including audiology, speech/language pathology, education of the deaf, psychology, social work, occupational and physical therapy and related consultative assistance from medical professionals. Education is tailored to meet the needs of the individual child. While there has been a debate over the best way to educate deaf children since the 16th century, the Lake Drive School agrees with a growing number of individuals who recognize that no one system of communication is right for all children. The choice of a communication system must be made on an individual basis, taking into consideration the characteristics of the child, the resources available, and the commitment of an individual family to a communication method. This careful approach has led to outstanding results: The first group of high school graduates who participated in the Early Intervention Program as infants and remained in the Lake Drive program through high school graduation, in June 2000, all went off to the colleges of their choice, many having been awarded academic scholarships to continue their education.

The philosophy of the Lake Drive Foundation is that students must be exposed to positive influences within a framework of activities and experiences that help both children and parents to flourish and reach their full potential. Our goal each day is to create such an environment.

It was this philosophy and the school's reputation for excellence in education that attracted the support of The Wilks Foundation, which provided the Lake Drive Foundation with $30,000 for a project. The project was designed to identify socioeconomically disadvantaged children between the ages of three and five years who were at risk for speech and language delay as a result of hearing loss previously unidentified and/or secondary to ear infections. Once children were identified, parents and teachers were instructed how to manage the hearing loss and how to foster speech and language development. The children themselves received speech therapy within their day-care programs. There was follow-up audiological testing and referral for medical intervention for children so identified. Spanish-language services were made available to families as needed. In addition, the project was designed to heighten public awareness of the importance of early identification of hearing loss. The grant has been renewed for two more years. Funds also have been received from Lucent Technologies, some of which have been used for a special project within the school to expand services for students with multiple disabilities through the initiation of a practical-skills approach to teaching core-content subjects. Other funds have been received from the Deaf Golfers Association, the Deaf Children's Association of America, Fleet Bank, and Synermed, Inc.

Research has shown that in the womb, foundation competencies for subsequent language and speech acquisition are already developing. By the age of three, the optimal period for the development of speech and language is closing, and a child who has never developed these skills by that age will forever lag behind his or her contemporaries, not only in speech and language but also in all social and educational areas that are dependent on speech and language. In fact, recent research reveals that if a hearing loss is identified and treated before age six months, the outcomes are significantly greater than at any period thereafter. Our capacity to identify hearing loss at very early ages has only recently begun to be used on a wide scale, as screening measures have become more accurate and cost-effective. Once hearing loss is identified, the costs for subsequent educational intervention have been partially provided through federal and state funds. In New Jersey, agencies providing services have had funding freezes, which result in a functional funding reduction at a time when service needs are increasing and becoming more complex.

Securing additional operational funding is crucial if the Lake Drive Foundation and the Lake Drive School are to fulfill their reason for being—to provide specialized differentiated education to deaf and hard-of-hearing children, allowing them to acquire academic skills needed to succeed in life.

The funds currently granted through state and federal agencies to the program for infants and toddlers (age birth to three years) are insufficient to provide the intensity and diversity of services needed for the children and their families. Funds are needed to pay for audiological diagnostic testing, auditory training, speech and language therapy, psychological counseling, occupational and physical therapies, transportation for families so that they can participate in group educational activities, language-therapy groups for children, sibling groups, and social-work services. As previously stated, many of the children the school serves have multiple disabilities, and their families have limited resources to cope with the demands of raising a child with special needs. Without additional funding, the comprehensive involvement of hearing-impaired youth in a variety of specialized learning systems is in jeopardy. The ongoing fund-raising goals of the Foundation will have to increase to continue to cover the costs needed to maintain effective program implementation.

We seek to secure additional funding to maintain a high level of quality programming and to provide entry to those on the waiting list. Because we would be serving more deaf and hard-of-hearing students on a budget much smaller than originally projected, and because costs continue to grow, money for general operations has dwindled precipitously low. A grant from your organization at this juncture would provide critical support for the Foundation and for the Lake Drive School's programs.

B.   NARRATIVE

   1.   **Agency Information—Agency history; agency's mission, goals and/or objectives, description of current programs, activities and accomplishments, overall plans for the coming year, description of organizational structure, board/staff responsibilities and level of volunteer involvement, agency affiliation with federated funds or public agencies.**

The Lake Drive Foundation for Deaf and Hard of Hearing Children, Inc., is a nonprofit, nonsectarian, 501(c)(3) tax-exempt organization funded by The Wilks Foundation, Lucent Technologies, the Deaf Golfers Association, the Deaf Children's Association of America, Fleet Bank, Synermed, Inc., the Lake Drive Home and School Association and private donations. The Foundation receives no money or other support from the United Way or similar organizations. The Foundation' s President, Marc Buro, has worked successfully with the Lake Drive School for Deaf and Hard of Hearing Children to develop and implement fund-raising programs for children with special needs. Since 1996, the Lake Drive Foundation has worked to fill gaps in financial support to help children get an early start to improve communication skills. Public funding for early intervention programs is somewhat of a Catch-22. The state funds up to a maximum of two hours a week of service per child but mandates that agencies receiving funds through state grants provide all the services a child needs. Somehow the programs are expected to obtain necessary resources to pay for the funding gaps. Experience has shown that as children reach the age of 18 months to two years, their language and speech development is enhanced if their direct therapies are more focused and frequent and sustained at approximately six hours per week. This six-hour figure does not include occupational or physical therapy for additional handicapping conditions. The current funding level is totally inadequate to give infants the intensive assistance they need to maximize speech and language skills.

Knowing that when a child has a hearing loss during the developmental years, all areas of development can be affected significantly, the Foundation believes that early identification of a hearing loss is critical to a child's academic and emotional adjustment. Since 1969, the Lake Drive School for Deaf and Hard of Hearing Children has implemented a continuum of programs that encourage parents and young people to develop the competencies they need to function competitively in the hearing world. This is accomplished using specialized teaching strategies; assistive listening devices to maximize use of residual hearing; speech, language and auditory therapies; and unique and evolving prescriptive curricula that foster literacy, scientific and mathematical knowledge and computer skills. In addition, a specialized curriculum is in development for children who need to learn basic skills through practical application. Education of children who are deaf or hard-of-hearing is a complex process. This process includes appropriate placement; selection of the mode(s) through which the children learn best (auditory, visual or tactile); curriculum; amplification; and decisions by families, schools and individuals about transition to other programs and services. The success of these elements depends on the availability of reliable evaluative information about each child. The communication, academic, intellectual, medical and audiological characteristics of a child combine to create an interconnected pattern of strengths and needs that parents and teachers must translate into classroom goals and objectives.

The Lake Drive School serves approximately 280 students, ages birth to high school graduation, from nearly 100 communities, including Newark, Paterson, Jersey City, New Brunswick, Elizabeth, the Oranges, Plainfield and Trenton. The school operates an itinerant program with the equivalent of 2.5 teachers of the deaf who travel throughout Northern New Jersey to provide services to deaf and hearing-impaired children in their home school districts. Among the 280 students served by the Lake Drive School, approximately 30 are enrolled in a specialized program of services within the Briarcliff Middle School in Mountain Lakes and 40 within the Mountain Lakes High School. In order for the children to perform successfully within these mainstream educational settings, a variety of support services are made available. These include hiring additional teachers of the deaf, sign-language interpreters, speech/language pathologists, counselors, school/clinical psychologists and student note-takers. Sensitivity training is made available to the students and staff within the mainstream schools to increase their awareness of the needs of the students with hearing loss and to foster interaction. Nearly every athletic team within the district includes students who are hearing-impaired as active participants, supported by after-school sign-language interpreters. There are nine interpreters available to meet the needs of in-school as well as after-school communication in a concerted attempt to make the program "communication accessible" to all participants. A sign-language class is offered at the high school for interested hearing students, and there are lunchtime and after-school opportunities for faculty to learn sign language. Many faculty members have participated in sign-language classes, including the principals of both the high school and the middle school. There is a genuine commitment in the community to include students with hearing loss in the richness of the educational programs of the district.

By focusing on the child, the family, the community and culture and education, the Lake Drive School strives to prepare its parents and students to make wise and productive educational choices. Within the School's nurturing environment, children learn both self-discipline and self-esteem, and the speech, language and academic skills that are critical for life. We believe the safe haven of the Lake Drive School for Deaf and Hard of Hearing

Children inspires children to achieve.

The school's programs, supported by the Lake Drive Foundation, are geared to developing the whole child. Academic-support systems are offered, as well as extracurricular activities. Parents are encouraged to participate in their child's programs and are viewed as partners in planning and implementing their child's educational program.

The Foundation has embarked on a campaign to raise community awareness of the effect of deafness on infants and children and to make the public aware of the Foundation's activities and the need for more financial support, in view of recent and continuing federal and state restrictions in funding for early intervention programs.

The Lake Drive Foundation is grateful to The Wilks Foundation for providing $30,000 for Lake Drive's research on the impact of ear infections on speech and language in children from birth to five years of age. The grant has been renewed for an additional two years.

Among the members of the Board of Directors are a retired New Jersey state senator, corporate executives, a certified public accountant, and local business owners, all volunteers.

2. **Purpose of Grant—The need or problem that your organization works to address, and the population that your agency serves, including geographic location, socioeconomic status, race, ethnicity, gender, sexual orientation, age, physical ability and language, description of planned program/activities to accomplish goals, timetable for implementation, other participating organizations, long-term sources/strategies for funding of this project at end of grant period, projected budget.**

The Need. The number of infants, children and adolescents who are being identified as having hearing impairment is increasing. The National Center for Health Statistics estimates that as many as 22.5 million Americans may have some degree of hearing loss. Of these individuals, at least 1,053,000 were under 18 years of age. This means that one of every six children has diminished hearing to some degree at any given point in time. Even more disturbing is the estimate that only about 46% of newborn infants in the United States and its territories are screened for hearing loss (please see attached chart). The state of New Jersey is scheduled to promulgate new regulations requiring screening of newborns for hearing competence. Mandatory screening will increase the need for the remedial services and training that the Lake Drive School provides. Many youth for whom hearing loss or impairment is detected could benefit significantly from early intervention strategies. In general, early intervention applies to children of school age or younger who are discovered to have or be at risk of developing a handicapping condition or other special need that may affect their development. Early intervention consists of the provision of services for children and their families for the purpose of lessening the effects of the condition. Early intervention can be remedial or preventive in nature—remediating existing developmental problems or preventing their occurrence. At the Lake Drive School, early intervention may begin at any time between birth and up to age three years. The Lake Drive Foundation is principally responsible for providing the bulk of necessary funding for the early intervention program.

There are three primary reasons for intervening early with a deaf or hard-of-hearing child: to enhance the child's development, to provide support and assistance to the family, and to maximize the child's and family's benefit to society.

Child-development research has established that the rate of human learning and development is most rapid in the preschool years. Timing of intervention becomes particularly important when a child runs the risk of missing an opportunity to learn during a state of maximum readiness. If the most teachable moments or stages of greatest readiness are not taken advantage of, a child may have difficulty learning a particular skill at a later time. Representatives of the Lake Drive School and the Foundation believe that only through early identification and participation in appropriate programming can children develop their full potential.

Early intervention services also have a significant impact on the parents and siblings of a deaf or hard-of-hearing child. The family of a young hearing-impaired child often feels disappointment, social isolation, added stress, frustration and helplessness. The compounded stress of the presence of a child with special hearing needs may affect the family's well-being and interfere with the child's development. Families of disabled children are found to experience increased instances of divorce and suicide, and the disabled child is more likely to be abused than is a non-handicapped child. Early intervention can result in parents' having improved attitudes about themselves and their child, improved information and skills for teaching their child, and more release time for leisure and employment. A third reason for intervening early is that society will reap maximum benefits. The child's increased developmental and educational gains and decreased dependence upon social institutions, the family's increased ability to cope with the presence of a hearing-impaired child, and perhaps the child's increased eligibility for employment, all provide economic as well as social benefits.

After more than 50 years of research, there is evidence—both quantitative (data-based) and qualitative (reports of parents and teachers)—that early intervention increases the developmental/educational gains for the child, improves the functioning of the family, and reaps long-term benefits for society. Early intervention has been shown to result in the child's: (a) needing fewer special-education and other habilitative services later in life; (b) being retained in grade less often; and (c) in some cases, being indistinguishable from normally hearing classmates in terms of academic achievement years after intervention.

The available data emphasize the long-term cost-effectiveness of early intervention. The highly specialized, comprehensive services necessary to produce the desired developmental gains are often, on a short-term basis, more costly than traditional school-age service-delivery models. However, significant long-term cost savings result from such early intervention programs.

Professionals at the Lake Drive School and the Foundation believe that providing early audiologial and speech and language services to children from birth to three years of age is critical. While there are no hard and fast rules, in general if there are no additional handicapping conditions, infants with hearing impairment up to the age of about nine months can benefit from about one hour a week of intervention, which takes the form of guidance to the family about how to use real-life experiences to develop early language, speech and hearing. Caregivers and family members often unconsciously stop using language and speech when interacting with the child with hearing loss. Modeling and explicit teaching are important tools for fostering auditory, language and speech development during this early period. In fact, there is some research to show that such intervention during the first six months of life can result in outcomes of normal to nearly normal language and speech development. Ongoing diagnostic evaluation to be sure the child has appropriate amplification allowing for learning through use of hearing is an integral component of the early intervention. Consistent exposure to speech and language in a form that is accessible to the child is modeled and practiced daily by the family to provide multiple opportunities for the child to learn. As the child becomes more receptive to direct teaching, the amount of professional time that is effective begins to increase. Other caregivers need instruction in meeting the young child's needs, as the child begins to participate in community-based activities such as day care or nursery school. Experience has shown that by the time the child has reached 18 months, six hours per week is required for therapy, up until the time for transition from early intervention at age three years. If additional therapies are needed, up to four additional hours per week may be required. The cost of such therapy today is $79 per hour per child, ranging from $158 per week per two-hour session for infants and toddlers to $474 per week for six-hour sessions for school-age youth. Unfortunately, these costs are expected to continue to escalate.

Historically, much of this cost has been borne by federal and state government. Awareness about early intervention services has grown, and the number of children and families eligible for these services has increased. Overall funding in New Jersey has failed to keep pace with the increased numbers of children in need of specialized service across the state. This has resulted in a period of virtual flat funding, which essentially amounts to a funding reduction, as more children are in need of the school's services. This is so, notwithstanding the fact that longitudinal studies of children who had participated in early intervention programs show that when schools invest $3,000 or more for one year in these programs, they immediately begin to recover their investment through savings in special-education services. Other benefits included hundreds of dollars acquired by parents who were able to work more productively while the child participated in the programs. Moreover, thousands of dollars were saved by public schools because children with early intervention had fewer years in grade, and tens-of-thousands of dollars more in lifetime earnings were projected for these children.

Other studies show total cumulative costs to age 18 of early intervention special-education services to a child beginning intervention at: (a) birth; (b) age two; (c) age six; and (d) age six with no eventual movement to regular education. The researchers found that the total costs were actually less if begun at birth. Total cost of special services begun at birth was $37,273, and total cost if begun at age six was between $46,816 and $53,340. The cost is less when intervention is earlier, because of the remediation and prevention of developmental problems that would have required special services later in life. In another study, a three-year follow-up showed that for every dollar spent on early treatment, $7 in savings was realized within 36 months.

The Lake Drive Foundation for Deaf and Hard of Hearing Children is aware of the tremendous risks that beset young deaf and hard-of-hearing people in the New Jersey and surrounding regions served by the Lake Drive School. Like investigators and researchers in the studies summarized above, Lake Drive School administration and faculty are aware of the dismal national outcome data that have repeatedly shown that at high school graduation, children who are deaf have attained reading comprehension at a fourth-grade level at best. The efforts of the Lake Drive program to intervene early and aggressively, in combination with the systematic, ongoing educational program that follows early intervention, have led to outcomes far different from those reported nationally. Lake Drive students, even students with multiple special needs, perform at much higher levels. All the hearing-impaired graduates of the Mountain Lakes High School exceeded national outcome expectation, and approximately 75% of students by age 13 exceed nationally reported average performance levels. Continued funding, particularly for the youngest children, is imperative to maintain these outcomes. Confirming its commitment to continue to provide intensive early intervention services for infants and school-age children within its component programs the Lake Drive School works cooperatively with the Lake Drive Foundation to meet the needs of its youth through fund-raising campaigns. The goal of the Foundation is to fill the gaps in financial support to help youngsters continue to secure a high level of early intervention and other communication-skills services.

The need is immediate, and the supporting funding will be required on an ongoing basis. Federal law mandates that there be multiple funding sources for children in the birth-to-age-three group. There is no guarantee of special education for children in this age group in spite of the benefits that are generally recognized.

Population Served. The Lake Drive Foundation and the Lake Drive School serve hearing-impaired youth and their parents. Students may range in age from as young as birth to 21 years. Forty infants and toddlers up to age three years participate in the early intervention program on a regular basis and reside in the northern half of New Jersey, covering a radius of approximately 100 miles in all directions from the school. Of the school-age population, which includes children from age three to high school graduation, approximately 17% are students eligible for free or reduced lunch, 16% are from Spanish-speaking families, and another 10% are from non-English-speaking families who use a variety of languages. There are also nine families who are themselves deaf and communicate in sign language. Many of the children come from troubled neighborhoods in cities such as Newark, Elizabeth, East Orange, Orange and Plainfield. The services are geared toward students who can benefit from a nonresidential school environment and youth whose parents may be unable to pay the full costs of the specialized care required to help develop communications skills that these hearing-impaired infants and school-age youth need.

Program Philosophy. The Lake Drive School welcomes deaf and hard-of-hearing youth from birth to high school graduation (up to age 21) and their parents to a dynamic, carefully structured program within an atmosphere that is supportive, safe and responsive to the needs of its students. The program's philosophy is to develop communication and literacy skills that will enable students to participate in the "hearing world."

An increasing number of positions in the work force will require technological experience, as the amount and breadth of technical training needed for many jobs have increased. Many jobs depend on the skills of symbolic analysis—abstraction, system-thinking, experimental inquiry and collaboration, areas that are dependent on well-developed linguistic and mathematical skills.

The Information Age is changing the occupational structure to one based on mental, not physical, abilities. To the technologically astute, the quality of life will be improved dramatically. This new age of technology calls for reading, math and scientific proficiency to prevent traditional barriers to advancement. We believe that by offering information technology as another component of the academic-training program and therapies, young people will have a more realistic chance to be independent. To this end, the school provides students with opportunities to learn through use of the computer from the earliest ages.

The Lake Drive School utilizes the team approach to serving students. The therapy and training teams are composed of professionals representing a variety of disciplines: special education; social work; psychology; child development; and physical, occupational, and speech and language therapy. All teams also involve the family in varying ways and degrees. Team members share common tasks, including the assessment of a child's developmental status and the development and implementation of a program plan to meet the assessed needs of the child within the context of the family. The underlying team philosophy is the earlier the intervention, the more effective it is. With intervention at birth or soon after the diagnosis of deafness or hearing impairment, the developmental gains are greater and the likelihood of exacerbation of problems is reduced.

In a world of budget restrictions for early intervention programs that has never seemed more threatening and devoid of promise for a disproportionate number of America's hearing-impaired children, the Lake Drive Foundation for Deaf and Hard of Hearing Children provides a tangible measure of hope. The programs offer young people what they need and want most: adults who respect and listen to them; a safe environment where they can have fun and be themselves; and interesting, constructive activities that channel youthful energy into challenging pursuits. A youth-development strategy that fosters a sense of belonging, competence, usefulness and influence underlies all Lake Drive programs, in order to build self-confidence, self-esteem and the skills children need to function independently.

For each child, early intervention services also include an assessment and a written individualized family service plan (IFSP) developed by a multidisciplinary team and the parents. Services provided are designed to meet the developmental needs of the child and to be in accordance with the IFSP. Case-management services are provided for each child and his or her parents. Professionals and support staff at the Lake Drive School possess a comprehensive knowledge base and a diversity of skills. Staff providing services to any one family often represent multiple disciplines. Moreover, collaboration among professionals from different agencies is often necessary. As a result, new definitions of "staff," "team" and "collaboration" are emerging within the context of Lake Drive School to better serve students.

The Lake Drive School and the Lake Drive Foundation support:

- Efforts to give deaf and hearing-impaired youth the head start they need to lead full and productive lives;
- A philosophy and practice of selection of the most effective means of establishing communication for an individual child, including auditory-oral approaches to learning language and total communication, the simultaneous use of sign and speech, and other modes of augmentative communication;
- Efforts to provide the best tools and educational enhancements for hearing-impaired youth;
- Fund-raising campaigns to provide replacement and supplementary funding to support early intervention and other programs for deaf and hard-of-hearing youth;
- Efforts to leverage Lake Drive School's 30-year tradition of support in the lives of youth and their parents.

The message is clear. It is critical for deaf and hearing-impaired students not only to stay in school, but also to succeed in school—hence the need to provide early intervention services.

Facilities. Lake Drive School is a public school building located at 10 Lake Drive within the Mountain Lakes Public School District, Mountain Lakes, New Jersey. It was the original stone schoolhouse for the community. As the school-age population of the town dwindled in the 1970s, the community opened its doors to children with hearing impairment from across the state, and, in the late 1970s, turned over the use of the Lake Drive School to the program for hearing-impaired children. Although the community now has an increased school-age population, it has maintained its commitment to hearing-impaired children from across the state and has continued to make the building and its other schools accessible to nonresident students with hearing impairment. The school is located near the crossroads of major highways, making it accessible to children who live long distances from it. Hence, the capability to serve children from across the northern half of New Jersey with commuting times of approximately one hour. The school itself is filled to capacity. In the near future, the Foundation may be faced with the very real prospect of playing a significant role in the identification and/or building of additional classroom space within the district. Students are also housed at Briarcliff Middle School and at Mountain Lakes High School, in classrooms dedicated for their use, as well as in classrooms throughout those two buildings.

3. Staffing—Number of paid full-time staff; number of paid part-time staff; number of volunteers.

The Foundation itself employs only a part-time paid secretary. Foundation board members are volunteers. The school is staffed by individuals who have had specialized or on-the-job training in working with children with hearing loss. In an effort to provide role models for our students, a number of staff members are hearing-impaired adults. In addition, in order to meet the needs of children from Spanish-speaking families, we currently employ three bilingual speech/language pathologists, a bilingual teacher of the deaf, and a bilingual social worker. The educational backgrounds of staff members range from the high school level of the paraprofessional to the doctorate level. An active program of in-service education is a hallmark of the school, to insure that all staff have state-of-the-art information and skills. The early intervention program is staffed by two speech/language pathologists and a teacher of the deaf, as well as a part-time audiologist, a social worker, and occupational and physical therapists. (The needed increase in hours of the part-time staff is limited by budget restrictions.) The school-age population is served by 27 teachers of the deaf, 14 speech/language pathologists, the equivalent of 1.5 social workers, a school psychologist, an art teacher, a music teacher, a physical-education teacher, a computer specialist, a computer technician, three occupational therapists, a physical therapist, an audiologist, an audiological technician, 14 classroom paraprofessionals, nine paraprofessionals dedicated to meeting the special needs of children with multiple disabilities, and nine sign-language interpreters. The daily staff-to-student ratio is 1:4 in general, but concentrated according to the age and needs of students.

During the 2000-2001 school year, as part of the itinerant program, the equivalent of 2.5 teachers of the deaf who travel throughout Northern New Jersey to provide services to deaf and hearing-impaired children in their home school districts were maintained. Lake Drive School now offers an early intervention program, preschool, school-age, high school and *mainstream* programs to its students.

4. Networking and Organizational Relationships

The Lake Drive School for Deaf and Hard of Hearing Children has successfully developed working relationships with school districts across the state of New Jersey and with audiological-testing facilities in New Jersey and New York. Regular communication and coordination with numerous local school districts takes place, and additional dialogue with administrators and child-study teams is routine. Itinerant teachers meet regularly with principals and teachers to discuss the students' progress, both academically and emotionally. School faculty work closely with cochlear-implant teams, audiological-test facilities and medical staffs, so that they can jointly support each child. Many members of the Lake Drive faculty are active members of the state early intervention network and participate in both state and local efforts for early intervention. They have served and continue to serve on the state's task force for early identification of hearing loss, and on the state task force to provide services to children with low-incidence disabilities, which include hearing loss. The school works closely with several universities to provide student teacher-training opportunities. In the past year, these include Columbia University, Kean University of New Jersey, Paterson University and Bloomsburg University. In an effort to contribute professionally, Lake Drive staff frequently present at national and statewide conferences regarding education of children with hearing loss and related disorders.

5. **Funding Request—Please describe the program for which you seek funding. If applying for general operating support, briefly describe how this grant would be used.**

The Lake Drive Foundation for Deaf and Hard of Hearing Children, Inc., is requesting a $5,000 grant as part of the approximately $141,000 we must raise to cover the operational-cost increases associated with a reduction in federal and state funding for early intervention programs and to serve additional youth and parents who wish to enroll in our programs.

The Foundation must find more funds to keep the infant/toddler and preschool programs alive, because these programs are critical to improved and more-effective remediation, both short and long term.

The key program goals are:

1. Early identification of hearing loss and aggressive intervention to maximize use of hearing, including:
   a. Helping the child understand the meaning of any sounds heard, including spoken language
   b. Teaching the child's parents how to make sound meaningful to the child throughout the day
   c. Helping the child learn to respond to and to use sound in the same way that children with normal hearing learn, when possible
   d. Working, when possible, to help children develop an inner auditory system, so that they are aware of their own voices, to match what they say with what they hear others say
2. Working with families in collaborative partnership to guide their children to meet their full potential
3. Guiding families so they can obtain appropriate medical care, amplification or other assistive technology to maximize use of residual hearing
4. Fostering the development of communication
5. Fostering the development of language
6. Fostering the development of oral speech production
7. Fostering the development of cognition
8. Identifying impediments to learning
9. Establishing solutions for identified problems and finding resources to implement the solutions
10. Establishing a baseline level of performance
11. Developing goals and objectives
12. Observing and evaluating the child's development in all areas and modifying intervention to address new needs
13. Guiding families to find ways of having their children participate socially and educationally with children who have normal hearing

Current staff members are stretched almost beyond capacity, and they are willing to give even more to help the school's students. However, to serve the best interests of new youth, the Foundation will be required to secure more funding to replace that lost through federal and state budget cuts, in order to maintain current staffing commitments and engage more professional consultants. We must maintain current staff, and we would bring in more teachers and consultants, not only to work day and night to serve our children, but also to train parents to become involved in skill development of their children. Our current staff work at capacity and beyond traditional school hours providing services in the evening, particularly to the families of our youngest participants. It is only with funding from the Foundation that existing services are possible. State and federal funds allow for only skeleton programming. In order to continue to meet our goals and to prepare our children to become full and productive citizens, we require the support of private funds.

6. Evaluation—Please explain how you will measure effectiveness of your activities.

We also seek funds to engage an independent third-party research firm to evaluate our program on a yearly basis. Outcome analysis of the program and its relationship to changed behavior will be the primary method used to evaluate the success of the early intervention program and other educational components of the Lake Drive School. Such evaluation data can then be used to support requests for funding the program's continuation.

The evaluation tools to be utilized for the program will seek to present objective outcome-evaluation data as clear evidence of whether program components are effective, efficient and cost-beneficial. The current and proposed programs will seek to prove outcome effectiveness through empirically demonstrated behavioral changes. Each early intervention participant by law has an Individual Family Service Plan, in which goals and objectives are stated. Analysis of percentage of goals met can serve as an objective measure of program effectiveness. In addition, a parent-satisfaction survey is administered annually for those children ages birth to three or at the time of transition, as many participants may not be identified until they are close to age three. Results of this survey can also serve as a measure of program effectiveness. The evaluation is expected to improve effective implementation of the program; to enable the project to demonstrate its value to the community at large, those in the deaf and hearing-impaired community, to parents and to potential funders; and to influence the formation and implementation of social policy, both locally and nationally.

Proposed Types of Evaluation. With respect to the Lake Drive School Programs, particularly the early intervention program, the three most basic questions to be asked are:

1. What are the program's results, and what does the program change?
2. What program qualities make it work or be effective?
3. Is the program cost-effective?

Four basic types of evaluation will be integrated into the proposed program structure to address these questions. They are needs assessment, outcome evaluation, process or monitoring evaluation, and cost-benefit analysis.

A Proposal From
NPower Michigan
Detroit, Michigan

To
Charles Stewart Mott Foundation
Flint, Michigan

Requested amount: $160,000 in each of two years; **Amount received:** $160,000 in each of two years

Funder's comments:

"This is an exemplary proposal in many ways. That said, we don't just fund a piece of paper; we fund the people and the leadership that stand behind it. That's a really important part of the equation. What you want to see in a proposal is the organization's ability to articulate its plans, and to do so hitting needs, goals and objectives, strategies, and evaluation. This document is very concise. I am wary of excessively long project proposals because one has a sense the grantseeker is not able to explain succinctly and clearly the need in the community, and the plan to address that need.

"At the Mott Foundation, a program officer will take 10 to 15 proposal pages and winnow them down to two pages (plus a third one for the budget) for senior management, grants administration, and the trustees of our foundation. So we have to synthesize enormous amounts of information and condense it to the key facts. And what helps most is clear, concise, energetic writing that signifies the nonprofit's leadership has thought this through well in advance. It is indicative of good thinking.

"This proposal contains an impressive need statement. I wrote on my own copy 'good, clear, specific, concrete.' It includes specific references to the needs of a number of nonprofits in Michigan, gathered through focus groups and interviews. This demonstrates attention to detail and command of the arena in which the grantee will be working.

"The information section on NPower Michigan is also strong. This project is barely out of the gate and already has specifics about first clients as well as donated computers and software. Someone already has done a lot of groundwork. And the organization is obviously building on experience and success.

"This proposal communicates a lot of energy. And, in fact, if you were to meet the director, you would see that's the way she is. It comes back to what I said earlier about funding the leaders and the people behind the proposal. We want experience, wisdom, intellect, and clarity. But we also want passion because that can drive the project and the organization.

"The section about the credibility of the organization is also good. It includes what's happened so far, and the expertise of the people. The short bios were really helpful.

"This is a technology proposal, but a novice can understand every word. That high level of clarity is also attractive. The introduction gives the reader a sense that this is technology aimed at serving people. The language is accessible and centered on how the grantseeker will help nonprofits in their communities.

"What I also like about this proposal is that it clearly refers to leveraging resources—money, talent, and time—something attractive to a funder. One other thing that made this proposal attractive to the Mott Foundation is that it is for multiyear funding. We like multiyear proposals because they provide for continuity of funding. This proposal asks for two-year support and clearly states the organization will come back for continued support for years three and four. As program officers we write it up for the full four years. The first two years are approved, but the second two years are noted as having been already foreseen. So that makes it much easier when we have to recommend renewal. In essence the foundation is saying 'We understand the idea; we like the idea; and when you come back for renewal, based on solid performance, the paperwork can be expedited.'

"This proposal contains an exemplary budget. Sometimes we get far too little or far too much detail on supplies or services, but this budget gave us just the right amount. It's good on support details that explain line items briefly. Once again, it's evident that someone has done a lot of homework well.

"Could this proposal have been better in any way? Maybe it could have been a little more explicit on the actual deliverables in years one and two. But that is always difficult in a multiyear start-up project, and certainly it's harder to be specific about the second year than the first year."

Elan D. Garonzik, Program Officer, Charles Stewart Mott Foundation

Notes:
The complete proposal included the following attachments: annual budget, funding projections, staff biographies, and IRS tax-exempt letter.
Proposal written by Kathleen F. Teodoro, then Executive Director, and the NPower Network; submitted to the funder by Kathleen F. Teodoro.

Putting technology know-how in the hands of Non-Profits

PHONE 866 / 41 NPower
FAX   313 / 237 8156

EMAIL Info@NPowerMichigan.org
WEB   www.NPowerMichigan.org

9 April 2002

Mr. Elan Garonzik
Charles Stewart Mott Foundation
Mott Foundation Building
503 S. Saginaw St., Suite 1200
Flint, MI 48502

Dear Mr. Garonzik:

Attached please find our proposal for a C.S. Mott Foundation grant, the purpose of which is to establish NPower Michigan's technology training and consulting services for Michigan nonprofits. We are asking the C.S. Mott Foundation to make a leadership gift of $160,000 each year for the first two years of NPower Michigan's operation, with plans to consider extending the support for an additional two years at the end of the initial granting period.

Your support during the planning stages of NPower Michigan demonstrates your awareness of the need for increasing the technology skills of the many people in the Michigan nonprofit community who work so very hard, but have so few resources. NPower Michigan is now poised to help these people stretch their organizations' resources by training them to use technology effectively and imaginatively. If agencies can streamline their paper work, automate their mailings or budget processes, set up interactive Web sites, or provide self-help opportunities for clients, they will be able to greatly expand their services without a significant expansion of personnel or other resources.

Many people in these agencies already know how they would like to use technology to achieve or extend their missions, but they lack the necessary skills and the funds needed to acquire the skills. Thus, the non-profit community tends to lag behind business and government in its use of technology. NPower Michigan can them help bridge that digital divide.

NPower Michigan's technology assistance is focused on and priced for non-profits. We envision a community of non-profits using technology with a resourcefulness and effectiveness equal (or superior) to the most technology-enabled businesses. That is the vision we are asking you to help us realize.

Thank you for considering our proposal. Please let me know if I can provide any further information that may assist you in your decision.

Yours truly,

Kathleen F. Teodoro,
Executive Director
NPower Michigan
Enclosure

DETROIT OFFICE
Penobscot Building
645 Griswold, Suite 1300
Detroit, MI 48226

GRAND RAPIDS OFFICE
118 Commerce SW
Grand Rapids, MI 49503-4106

ANN ARBOR OFFICE
AA IT Zone
330 East Liberty
Ann Arbor, MI 48104

NPower Michigan – "Putting Technology Know-How in the Hands of Non-Profits"

General Purposes Request – The C.S. Mott Foundation

INTRODUCTION

NPower Michigan was founded to help non-profits achieve their missions by integrating the appropriate use of technology into their day-to-day work and direct service delivery. Because of our mission, technology looks a little different to us. Web sites are vehicles for action alerts about groundbreaking cancer research. Databases track dedicated arts patrons and are linked up via email so patrons can learn about their favorite art exhibits or performances. File sharing between remote locations means that a child rights advocate in Detroit can access legal documents for a case in its Lansing field office. Some may see technology as cold and impersonal, but in the non-profit sector, we have witnessed the advent of technology chart a very human-centered course.

NARRATIVE

Statement of need

"Technology is a critical tool for non-profits to use to effectively mobilize their constituencies, develop collaborative partnerships, raise money and generally forward their organizational goals...most non-profits could benefit from IT that goes beyond just equipment – to include strategic support for organizational capacity building in such areas as staff training, long-term maintenance and technical assistance."

> ~ Rick Cohen, President
> *National Committee for Responsive Philanthropy*

Non-profits shape our communities, and the work of Michigan's non-profit community is diverse: housing the homeless, feeding the hungry, aiding the elderly and sick, sheltering the abused, protecting our wildlands, enriching and illuminating our lives with art. When taken as a whole, the daily work of Michigan's 21,135 non-profit organizations serves as a catalyst for social change. Ironically, non-profits take on society's most pressing issues, but rarely have access to powerful tools to solve these societal problems. Most often this reality leaves non-profits on the negative side of the organizational divide – "the gap between those organizations that have the ability to use technology to further their missions and those that do not."[1]

In 1999, the United Way Community Services and the University of Michigan School of Social Work conducted a study to discover information technology perceptions, capacities and needs of non-profit organizations in the state of Michigan. The report concluded that the technological advances needed should focus on the areas of low-cost training, technical assistance and information brokering—not merely the acquisition of additional hardware. The majority of respondents felt that "Michigan non-profits are not ready for the information age".

It is this service void that will be filled by NPower Michigan, a new non-profit which will provide comprehensive technology support services to 501(c)(3) non-profits (excepting K-16 schools and places of worship) throughout Michigan. We are asking the C.S. Mott Foundation to make a leadership gift of $160,000 each year for the first two years of NPower Michigan's operation, with plans to consider extending the support for an additional two years at the end of the initial granting period

---

[1] Beyond Access: A Foundation Guide to Ending the Organization Divide." National Committee for Responsive Philanthropy. A report by Bethany Robertson, December 2001.

Mission statement

NPower Michigan is dedicated to helping other non-profits in Michigan use information technology to deliver their services more effectively and efficiently. NPower Michigan will provide a continuum of affordable, high-quality technology assistance services that are solidly anchored in knowledge of non-profit strengths, needs, and constraints.

NPower Michigan's staff have extensive non-profit experience. They are also highly knowledgeable and enthusiastic about technology. Yet we do not believe in technology for technology's sake: we care about technology's role in enabling solutions, its role in helping non-profits do more of what they set out to do.

NPower Michigan's conviction is that technology, appropriately employed, can help non-profit groups:

♦ Redirect energies from time-intensive administrative work to more focused and creative direct service delivery.

♦ Improve services by turning information into knowledge, and knowledge into power and action.

♦ Secure new resources by more convincingly documenting how their services effect positive change.

♦ Better collaborate with other non-profits, the private sector, and government in providing services that are non-duplicative, holistic and respectful of the clients served.

Service offerings

Guided by our principle freely sharing tools and lessons learned within the NPower Network and with sister organizations, NPower continually innovates and improves our service offerings. NPower Michigan uses both on-land and on-line approaches in our service delivery. Our on-land services include:

♦ Consultation and guidance in technology assessment and planning.

♦ Hands-on assistance with jobs like building a database, launching a Web site, or configuring a computer network.

♦ Technology training classes covering strategic technology use, widely-used operating systems and software applications, technology troubleshooting, and computer networking.

♦ Volunteer matchmaking that links tech-savvy community volunteers and non-profits needing short-term help with technology basics.

NPower's on-line services include:

♦ Web-based tools, resources, tips, and tricks to arm non-profits with the technology know-how to tackle their work. We have extensive resource pages on topics ranging from the life cycle of a technology project, to using the Internet as a fundraising resource, to protecting your computers against attacks from nasty viruses.

♦ Interactive, on-line tools to help non-profits take an inventory of their existing technology assets (including hardware, software and staff skills), identify technology opportunities to help them integrate technology as a mission-support tool, and understand and project the resources that will be required to successfully implement their plan. NPower has developed our online tools in partnership with TechRocks and other sister organizations.

♦ A range of web-based software tools that meet most non-profits' essential computing needs, coupled with technology training and support services. Currently, NPower provides non-profits with: web-based file sharing, e-mail, fund development tools, an intake application that runs on mobile hand-held devices for homeless shelter providers as well as data backup and virus protection services.[2]

NPower targets our on-land and on-line services to small and mid-sized non-profit organizations. Currently 75% of all NPower customers around the country are non-profit organizations with annual budgets under $1.5 million. It is this group of non-profit organizations that tend to have the most significant need for technology assistance, but do not have the resources to get this help. Having both on-land and on-line services ensures that, regardless of budget, staff size, or geographic location, non-profits have access to technology support services that meet at least some of their needs.

Accomplishments to date

NPower Seattle

We are modeling our program offerings after NPower Seattle, which opened its doors in March 1999. NPower Seattle provides services to the full gamut of non-profit organizations; however, the majority of their clients are smaller agencies with budgets of under $500,000 and a staff size of less than ten. From training to consulting to volunteer matching, they work on a daily basis with organizations possessing few technology resources and a huge technology need. The graphs below give a visual representation of the NPower Seattle client base.

NPower Seattle's accomplishments since opening include:

♦ As of February 2002, NPower Seattle celebrates 327 members.

♦ In 2001, NPower consultants delivered close to 7,500 hours of hands-on assistance on jobs like technology needs assessments and planning, computer networking, database design, and scheduled technical support. This number is up from 2,800 hours in 1999 and 3,900 hours in 2000.

♦ 1,403 people have received over 6,000 hours of instruction in the NPowerTrain Seattle lab, learning skills including word processing, Web site design, database development, spreadsheet modeling, desktop publishing, and computer networking. Like the consulting

---

[2] Our ASP pilot program is housed in Seattle and is also funded largely by the C.S. Mott Foundation.

numbers, these training figures demonstrate significant growth from the 1,700 hours of training delivered in year one.

♦ Also in 2001, 280 community members have shared their technical skills with 180 Puget Sound non-profits through NPower's volunteer matchmaking program, principally via two highly successful community Days of Service.

♦ Through the InterNPower program, four interns worked over 700 hours providing 440 hours of direct support to 14 area non-profits.

♦ 20 non-profit groups (in Washington, New York, Indiana and Michigan) have access to a suite of Web-based applications via NPower Seattle's Application Service Provider pilot program.

Building on the experience of NPower Seattle, NPower Michigan has high hopes of performing as notably, even in this very different climate.

The NPower Network

By the end of 2003, NPower will be providing services in 13 communities across the country. Through the NPower & Microsoft National Partnership, the NPower Network has already branched out into five communities outside of the Puget Sound area, including Michigan, New York, the San Francisco Bay Area, Atlanta, and Indianapolis. Portland, Oregon will soon join the Network, with Denver and Minneapolis/St. Paul likely to follow in late 2002. Each affiliate localizes its service offerings to meet the needs of its community. New York, for example, developed a unique work force development program, published cutting edge reports on wireless technologies, and participated actively in the city's post-September 11th rebuilding efforts. NPower Michigan is proud to be a part of this talented, energetic, and diverse learning community.

NPower Michigan

NPower Michigan is now ready to open its doors, thanks to the energetic work of its talented staff and Board of Directors. (See Appendix 1.) We have welcomed our first members, embarked on our first consulting engagements, and registered our first students. NPower Michigan's first clients include:

♦ Accounting Aid Society
♦ Affirmations Lesbian & Gay Community Center
♦ Boysville
♦ Greater Oakland Nurses Association
♦ Michigan Parkinson Foundation
♦ Southfield Community Foundation
♦ Wayne County Kidspace Inc

NPower Michigan has received initial funding from the Microsoft Corporation and the W.K. Kellogg Foundation. We are currently working out of a temporary space at the Samaritan Center, home to over 40 non-profits in Detroit's Warren-Conner empowerment zone. Concurrently, we are working with the new Non-profit Facilities Center and the Detroit Collaborative Design Center to remodel space within the Samaritan Center to house our offices and training facility; the Compaq Corporation is providing computers for the 12-person training lab. In addition, the Symantec Corporation has agreed to donate up to 100 seats of their well-respected *Norton AntiVirus* software to distribute to local non-profit agencies via our upcoming Virus Vaccination Day of Service, a community service project we are planning in partnership with Comnet .

In addition to inviting Comnet to work with us on the Day of Service, we are facilitating the Web design classes that Comnet offers. (See our newsletter, enclosed.) NPower Michigan is committed to supporting the successful work of sister agencies and identifying opportunities to leverage our service capacity through creative partnerships. To this end, we have begun working with the Grand Rapids Community Media Center and with Ann Arbor's Non-profit Enterprises at Work in anticipation of our fourth quarter plans to launch satellite operations in those cities.

GOALS & EVALUATION

Goals for years one and two

Over the next two years, NPower Michigan plans to accomplish the following:

- ◆ Expand our Board of Directors to include representatives from Grand Rapids and Lansing.

- ◆ Hire an Operations Manager for each satellite city; hire additional consulting and training staff in response to service demand.

- ◆ Establish satellite offices in Ann Arbor and Grand Rapids to begin delivering consulting & training services in those cities.

- ◆ Deliver 2,000 billable hours of consulting services in year one; evaluate year one performance, set and attain year two targets.

- ◆ Deliver 1,700 student hours of training in year one; evaluate year one performance, set and attain year two targets.

- ◆ Revise course offerings and curricula in response to local feedback.

- ◆ Plan and carry out a Day of Service event serving at least 25 non-profits in metropolitan Detroit during year one; in year two, stage a similar event to include Ann Arbor and Grand Rapids.

Project evaluation

Since our inception 1999, NPower has made evaluation an integral part of our daily work. All NPower services are carefully evaluated with respect to service quality, customer satisfaction and the extent to which technology know-how is effectively transferred to non-profits. Depending on the specific service provided, methods of evaluation include surveys, interviews, case studies and focus groups. The lessons learned from our evaluation efforts inform program design changes and new program development.

At the macro level, NPower is concerned with four evaluation questions. They are:

1. *Are our services meeting the needs of the non-profit community?*
2. *Are we maximizing our ability to provide high quality direct services and resources?*
3. *Are we transferring technology know-how to the non-profit community?*
4. *Do our services and tools help non-profits meet their missions?*

The NPower Network is contracting with Innonet, a non-profit based in Washington D.C., to manage our evaluation efforts.

Dissemination of Lessons Learned

One of NPower's core values is sharing lessons learned to maximize the knowledge base of organizations and individuals working toward the common goal of using technology to strengthen our communities. Thanks to the NPower Network, we will be able to share the lessons working with our partners here in Michigan with other NPowers around the country; the Microsoft Corporation will host an annual meeting of NPower affiliates to encourage this sharing. In addition, we will ensure that they are made widely available by posting them on our Web site and alerting interested parties that these resources are available. Any lessons learned from work supported by the C.S. Mott Foundation would be disseminated with the same spirit of shared learning.

BUDGET

Commentary

The revenue projections used in NPower Michigan's 2002 budget were based on the experience of NPowers in Seattle and New York, as well as market research conducted for the NPower Michigan business plan. Unless otherwise indicated, costs associated with each line item are based on the startup experience of NPower Seattle.

The figures provided for rent and renovations are based on the prospect that our landlord will bear a portion of the cost of building improvements, passing the cost back on to us as a rent increase. The schematic design for the renovation is being developed, but the final proposal has not yet been approved by our Board of Directors.

Budget detail

See Appendix 2.

FUNDING

See Appendix 3.

IRS DETERMINATION

See Appendix 4.

new budget e-mailed to me 5/15/02

NPower Michigan
Financial Analysis
Funding, 2002 - 2004

Date: May-02

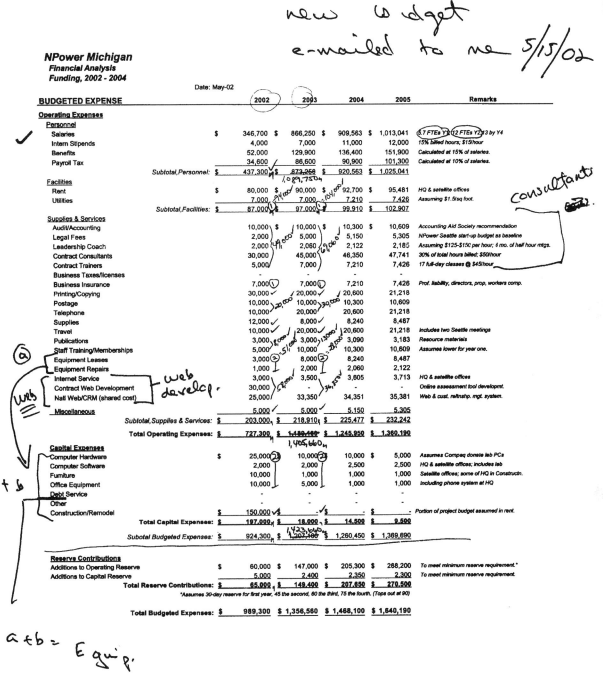

BUDGETED EXPENSE		2002	2003	2004	2005	Remarks
Operating Expenses						
Personnel						
Salaries	$	346,700 $	866,250 $	909,563 $	1,013,041	5.7 FTEs Y1; 12 FTEs Y2; 13 by Y4
Intern Stipends		4,000	7,000	11,000	12,000	15% billed hours; $15/hour
Benefits		52,000	129,900	136,400	151,900	Calculated at 15% of salaries.
Payroll Tax		34,600	86,600	90,900	101,300	Calculated at 10% of salaries.
Subtotal, Personnel:	$	437,300 $	873,250 $	920,563 $	1,025,041	
			1,089,750			
Facilities						
Rent	$	80,000 $	90,000 $	92,700 $	95,481	HQ & satellite offices
Utilities		7,000	7,000	7,210	7,426	Assuming $1.5/sq foot.
Subtotal, Facilities:	$	87,000 $	97,000 $	99,910 $	102,907	
Supplies & Services						
Audit/Accounting		10,000 $	10,000 $	10,300 $	10,609	Accounting Aid Society recommendation
Legal Fees		2,000	5,000	5,150	5,305	NPower Seattle start-up budget as baseline
Leadership Coach		2,000	2,060	2,122	2,185	Assuming $125-$150 per hour; 4 mo. of half hour mtgs.
Contract Consultants		30,000	45,000	46,350	47,741	30% of total hours billed; $50/hour
Contract Trainers		5,000	7,000	7,210	7,426	17 full-day classes @ $45/hour
Business Taxes/licenses		-	-	-	-	
Business Insurance		7,000	7,000	7,210	7,426	Prof. liability, directors, prop, workers comp.
Printing/Copying		30,000	20,000	20,600	21,218	
Postage		10,000	10,000	10,300	10,609	
Telephone		10,000	20,000	20,600	21,218	
Supplies		12,000	8,000	8,240	8,487	
Travel		10,000	20,000	20,600	21,218	Includes two Seattle meetings
Publications		3,000	3,000	3,090	3,183	Resource materials
Staff Training/Memberships		5,000	10,000	10,300	10,609	Assumes lower for year one.
Equipment Leases		3,000	8,000	8,240	8,487	
Equipment Repairs		1,000	2,000	2,060	2,122	
Internet Service		3,000	3,500	3,605	3,713	HQ & satellite offices
Contract Web Development		30,000	-	-	-	Online assessment tool developmt.
Nat'l Web/CRM (shared cost)		25,000	33,350	34,351	35,381	Web & cust. reltnshp. mgt. system.
Miscellaneous		5,000	5,000	5,150	5,305	
Subtotal, Supplies & Services:	$	203,000 $	218,910 $	225,477 $	232,242	
Total Operating Expenses:	$	727,300 $	1,189,160 $	1,245,950 $	1,360,190	
			1,405,660			
Capital Expenses						
Computer Hardware	$	25,000	10,000	10,000 $	5,000	Assumes Compaq donate lab PCs
Computer Software		2,000	2,000	2,500	2,500	HQ & satellite offices; includes lab
Furniture		10,000	1,000	1,000	1,000	Satellite offices; some of HQ in Constructn.
Office Equipment		10,000	5,000	1,000	1,000	Including phone system at HQ
Debt Service		-	-	-	-	
Other		-	-	-	-	
Construction/Remodel	$	150,000 $	- $	- $	-	Portion of project budget assumed in rent.
Total Capital Expenses:	$	197,000 $	18,000 $	14,500 $	9,500	
Subtotal Budgeted Expenses:	$	924,300 $	1,207,160 $	1,260,450 $	1,389,690	
			1,423,660			
Reserve Contributions						
Additions to Operating Reserve	$	60,000 $	147,000 $	205,300 $	268,200	To meet minimum reserve requirement.*
Additions to Capital Reserve		5,000	2,400	2,350	2,300	To meet minimum reserve requirement.
Total Reserve Contributions:	$	65,000 $	149,400 $	207,650 $	270,500	
		Assumes 30-day reserve for first year, 45 the second, 60 the third, 75 the fourth. (Tops out at 90)				
Total Budgeted Expenses:	$	989,300 $	1,356,560 $	1,468,100 $	1,640,190	

consultants

web develop.

a + b = Equip.

[Notations were made by the funder in reviewing the proposal.]

NPower Michigan
Financial Analysis
Funding, 2002 - 2004

Date: May-02

BUDGETED REVENUE		2002		2003		2004		2005	Remarks
<u>Earned Operating Revenue</u>									
Consulting	$	147,500	$	301,850	$	564,300	$	709,750	*Assumes 4000 billed hours.*
Education		24,560		72,290		94,443		96,332	*6 full-day classes monthly; ave. 4 students*
Membership		35,795		70,519		71,058		74,366	*Based on Seattle and market; 180 memberships*
Total Earned Operating Revenue:	$	207,855	$	444,658	$	729,802	$	880,448	

Numbers revised to reflect working partnerships with existing agencies and perceived changes in the economy.

		2002		2003		2004		2005	Remarks
<u>Unearned Operating Revenue</u>									
Interest Earnings	$	30,120	$	26,898	$	25,588	$	4,305	
Committed Funder Support		640,000		580,000		270,000		-	
Microsoft		240,000		250,000		250,000			
Kellogg		140,000		150,000					
Mott		160,000		160,000					
SBC Ameritech		80,000							
Metro Health Foundation		20,000		20,000		20,000			*Scholarship program*
To Be Identified		111,325		305,004		442,710		755,436	*$285,000 grants pending*
Total Unearned Operating Revenue:	$	781,445	$	1,491,902	$	1,008,298	$	759,741	
Total Projected Revenue:	$	989,300	$	1,936,560	$	1,738,100	$	1,640,190	
% Expenses Recovered Through Earned Revenue		24.1%		34.8%		51.5%		53.9%	

		2002		2003		2004		2005	
TOTAL BUDGETED EXPENSES:	$	989,300	$	1,356,560	$	1,468,100	$	1,640,190	
TOTAL PROJECTED REVENUE:	$	237,975	$	471,556	$	755,390	$	884,753	
REQUIRED FUNDER SUPPORT:	$	751,325	$	885,004	$	712,710	$	755,436	
ANNUAL FUNDING COMMITTED	$	640,000	$	580,000	$	270,000	$	-	
ADDITIONAL FUNDING NEEDED FOR 2002	$	111,325	$	305,004	$	442,710	$	755,436	
ANNUAL FUNDING PENDING:	$	285,000	$	325,000	$	575,000	$	350,000	*To meet minimum budget for year one.*
% Expenses Recovered Through Earned Revenue		24.1%		36.8%		57.8%		67.5%	

KATHLEEN TEODORO, *Executive Director.* A native of Grand Rapids, Kathleen comes to NPower Michigan after serving as Director of Education for NPower Seattle. Kathleen was part of the first NPower management team and guided the startup of NPower Seattle's training program. She brings to Michigan the commitment to top quality service for non-profits that helped make NPower Seattle a marked success. Kathleen came to NPower from Adobe Systems, a California-based software company, where she worked in technical support and training. She was also a member of the Access.adobe.com team, a small group of employees who managed Adobe's Internet portal for blind and visually-impaired users. Kathleen's prior work also includes service with a wide array of non-profits—from a children's theater to a group home for developmentally delayed Deaf adults to an advocacy organization for organic farmers. She has a degree in Philosophy from Seattle University and performed with the School of Hard Knocks in New York City. (Both proved to be pivotal educational opportunities!)

BRAD JENSEN, *Web Services Coordinator and Technology Consultant.* Brad earned a Master's degree from the University of Michigan's School of Information, where he concentrated on the Information Needs of Non-Profit Organizations and Usability Engineering. He is a Rotary Ambassadorial Scholar and spent a year studying the role of information technology in social and economic development at the University of Pretoria, South Africa. After years living in South Africa and Germany, Brad finally decided to give up his nomadic life style and settle down back where he started off—in Detroit. He returns to Michigan with a keen understanding of the digital divide and computer refurbishing and re-deployment.

ANNA LEAVITT, *Web Services Coordinator and Account Manager.* Prior to working for NPower Michigan, Anna spent three years at the Bill and Melinda Gates Foundation supporting the US Library Program. She was instrumental in building and managing the Logistics Department, an experience that sparked her interest in information and knowledge management practices for non-profits. She feels lucky to have worked for such an amazing foundation, and even more fortunate to have the opportunity to apply her lessons learned as a member of the startup team at NPower Michigan. In addition to coordinating NPower's Web-based computing pilot program in metropolitan Detroit, Anna attends the University of Michigan where she is working towards her Master's of Science in Information with a focus on Public Policy.

NPower Michigan ◆ The Samaritan Center ◆ 5555 Conner Avenue ◆ Detroit, MI 48213
Main Line: (313) 267-9550 ◆ Training Line: (313) 267-9554 ◆ Fax: (313) 267-9556 ◆ On the Web at: www.NPowerMichigan.org

Staff

SHARON PETERS HARDEN, *Director of Education.* Sharon brings with her over ten years experience working in the non-profit sector. Her experience includes non-profit management, program planning and development, and adult and community education. A native Detroiter, Sharon has worked in a number of adult training and job skills programs, most recently as the Branch Manager for the Metro Detroit YWCA. As a volunteer, she has worked with non-profit programs to provide leadership skills, life skills, and other training. Sharon believes in the abundant rewards of being in service to others and helping people reach their potential.

HAVEN PFEFFER, *Office Manager.* With more than 5 years experience working in a variety of different roles at local non-profits, Haven has worn many hats, assisting organizations with administrative support, database management, event coordination, fund developement and communications. She has worked with a variety of organizations, including the Eight Mile Boulevard Association, the United Way of Oakland County, and...er...HAVEN. (Can't help but get a kick out of that bit of trivia!) Thanks to her work with these and other local agencies, Haven possesses a deep understanding of the benefits technology can bring to a non-profit organization. She holds a BA in Public Relations from Wayne State University.

ANDY WOLBER, *Director of Consulting and Operations.* Prior to joining NPower Michigan, Andy worked for USWeb/CKS, managing to remain employed through its tumultuous history of mergers and name changes until he found himself working for the Dallas branch of divine. Through it all, Andy played a key role in developing internet technology and brand strategies for clients such as AIMCO, JC Penney and Good Shepherd Medical System. He has also applied his extensive technology know-how in service to numerous non-profits, including the Center for Nonprofit Management, The Jewish Community Center, and the National Alliance for the Mentally Ill. He served for many years as the Executive Director of the Dallas Historical Society and board chairman of the Arts District Friends (Dallas). Originally from Parma, Michigan, Andy acquired a B.A. in Music Theory and Composition from Spring Arbor College before moving to Texas, where he earned an MBA and an MA in Arts Administration from Southern Methodist University.

NPower Michigan ◆ The Samaritan Center ◆ 5555 Conner Avenue ◆ Detroit, MI 48213
Main Line: (313) 267-9550 ◆ Training Line: (313) 267-9554 ◆ Fax: (313) 267-9556 ◆ On the Web at: www.NPowerMichigan.org

230   GUIDE TO WINNING PROPOSALS

A Proposal From

San Francisco Court Appointed Special Advocate Program
San Francisco, California

To

Pottruck Family Foundation
San Francisco, California

Requested amount: $15,000; **Amount received:** $60,000 over three years

Funder's comments:

"The short cover letter clearly and succinctly communicates the amount requested and what the funds will be used for. The proposal begins with the history and purpose of the organization and a discussion of the needs—the human needs—that the San Francisco Court Appointed Special Advocate Program (SFCASA) addresses.

"The proposal successfully conveys the environment in which SFCASA operates and discusses SFCASA's relationships with other agencies. The proposal describes how the program works, offers specific goals and objectives for the coming year, and how the program will be evaluated. Finally, they offer a narrative budget section, sources of support, and a discussion of their values and management principles.

"The attachments tell the rest of the story. The budget and financial information is clear and the client profiles provide a sense of the challenges faced by the children the agency serves.

"I would have formatted the document with more breaks between sections for better readability. Under funding sources, I prefer to have each listed and categorized as received or pending; I'd also like to know if any were declined."

Nancy Wiltsek, MNA, Executive Director, Pottruck Family Foundation

Notes:

The complete proposal included the following attachments: list of attachments, list of board members, projected organizational budget, several letters of support from court officials and government agencies, a training schedule, client profiles, IRS tax-exempt letter, newsletters, and audited financial statements. The foundation was formerly named the Pottruck/Scott Family Foundation.

Proposal written and submitted to the funder by Karen Miller Wood, Director of Development.

A child's voice in court.®
San Francisco Court Appointed Special Advocate Program

November 19, 1999

Ms. Nancy Wiltsek, Director
Pottruck/Scott Family Foundation
2269 Chestnut Street, #800
San Francisco, CA 94123

Dear Ms. Wiltsek,

The **San Francisco Court Appointed Special Advocate (SFCASA) Program**
recruits, screens, trains, and supervises community volunteers to become court officers
providing comprehensive advocacy and mentorship services to abused and neglected
children under the jurisdiction of San Francisco's Juvenile Dependency Court.

The attached proposal is in request of **$15,000** to support general operations in
1999-2000 enabling SFCASA Program volunteers to serve a total of 250 client children
during the funding year.

SFCASA is grateful to the Pottruck/Scott Family Foundation for its consideration
of our request.

Very truly yours,

Karen Miller Wood

Karen Miller Wood, Director of Development

833 Market Street, Suite 1004 San Francisco, CA 94103   415.398.8001 Fax: 415.398.8068
E-mail: info@sfcasa.org   http://www.sfcasa.org

A child's voice in court.®
San Francisco Court Appointed Special Advocate Program

Request to the Pottruck/Scott Family Foundation
1999-2000 SFCASA Client Caseload Expansion

The History of SFCASA

The existence of a CASA Program in San Francisco reflects a community will to improve quality of life, expand opportunities, and prevent delinquency for abused and neglected children. In 1989, Supervising Juvenile Court Judge Roy Wonder established a task force to explore the possibility of beginning a new CASA program to serve dependent children in San Francisco. This task force, which evolved into the SFCASA Board of Directors, organized an Advisory Council to be composed of representatives from the Juvenile Court, the Department of Social Services, attorney groups, child welfare agencies, and representatives from the SFCASA Board of Directors and staff. Initially meeting each month, the Council now meets quarterly to optimize interagency cooperation and service delivery to children

In 1991, SFCASA trained its first class of 11 volunteers. Since that time, SFCASA volunteers have provided comprehensive mentorship and advocacy services to over 500 high risk abused and neglected client children. In FY 1998-1999, SFCASA volunteers served a total of 190 client children and provided approximately 40,000 logged hours of comprehensive mentorship and advocacy service to client children. SFCASA's goal for 1999-2000 is to expand volunteer services to serve 66 new client children with a total of 250 served in that fiscal year.

In addition, we have enhanced our ability to supervise volunteers in their advocacy for youth in the schools and have established significant new links with the San Francisco Unified School District. Increasing numbers of SFCASA volunteers are being trained and appointed as Parent Surrogates for Educational Purposes (as provided in California's Education Code) when client youth have no family member able to serve in that capacity. We have significantly increased our knowledge of strategies for helping client youth and their caregivers to obtain access to the wide array of services available through the San Francisco Unified School District. We have also increased our knowledge of the appropriate circumstances under which to request services from non-public schools. In addition, collaboration with agencies affiliated with the Mayor's Criminal Justice Council and with the Mayor's Office of Children, Youth and Their Families has increased our effectiveness in providing appropriate service referrals for our youth. SFCASA has initiated a new project designed to promote successful participation of pre-emancipation client youth in the Independent Living Skills Program of the Department of Human Services. Improved collaboration with the Juvenile Dependency Court has resulted in the Court referring clients to SFCASA sooner than previously upon establishment of jurisdiction, with the result that our volunteers have been able to provide urgently needed support to client youth during periods of acute stress.

Also since the formation of its non-fiscal collaborations with the Juvenile Dependency Court and with the Department of Human Services, SFCASA has developed collaborative relationships with the Southeast Family Support Network, the San Francisco Child Abuse Council, California Youth Connections, Alternative Family Services, Sojourner Truth Foster Family Service, Aspira Foster Family Services, and other foster family agencies, Superior Court Mediation Services, the San Francisco Mentoring Coalition, the University of California, School

833 Market Street, Suite 1004 San Francisco, CA 94103   415.398.8001 Fax: 415.398.8068
E-mail: info@sfcasa.org   http://www.sfcasa.org

of Nursing, Department of Family Healthcare Nursing, the Department of Public Health, the Bay Area CASA Collaborative, the California CASA Association, and the National CASA Association.

The San Francisco Court Appointed Special Advocate Program

Today, approximately 3,400 of San Francisco's children have been subjected to abuse and neglect and have been placed under the jurisdiction of the Juvenile Dependency Court. The San Francisco Court Appointed Special Advocate (SFCASA) Program recruits, screens, trains, and supervises community volunteers to serve as advocates and mentors for these children. SFCASA volunteers, sworn officers of the Court, provide judges with information to which they lack other access and which they need to make sound decisions for children in their courts' care. SFCASA volunteers are trained to assess their individual clients' needs and to address those needs which, if unaddressed, block achievement in school, lead to delinquency, and substance abuse, and ultimately mitigate against productive citizenship. SFCASA is the only agency operating in San Francisco dedicated exclusively to serving this client population.

San Francisco's dependency population has the highest percentage (76%) of children and youth in Long Term Placement of all California counties which have 1,000 or more children and which are documented in the State Foster Care Information System. These young people spend an average of 5 years in foster care and are moved from one residential placement to another an average of 5 times. This frequent change of residence results in serious disruptions of educational program, healthcare, and record keeping, as well as in the trauma of separation from familiar people and places and in the unrelenting necessity to accommodate new rules and many daunting situations. Court dependent children, designated high risk and homeless by the federal government, comprise a disenfranchised population for whom, without the intervention of SFCASA volunteers, equal opportunity, needed and available services, and consistent adult support are inaccessible.

The most compelling needs of children in foster care are **1)** for a safe and permanent home; **2)** for appropriate educational services; **3)** for good preventive and indicated healthcare; **4)** for after school activities which build self-esteem and community, while also offering alternatives to delinquent behaviors; and **5)** for a culturally appropriate caring, consistent, and responsible adult mentor. While advocating for services which will address these needs, the SFCASA volunteer also teaches and models constructive alternatives of behavior and establishes a relationship of trust with the client child which helps him or her to steer away from high risk activities. SFCASA volunteers and their client children have found participating together in volunteer activities to be enriching and rewarding--as well as bonding--experiences. These activities provide educational enrichment and play a significant role in the child's development of self-esteem, ability to trust others, and connection to the community.

The ethnic composition of SFCASA's target population is 68% African American, 4% Asian/Pacific Islander, 12% Latino/a, 12% white (non-Latino/a), 1% Native American, and 3% undesignated. These children are 49% female and 51% male.

SFCASA currently serves **155** abused and neglected children with **133** active volunteers. The 7.75 FTE member SFCASA staff consists of six full time and two part time members. The Executive Director (100% FTE), the Office Manager (100% FTE), two 100% FTE Case Supervisors, one 50% FTE Case Supervisor, the Program Director (100% FTE) ,the Volunteer Training Coordinator (100% FTE), the Program Assistant (50% FTE), and the Director of

Development (75% FTE). An MIS Specialist volunteers to serve as SFCASA COMET Database Administrator, recording case related data in and managing the COMET database.

SFCASA volunteers' roles and responsibilities are **1)** to support the client child throughout the court proceedings; **2)** to explain the court proceedings to the child; **3)** to establish a relationship with the child enabling the volunteer to gain maximum understanding of that child's needs and desires; **4)** to review all available records relevant to the client child's family, school, health, social, and residential history; **5)** to identify, explore, and make available community resources able to facilitate family preservation, family reunification, or alternative permanency planning; **6)** to explain the SFCASA's role, duties, and responsibilities to all parties associated with the client child's case; **7)** to communicate the client child's needs to the court thorough written reports and recommendations; **8)** to ensure implementation of court-approved plans for the child; **9)** to investigate the interests of the child in judicial or administrative proceedings outside of court; **10)** to communicate and coordinate efforts of the client child's social worker, and attorney; **11)** and to perform other duties as determined by the presiding juvenile court judge or a designee. SFCASA volunteers are assigned subsequent to the establishment of Juvenile Dependency Court jurisdiction over a case.

Program volunteers provide one-on-one after school enrichment activities such as hiking, skating, and visits to museums and libraries. They secure enrollment for their young clients in after-school enrichment activities and make every effort, when indicated, to involve clients in alternative schools, job training and Independent Living Skills programs. Volunteers are assigned to in-home, kinship, and foster care placements. SFCASA is a community based organization with demonstrated expertise in case management and with experience working with high risk youth and their families, as well as with the juvenile justice system, the San Francisco Department of Public Health, the San Francisco Unified School District, and community based organizations serving foster children in San Francisco.

Recruitment: SFCASA actively recruits volunteers from San Francisco's racially, ethnically, and linguistically diverse as well as gay and lesbian communities through the implementation of a comprehensive diversity outreach effort managed by the Volunteer Training/Diversity Recruitment Coordinator. SFCASA also strives to recruit volunteers able to work effectively with children having special needs. To accommodate volunteers from the City's diverse communities, SFCASA's Volunteer Training is held in San Francisco's culturally diverse Portola and Bayview neighborhoods.

Screening: SFCASA volunteer screening includes a phone intake procedure clearly describing the purpose of the SFCASA Program, its role on behalf of children in Dependency Court proceedings, the role and responsibilities of SFCASA volunteers in such proceedings, the required eighteen-month and estimated four to six hour per week casework commitment, and the forty hour classroom training program. SFCASA applicants are required to submit a minimum of four references--two professional and two personal--regarding their character, competence, reliability, and suitability to assume the role of an SFCASA volunteer. The applicant is interviewed by at least two SFCASA Program Department staff who assess his or her suitability to enter Volunteer Training.

Volunteer Training: SFCASA Volunteer Training consists of 40 hours of comprehensive classroom education in the major areas relating to the Juvenile Dependency Court process. The Program Director, Case Supervisors, and Executive Director participate in the classroom instruction, as do judges and commissioners of the Juvenile Dependency Court, staff of the

The San Francisco Court Appointed Special Advocate (SFCASA) Program/4

Department of Human Services, Deputy City Attorneys, and other qualified professionals with substantial knowledge and experience in their respective fields who are competent to provide technical training to lay persons and who donate their time to the Program. *[See attached Volunteer Training Schedule]* Volunteer candidates are required to complete three hours of Juvenile Dependency Court observation and twelve hours annually of inservice education. SFCASA professional staff attend all Training sessions to assess volunteer candidates' progress and appropriateness to the Program. Each volunteer receives a copy of the *SFCASA Comprehensive Training Manual* covering the Training curriculum.

Assignment: At the conclusion of each forty hour classroom Volunteer Training and upon final screening, SFCASA Case Supervisors and Program Director discuss cases awaiting assignment and distribute them, as appropriate, to the Case Supervisor with expertise called for by each respective case. Each individual SFCASA Case Supervisor has special expertise, respectively, in psychotherapy, mentoring, and the law. The Case Supervision team then selects 2-3 cases appropriate to each volunteer awaiting assignment, taking into consideration individual volunteers' skills, background, and preferences.

Supervision: The newly assigned volunteer meets with the client child, examines the child's Department of Human Services file, and gathers information from family members, teachers, foster parents, and others able to provide information about that child's background and needs. Under the supervision of his or her assigned Case Supervisor, the volunteer prepares a written Case Plan for the client child based on the careful assessment of that child's needs. Volunteers report to Case Supervisors at least bi-monthly, and case review meetings between volunteers and supervisors are held at least every 60 days. Volunteers also receive case supervision at monthly case support meetings held in the SFCASA office and have 24 hour access to Case Supervisors by pager and by a voice mail system. Volunteers record their case activity in monthly Case Logs which, along with all Court Reports, are reviewed by Program staff. The presiding Juvenile Court judge and commissioners have open and regular channels of communication both to SFCASA staff and Executive Director and to information regarding SFCASA cases. Monthly inservice meetings provide additional training to volunteers and may be used to fulfill the annual 12 hour continuing education requirement. SFCASA volunteers report at six month intervals to the Court regarding their individual client children's status and needs.

The Court has ready access to information regarding SFCASA case work. In addition to the communication made possible through the SFCASA Advisory Council, SFCASA Executive Director and staff meet informally and have frequent phone contact with judges and commissioners. SFCASA staff communicates with the court by memo and attends court sponsored Bar Association and Panel attorney trainings. Either the SFCASA Program Director or a Case Supervisor attends Juvenile Dependency Court hearings of SFCASA cases. SFCASA Executive Director, Program Directors, and staff attend the annual Judicial Council of California Beyond the Bench Conference.

SFCASA receives case referrals not only from the Court, but also from the Department of Human Services (DHS) and from Panel attorneys representing children involved in Dependency Court proceedings. DHS staff participate in SFCASA Volunteer Training, and SFCASA staff trains DHS Child Welfare Workers on the role of the SFCASA volunteer. SFCASA volunteers consult DHS Child Welfare Workers concerning client children's needs. The Senior Data Analyst at DHS provides SFCASA with necessary data about our target population, as do DHS department managers from whom we have requested information.

The San Francisco Court Appointed Special Advocate (SFCASA) Program/5

Goals and Objectives

SFCASA is requesting a grant in general support of Program volunteer advocacy and mentorship services to meet continuing client service as well as client caseload expansion needs during 1999-2000. The goal of the SFCASA Program is both to improve quality of life, prevent delinquency, and expand opportunity for an annually increasing number of Dependent children through the fulfillment of the following 1999-2000 objectives:

Objective 1: to provide intensive individualized advocacy for children in the Juvenile Dependency Court system by recruiting, screening, training, and supervising **66** new Program volunteers and the assignment of these volunteers to **66** client children not previously served by SFCASA;

Objective 2: through the activities of Program volunteers, to provide services leading to family preservation, reunification, kinship placement, or a safe, stable, and nurturing foster or adoptive home;

Objective 3: to provide comprehensive assessment of the healthcare, educational, and recreational needs of individual client children, and thus to promote clients' optimal health, improved academic performance, and self-esteem;

Objective 4: to increase participation in the SFCASA Program of culturally diverse volunteers, thus to provide, to the maximum extent possible, culturally appropriate mentorship to each client child.

Measurement Instruments

Quantitative outcome measurements of the effectiveness of the Client Caseload Expansion Project will be the number of new volunteers trained, the percentage of culturally diverse new volunteers trained, and the number of children served. SFCASA records this information in a COMET software data collection system. Hard copy records are contained Volunteer Files containing all application and screening records (including Volunteer Assessment forms completed by two staff members immediately after each initial and post-Training volunteer screening interview, security check data, DMV printouts, signed applications, references, signed Volunteer Agreement, and court appointment order), in Case Activity files; in Volunteer Training and inservice education attendance records; in monthly Volunteer Case Activity Logs; in quarterly written Case Plan reviews, and in Court Reports written and presented to the Court every six months.

Project Budget

SFCASA is applying to the Pottruck/Scott Family Foundation for **$15,000** in general operational support to recruit, screen, train, and supervise community volunteers who, as Court Officers, advocate for and mentor abused and neglected children under the jurisdiction of San Francisco's Juvenile Dependency Court. In FY 1999-2000, SFCASA plans to serve a total of 250 children. This number reflects a 31% increase over the total number of client children served in 1998-1999. The funding requested from the Pottruck/Scott Family Foundation, if granted, would comprise 2.7% of SFCASA's projected 1999-2000 annual budget. As the attached 1999-2000 SFCASA projected annual organizational budget shows, current funding for SFCASA derives from government and foundation grants and from corporate and individual gifts. Future funding is planned to derive from these sources, but with decreasing reliance on grants and increased reliance on individual and corporate gifts.

1999-2000 Funding Sources

Funding sources for FY 1999-2000 (revised from FY 1999-2000 Projected Budget) are as follows: the Mayor's Criminal Justice Council ($46,100), Charles and Helen Schwab Family Foundation ($20,000 remainder of $40,000), Stuart Foundations/California CASA Association ($32,500), United Way of the Bay Area ($25,000 for each of three years, 1999-2002), San Francisco Foundation ($15,000), Mayor's Office of Children, Youth, and Their Families ($25,000), Louis R. Lurie Foundation ($25,000), Sara H. and William R. Kimball Foundation ($20,000), Richard and Rhoda Goldman Fund ($15,000), Van Loben Sels Foundation ($15,000), Fremont Group ($10,000), Transamerica Foundation ($5,000), Bernard and Alba Witkin Charitable Trust ($2,000), Proposition 10 (pending with amount of request undetermined at this time), PacifiCare Foundation ($10,000, pending), Dresdner RCM Global Investors ($10,000, pending), Judicial Council of California ($50,000, pending), Bothin Foundation ($21,900, pending), Pottruck/Scott Family Foundation ($15,000, pending) Charles Schwab Corporation Foundation ($5,000, pending), individual gifts ($45,000, projected), Annual Major Fundraiser ($40,000), workplace giving ($10,000. projected), holiday card sales ($9,000). In-kind and donated support is currently projected at approximately $32,900. SFCASA, is supported by grants and gifts and raises its entire operational budget annually.

Management Principles and Strategic Plan

SFCASA makes every effort to incur only those overhead costs which are necessary to support case related activities. Personnel and fiscal management practices are designed to promote fairness, consistency, accountability, and the continuation of SFCASA Program volunteer services. SFCASA operates in compliance with National CASA Association Program Standards and Recommended Management Practices, Judicial Council of California Rule #1424, local rules of court and according to Memoranda of Understanding with the Juvenile Dependency Court and the Department of Human Services. Written program policies defining the roles and responsibilities of SFCASA volunteers and other parties in the Juvenile Dependency Court system have been developed in consultation with members of the SFCASA Advisory Council and the Supervising Judge of the Juvenile Court. To ensure both quality and continuity of program management, SFCASA has developed the following policy manuals: *The SFCASA Procedures Guide For Case Management, Employees' Policies and Procedures, Financial Procedures,* and *The Revised Board of Directors Manual.* Operating under the organization's by-laws, SFCASA's Board of Directors has fiduciary and governance responsibility for the Program, with the President overseeing all resource development activities and fundraising committees. The Board establishes policy and delegates responsibility for implementation to the Executive Director. Fiscal oversight of the Program is managed by the Board Treasurer and the Board Budget and Finance Committee. SFCASA fiscal management procedures are set forth in the organization by-laws and comply with federal and State regulations for private non-profit organizations.

Financial records are maintained in an MYOB Bookkeeping system and are reconciled monthly by an independent bookkeeper. Taxes and SFCASA's annual audited statement are prepared according to standard accounting procedures by an independent Certified Public Accountant. SFCASA is a 501 (c) (3) organization with an eight year history of effective administration of grants from federal, State, local, private foundation, and corporate funding sources.

The San Francisco Court Appointed Special Advocate (SFCASA) Program/7

In FY 1997-1998, responding to the need for expanded SFCASA volunteer services, SFCASA's Board of Directors developed a Strategic Plan for phased program growth. The Plan resulted from six months of collaborative work on the part of the Board of Directors and staff guided by a development professional with over 20 years experience in the field of non-profit fund development and who provided *pro bono* service. SFCASA's Strategic Plan provides for Program continuity and expansion through the development of a diversified and expanding funding base to support planned phased increase of staff to accommodate a growing caseload. The Board of Directors and staff have worked together to enlarge and to diversify SFCASA's funding base and to coordinate caseload growth, staff capacity, administrative support, and income as called for in the Plan.

The SFCASA Program is grateful to the Pottruck/Scott Family Foundation for its consideration of our request.

A child's voice in court.®
San Francisco Court Appointed Special Advocate Program

SFCASA Client Profiles

1. Arturo, 12, is a Latino boy who entered court jurisdiction one year ago. One of six children, he was the only child in his family subject to his father's verbal abuse and physical violence. He repeatedly ran away from home. When placed in foster care, he continued to run away from the foster placement. Attempts at reunification, such as weekend visits with his family, have been unsuccessful so far. Arturo is often AWOL from his current group home, is highly disruptive at school, was expelled from one school, and was suspended from the school in which he was subsequently enrolled. His math and science skills are well below grade level. He has poor study and personal hygiene habits, has become friends with a boys who engage in delinquent behavior, and often misses his therapy sessions.

Arturo's SFCASA volunteer visits Arturo regularly at the group home where Arturo currently resides, takes Arturo out for various constructive activities, and visits him at school. The volunteer recently began taking Arturo to a public swimming pool where he arranged for Arturo to have swimming lessons. Arturo and his SFCASA volunteer now swim weekly, and the volunteer hopes to interest Arturo in eventually joining a swim team. The volunteer is currently advocating for Arturo to be placed in a special home for disturbed children where the problems symptomized in his disruptive behavior can be effectively addressed. He continues to model positive and constructive behavior for Arturo and to be a friend for him.

2. Nyeisha, 12, is an African American girl who, at the time of her assignment to an SFCASA volunteer, was at high risk for pregnancy, having consistently expressed the strong desire to have a baby. Her father is an alcoholic living out of state and her mother is a cocaine addict. Nyeisha has lived in several foster homes and now lives in kinship care.

At the time of her referral to SFCASA, Nyeisha's behavior was intensely angry and often involved her in inappropriate outbursts directed towards other children. At one point, Nyeisha threatened to kill a school staff person. At the time of assignment to an SFCASA volunteer, Nyeisha was living in foster care in the home of a relative whose negative personal style aggravated Nyeisha's fear and anger.

Nyeisha's SFCASA volunteer works with Nyeisha's relative/caregivers in applying positive discipline strategies in the home. Nyeisha responds well to a disciplinary system based on rewards and praise. The volunteer picks Nyeisha up from school one day each week and spends the afternoon with her. As the result of a report prepared by the volunteer, the court investigated allegations of borderline abuse in the kinship placement and ordered modification of inappropriate disciplines. The volunteer has spent many hours in conversation with Nyeisha about positive alternatives and staying in school, and has enrolled Nyeisha in a well supervised extended care after school program. A milestone for Nyeisha is that her self-esteem and sense of improved prospects for the future have increased such that she has told her SFCASA volunteer that she wants to wait until she is in her twenties to have a baby.

3. Mark, 12, is a Caucasian boy whose mother is heroin addicted and who for several years lived in kinship care with relatives who abused him. He was removed from their home and placed with a foster family. He is an intelligent boy who seems to act out for attention. He presented disciplinary problems in his first foster home.

833 Market Street, Suite 1004 San Francisco, CA   94103   415 . 398 . 8001   Fax: 415 . 398 . 8068
E-mail: sfcasa@aol.com   http://www.sfcasa.com

SFCASAClientProfiles/2

Mark's DHS worker had planned to move him to another county, but Mark's SFCASA volunteer, concerned about the damaging effects on Mark of a move to a completely unfamiliar place, worked with Mark's attorney to obtain a court order preventing the relocation out of the county and allowing preservation of positive contacts within the San Francisco community,. The volunteer also advocated for a new foster family home. The DHS worker was able to find such a placement for Mark, and Mark adjusted well to the new home, although he was at first uncomfortable being the only Caucasian boy in an African American neighborhood and taking the bus to school. The success of Mark's current school placement, for which his SFCASA volunteer also advocated, is measurable in Mark's current good attendance and improved grades and behavior. The son of Mark's foster mother has begun to watch over Mark and walks to and from the bus with him. Mark is developing a close bond with this older boy, is doing well at his current home, and is liked by everyone there.

4. **Trevor, 14** and Caucasian, is the child of a heroin addicted mother and was diagnosed as depressed at 4 years of age. He lived with his grandmother for several years and now is in kinship care in the home of an uncle. Trevor was referred to the SFCASA Program after another child in his foster home died and Trevor began to be seriously out of control. His school attendance was poor, he was disruptive in school, often refused to go home, and engaged in altercations with his uncle, some of which were physically violent. Trevor blamed himself for his friend's death.

Trevor's SFCASA volunteer has befriended him and gotten to know Trevor's extended family, counselors, and teachers. He phones Trevor in the morning to make sure that Trevor is up and at school on time. The volunteer also monitors Trevor's homework and provides much needed encouragement regarding school and other areas of the young man's life; he attends Trevor's basketball games, plays basketball with him after school, and spends time--sometimes daily--in local parks, chatting and playing sports. The volunteer has also cooperated with Trevor's DHS worker to address the problems in the foster home and obtained a temporary placement in the home of Trevor's aunt. While living with this aunt, Trevor's behavior and school attendance have improved dramatically. The SFCASA volunteer is currently developing a formal and objective assessment of the desirability of placing Trevor permanently with his aunt.

5. When **Gerard, 14** and African American, was referred to the SFCASA Program, he spent much of his time on the streets of the Mission District and in a state of acute stress owing to gang harassment, for which reason he was afraid to go to school and rarely attended. He was doing poorly in all areas. In addition, he had been trying to care both for his drug addicted father and for his young half siblings, who were living at a different residence with his mother.

Gerard's SFCASA volunteer, when first assigned, would have to walk through the streets of the Mission District trying to find Gerard. Gerard's SFCASA has been instrumental in researching and obtaining a placement for Gerard in a residential school for troubled youth where Gerard has broken his failure cycle. He completed two grades in one year, is happy and carefree. He enjoys working on a reward system and gets along well with the other children in the school. The SFCASA volunteer has facilitated four visits for Gerard with his grandmother in San Mateo County and is evaluating the possibility of Gerard's living with her when he is ready to leave the residential school.

[The names of the SFCASA Program clients have been changed in compliance with Program confidentiality requirements.]

SFCASA PROJECTED BUDGET
1999 - 2000

REVENUE

GRANTS AND GIFTS	
Bank of the West	1,500
Charles Schwab Family Fund	40,000
Dresdner RCM	10,000
Fremont Group	10,000
GATX Corp.	5,000
Goldman Fund	15,000
Jr. League	3,000
Judicial Council 98-99 *	6,000
Judicial Council 99-2000 **	41,000
Judicial Council 2000-01 ***	23,750
Lurie Foundation	25,000
Mayor's Criminal Justice Council	46,100
MOCYF	25,000
PacificCare Foundation	10,000
S.F. Foundation	15,000
SFES Mentoring Project	30,000
Stuart - I & T	32,500
Stulsaft Foundation	5,000
Transamerica Foundation	5,000
United Way	25,000
Van Loben Sels Foundation	15,000
Whitkin Trust	2,000
DONATIONS	
Annual Giving	15,000
Board Initiative	31,447
Donor Development Projects	25,000
In Kind Giving	25,000
Volunteer Initiative	10,000
Workplace Giving	10,000
FUNDRAISING	
Board Event	40,000
E-Commerce	750
Interest Income	1,000
Kids for Kids Cards	10,000
Vigil	1,000
TOTAL:	560,047

SFCASA PROJECTED BUDGET
1999 - 2000

EXPENSES

Advertising	500
AOL/Website	500
Banking Service Charge	1,500
Board Training and Meetings	250
Conference Expenses	3,500
Misc. Contributions	100
Development Projects	15,000
Dues and Subscriptions	500
Equipment Rental	500
Fundraising Expense	20,000
In Kind Giving	25,000
Insurance Stipend	9,600
Insurance/Liability/D&O	4,200
Insurance/Workman's Comp	4,300
Legal and Accounting	4,000
Maintenance and Repair	1,000
Postage	4,000
Printing and Stationary	3,500
Rent	27,192
Staff Gross Wages	323,160
Staff Payroll Tax (15%)	48,474
Staff Payroll Raises	9,695
Staff Payroll Raises Tax (15%)	1,454
Staff Training & Reimbursements	2,000
Supplies.	5,000
Tax/Licenses/Permits	250
Telephone	9,800
Volunteer Recognition Event	2,000
Volunteer Recruitment & Training	12,000
SUBTOTAL	*538,975*

OFFICE MOVE (ONE-TIME EXPENSE)	
Computers & Networking	7,500
Movers	2,000
Phone System	9,100
Rent Deposit	2,472
SUBTOTAL:	*21,072*

TOTAL:	560,047

A Proposal From
VolunteerMatch
San Francisco, California

To
The John S. and James L. Knight Foundation
Miami, Florida

Requested amount: Unspecified; **Amount received:** Three-year commitment to general/operating support: $250,000 in 2002, 2003, and 2004.

Funder's comments:

"The proposal followed our foundation application form, as we require, and included all of the components I would expect in a well-developed proposal. It is specific about goals. The anticipated outcomes (section 5) was the strongest feature of the proposal. The writing style was clear and jargon-free, and the graphics were appropriate. It contained relevant detail and didn't simply bury the reader in information. It includes a serious business plan to address long-term sustainability after the Knight Foundation grant expires. The VolunteerMatch budget was clearly presented, though it did not contain an income statement. However, the expense statement was quite clear. After seeking clarification regarding income, we had sufficient detail in the budget to make our funding decision. The attachments were helpful and relevant, and included a comprehensive evaluation plan."

Penelope McPhee, Vice President and Chief Program Officer,
The John S. and James L. Knight Foundation

Notes:

The complete proposal included the following attachments: reports by the Bridgespan Group and Harder+Company Community Research, financial reports, and list of committed and prospective funders. The evaluation plan referenced above by the funder is not included here.

Proposal written and submitted to the funder by Andrew Smiles, Chief Financial Officer.

October 31, 2001

Penny McPhee
Vice President & Chief Program Officer
The John S. and James L. Knight Foundation
One Biscayne Tower, Suite 3800
2 South Biscayne Boulevard
Miami, FL 33131-1803

Dear Ms. McPhee,

I hope this note finds you well. I have put together this packet to bring you up to speed on recent developments here at VolunteerMatch. While the Q3-01 Report (*See Tab 1, in the attached binder*) provides a concise overview, I wanted to provide a more detailed outline of recent news and events. VolunteerMatch has been busier than ever over the past few quarters.

> **Fundraising Progress**
> As you know, since February 2001, VolunteerMatch has been driving to raise funds for a three-year plan to expand the reach, impact, and sustainability of the organization and the service. Our plan, vetted by independent consultants at The Bridgespan Group, called for $12.7 million in philanthropy investments over the next three years (*See Tab 2 for Financial Pro Forma*). With a challenge grant from The Atlantic Philanthropies, nearly $6 million was raised between February and July, constituting Phase I.
>
> Now in Phase II of the fundraising progress, our current goal is to raise $3.8 million by the end of Q1-02, in order to leverage the remaining $1.25 million from Atlantic Philanthropies. This will bring us to the final stretch of our three-year goal (*See Tab 3 for a list of committed and prospective funders*).

> **Product News**

In August, VolunteerMatch re-launched its website with a visual re-design, as well as improvements for both individuals and nonprofit users. Concurrently, we launched a national marketing campaign to celebrate the people and nonprofits behind VM.

> **Evaluation and Metrics for Effectiveness**

VolunteerMatch completed a survey and evaluation process with an independent firm, Harder + Company Community Research. The result was a report, titled "Valuing VolunteerMatch: An Evaluation of Services Provided to Nonprofits and Volunteers," which helped us objectively measure our Social Return on Investment. In addition, we have enclosed a copy of a document requested by Vince Stehle, Program Officer at the Surnda Foundation, to discuss how VolunteerMatch measures its success (*See Tab 4 for both of these documents*).

> **Sustainability**

In Q3, earned revenue covered 36% of overall expenses through sales of VolunteerMatch Corporate and licensing deals. With the goal of growing this percentage in future quarters, VolunteerMatch recently contracted The Bridgespan Group to explore new earned-revenue streams to increase long-term financial sustainability (*See Tab 5 for A report on earned revenue, as well as the "Scope of Services" for our work with The Bridgespan Group).*

> ### Recent Publicity
In July, VolunteerMatch was awarded two Webby Awards, in the categories of Activism and Services, which generated press mentions in *The New York Times, The Washington Post, The San Francisco Chronicle, The Los Angeles Times,* among many others.

> ### Board Development
VolunteerMatch expanded its Board of Directors with the addition of Vince Stehle, Program Officer from the Surdna Foundation. In addition, we expanded our National Board of Advisors with the addition of Peter Hero, President of The Community Foundation of Silicon Valley, and William Hearst III, Partner with the venture capital firm, Kleiner Perkins Caufield & Byers.

> ### September 11th
Finally, VolunteerMatch joined the nation in expressing its condolences to all those effected by the tragedies of September 11th. In response to the attacks, VolunteerMatch dedicated its talents and resources to the volunteers and agencies directly responsible for helping our nation recover. Thousands of individuals turned to VolunteerMatch as an avenue to help out in a time of need. As a result, VolunteerMatch experienced a 700% increase in traffic and September was recorded as VM's most active month ever for volunteer referrals.

While we have been busy on all fronts, there is still much work to be done. On November 15th we will be launching a National Public Service Campaign to reach out to people and nonprofits nationwide and to invite them to join the VolunteerMatch service. In the months ahead, we hope that our clear vision, our track record of success, and the strong philanthropic support we have received to date will give confidence to the Knight Foundation to participate in the current funding round. To that end, I have enclosed a full Proposal Summary (see Tab 8), which I look forward to discussing in the near future.

Sincerely,

Andrew Smiles
Executive Officer, Development

Proposal Summary
For The John S. and James L. Knight Foundation

I.   The Mission:

Founded in 1994, VolunteerMatch's mission is to help everyone find a great place to volunteer.

II.   The Service:

VolunteerMatch is an online service that helps nonprofits recruit, manage, and communicate with volunteers over the Internet. At its core, VolunteerMatch is a database, accessible over the web, which includes current listings and descriptions of nonprofit organizations and their volunteer opportunities. Over 17,000 nonprofit organizations have published over 55,000 volunteer opportunities through VolunteerMatch. Using VolunteerMatch as their "doorway" to the Internet, nonprofits post and edit vital information (such as their mission statement, programs, address, phone number, email, and web address) to solicit volunteers and supporters for their work.

For individuals, all of the information they need to get involved as a volunteer is available in one place. Users simply log on to www.volunteermatch.org and input their zip code, their volunteer preferences, time frame, and click on the "find" button. The VM database will automatically return a list of current, up-to-date volunteer opportunities that match their search criteria. Thus, with several clicks of a button, local residents can find an opportunity that matches their particular strengths with a specific need in their community. The result is an open, participatory network that offers a universally accessible database for people who want information about nonprofits and volunteering.

In addition to connecting volunteers to nonprofits, VolunteerMatch customizes its service for use by Fortune 1000 companies, in an effort to leverage the skills and capacities of corporate employees on behalf of community needs. Through VolunteerMatch Corporate™, in exchange for a membership fee, corporations are offered a customized web service that links employees directly with nonprofit organizations. This service tracks the "who, when, and where" of the company's volunteering efforts and is available to all employees through a link from the corporation's Intranet. The VolunteerMatch Corporate™ initiative, therefore, serves VolunteerMatch's mission to increase community involvement (among corporate employees, in this case) and enhance nonprofit organizational effectiveness, while also contributing to the important goal of diversifying the VolunteerMatch funding base to sustain the service over time.

III.   The Context and the Need:

With the proliferation of the Internet over the past five years, our nation has witnessed an extraordinary communications revolution. More than two-thirds of Americans now have access to the Internet (over 100 million people) and roughly 55,000 *new* users log on each day.[1] The Internet has become the fastest growing technology in history, requiring only seven years to reach 30% of American households. By comparison, 38 years passed before the telephone reached 30% of households, and 17 years for the television.[2] It is clear that the new Internet medium is fundamentally changing the way individuals, businesses, and nonprofits work and communicate.

---

[1] UCLA Center for Communication Policy, "The UCLA Internet Report: Surveying the Digital Future," November, 2000, p.4-5, 10.
[2] Ibid, p. 5.

VolunteerMatch Proposal Summary

Nonprofit organizations have been slow to adopt the new communication technologies offered by the Internet, but they are clearly not exempt from this sea change. The technology revolution continues to hold the promise of new efficiencies and increased productivity for nonprofit and charitable organizations. In a recent study, The Center for Excellence in Nonprofits concluded, "it is generally accepted that nonprofits…are not fully utilizing the technologies that could streamline and improve operations."[3] New technology tools connecting people, ideas, and organizations on a local level can transform the practice of nonprofit management, including volunteer-recruitment, advocacy, and fundraising.

In addition to new opportunities presented to nonprofits by the advent of the Internet, there also is a palpable demand among Americans for more and better information about nonprofit organizations and community involvement. A recent study on E-philanthropy by Cone, Inc. reports that, "70 million Americans want to be more involved in charitable activities, yet many feel hampered by a lack of available information."[4] For individuals, finding the right organization or volunteer opportunity can be a laborious, complicated, and often frustrating experience. As for nonprofits, most are focused squarely on their missions and while many nonprofit organizations devote significant resources to advertising, public service announcements and awareness campaigns, these promotions often fail to reach the appropriate target audience of potential volunteers. The result is a communication gap between individuals who want to help, and non-profits that need help. VolunteerMatch is a web-based solution attempting to bridge this communication gap.

IV. Goals:

VolunteerMatch has three overarching goals: 1) to increase civic participation with community service organizations nationwide, 2) to enhance the capacity of those organizations to engage the support of their communities, and 3) to generate earned revenue so as to build a bridge to financial sustainability. To achieve these broad goals, VolunteerMatch focuses on three clear objectives:

1) **Increase the number of volunteers** recruited through the VolunteerMatch network,

2) **Increase nonprofit participation** with the VolunteerMatch service, and

3) **Increase earned revenue** through VolunteerMatch Corporate™ and licensing deals.

As an Internet-based organization, VolunteerMatch is fortunate to have the ability to track the outcomes of these goals with its proprietary technology. Every week, database and web-log reports track the number of new volunteers referred and the number of new organizations registered. These metrics, together with benchmarks for VolunteerMatch Corporate™ adoption and earned revenue, will be measured against the following quantitative goals for 2001, 2002, and 2003:

---

[3] Wired for Good: A Joint Venture of Center for Excellence in Nonprofits and Smart Valley, Inc., "Technology Survey Final Report," February, 1999, p.3

[4] "Of those surveyed, 76% could not find enough information about the organization's goals, 67% wanted more information about which groups were the neediest, 58% were unable to find organizations supporting issues important to them, and 51% were unable to find local organizations." Cone, Inc., "E-Philanthropy Report 2000: A Look at the Current State of Philanthropy and Cause Related Marketing Online," Fall, 2000, p.21

V.   Quantitative Outcomes:

By the end of 2001:
- o   Generate a total of 640,800 volunteer referrals (310,000 new referrals in 2001)
- o   Serve a total of 20,800 nonprofit partners using the VolunteerMatch service (roughly 8,000 new organizations in 2001)
- o   Expand the membership base of VolunteerMatch Corporate™ and increase the number of VolunteerMatch licensing partners to generate $1 million in earned revenue in 2001.

By the end of 2002:
- o   Generate a total of 1 million volunteer referrals (408,000 new referrals in 2002)
- o   Serve a total of 31,200 nonprofit partners (10,000 new organizations)
- o   Generate $1.25 million in earned revenue through licensing and VolunteerMatch Corporate™ in 2002.

By the end of 2003:
- o   Generate a total of 1.5 million volunteers (507,000 new referrals in 2003)
- o   Serve a total of 43,800 non-profit partners (10,000 new organizations)
- o   Generate $1.95 million in earned revenue through licensing and VolunteerMatch Corporate™ in 2003.

Achieving these goals will be contingent upon reaching our fundraising objectives for the coming three years.

VI.   Project Activities:

The VolunteerMatch service is made possible by the collective work of six tightly interwoven departments. All activities performed by these departments are ongoing efforts to drive at the same three metrics: 1) the number of volunteers recruited through the service, 2) the number of nonprofit organizations actively participating with the service, and 3) the amount of earned-revenue generated from licensing deals and corporate membership through VMC.

- a.)   *Client Relations:* Responsible for all contact with nonprofit partners and individual users. Client Relations manages strategic relations, quality control, and day-to-day communication with and education of our nonprofit and volunteer users.
- b.)   *Web Production and Development:* Responsible for product conceptualization and development; front-end web development, user-interface, HTML, and prioritizing technology development operations.
- c.)   *Engineering:* Responsible for database architecture engineering, business-logic and Linux-administrator-level development to customize the VolunteerMatch database to ensure scalability and performance.
- d.)   *Marketing and Public Relations:* Responsible for branding and promoting the wide-scale adoption of the VolunteerMatch service among nonprofits, volunteers, and paying corporate clients.
- e.)   *Business Services and VolunteerMatch Corporate™ (VMC):* Responsible for developing earned revenue through corporate membership with Fortune 1000 companies. The team develops and maintains a growing corporate-client base through VMC outreach, sales, consulting, and ongoing client relations.
- f.)   *Management/Administrative:* Responsible for fundraising for the VM service as well as developing internal systems and budgeting processes to prepare for rapid organizational growth on all fronts.

VII.   Dissemination Plan:

To serve the broadest possible audience of nonprofits, VolunteerMatch's Director of Nonprofit Relations and the Client Relations Team have worked to expand nonprofit participation with the service while ensuring that each nonprofit customer is treated with a high level of professional service. The following are a few strategies to gain new nonprofit customers:

Viral Marketing

The Client Relations Team has found it extremely effective to enlist the support of our existing nonprofit and volunteer partners to spread the word. VM sends a monthly alert to volunteers and nonprofits, apprizing them of new services and offerings from VM. The network effects that result from this kind of "viral marketing" approach have been extraordinary; people forward e-mails to friends, family, and other nonprofits to help spread the word. A monthly volunteer newsletter goes to over 150,000 volunteers, and a monthly nonprofit newsletter goes to all 14,000 nonprofit members.

Outreach

The Client Relations Team attends up to fifteen national conferences each year, such as the Independent Sector Conference, the National Conference on Community Service, National Council of Nonprofit Administrators, and others. These person-to-person interactions have been extremely useful tools for acquiring new clients into the VolunteerMatch network.

Partnering with National Nonprofits

One important strategy for expanding the VolunteerMatch nonprofit network is to deliver a customized version of the VolunteerMatch tool to help national nonprofits deliver a specific subset of information to their users. By creating a co-branded website that provides an online volunteer-matching solution for national nonprofits, VolunteerMatch has been able to gain endorsements from the national offices of twelve national organizations, while expanding participation among their local affiliates. For example, visitors to the National CASA website (www.nationalcasa.org) can search for and sign up for volunteer opportunities with a National CASA affiliate in their own community. The technology behind this functionality is provided by the VolunteerMatch service. By means of this co-branding strategy with national nonprofits, VolunteerMatch has expanded participation to several hundred new affiliates nationwide.

Tech Developments

VolunteerMatch's Tech and Product Development teams are consistently working on site improvements to help extend VolunteerMatch's reach. For example, VolunteerMatch recently re-launched its website in August of 2001 with new and improved tools for nonprofits and for volunteers. One new tool is the "Email a Friend" function that allows individuals to share volunteer opportunities with acquaintances. This feature enables volunteers to spread the word about exciting opportunities in the VolunteerMatch network, hopefully drawing more people and nonprofits to the service.

VIII.   Sustainability:

At VolunteerMatch, we are constantly striving to diversify our funding base and wean ourselves from long-term philanthropy support to become increasingly self-reliant. Over the next three years, VolunteerMatch will dedicate significant resources to expanding its business services unit in order to build earned revenue engines capable of sustaining VolunteerMatch into the future. To do this, VolunteerMatch will rely on its scalable technology infrastructure and focus new resources on marketing and sales to support its revenue generating products.

VolunteerMatch has already begun the march toward sustainability. Over the past two years, earned revenue from licensing and VolunteerMatch Corporate™ has covered an increasing share of VM's operating budget. In 2000, VM reported earned-income accounting for roughly 49% of total expenses. To continue to build on this sustainability model, VolunteerMatch expects to increase both its level of spending and its earned-revenue income.

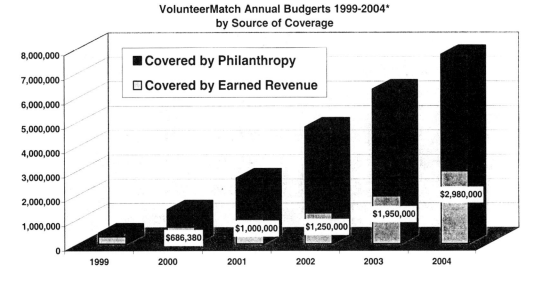

VolunteerMatch relies on two models for generating income: 1) sales of the VolunteerMatch Corporate™ Service, and 2) licensing of the VolunteerMatch database and content.
So far, VolunteerMatch has realized approximately $1.43 million in earned revenue over the past two years from these two revenue models, outlined below.

1.   Sales of VolunteerMatch Corporate™ Service

VolunteerMatch Corporate™ (VMC) is an online service designed to help large corporations get their employees involved in their communities. VMC enables Fortune 1000 corporate community affairs officers to track the "who, when, and where" of their employee volunteer programs, while automating tasks related to volunteer publication and recruitment for company-wide events. The result of these partnerships is greater corporate volunteerism and additional revenue that has been re-invested in VolunteerMatch.

Table 1: Earned Revenues from Corporate Sales of VolunteerMatch Corporate™

Year	Revenue
1999	$123,338
2000	$458,580
2001 (thru Q3)	$338,250
Total	**$920,168**

2. *Licensing of VolunteerMatch Content*

VolunteerMatch licenses the VolunteerMatch database, content, and technology to Internet portals that want access to a volunteer referral tool for their online customers. This strategy has already earned over $460,000 in revenue through licensing deals with partners such as: AOL Time Warner's Helping.org, Oxygen.com, Community-Service.com, KOIT, Shine365, and Environmental Defense.

Table 2: Earned Revenues from Licensing Contracts

Year	Revenue
1999	$175,000
2000	$227,800
2001 (thru Q3)	$110,600
Total	**$513,400**

In the future, VolunteerMatch plans to retain these clients and sign new licensing contracts with additional Internet portals.

IX. Social Return on Investment (SROI):

Delivering Social Value Returns on Philanthropy Investments

It goes without saying that VolunteerMatch is highly concerned with positive impacts created by the VolunteerMatch service. The SROI is our best attempt to quantitatively capture the value created (through volunteer recruitment savings and volunteer hours delivered) through the VolunteerMatch service. A 2001 independent survey conducted by Harder + Co. Community Research has helped VolunteerMatch to ascertain some estimates of the value-added provided by the VolunteerMatch network. In Q3-01, the value of labor from the volunteer referrals, combined with the recruitment cost savings, amounts to an estimated $62 in social value being returned for every dollar spent on VolunteerMatch. This ration is measured each quarter to provide a consistent measurement of the value of the VolunteerMatch service.

Beyond the SROI, we consider the big picture benefits of the VolunteerMatch service by asking: What would be the ultimate price tag if each of the over 17,000 VolunteerMatch nonprofits decided to build *their own* interactive database and web-service to recruit and manage volunteers? And further, assuming individual nonprofits were able to make such an investment, would they be able to gain the Internet traffic and media exposure that VolunteerMatch provides them? While it may be difficult to ascertain actual "social value delivered" it is clear that investments in VolunteerMatch have the potential to create enormous multiplier effects by providing a single solution delivering online volunteer resources to the entire sector.

X. Partnerships:

Building strong partnerships is a key piece of the VolunteerMatch strategic plan. By sharing ownership with local and national nonprofits, corporations, Internet portals, and individuals, the network has grown organically and exponentially. VolunteerMatch partners with other entities that can appreciate the value of the VolunteerMatch service, while adding value through their relationship with the network. The simplest example is a national nonprofit like National CASA, which uses the VolunteerMatch network to perform massive volunteer recruitment (over 20,000 volunteers referred through VM). In return, VolunteerMatch has gained over 700 new participating affiliates in the VM database through this partnership.

Local Nonprofit Partners:

Local nonprofit partners help build the base of available volunteer opportunities with the VolunteerMatch service. In turn, they use VolunteerMatch as a marketing and publicity channel and a place to publish their organization's information on the Internet. According to an independent assessment of VM, 63% of the organizations served by VM have ten or fewer full-time paid staff members.[5] Many of these "mom and pop" organizations rely heavily on volunteers to get their work done, and make up the majority of 17,300 nonprofits in the VM network.

National Nonprofit Partners:

VolunteerMatch partners with national nonprofit organizations in order to increase participation with the network. In return, they receive a customized integration to help solicit human resources (volunteers) in the most efficient and cost-effective manner. By partnering with VolunteerMatch, these organizations are able to direct visitors from their own websites to specific opportunities with their own local affiliates. Current national nonprofit partners include:

- The American Red Cross
- The American Humane Association
- National Court Appointed Special Advocates (CASA)
- Junior Achievement
- Rolling Readers
- Hostelling International
- America's Second Harvest
- Camp Fire Boys & Girls
- National 4-H Council
- Save the Children/YouthNoise
- Goodwill Industries
- ASDVS-American Hospital Association

Internet Portal Partners:

Internet partnerships are crucial to the marketing and dissemination of the VolunteerMatch message. Internet partners provide pro-bono banner advertising space, direct traffic to VolunteerMatch, and have carved out a niche for volunteerism on their sites. Internet partners include:

- America Online (Helping.org)
- NBCi
- LookSmart
- iVillage
- Oxygen.com
- Community-Service.com
- Shine 365
- Environmental Defense

---

[5] Harder + Company Community Research, "Evaluating VolunteerMatch Service," August, 2000, p.3

VolunteerMatch Proposal Summary   October, 2001
                                                                    page 7 of 9

Corporate Members:

VolunteerMatch views its corporate members as partners in promoting volunteerism nationwide, and building a robust VolunteerMatch network. VolunteerMatch Corporate™ provides the tool for corporations to have a direct link between their employees and their communities, through a customized integration, under their own corporate interface. VMC gives corporations a powerful, innovative web-based service to increase employee volunteerism, fulfill community outreach goals, and measure results. Current VolunteerMatch Corporate™ members include:

- Gap, Inc.
- Nike
- Levi Strauss & Co.
- The Coca-Cola Company
- SGI
- Charles Schwab & Co., Inc
- Garage.com
- LAM Research
- Paine Webber
- Macromedia
- Bank of America
- Dell Corporation
- MarchFirst
- Arthur Anderson LLP
- Dun & Bradstreet
- Duke Energy
- Lexmark International, Inc.
- Merrill Lynch
- Microsoft (SVN)
- Verizon Information Services

Volunteers

Not mentioned above, but of extreme importance, are the hundreds of thousand volunteers who visit VolunteerMatch every month to enlist themselves to serve the needs of their local communities. To date, these volunteers have used VolunteerMatch to generate over 540,000 referrals for nonprofits in need. As more individuals, organizations, and corporations receive value from the service, the network will become stronger and stronger. In short, by helping its partners achieve their missions, VolunteerMatch achieves its mission too.

XII.   Financial Need:

While we are proud of the record of success of VolunteerMatch to date, it is increasingly clear that significant resources are required to continue offering professional technology services to nonprofits, volunteers, and community-minded corporations.

In February of 2001, VolunteerMatch completed an in-depth strategic planning and budgeting process, with significant guidance and support from the independent consulting firm, The Bridgespan Group. As a result of this planning process, VolunteerMatch developed a long-term plan calling for roughly $18.8 million to build and sustain the VolunteerMatch service over the next three years. Of this sum, VolunteerMatch projects that roughly $6.1 million will be realized over three years from earned-revenue sources, including licensing contracts and VolunteerMatch Corporate™ membership fees. Since last February, we have raised nearly $6 million in philanthropy support. With a challenge grant in place, we are $3.8 million from meeting our three-year goal so as to execute on our plan.

XIII. Next Steps:

With four years of experience and more than $3 million invested in technology, VolunteerMatch is now ready to build on its past successes. VolunteerMatch is poised to execute on its aggressive goals for increasing civic participation, enhancing nonprofit effectiveness, and expanding sustainability models. With a three-year plan vetted by The Bridgespan Group, the only remaining hurdle is to raise the necessary financial capital to execute.

For this reason, we are making a pro-active investment in technology tools to help *all* nonprofits better achieve their goals. While we are proud of our success thus far, we also recognize that the 17,300 participating nonprofits represent less than 3% of all nonprofits in the sector (approximately 800,000). We believe we can do more. Our hope is that foundations and philanthropists will see an opportunity to make VolunteerMatch a permanent service on the Internet, whose benefits can be shared by organizations across the sector.

VOLUNTEERMATCH BUDGET:

		2002

PERSONNEL COSTS:
(figures include health, 403(b), and other benefits @25%)

Management and Admin

President @ .5FTE XXXXX	$	XXXXX
Chief of Staff @ 1 FTE XXXXX	$	XXXXX
Executive Officer (Development) @ 1FTE XXXXX	$	XXXXX
Financial Manager XXXXX	$	XXXXX
Development 1 XXXXX	$	XXXXX
Engineering Admin @ .1FTE XXXXX	$	XXXXX
Senior Management 1	$	XXXXX
Senior Management 2	$	XXXXX
Bonus Allocations	$	19,440
TOTAL	$	642,006

Client Services

President @ .25FTE XXXXX	$	XXXXX
Client Relations 1 XXXXX	$	XXXXX
Client Relations 2 XXXXX	$	XXXXX
Client Relations 3 XXXXX	$	XXXXX
Client Relations 4/Intern	$	XXXXX
Client Relations 5	$	XXXXX
Client Relations 6	$	XXXXX
Senior Management Needed for all Client Relations Staff	$	XXXXX
Director National Nonprofit XXXXX	$	XXXXX
Bonus Allocations	$	14,993
TOTAL	$	561,034

Web Production & Development

Product Development Manager XXXXX	$	XXXXX
Bonus Allocations	$	XXXXX
TOTAL	$	XXXXX

Engineering

Chief Engineer @ .9FTE XXXXX	$	XXXXX
System Admin 1 XXXXX	$	XXXXX
Senior Engineer 1 (Business Logic/ Java) XXXXX	$	XXXXX
Engineer XXXXX	$	XXXXX
Bonus Allocations	$	13,926
TOTAL	$	428,655

Marketing & Business Development

President @ .15FTE XXXXX	$	XXXXX
PR Director XXXXX	$	XXXXX
Bonus Allocations	$	4,093
TOTAL	$	115,407

Business Services

President @ .1FTE XXXXX	$	XXXXX
Director of New Accounts XXXXX	$	XXXXX
New Hire: Director Level	$	XXXXX
Director of Client Relations XXXXX	$	XXXXX
Client Relations Associate 1 XXXXX	$	XXXXX
Client Relations Associate 2	$	XXXXX
Bonus Allocations	$	12,945
TOTAL	$	380,978

TOTAL PERSONNEL COSTS:	$	**2,240,850**

NON-PERSONNEL COSTS:

Engineering: Site Infrastructure (Hardware, Software & Service)
Carrier - bandwidth
Hosting facility
DNS service
Operating system
Web server
Application server
Template language
Database server
Database interface
Email server
Outbound email management system
Load balancing
Hub / switch
Storage system
Security
Caching
Production CPU's
Development CPU's
Site tracking & analysis
7/24 site monitoring
Configuration management
Other

	$	70,000
TOTAL	$	70,000

Website Development
Feature development
Java apps
Creative
User interface
Other

	$	170,000
TOTAL	$	170,000

Marketing
Professional
Distribution costs
Online marketing
Creative
Branding alignment
Collateral development
Other
PSA/ 30 sec. spot

Other	$	350,000
TOTAL	$	350,000

Travel, Conferences, Expense

Travel	$	79,000
Conferences	$	70,000
TOTAL	$	149,000

Unallocated Costs

Professional services	$	156,000
Consulting	$	60,000
Training	$	20,000
Office infrastructure	$	295,052
Local / long distance phone service		
Personal voice mail system		
Switchboard system		
Internet connection		
Fast Ethernet switch		
Business workstations		
Engineering workstations		
Laser printers		
Color inkjet		
Copy machine		
Conference phone		
Security system		
Harder survey / evaluations	$	15,000
Legal / Accounting	$	43,000
Rent	$	201,600
Other	$	1,986
TOTAL	$	792,638

TOTAL NON-PERSONNEL COSTS:	$	1,531,638

TOTAL ORGANIZATIONAL COSTS:	$	3,772,489

6

Seed Money

How does a new organization, without an extensive track record of success, secure foundation funding to establish its programs? Often this is accomplished by applying for the type of support called seed money. Usually defined as grants to start, establish, or initiate new projects or organizations, they may also be called "start-up funds," and they may cover salaries and other operating expenses.

Awarding seed money entails a greater exposure to risk for a foundation than does giving to more established organizations. Consequently, this type of support is not appropriate for all grantmakers. Grantseekers who are just beginning to formalize their nonprofits' programs need to search for funders interested in their subject area, their community, and/or the audience they serve, who also will consider seed money grants.

In the case of the two proposals shown in this chapter, the writers succeeded in translating their particular passion for a cause into persuasive documents. The narratives are quite different from each other in tone, length, and subject, but each represents a transition from the initiative of one community activist into a formal organizational structure that will ensure continuity of effort. Echoing Green provides two-year fellowships in order to identify visionary individuals and to support their new and innovative organizations. This grantmaker embraces risk and looks for social change agents who are deeply committed to their communities. Represented here are two examples of proposals for the Public Service Fellows program of Echoing Green. The proposals are for different years, and therefore the application formats differ from each other (and from the current application form, which is now submitted electronically at the foundation's Web site).

Toni Blackman established Freestyle Union in order to reach young people through hip-hop and to utilize this medium of musical expression to enhance social consciousness. Matthew Lee sought to assist lower-income communities by ensuring access to equitable financial services. His efforts culminated in the establishment of Fair Finance Watch. Both applicants had arranged for fiscal sponsorship through an existing nonprofit organization, and we have included the agreement that Matthew Lee signed with Inner City Press as an example of this type of document.

Toni Blackman and Freestyle Union
Washington, D.C.

To
Echoing Green
New York, New York

Requested amount: $30,000 for each year of a two-year fellowship;
Amount received: $30,000 for each year of a two-year fellowship

Funder's comments:

"At Echoing Green, our application guidelines may vary from year to year, so it's very important that grantseekers check for the current version. Today's applicants can only submit their initial applications from our Web site (www.echoinggreen.org). We're strict about adherence to our guidelines, since this is one way to level the playing field for all applicants. For example, if someone submits more than the required number of letters of recommendation, we will not include the additional letters in the grant application package.

"At Echoing Green we help launch leaders, and people are starting off at different places in the process. We assess proposals on a case-by-case basis; so that could mean that a start-up is just an idea on a scrap of paper, or it could be a recognized 501(c)(3). In general, two years of formalized activity is the maximum to qualify for our fellowships. What matters to us is seeing passion, energy, leadership, and strong community ties. And it's not just, 'Oh, I love children.' It's taking a stance on something that's more specific, because our interest is to seed new and innovative ideas that will address seemingly intractable social problems.

"Toni's application was exemplary in all those ways. Her writing style is future-oriented, and she openly shares her opinions. Her statement of experience is very impressive. It is written in such a way that I'd want to participate in her endeavors whether or not I was interested in poetry. I think that the grantmaker should feel that type of energy from every single proposal that's funded, whether the applicant is a rock specialist, a poet, a tax lawyer, or whatever.

"Her action plan laid out the design for the year ahead with measurable outcomes. This is important, since we will hold our Fellows accountable to their plan. The action plan also helps us to assess how realistic the applicant is about his or her role. The resume is an essential addition to seed grant proposals, and hers was very comprehensive, giving credence to her leadership, creativity, and organizational abilities by enabling us to trace her entrepreneurial work.

"Toni's letters of recommendation were also very powerful. A generic, nonspecific letter of recommendation from a notable person does not necessarily provide necessary and relevant information. We think the most compelling letters come from people who know the applicants in their leadership roles—have experienced their leadership, even. For example, if the request relates to a youth organization, I like to see letters from young people, or their parents."

Lara Galinsky, Vice President, Strategy, Echoing Green

Notes:
The complete proposal included the following attachments: resume and letters of recommendation, which are not included here. The foundation was formerly known as echoing green.
Proposal written and submitted to the funder by Toni Blackman.

cover sheet

echoing green

1999 Fellowship Application

> Submit your completed
> application to your
> Fellowship Coordinator.

> Please type or print this form.

Toni   Blackman
FIRST NAME   LAST NAME

1701   New Jersey Avenue NW
STREET ADDRESS *(Please provide an address that can receive normal and express mail.)*

Washington   DC   20001
CITY   STATE   ZIP

202-387-1248   202-387-1248
DAY PHONE   NIGHT PHONE

202-387-2716
FAX   E-MAIL

Through which Participating Institution are you applying?

HOWARD UNIVERSITY

☐ Community-Based Organization   ☑ Undergraduate College/University
☐ Graduate Program

Have you applied to echoing green before?   ☐ yes   ☑ no   If yes, when: _____

If applying with a partner, what is your partner's name?

_____

What is your organization or project name?

FREESTYLE UNION

Where will your organization or project be based?

Washington   DC
CITY   STATE   COUNTRY

Where are the communities or constituencies that your organization or project will serve?

Washington   DC
CITY   STATE   COUNTRY
Maryland & VA Suburbs

more >>

Which of the following best describe the *subject areas* in which your organization or project will focus *(check all that apply)*?

☑ Arts
☐ Civil rights
☑ Community empowerment
☐ Criminal justice
☐ Disabilities
☐ Early childhood development
☐ Economic development

☐ Economic justice
☑ Education
☐ Environment
☐ Health
☐ Homelessness
☐ Housing
☐ Human rights

☐ Job training, creation and conditions
☑ Skills development & training
☑ Violence prevention
☑ Youth development
☐ Other _____
_____

echoing green

198 Madison Avenue

8th Floor

New York, New York 10016

212.689.1165

general@echoinggreen.org

www.echoinggreen.org

Which of the following best describes the *type of work* that you propose to do *(check all that apply)*?

☑ Advocacy
☐ Counseling
☑ Community organizing
☑ Community outreach
☑ Community service

☑ Educating
☑ Helping others find their expressive voice
☐ Litigating
☑ Mentoring

☑ Training and Technical Assistance
☐ Other _____
_____

What are the *primary target constituencies, communities or populations* you propose to serve *(check all that apply)*?

☑ Adolescents: 13-18 years
☑ African Americans
☑ Asian and Pacific Americans
☐ Caucasians
☑ College students
☐ Communities outside the U.S.
☐ Consumers
☐ Domestic violence survivors
☑ Children: ☐ 0-5 years
    ☐ 6-12 years

☐ Gay men, lesbians, bisexuals or transgendered people
☐ Immigrants
☐ Indigenous people
☑ Latino/as
☐ Low income communities
☐ Men
☐ Native Americans
☐ Parents
☐ People affected by HIV/AIDS

☐ People with disabilities
☐ Political violence survivors
☐ Refugees
☑ Rural communities
☑ Urban communities
☑ Women *& girls*
☐ Workers
☑ Other *the arts community the hip-hop community*

How did you hear about the echoing green Fellowship *(check all that apply)*?

☐ Through the echoing green Fellowship Coordinator
☐ Through your work
☑ Through an echoing green Fellow

☐ Publication: Which one? _____
_____
☐ Flyer
☐ Word of mouth/friends

☐ echoing green web site
☐ Other _____
_____

echoing green
1999 Fellowship Application

Section II. Short Answer Questions

1.Organization/Project Profile

Freestyle Union's mission is to not only use hip-hop as a form of artistic and cultural expression, but to promote positive images within the rap community, to encourage activism and to inspire young people to transform their creativity into a powerful tool to benefit themselves personally and their world. FSU addresses its mission by providing: 1) artistic development through its cipher workshops and performance opportunities where participants acquire discipline, presentation and critical thinking skills; 2) leadership training to prepare hip-hop artists to function as educators; 3) encouraging social activism and community responsibility through things like the "End the Silence" Cipher where each artists had to improvise on topics related to ending violence against women; and 4) a range of educational activities that expose students and the public to the artistry, meaning, and cultural background of hip-hop. Millions of records sell every year demonstrating the power of the music, the size of the market and the desperate need for balance in what's being offered to listeners-- by working with a host of community partners in Washington, DC, Maryland and Virginia, FSU provides a safe and supportive environment for conceptual thinking and innovation to raise standards for artists and audiences alike. There are few creative outlets for young hip-hop artists and few places in the streets that demand excellence, growth and confidence from within. When one is confident the need for excessive aggression decreases, reliance on expletives reduces and creativity meets the brain. My experience has shown that artistic mechanisms directing young people to focus on their self-development empowers them to develop as artists that use language and content in more creative and less stereotypical ways. It also increases their social consciousness and sense of community responsibility as hip-hop becomes the best method of social change for artists who may not feel at home within the boundaries of traditional arts programs .

2.Future Plans

I want to look creatively at social issues and concerns to inspire community dialogue about societal issues that need examining--to take street corner conversations and put them into my theater work. I want to create and perform, incorporating hip-hop into what I do as an artist and author, getting beyond sex and violence as content for art--to present socially conscious work in an enlightened way that informs but also entertains. I want to do more than talk about the . potential of hip-hop as a vehicle for social change by showing *we are doing it* (even with little money) through cipher workshops dealing with pressing issues like domestic violence and AIDS prevention. I want to reach other artists globally--my interactions with other hip-hop artists in other countries have opened up possibilities for the exchange and development of new work and to build broader-based understanding of and community for hip-hop. Five years from now, I will have a healthy, financially stable organization with a solid staff of committed artist/educators. We will have collectively demonstrated that it is possible to combine personal integrity and social activism with financial success.   Finally, I hope to serve as a mentor and an example for younger artists-to empower them to see that they have the potential for growth and development in a world that stretches far beyond their own block.

echoing green Fellowship Application
Toni Blackman/Freestyle Union, Page 2

Section III. Statement of Experience and Commitment

I created **Freestyle Union** (FSU) as an integral part of the hip hop movement, a continuum of the African American and Latino oral traditions. While directly related to forms of cultural expression that are only 20 years old, hip-hop connects to a 1,000-year-old tradition of poetry and storytelling. The term hip-hop describes this art culture overall as well as its four main components: 1) rhyming, 2) dance, 3) visual/graffiti art, and 4) DJing (using two turntables to mix and manipulate records). Though perhaps not evident to mainstream America, over the past two decades a sub-culture of young artists have explored and celebrated hip-hop in all of its diversity, both with the U.S. and internationally. With my commitment, Freestyle Union is and has been a part of that subculture.

During the past two decades, while mainstream media may not have publicized the creative aspects of hip-hop, an "underground" subculture kept hip-hop music and culture alive as a vital and relevant art form. As the founder of Freestyle Union, I had envisioned a collective for hip-hop artists in DC since she chartered the United Rappers' Organization at Howard University in 1989 and later founded the Hip Hop Arts Movement, a performance ensemble, in 1993. An outgrowth of these earlier groups, **FSU attempted to create a safe, supportive environment for rap poets who wanted to grow artistically.** *Rooted in this legacy, I founded Freestyle Union (FSU) in February of 1994 in order to develop hip-hop artistry, build a sense of community for artists and audiences, and create leaders who, as dedicated keepers of the tradition, preserve and develop all facets of the hip hop art form through their performing and teaching.*

Since its founding, FSU has focused primarily on its weekly hip-hop "freestyle" poetry workshops in DC or, as they would later would become known, the *ciphers*. *Freestyling*, a form of improvisational poetry, is an interactive mental sport which demands great mental concentration and an outstanding ability to use language rhythmically and creatively. Organized solely by volunteers, within five months freestyle workshops regularly drew through word-of-mouth as many as 80 young people of diverse backgrounds from all over the metro area—including teens, college students, architects, lawyers, teachers, and even postal workers.

Both my motivation—and my challenge—for FSU dates back to the time in hip hop history when *the media neglected to make the distinction between us, the artists who were committed to developing the art form, from them, the entertainers whose sole goal was to make money through producing and selling gangsta rap*. Freestyle Union began when gangsta rap was at the height of its popularity, partially as a response to, and reaction against, more violent forms of rap expression. At this same time, select political leaders and media began to attack rap music calling for a ban against it (some radio stations were so anti-rap that their announcers would advertise their commitment to not playing rap music). However, since the media inaccurately associated all forms of rap, rather than just gangsta rap, with violence, most clubs refused to book any rap acts, including those with a positive image and high level of artistry. *Artist-keepers-of-the-culture* were frustrated--the recording industry had chosen to exploit the violent, negative types of rap, shutting the door on artists and ideas that weren't considered "hard enough."

Since then, I am proud to cite Freestyle Union's numerous accomplishments, both artistically and educationally—a track record of accomplishments that positions me to succeed. In fact it was at one of the freestyle workshops in 1994 that jazz saxophonist Steve Coleman (BMG/Novus) first watched three of Freestyle Union's original members; since meeting, they've toured over thirteen countries, recorded professionally, and released their own album as "Opus Akoben" in Europe on BMG/RCA. These artists are no longer with FSU, but being involved with hip-hop in an organized community-focused way has been instrumental in the actualization process and the developing their identity as people who count. In 1995 I, along with Freestyle Union, received the Washington Area Music Association's Community Achievement Award and in 1996, a $5,000 individual City Arts Project grant from DC Commission on the Arts and Humanities.

As Freestyle Union had led the way in reaching young people through hip-hop, over time the organization has attracted and developed a series partnerships with local educators who see the importance of using hip-hop as a medium to discuss challenges and activate social consciousness. FSU has also sponsored workshops for a growing and diverse range of community partners, including Washington Performing Arts Society (WPAS), WritersCorps, Howard University, George Mason University, the Smithsonian Institution, the DC Area Writing Project, City Lights Project, and BMG/Rock the Vote. Out of one such partnership with the Network of Educators on the Americas (NECA), FSU established its own Educational Division. NECA, a grassroots leader in teacher re-training and anti-bias teaching, included FSU facilitators in the National Coalition of Educational Activists conference when it came to DC. They met with some of the country's most progressive educators and researchers to discuss the ways FSU addresses a new generation agenda and allows young people to have discourse about their communities..

I also look back with pride about my own artistic accomplishments. As my artistic voice has developed and been recognized, my artistry has grown and informed the work of FSU. Most recently, I was awarded the Mayor's Art Award for Outstanding Emerging Artist. As an avid and committed practitioner and scholar in hip-hop, I strive to lend credibility to my voice as a woman within the male-dominated rap world. I co-authored and performed in ACTCo's Arena Stage production of the *Hip Hop Nightmares of Jujube Brown*. My musical act has opened for a diverse range of pop artists incl. Ricki Lee Jones, the Lilith Fair, Wu Tang Clan, and Regina Belle and the Manhattans. I have a Master of Arts in organizational communication from Howard University-officially this May. My travels to international cities such as London were eye-opening--I have had the opportunity to witness and experience how much those of us in the U.S. hip hop movement have influenced artists in other places. My international experiences provide me with new artist/friends and connections, and with a more open attitude about the possibilities for developing hip hop in other countries.

Section IV. Organization/Project Proposal

1. Organization/Project Description

FSU works to achieve its mission through two components which serve hip hop artists, educators, and the broader public. Our main emphasis continues to be young people.

1.EDUCATIONAL DIVISION----

A) The Cipher Workshop continues to be the most important core activity. Since its inception in 1994, Freestyle Union has successfully sponsored and produced over 100 ciphers. Growing out of the original freestyle workshops, ciphers provide a creative training ground for artists to grow professionally, develop a sense of their own community, but also to furnish a meeting place where new artists are exposed to those who are established and touring. By sponsoring these monthly grassroots events held at locations throughout the metropolitan area, FSU continues to meet its mission to fill a vital social and artistic void for young people, particularly for developing artists. In the open, safe, non-competitive environment, I challenge artists to use rap poetry to analyze proverbs, debate current events, and practice storytelling. Over time, FSU has developed a unique menu of exercises to hone performance skills such as timing, focus, and rhythm, which include Bounce, First-word-last-word, Pick-it-up, and Quest Rhyme. As always, the challenge is to freestyle (improvise) on the spot. These exercises and related ground rules challenge and support participants rather than pressuring them to win.

The FSU Cipher has been covered by Fox News, local press, and national magazines. Such exposure prompted interest from hip-hop community organizers all over the country in cities such as Nashville, Sacramento, Raleigh, and Little Rock, who are interested in running their own ciphers.

The FSU cipher has converted a host of non-believers to understanding the power of hip-hop poetry. Teachers, poets, musicians and family members have attended ciphers and marveled at the verbal dexterity, poetic style and outstanding artistic skills involved in free-styling. Many have become advocates of hip-hop and supporters of Freestyle Union. Teachers have invited FSU artists to speak in their classrooms, asked for recommendations on music, and have even brought students to ciphers. The message that I convey is this: There are many young people who, for some reason, don't realize that the lyrics don't have to be violent to be cool. FSU says to them that it's okay to be who you are, to do what we do. Artists stay excited because they realize they are always opening eyes. There are parents and teachers who think that they hate rap. Once they understand it, they realize that rap has another side.

B)"Understanding Hip Hop" was developed to expose adult educators to the rich history and traditions of hip-hop music and increase understanding of contemporary youth culture. Inspired by working with Network of Educators on the Americas (NECA) in conjunction with their executive director Deborah Menkart, FSU has integrated its philosophy and experience by training a group of <u>facilitators</u>, or young artist/educators to conduct workshops about hip-hop and freestyling suitable for both adult educators and children. Menkart integrated these workshops into her teacher re-certification programs in DC Public and Montgomery County, MD school systems and also included them in conferences for educators. Since then, educators who wish to expose their students to positive aspects of rap music have invited FSU facilitators to conduct lecture demonstrations in their schools. The Educational Division 's workshops cover topics such as "Understanding Hip-hop" and the "Art of Freestyling." Recently FSU worked with 500 10th graders at Blair High School to understand the connections between hip-hop and Homer's <u>Odyssey</u>; out of this experience, the teacher has requested that Blair become a site for a national hip hop festival sponsored by the Washington Performing Arts Society, to take place in 1999. FSU's facilitators have held educational sessions with numerous groups including the Stanford Jazz Workshop in Palo Alto, California, Project Create, the WPAS' Nuyorican Residency, the Arlington Cultural Affairs Division, DC Public School Systems, George Mason University's PACE program, and at Musicwork's GhettoGrammar and the Oval Theater in London.

I know the role that education can play in building meaningful connections between hip hop, young people, and adults. Most of the facilitators came through the cyphers, so there is a constant connection to the culture--to create a stronger voice and sense of community understanding for hip hop that crosses age groups from young people to parents, from artists to teachers and venues from, schools to clubs to parks…We don't call it community service—we strive to create a whole, complete artist, whos understand the power of art, who take control of their community. With financial support we are going to be able to strengthen our curriculum concepts and ideas and better train youth educators.

New Developments in Education
Next summer, FSU will partner with the Empower Program, a nonprofit organization that addresses gender violence prevention, and the African Continuum Theater Company (ACTCo) to sponsor a 12-week *Girls Hip Hop Project*. By combining theater and improvisational poetry in a summer program, the Project will support and nurture female relationships and develop leadership within the hip-hop community. In addition to writing and performance workshops, the girls will meet with celebrity guest speakers monthly, culminating in a performance at Lincoln Theater. Next spring, the Education Division embarks on a new partnership with the **Arlington AIDS Project** to run a 10 week *hip-hop poetry series* for teen aged girls and boys, where they will be exposed to hip-hop culture, creative writing techniques, and receive risk reduction education with a culminating performance on World AIDS Day in December.

C) The Literary Division is a select group of artists within the corps who seek to document, publish and archive hip hop, capturing its unique perspectives and teachings. By proactively documenting their own art, the Literacy Division will capture the oral tradition of hip-hop in its truest and most accurate spirit. The Literary Division strives to convert the "source material" of hip-hop, such as street corner conversations and coffee shop chats, as well as the artistic process of hip hop--what artists do and how they do it-- into written form that can be shared with others. Because historically hip hop has not been documented by its own practitioners, there exists a gap in relevance and authenticity between academic writings which may be difficult to understand, if not irrelevant, as well as writings which promote a certain political agenda. To date, the activities of the Literary Division include:

- Toni Blackman has self-published three pieces on the art of freestyling.
- Jabari Exum, 16 yr. old artist/educator, is editing a booklet on what makes a good MC (rapper) to be distributed at the WPAS/Smithsonian Hip-hop Festival-Fall '99.

2. THE PERFORMANCE CORPS is a smaller ensemble of 15 artists who perform at community events, festivals and cipher demonstrations. Performance Corps artists are required to be 1)highly skilled lyricists, 2)show a commitment to the ideals and philosophies of FSU, and 3)go through FSU's ongoing artist development and training. In addition to attending intensive, advanced-level training sessions every other week. Any artist that benefits from FSU performance experiences must also commit teaching an agreed upon number of community workshops. The Freestyle Union Performance Corps has opened for the Last Poets (a poetry group famous since the 1960's), for Wu Tang Clan, the Georgia Aveune Festival, and at the Smithsonian Institutions 1998 Kwanzaa program. Each quarter Corps members volunteer to perform at community events and over the past two years have regularly done the DC Rape Crisis Center's *Take Back the Night Vigil*, several neighborhood Block parties for Peace, Martin Luther King Day events, Kwanzaa events, and fundraisers for non-profit organizations. We recently did the War Resisters League 75th Anniversary and committed to the Black-Latino Unity Fest

Purpose of Funding

FSU is requesting funding to support program development, staffing and general operations. In 1998-99, Freestyle Union is at a critical juncture where, with increased financial support, it is poised to take the next step towards stabilizing its internal structure. It is critical that until recently, Freestyle Union has been run solely by volunteers: Founding Artistic Director Toni Blackman, Administrator Adrea Parker, and Manager Janice Carrol. FSU is finalizing a 12-member advisory board, many of whom may become part of its official board. FSU's uniqueness has enabled it to attract dynamic interns and volunteer staff to help run ciphers, plan shows, coordinate community youth workshops, book community performances, write marketing materials, design graphics, and set-up collaborations between record companies and promoters.
By establishing a paid full-time position for me as founding artistic director and upgrading computer and administrative systems, FSU will ensure its continued growth. Within the next calendar year FSU intends to implement the following plan:

- Secure funding for the full-time paid position of executive director and other costs associated with staff growth.

- Establish systems for information and financial management, including database and other computerized forms.
- Develop new partnerships to generate earned income with such organizations as Empower, ACTCo, and WPAS.
- Maintain a schedule of regular meetings and communication with facilitators and the Performance Corps.
- Enhance, update and print marketing materials for wider and regular distribution.
- Through new communication mechanisms, such as a quarterly newsletter and website, increase communication with and support from friends, supporters, and parents.
- Provide professional development and training for select facilitators who will then conduct workshops and represent FSU publicly.

FSU is currently in the process of incorporating and filing for nonprofit status, which should be complete in the next several months (until then, FSU has arranged for fiscal sponsorship through another nonprofit organization). The advisory board will help with identifying funding strategies and sources as well as potential board members. Longer term goals are to:

- Hire booking personnel.
- Document FSU's work more extensively on video tape and audio tape.
- Purchasing four-track equipment in order to document the ciphers.
- Set up an intern training program to train young people to run grassroots arts organizations.
- Develop curriculum, research, teacher training materials for the Educational Division, about topics such as using hip hop to teach literature such as Odyssey.

Throughout the process of planning for Freestyle Union's organizational growth, it is vital for me to remember the importance of developing my own artistic voice. I wish to continue writing for theater as well as critical essays about hip-hop. I want to continue to perform music in both traditional and nontraditional settings, and to consider recording my music.

2. Community/Constituency Ties and Connections

Existing Community Partners
Earlier sections of this proposal cite numerous past successful partnerships with
community organizations (see page 3). Currently, Freestyle Union brings existing
relationships with the following community partners.

African Continuum Theater Company (*ACTCo*). *ActCo* will provide drama training for
the Girls Hip-Hop Program; a collaboration with Empower. ActCo will also produce a
new performance work, *Blowin' Up,* in the spring of 1999.

Arlington County Cultural Affairs Division and Arlington AIDS Project. These two
divisions of the county government partnered with FSU to bring in Toni Blackman and
younger FSU educator, J. Brisbane, as Artist-in-Residence. FSU teen members will also
be a part of this fall's series of workshops. The Cultural Affairs Division has also booked
corps members for its "Say the Word" Performance Series.

Empower Program (*Empower)* will provide the gender violence prevention component of
the Girls Hip-Hop Program. The FSU male trainers will go through their male program
prior to the start of the project.

Network of Educators on the Americas (*NECA*) NECA will continue to serve as an
advisor to the Educational Division of FSU and has offered to serve as the fiscal agent for
FSU while it goes through the 501C(3) filing process.

Washington Performing Arts Society (*WPAS*) The Washington Performing Arts Society
identified FSU as a partner for the Nuyorican Residency and $400,000 Lila Wallace
Community Partnership grant. This WPAS initiative connected FSU with key advisor Liz
Lerman and Carla Perlo of Dance Place who subsequently is bringing in FSU to work with
their summer youth program, the Energizers. WPAS has been and will continue to be
instrumental in widening FSU's audience demographics.

Support with Organizational Development: Key Advisors
*   Melissa Bradley, formerly of The Entreprenuerial Development Institute-TEDI,
    serves as my business advisor.
*   Lisa Sullivan of L.I.S.T.E.N. functions as an organizational consultant and Liz
    Lerman of Dance Exchange a mentor.
*   Suzanne Callahan of Callahan Consulting for the Arts (formerly of the NEA) offers
    pro-bono services and Kim Chan of WPAS have been instrumental in this phase of
    Freestyle Union's development. Callahan has assisted with resource development
    and Chan with administrative planning.

Action Plan

Fall
-Participate in the 3wk. WPAS/Smithsonian Hip Hop, Spoken Word, Dance Festival
-Host Cipher Workshop in October for "Domestic Violence Awareness Month"
-Continue Program Development: Have Curriculum reviewed by consultants and advisors
-Interview and Hire Organizational Intern
-Formalize Board Set-up
-Complete Fundraising for StepAfrica Festival Trip to South Africa
-Develop Marketing Materials for 2000
-Develop Train-the-trainer curriculum for artist-educators in the corps
-Meet with advisors to critique overall plan, solidify financial mgmt. system and research funding
-Monthly organizational meetings with artists
-Research Possibilities for Summer 2000 cultural exchange w/ London, U.K.

Winter
-Continue marketing, organizational planning & monthly meetings
-Have successful performance & community workshops in South Africa (Dec.)
-Begin Intensive Train-the-trainer training with corps artists (Public Speaking/ Teaching/Conflict Resolution/ Sound Labs/Artist Development/Gender Violence Prev.)
-Expand fundraising efforts
-Meet with community based organizations and identify potential sites for FSU workshops
-Artist Residency w/ University of Michigan (Toni and 2 FSU facilitators/Work in Detroit Area)

Spring
-Participate & Consult w/ Latino International Hip-Hop Conference @ Miami-Dade College in Miami (Toni and FSU Facilitators)
-Finalize curriculum
-Spring programs begin: Potential partners incl. Us Helping Us, an AIDS prevention project for African-American Males and the Independent Living Program
-Review organizational goals and identify strategic planning consultant
-Professional Development for Executive Director

Summer
-Identify and/or hire booking personnel (for workshops & performances)
-Run the Girls Hip Hop Project w/ the Empower Program
-Update print marketing materials
-FSU facilitators and youth educators participate in cultural exchange with London artists
-Solidify bookings for community workshops, lectures, & schools
-Enhance performance calendar
-identify new youth to bring into the fold

Freestyle Union Budget

	TOTALS	Notes
Expenses:		
Salaries	28,200.00	$XXXXX for Executive Director and $XXXXX for p/t admin $XXXXX in honoraria for ED
Fringe Benefits	4,250.00	For Executive Director
Consultant & Professional Fees	25,150.00	Consultants & honoraria for resource dev., database design, workshop facilitators, newsletter writers, Web design & maintenance, & staff @ ciphers
Travel	8,092.00	Roundtrip btwn. DC & Balt., NYC, S.Africa & various univeristies
Euqipment	3,000.00	To purchase state of the art computer & laser printer
Supplies	177.00	ADAT tape to record/produce Freestyle U. CD/cassette
Printing & Copying	5,573.00	For quarterly newsletter & FSU marketing materials to generate performance & educational work & for audiences & for workshop materials in Baltimore & DC
Telephone & Fax	2,100.00	avg. 180 per/mos. (Booking/Workshop Planning)
Postage & Delivery	2,978.00	To distribute new communication mechanisms (newsletters, press kits, communication w/ FSU members & solicit individual donors)
Rent	4,170.00	For meetings, ciphers, workshops, rehearsals, events
Utilities		
Maintenance		
Evaluation		
Other (specify)		
Publicity (photos/promo)	400.00	For CD & Cassette
CD/Cassette Manufacturing	3,040.00	
Hospitality	500.00	For individual donor event
World Wide Web Server	500.00	Est. @ $50/month for 12 months
Computer Software	500.00	For web-site software, Quicken, Excel & Access
Computer Training	1,200.00	2 days of training in ea. Software for E.D. est. @ 150 per/day
Total Expenses	90,190.00	

Revenue:

Grants& Contracts		
Government	10,000.00	From DC Commission for ARTS EDUCATION work
Fellowships	30,000.00	echoing green
Foundations	28,000.00	$15,000 secured from Meyer; estimated $5000 -Community Foundation; $3,000-George Preston Marshall Foundation; $5000-Ms.Foundation;
Corporations		
United Way/Combined		
Earned Income		
Individuals	1200.00	From individual donor event
Events	360.00	For 2 ciphers
Publications/Products	4,800.00	For CD/Cassette Sales (estimate 400 @ $12)
ACTCO & Empower	8,000.00	For community workshops & performances (secured)
WPAS	4,000.00	For co-producing festival & participating in cultural exchange (secured)
NECA	800.00	Honoria for 5 events @ $250 ea.
NYC Nuyorican Cafe	1,400.00	Artist Fees for 4 performances
In-Kind Support	1,630.00	From Dance Exchange for space at ciphers
Total Revenue	90,190.00	

A Proposal From
Matthew Lee and Fair Finance Watch
Bronx, New York

To
Echoing Green
New York, New York

Requested amount: $30,000 for each year of a two-year fellowship;
Amount received: $30,000 for each year of a two-year fellowship

Funder's comments:

"At Echoing Green, our application guidelines may vary from year to year, so it's very important that grantseekers check for the current version. Today's applicants can only submit their initial applications from our Web site (www.echoinggreen.org). We're strict about adherence to our guidelines, since this is one way to level the playing field for all applicants. For example, if someone submits more than the required number of letters of recommendation we will not include the additional letters in the grant application package.

"At Echoing Green we help launch leaders, and people are starting off at different places in the process. We assess proposals on a case-by-case basis; so that could mean that a start-up is just an idea on a scrap of paper, or it could be a recognized 501(c)(3). In general, two years of formalized activity is the maximum to qualify for our fellowships. What matters to us is seeing passion, energy, leadership, and strong community ties. And it's not just, 'Oh, I love children.' It's taking a stance on something that's more specific, because our interest is to seed new and innovative ideas that will address seemingly intractable social problems.

"Matthew's application is very concise and very clear. He has incorporated a statement of need into the section entitled 'The Communities and Constituencies To Be Served.' His use of statistics is excellent, revealing that he had done original research to document the need. He is educating us by giving background about the community. Our grant applications are read by both generalists and by topic specialists, so providing background information on a topic is important. Matthew's application makes perfect sense, even to someone who does not have a financial background. He is careful to explain any acronyms he uses.

"His quarterly timeline is also excellent. He has sequenced the steps in the process, and we look closely at this practical aspect of the application.

"Though we'd prefer not to see anything handwritten on the budget, this budget showed where he intends to seek additional funding, or has already, as well as in-kind support. So he's demonstrating in the budget that other funders know and respect his work.

"Matthew's letters of recommendation were amazing. Applicants need to think closely about letters of recommendation. A generic, nonspecific letter of recommendation from a notable person does not necessarily provide necessary and relevant information. The most compelling letters come from people who know the applicants in their leadership roles—have experienced their leadership, even. For example, if the request relates to a youth organization, I like to see letters from young people, or their parents."

Lara Galinsky, Vice President, Strategy, Echoing Green

Notes:
The complete proposal included the following attachments: resume and letters of recommendation, which are not included here.
Proposal written and submitted to the funder by Matthew Lee.

Echoing Green Public Service Fellowship 2000 – 2002
Application Cover Sheet

Last Name Lee   First Name Matthew

Street Address 703 East 187th Street, #1D

City Bronx   State NY   Country U.S.A.   Zip 10458

Day phone 718-716-2700   Evening phone 718-364-2092

Fax 718-716-3161 (c/o)   E-mail innercity1@aol.com

◆ ◆ ◆ ◆ ◆ ◆

Complete if you are applying through a 501(c)(3) organization, including fiscal sponsor:

Name of Organization (Fiscal sponsor) Inner City Press / Community on the Move, Inc.

Street Address 1919 Washington Avenue

City Bronx   State NY   Country U.S.A.   Zip 10457

Day phone 718-716-3540   Evening phone

Fax 718-716-3161   E-mail

◆ ◆ ◆ ◆ ◆ ◆

Where is your project based?

City Bronx   State NY   Country U.S.A.

Where are the communities or constituencies your project serves?

City _____ Low income communities in New York and beyond. _____
            State _____ Country _____

Please check the **one** category that most accurately describes your project:

❑ Arts, culture, humanities   ❑ Employment   ❑ Civil and Human Rights
❑ Education   ❑ Food, nutrition, agriculture ☒ Community improvement/Economic
❑ Environment   ❑ Housing   development
❑ Health   ❑ Youth development

Please check the **one** population served that best fits your constituency:

❑ Senior Citizens   ☒ Economically Disadvantaged   ❑ Racial/
❑ Alcohol/Drug Abusers   ❑ Sexual Minorities   Ethnic Minorities
❑ Children and Adolescents   ❑ Immigrants and Refugees   ❑ Offenders and Ex-Offenders
❑ Persons with Disabilities ❑ Men and boys   ❑ People with AIDS
                             ❑ Women and girls   ❑ Parents

If none of the above categories apply, please leave the section blank.

Fiscal Sponsor Form

Inner City Press/Community ^{on the} (the "Fiscal Sponsor") hereby acknowledges that it has entered
(Name of Fiscal Sponsor) Move, Inc.

into an agreement with _____Matthew Lee_____ (the "Fellow") to take on the Fellow's
(Name of Fellow)

project, Inner City Public Interest Law Center (the "Project"). The Fiscal Sponsor agrees that
(Name of Fellow's Project)

all funds distributed to it by the Echoing Green Foundation are to be expended solely for the purposes

stated in the Fellow's Echoing Green Fellowship Application. The Fiscal Sponsor also agrees that the

expenditure of such funds will be controlled exclusively by the Fellow, except for fees of the Fiscal

Sponsor expressly stated in the attached written agreement between the Fiscal Sponsor and the Fellow.

Name of fiscal sponsor: Inner City Press/Community on the Move

_____
~~(Name of Fiscal Sponsor)~~

_____
~~(Signature of Authorized Officer)~~
Iliana Itzkowitz

_____Chairperson_____
~~(Print Name)~~ Title

_____
(Title)

Attach a copy of (1) the written sponsorship agreement between the Fiscal Sponsor and the Fellow and (2) the
Fiscal Sponsor's letter from the Internal Revenue Service determining the Fiscal Sponsor to be an organization
described in Section 501(c)(3) of the Internal Revenue Code.

Concept Paper to Echoing Green (Revised, February 16, 2000)

Matthew Lee: Inner City Public Interest Law Institute

I.   Project Goals

My project will enforce the New York State and federal Community Reinvestment Acts ("CRA" -- laws requiring banks to serve low- and moderate-income ["LMI"] neighborhoods), particularly on cutting-edge issues that might not otherwise be worked on: Internet banks (which have the potential to exclude most residents of LMI neighborhoods), high interest rate, predatory mortgage lending, and discrimination in the provision of homeowners and other types of insurance. I have resided and been a community activist in the South Bronx since 1987, and became a lawyer in 1997. Longer term, the Inner City Public Interest Law Institute I plan to establish will also work on the problem of the "digital divide" (communities being left behind by the information super-highway), and even on banking-related human rights issues.

II.   The Communities and Constituencies To Be Served

In the first instance, and at a minimum, my project will act to enforce the CRA in the lower-income communities of color in New York City: the South Bronx, Upper Manhattan, North Brooklyn. While credit and insurance may be fairly available in New York City in the borough of Manhattan below 96th Street, and in pockets of the outer boroughs, in the above-named sections of New York City, there are few bank branches or insurance agents, but numerous check cashiers, loan sharks, and other high interest rate lenders. I recently completed a study of bank branches by borough. Here is a summary:

1

Area	Population	Branches	Pop / Branch
Manhattan	1,428,000	481	2,969
Bronx	1,169,000	102	11,461
S. Bronx	450,000	23	19,565
Brooklyn	2,301,000	244	9,430
Queens	1,952,000	328	5,951

Due to the lack of bank branches among other factors, it is more difficult for the residents of the South Bronx, Upper Manhattan and Northern Brooklyn to obtain credit at normal terms. These areas have become targeted for higher than normal interest rate credit, even to people who would qualify for normal interest rate loans. When people cannot buy a home or an apartment, when businesses cannot get loans or insurance to expand, communities decline, along with employment and educational opportunities. I intend to use administrative advocacy, public education, investigative journalism, and litigation, to focus and raise the profile of these issues, seeking their solution.

My project will also enforce CRA in other low-income and minorities communities (I intend to provide legal representation and advice to community groups in other cities, and will expand that work beyond CRA to also address the digital divide); the later human rights initiative I am planning would have an even wider focus. But the South Bronx will be its base.

III.   **Project Description: Process and Action Plan**

I will attack these problems by documenting the lack of access to fair credit and insurance in low income communities of color in NYC: the South Bronx, Upper Manhattan, and North Brooklyn, and filing administrative challenges with NYS and federal regulators on applications by institutions which are part of the problem.

2

The process: Community Reinvestment Act advocacy at present centers around challenges to particular bank mergers. While a community group may be concerned about the performance of a number of banks in its area, the opportunity for most effective advocacy arrives when one of these banks seeks to expand, most often by merger. (In fact, the CRA is **only** enforced in connection with bank expansion proposals. *See* 12 U.S.C. § 2903 (2)). The work involves researching and analyzing the bank's lending record, using Home Mortgage Disclosure Act ("HMDA") and CRA (small business lending) data, reviewing the bank's merger application, and, where applicable, submitting a formal challenge within the 30 day comment period. Often, before or after such a challenge is filed, a community group will meet and negotiate with the bank, seeking to address the deficiencies in the bank's lending record. If an agreement is reached, this should be reduced to clear, legally-enforceable language. The Financial Services Modernization Act (signed into law in November 1999) now allows bank and insurance company mergers, and requires the community groups engaged in advocacy report to bank regulators on their activities, making it even more important for grassroots community groups to have legal advice and/or representation, and making the Echoing Green fellowship I am applying for particularly timely.

I track the Federal Register, business news wires, and regulatory agency announcements and rule-making daily on the Internet, and will bring opportunities to the attention of community groups and neighborhood residents. I will launch a project-specific web site, to perform information dissemination and other functions. The site will have a how-to guide to enforcing the CRA and fair lending laws, links to the regulatory agencies' lists of pending merger applications, and to sources of HMDA and other useful data. The site will also cover the emerging issue of how communities can obtain data reflecting the fairness of insurance underwriting in their neighborhoods, and how communities can seek to address the issue of the digital divide.

3

Since submitting my initial Concept Paper in October 1999, I have filed and/or provided legal representation for other grassroots community groups to file, challenges to four banks and their lending records, as well as a "digital divide" (and antitrust) challenge to the pending MCI WorldCom - Sprint merger. I have written for publication in the American Banker newspaper an article about Internet banks and CRA: I am slated to make a presentation on this topic in Washington on March 21, 2000, at the annual conference of the National Community Reinvestment Coalition, on whose board of directors I serve. The federal Office of Thrift Supervision has granted the hearing request I filed on an insurance company's application for a new Internet bank. I am conferring with community groups in Alaska, preparing to file the first CRA challenge from that state, on a pending merger. The major policy issue is that the largest bank in Alaska limited its CRA assessment area (and duty) to only the cities, while soliciting deposits from rural areas, without serving these communities' credit needs. I am also preparing comments on the first cross-industry merger triggered by the financial deregulation legislation, stock brokerage Schwab's proposal to acquire U.S. Trust Corporation and its bank, which is focused only on the most affluent customers. As reflected in the attached budget, "revenues in hand" include $15,000 from the Surdna Foundation, received in February 2000, for nationwide CRA advocacy, with particular focus on such cross-industry mergers. The time is propitious for the requested seed money from echoing green. Here is the plan of action:

IV.   Evaluation -- **Timeline of Project Activities**

The impact of the project will be measured quarterly, against the following goals:

Months 1-3 (Q1): represent at least two groups/communities in bank challenges or other CRA advocacy, reaching at least one lending commitment; represent one group/community on insurance or telecommunications challenges; begin project-specific web site.

4

Months 4-6 (Q2): represent at least two groups/communities in bank challenges or other CRA advocacy, reaching at least one lending commitment; represent two groups/communities on insurance or telecommunications challenges, resulting in at least one agreement.

Months 7-9 (Q3): represent at least two more groups/communities in CRA and/or telecom advocacy, reaching at least one agreement; intervene / participate in another insurance proceeding, either on a merger / conversion or as a complaint filed with HUD under the Fair Housing Act.

Months 10-12 (Q4): complete training of three community groups, and/or help them establish an ongoing relationship with a local Legal Service / public interest law office; represent two new groups in CRA / insurance / telecom advocacy, reaching at least one agreement.

Months 13-15 (Q5): represent three groups (two from previous "CRA" clients) in telecom and insurance advocacy; have established more funding streams: foundation grants, attorneys fees, sliding scale retainers.

Months 16-18 (Q6): complete training of three more community groups, and/or help them establish an ongoing relationship with a local Legal Service / public interest law office; represent three new groups in CRA / insurance / telecom advocacy, reaching two agreements; complete and publish a how-to reinvestment law manual (two versions: one for lawyers, another for *pro se* community activists).

In months 19-24, I will use the lessons and successes of the first six quarters to push the work further, ideally registering the Institute as a non-governmental organization in consultancy with the United Nations and its Committee on Economic, Social and Cultural Rights. An issue I am already tracking and researching is how to bring scrutiny to multinational banks' and investment banks' undue control over developing nations, through their status as holders of Brady bonds and otherwise. CRA and regulatory expertise will be helpful in bringing these banking/human rights issues into the public debate.

5

h. Lee

Echoing Green Public Service Fellowship 2000

BUDGET FORM FOR PHASE II OF APPLICATION

REVENUES AND EXPENSES FOR TWO PROJECT YEARS: SEPTEMBER 1, 2000 – AUGUST 31, 2002					
	2000-01	2001-02		2000-01	2001-02
Revenues			**Expenses**		
A. Current Revenues					
Revenues in hand (list sources and amounts)			Salaries (specify)		
Surdna Foundation(2/00)	15,000		Attorney-director	XXXXX	XXXXX
			Assistant		XXXXX
			Professional Services		
			Rent	in-kind	12,000
Current in-kind support (list type of support and sources)			Utilities	in-kind	2,000
			Telephone	3,000	3,000
			Insurance	1,000	1,000
Inner City Press (space	4,000		Furnishings and supplies	1,500	2,000
Richard Pinner (compu-			Equipment	1,000	4,000
ter 2/2000)	500		Other (specify)		
B. Projected revenues			Research & web	1,000	2,000
Echoing Green	30,000	30,000	Travel	1,000	3,000
Other (list sources and amounts)					
Open Society Inst. Fellowship (app. 2/25	30,000	30,000			
Stanford PILF (app. due 3/1/00)	5,000				
Surdna		15,000			
OSI Law & Society		40,000			
Projected in-kind support (list type of support and sources)					
Inner City Press					
Vol. law students					
Vol. Bronx residents					
(also "in hand")					
Total revenues	84,500*	115,000	Total expenses	XXXXX	XXXXX
*- incl. projected/hoped for in hand = $19,500					XXXXX

NOTE: The first year budget is bare-bones; while the work would be possible at this amount, I anticipate raising other funds (incl. attorneys fees) - I could use Echoing Green's advice on further fundraising.

7

Planning Grant

Planning grants typically support efforts such as goal setting, information gathering, needs assessment, consensus and coalition building, or planning for a larger project. The projects under consideration may involve complex community collaborations.

Some foundations may follow up a planning grant with funds to carry out the actual implementation. In that case, the planning grant proposal is one step in the establishment of a partnership. But other funders do not feel the need to assist in the implementation phase and simply provide support for the planning. Grantseekers will want to inquire about the possibility of follow-up funding in advance of submitting the proposal.

For the grantseeker working on a proposal for a planning grant, the challenge is that much is unknown, and therefore it is difficult to predict tangible outcomes, timing, and costs. Indeed, determining these details may well be one of the objectives of the planning process.

This chapter reprints the application from Community Food Resource Center in New York to the New York Foundation for a planning grant in the amount of $35,000. The Resource Center sought to design an advocacy initiative that would promote earned income tax credits for low income citizens. It utilized the New York/New Jersey Area Common Application Form to present the request.

A Proposal From

Community Food Resource Center, Inc.

New York, New York

To

New York Foundation

New York, New York

Requested amount: $35,000; **Amount received:** $35,000

Funder's comments:

"The organization used the New York/New Jersey Area Common Application Form but didn't stick to it entirely. Where they veered from the format, they actually made the proposal stronger. The Common Application Form is a useful tool, but groups should not feel a slave to it! This is a case where the group had to talk about a very complicated, mind-numbing issue—earned income tax credits. How do you make that at all interesting and compelling? Some of the hardest proposals to read are those that use a lot of jargon or require the reader to have a certain level of expertise in order to even understand the basic premise. This proposal managed to educate the reader about a complex technical issue, make a case for its importance, and even convince you that they had a solid plan to tackle the problem.

"The components of the proposal were very well-balanced. This is a great example of how you can say a great deal in only five pages. They zeroed right in on what the problem was and how they proposed to deal with it. Even though they needed to set the context using a lot of statistics and technical terms, the need statement couldn't be clearer. The proposal didn't need to make use of any particular graphics or presentation tricks to make its point. The budget could have used more detail—the scope of work seems much broader than the budget reflects. In fact, this project has grown, and in its second year the budget topped $300,000!

"Attachments focused on a national campaign to get people to file for EI tax credits. This was helpful because it made it clear that Community Food Resource Center was not operating in a vacuum but was collaborating with similar efforts across the country. It also helped to know they were getting their information from credible experts on the federal level."

Maria Mottola, Executive Director, New York Foundation

Notes:

This proposal was written using the New York/New Jersey Area Common Application Form. The complete proposal included the following attachments: list of board members, IRS tax-exempt letter, current organization budget, project budget, brief resumes of key staff, copies of English and Spanish language brochures, copies of texts of radio ads and hotline message, article from *Newsday*, and the Center on Budget and Policy Priorities' EITC campaign kit.

Proposal written and submitted to the funder by Amy Brown, Director of Program Planning.

New York Area Common Application Form
Cover Sheet
Please feel free to make copies of this form or generate this one-page
cover sheet on your computer.

Date of application: <u>August 21, 2001</u>

Name of organization to which grant would be paid. Please list exact legal name.
<u>Community Food Resource Center, Inc.</u>

Purpose of grant (one sentence): <u>CFRC is requesting a $35,000 planning grant to enable us to design an</u>
<u>organizing and advocacy initiative to promote tax credits (especially the Earned Income Tax Credit) for</u>
<u>low-income New Yorkers.</u>

Address of organization: <u>39 Broadway, 10th floor, New York, NY 10006</u>

Telephone number: <u>212-894-8094</u>

Executive Director: <u>Kathy Goldman</u>

Contact person and title (if not Executive Director): <u>Amy Brown, Director of Program Planning</u>

Is your organization an IRS 501(c)(3) not-for-profit? (yes or no) <u>yes</u>

If no, please explain:

Grant request: <u>$35,000 planning grant</u>

Check one: General support   Project support X

Total organization budget (for current year): <u>$5.5 million</u>

Dates covered by this budget (mo/day/year): <u>July 1, 2001 – June 30, 2002</u>

Total project budget (if requesting project support): <u>$35,114</u>

Dates covered by project budget (mo/day/year): <u>November 2001 – April 2002</u>

Project name (if applicable): <u>EITC Campaign</u>

I. PROPOSAL SUMMARY

Founded in 1980 to fight hunger, CFRC has grown to become one of the city's leading advocates for equitable policies and practices affecting poor New Yorkers. CFRC is requesting a $35,000 planning grant to develop a new advocacy initiative to promote tax credits (especially the Earned Income Tax Credit) for low-income New Yorkers. A six-month planning grant will allow us to design an organizing and advocacy initiative aimed at achieving the following five goals:

1) Increasing the number of low-income New Yorkers who receive tax credits by promoting outreach efforts to populations less likely to receive them, such as immigrants and families moving from welfare to work.

2) Allowing low-income New Yorkers easier access to the credits by developing a structure for expanding the availability of free tax-filing assistance in low-income neighborhoods.

3) Increasing the dollar value of tax credits available to low-income New Yorkers by promoting the creation of a city Earned Income Tax Credit (EITC) and expansion of state credits.

4) Building recognition of the role tax credits play in anti-poverty efforts and creating a local constituency for advocacy around these benefits.

5) Coordinating with efforts on the federal level, in particular by the Center on Budget and Policy Priorities, to improve tax benefits for low-income filers and simplify the tax code.

Because of the large number of eligible workers and the significant size of refunds available, an EITC organizing and advocacy initiative has the potential to have a far-reaching effect on poverty in New York City. Over the past several months, CFRC has laid the groundwork for a campaign by researching the issues, learning more about efforts in Washington and across the country, and meeting with unions, community groups and other potential partners. Our initial efforts have made clear both the need for this initiative and the potential for its impact. *We believe that a significant and focused EITC initiative is a critical missing element in New York City anti-poverty efforts.*

II. NARRATIVE

A. Background

Community Food Resource Center (CFRC) is dedicated to helping low-income New Yorkers gain and maintain access to nutritious food, adequate income, and decent housing. Founded in 1980 to fight hunger, CFRC has grown to become one of the city's leading advocates for equitable government policies and practices affecting poor New Yorkers. We promote Food Stamps and public assistance benefits as well as children's food programs as essential benefits for families and individuals who do not earn enough through wages, are not able to work, or are transitioning from welfare to work.

Generally speaking, the population that we serve is the two million poorest residents of New York City. These "clients" are mostly minorities (African American, Latino, and Asian) who do not have enough income to support themselves and their families and are facing the brunt of federal, state, and city welfare reform measures. Included among them are the homeless, elderly, disabled, single parents, children, unemployed, working poor, and immigrants.

Our programs fall into two categories: advocacy and direct service. Our advocacy programs are directed in the areas of:

- *Access to Benefits* — analyzes legislation, regulations, and administrative practices associated with poverty, welfare, and Food Stamp issues to determine their impact on the two million New Yorkers living in poverty.
- *Child Nutrition* — works to ensure greater access and use of breakfast and lunch in the public schools and in the summer meals program and to improve children's eating habits.
- *Community Media Project* — this award-winning project produces programs for airing on Manhattan Neighborhood Network, submits articles to community newspapers discussing important issues for low-income New Yorkers, and provides training in video production to community members.

Our direct service programs include:

- *Community Kitchen of West Harlem (252 W. 116th St.)* — in operation since 1984, offers 600+ free, nutritious dinner meals each weekday evening, including 100 meals delivered to homebound seniors.
- *Entitlements Clinic (next to Kitchen)* — provides information, referral, and direct case assistance on Food Stamps, housing, SSI, and other issues to 500 Harlem households yearly.
- *Community Culinary Training Center* — started in January 2001, this project trains approximately 40 adults annually for entry-level employment in the food service industry using our kitchen facility. Eighteen adults graduated in the first six months, and graduates are earning between $7.50 and $15.00 per hour.
- *Eviction Prevention Teams (located in welfare centers)* — provide crisis intervention to assistance families with children at risk of becoming homeless each year to prevent their having to enter the city's shelter system. In 2000, staff handled 3,976 cases, closing 1,999 and preventing the evictions of 1,770 families.
- *Food Stamp Outreach Teams* — travel to more than 400 food pantries, senior and day care centers, and other public sites citywide to pre-screen people for Food Stamps and other benefit eligibility. During 2000, staff provided almost 25,000 households with information about Food Stamps and computer pre-screened 8,068 households. Of these, we anticipate that 6,813 are potentially eligible for Food Stamps.
- *Senior Meals Program* — operates two dinner programs, one each in Harlem and the Lower East Side, serving 225 meals a day using public school facilities and providing educational and recreational activities. The Harlem site includes an Intergenerational Program, which

2

provides educational, cultural, and recreational activities for 42 youngsters between the ages of 6 and 15 years.

CFRC has 69 full-time staff; 19 part-time staff; 15 other staff who receive stipends (such as our teen interns who work at the Community Kitchen); and 5 volunteers.

CFRC staff provides leadership and time to a number of coalitions comprised of advocacy, legal, housing, educational, health, and social service organizations, and occasionally, government agencies. For some of these coalitions, this effort requires reviewing data, identifying significant issues, meeting with government representatives and elected officials, talking with the media, preparing information packages, and chairing coalition meetings. These coalitions include the Welfare Reform Network, New York City Food Stamp and Welfare Task Forces, the New York City Coalition Against Hunger, the Ad Hoc Coalition for Real Jobs, and WIC Coalition.

We differ from other organizations in that we combine advocacy/policy and direct service to address the underlying issues that prevent poor New Yorkers from meeting their basic needs for food and nutrition, income support, and decent housing. Through our ongoing contact with thousands of low-income families and individuals, we develop advocacy/policy positions and propose changes to government programs affecting poor New Yorkers. Our statistical and anecdotal information is crucial to CFRC's development of new ways of addressing the needs of people living in poverty.

B. Funding Request

Purpose, Need and Population to Benefit

In the past few years, as welfare rolls have plummeted, we have begun to focus more on the working poor. These New Yorkers work sporadically, part-time, or even full-time at low-wage jobs. Reductions in government benefits, combined with the added costs of going to work (such as childcare, transportation, and clothing) mean that they are often worse off than families who remain on welfare.

The Earned Income Tax Credit (EITC) is the largest single income boost available to working poor families. The federal EITC was worth up to $3,888 for tax year 2000, and New York State offers its own credit worth 22.5% of the federal EITC. (Workers may be single or married, with or without children. Workers do not need to be employed full-time or year-round.) In addition, the recent tax cuts passed by Congress include expansion of the EITC for married families and a significant new Refundable Child Tax Credit available to most of the same families who are eligible for the EITC. Furthermore, because the credits are refundable, even workers who do not owe taxes can get a check from the IRS.

Last year, 1.2 million families in New York State received over $2 billion from the federal EITC. But they are only a portion of those eligible, and many groups are especially unlikely to request an EITC. A recent survey found, for example, that only 4% of non-English speaking low-income Hispanic parents had ever received the EITC, compared with 43% of all low-income parents. New workers are also less likely to receive the credit, including the more than half a million New Yorkers who have left welfare in the past five years.

A related issue is the need for free tax filing assistance. Tax forms can be intimidating to the most experienced filer, and many workers are afraid to claim tax credits for fear of doing something wrong. The recent tax changes bring new rules and additional forms, exponentially increasing the complexity of filing. Last year the IRS listed only 15 sites in Manhattan and the Bronx offering free income tax assistance. Many were open only a few hours each week. Because free filing is not

3

available, many low-income workers use paid tax preparers who charge high fees (as much as $65 per page or form) and encourage filers to take out loans — at interest rates of up to 180% — in anticipation of a refund.

While tax credits are not new, this issue is especially important *now* because of two critical factors:

1) An increasing number of low-income working families are struggling to make ends meet, and the EITC is the single most significant government program that can move these families out of poverty. (A study by the National Center for Children in Poverty found that the EITC reduces poverty among young children by nearly one-fourth.)

2) The large tax-cut recently signed by President Bush significantly expands federal tax credits (including a *new* Refundable Child Tax Credit and increases in the EITC for married families) but also *greatly* complicates the rules for filing, making it more difficult for families — especially immigrant and non-traditional families — to access the benefits.

Activities to Date

CFRC has already done a great deal of legwork towards developing an EITC organizing and advocacy initiative. This work has given us insight into how the credits operate and where the advocacy needs lie. Activities to date include research and analysis, conversations with potential partners, and small-scale outreach and tax preparation assistance.

- **Research and analysis:** We began by learning about the EITC, how it works, who is eligible and how much money they can receive. We met with staff from the Center on Budget and Policy Priorities, a Washington-based organization that coordinates a national campaign to get local groups to promote the EITC. The Center has encouraged CFRC to pursue a New York-based effort and has offered to provide advice and materials. Most recently, we participated in a meeting in Washington with representatives from 25 initiatives from around the country to discuss the increasing importance of EITC advocacy and future challenges for EITC campaigns.

- **Meetings and conversations with potential local partners:** We met with a variety of individuals and groups to inform them about the EITC and discuss opportunities to work together. These groups include elected officials, community-based organizations and advocacy groups, and several labor unions. Most people were only vaguely familiar with the tax credits and were surprised by the amount of money workers could potentially receive. All expressed an interest in finding ways to work together on an EITC initiative.

- **Media work:** We publicized the EITC through our Community Media Project, including distributing an article about the credit in multiple languages to our database of over 400 community newspapers. Several articles were published in a variety of languages, including English, Spanish and Bengali. The response was so strong that the IRS asked us to stop providing their EITC information number — they were deluged with calls as a result of our media exposure!

- **Outreach and tax preparation assistance:** We trained more than 20 line staff in the EITC and distributed information about the EITC through our Food Force (Food Stamp outreach), CHAT (eviction prevention), and Entitlements Clinic projects, which together see thousands of clients each month. We coordinated with the IRS and the Retired Senior Volunteer Program to provide free tax filing assistance at our Entitlements Clinic, which is located in Harlem. We had a great response from community members, many of whom would otherwise have had to pay a large portion of their refund to a for-profit tax preparation service.

4

Proposed Activities

CFRC will use the planning grant from the New York Foundation to develop an EITC advocacy initiative. The following activities will lay the groundwork for a campaign with the potential to bring millions of dollars to hundreds of thousands of low-income New Yorkers.

1. **Research and data analysis to:**
   - identify all tax benefits available to working poor New Yorkers and, in particular, which groups of New Yorkers are least likely to receive them.
   - calculate the financial benefit that the EITC provides to New York's low-income communities as well as the financial loss from less-than-full use of the credits.
   - understand why so few sites provide free tax-filing assistance to low-income New Yorkers, the extent to which they are used, and how this service might be expanded.

2. **Organizing and outreach, including:**
   - outreach to national groups and groups in other regions to learn more about successful models and best practices for EITC organizing and advocacy.
   - raising awareness among elected officials, the public, and the private sector of the role tax credits play in reducing poverty and supporting the local economy.
   - organizing among potential local partners, including anti-poverty organizations, immigrant groups, labor unions, utilities, supermarkets and other groups.
   - conversations with local IRS offices and their EITC staff to learn of their activities and plans and coordinate future efforts.

3. **Identification of strategies that might be part of a large campaign, for example:**
   - increasing EITC information and outreach, especially during tax season, through the media and in partnership with groups that reach a wide audience (e.g., inserts in utility bills).
   - creating a local toll-free hotline for tax credit information and assistance. (Currently, residents must dial the general IRS number, which handles all tax issues and is constantly busy.)
   - working with unions that represent large numbers of low-wage workers (e.g., 1199-SEIU represents 40,000 home health care workers who earn approximately $7.00 per hour).
   - sending notices to targeted groups likely to be eligible for the credits (such as those who have left welfare or those receiving childcare or health insurance through a government program).
   - enacting a New York City EITC and increasing the credit available to workers without children.
   - simplifying the tax code, including coordinating eligibility rules for the various credits and allowing families to file as part of the EZ form.
   - expanding funding for and availability of free tax filing assistance in low-income neighborhoods and in a variety of languages (e.g., by using public libraries and community-based organizations and coordinating with the IRS to train staff and volunteers).
   - partnering with accounting firms, trade associations, and/or colleges to recruit volunteer tax preparers and assign them to community-based sites.
   - replicating CFRC's successful Food Force model (in which a multi-lingual team of outreach workers with laptop computers fan out to community sites throughout the city to pre-screen potential Food Stamp recipients) to provide both EITC outreach and tax-filing assistance.

5

4. **Development of a full proposal for an EITC advocacy initiative, to begin in 2002,** and exploration of potential funding sources, including both government and private sources, as well as support through collaboration with other groups.

Proposed Project Length and Staffing

CFRC proposes to undertake a six-month planning period in order to develop an EITC advocacy campaign. Three primary staff will be involved in the planning effort: Kathy Goldman, CFRC's Executive Director; Amy Brown, Director of Program Planning; and a policy analyst, who will come on board in the second month of the grant and continue to work on the project after the planning period.

C. Evaluation

CFRC is requesting a grant to plan for the development of a significant organizing and advocacy initiative. As such, our assessment of the planning project's success will be based on our ability to:

- collect a solid foundation of research and information detailing the need for and opportunities presented by an EITC campaign.
- develop a clear and specific EITC agenda for the future.
- prepare a full proposal for conducting an EITC campaign, including committed and potential partners for related efforts.

6

Community Food Resource Center
EITC Campaign
November 2001 - April 2002

Personnel:

Executive Director (6 months @ 5% in kind)	$	
Director of Program Planning (6 months @ 20%)	$	XXXXX
Policy Analyst (4 months @ 100%)	$	XXXXX
Subtotal Salary	$	19,740
Fringe @ 25%	$	XXXXX
Administrative Overhead @ 20%	$	XXXXX
Subtotal Salary and Fringe	*$*	*29,610*

OTPS:

Rent/Utilities	$	3,208
Printing and Copying	$	200
Telephone	$	260
Travel	$	500
Office Supplies	$	250
Administrative OTPS Overhead	$	1,086
Subtotal OTPS	*$*	*5,504*
TOTAL	*$*	*35,114*

8

Letter of Inquiry

Many foundations prefer the first approach to be a letter of inquiry, rather than a full proposal. A few foundations will make funding decisions based solely on the letter of inquiry, though this practice is rare. Usually this letter is the first stage of a multiphase application process, sometimes involving subsequent conversations, submission of a full proposal or other forms of follow-up, and perhaps face-to-face meetings with the funder.

Grantseekers should view the letter of inquiry as a mini-version of the final proposal, since the details of the project—such as anticipated expenses, time frame, and other aspects—must be included in the letter, and therefore need to have been fully thought through. The letter of inquiry responds to the same "who, what, where, when, why, and how much" questions that a full proposal does, but in a much more abbreviated form.

A standard letter of inquiry is up to three pages in length, followed by a one-page budget. This shorter form allows grantmakers to make a preliminary assessment of the appropriateness and attractiveness of the project. With a few exceptions, this application format usually *is* a letter, beginning with a salutation and ending with a closing. For ease of review by the funder, these letters often include subheadings for the component sections.

The Esperanza Community Housing Corporation's letter of inquiry to the W.M. Keck Foundation requested $387,500 to help establish the Mercado La Paloma. This community revitalization effort in Los Angeles involved rehabilitation of an abandoned building to turn it into a neighborhood center.

The letter from the United Cerebral Palsy Association of Santa Clara/San Mateo Counties asked the Peninsula Community Foundation for $20,000 to help build a playground. The request was for part of the funds needed to construct a facility for disabled children and their families, and was a collaborative effort with several public and private agencies.

The Volunteer Legal Services Program of the Bar Association of San Francisco requested $5,000 from the Lisa and Douglas Goldman Fund for support toward the organization's work in assisting disabled children to qualify for Supplemental Security Income in the face of new government regulations.

The Westside Children's Center's letter to the W.M. Keck Foundation requested $500,000 for construction of the Early Learning Program of the Child Development Center. The organization sought to increase the number of low-income parents and children that it could serve in its neighborhood in west Los Angeles.

A Letter of Inquiry From
Esperanza Community Housing Corporation
Los Angeles, California

To
W.M. Keck Foundation
Los Angeles, California

Requested amount: $387,500; **Amount received:** Invited to submit full proposal and subsequently awarded $300,000

Funder's comments:

"It should be noted that we strongly encourage applicants to contact the foundation prior to submitting a letter of inquiry, and we often schedule a telephone or face-to-face consultation in advance of a formal submission. This is Phase I, the first step in our process.

"The foundation's Statement of Policy and Procedures asks for a narrative on letterhead, not to exceed three pages, signed by the applicant's chief executive, and a one-page budget. We also request a full, certified audit and copies of the organization's determination letters from the Internal Revenue Service and the California Franchise Tax Board stating that it is tax exempt. We indicate eight topics to be covered in the letter—the amount requested from the foundation; the institution's background; a project description; if a capital project, information on the permit status, the facility to be constructed, and programs to be offered; need statement; timetable for implementation; amount raised and fundraising plans; and justification for why this request is submitted to this foundation as opposed to other private or public funding sources. This is the first step in our process, and we look for strong organizations, substantiated need for the project, evidence of thorough planning, demonstrated capacity for implementation, impact, and justification for philanthropic support. A full proposal is required if the applicant is invited to Phase II. The review process also includes a site visit and input from experts. The foundation's board of directors is involved in both Phase I and Phase II decisions.

"This is the first request of its type received by the W.M. Keck Foundation, and it presented an interesting opportunity to build on previous foundation investments in the inner city. The letter of inquiry from the Esperanza Community Housing Corporation addressed all required components and used subheadings, making it easy to read. The organizational background section gave a clear description of the organization's accomplishments. The project description gave sufficient detail to describe the project, and identified specific organizations that had committed to lease space on the second floor.

"The need statement was compelling since it offered details about the characteristics of the neighborhood, providing a rationale for a community revitalization strategy. The timeline fit in with the foundation's grant cycle. The letter evidenced successful fundraising to date. The budget offered specifics about how our foundation's support would be used.

"The letter might have been improved by indicating that Esperanza had a long-term lease on the property with an option to buy and had the right of first refusal. (This was clarified in a follow-up call to the agency.) The need statement could have made a stronger case by citing data documenting the community's need for/likelihood of using the business, cultural, and service resources to be located at the Mercado."

Dorothy Fleisher, Program Director, W.M. Keck Foundation

Notes:

The complete proposal included the following attachments: audited financial statement, IRS tax-exempt letter, California Tax Board letter, five-year fundraising history, names of three expert references, and a list of board members.

Letter of inquiry written and submitted to the funder by Melanie Stephens, then Project Director and Economic Development Coordinator, and Sister Diane Donoghue, Executive Director.

Esperanza Community Housing Corporation
2337 South Figueroa Street · Los Angeles, California 90007

tel: (213) 748-7285
fax: (213) 748-9630
www.esperanzachc.org

May 15, 2000

Dr. Dorothy Fleisher and Ms. Anneli Klump
W.M. Keck Foundation
550 South Hope Street
Los Angeles, California 90071

Dear Dorothy and Anneli:

On behalf of Esperanza Community Housing Corporation, we are pleased to submit this letter of inquiry to the W.M. Keck Foundation for a **$387,500** grant to create 16,000 square feet of office, training and meeting space for health- and family-focused non-profit organizations in South Central Los Angeles.

Organizational Background: Founded in 1989, Esperanza Community Housing Corporation's mission is to achieve comprehensive and long-term community development in the Maple/Adams-Hoover/Adams neighborhood of South Central Los Angeles. Community residents of all ages and ethnicities are the foundation of Esperanza's grassroots work. Esperanza Community Housing seeks to create opportunities for residents' growth, security, participation, and recognition and ownership through developing and preserving affordable housing, creating opportunities for child care, ensuring quality education, promoting accessible health care, stimulating involvement in arts and culture, and pursuing economic development. Through partnerships with churches, schools, health agencies, block clubs and other community institutions, Esperanza helps to strengthen the social infrastructure of the neighborhood. In all of our actions, Esperanza strives always to build hope with the community.

Esperanza has an 11-year track record of multi-disciplinary work focused on creating a healthy neighborhood. Esperanza has completed the new construction and rehabilitation of 7 affordable housing developments, 2 child care centers, 2 community centers and a community park. We are under construction on two additional affordable housing projects, as well as the *Mercado La Paloma* described below. At our community facilities, Esperanza offers English as a Second Language classes; adult literacy classes; after-school and off-track tutoring for youth; painting, ceramics and crafts classes; and computer classes. Esperanza also created and runs the Community Health Promoters Program, which trains bilingual community residents to provide essential health education and access to health care for neighborhood residents. To carry out this work, Esperanza has raised over $ 15,000,000 in capital grants and long-term, low-interest financing to develop cultural/community centers, affordable housing, childcare centers and recreational facilities for our community.

The dedication and creativity of Esperanza's staff have been recognized by a wide variety of institutions; the following are a few examples. Esperanza's Executive Director has been awarded an Honorary Doctorate by Occidental College, the Alumni Award for Community Service by UCLA, and the Lifetime Achievement Award by the Southern California Association for Non-Profit Housing. Our Community Health Programs Director was invited to discuss Esperanza's community health promotion work with the National Coordinating Council on Juvenile Justice, chaired by Attorney General Janet Reno. Our Director of Community Development lectured about Esperanza's Mercado project at the 4th International Public Market Conference. Esperanza's Housing Director received the "Do Something Brick Award" through a national competition. The Getty Center requested our Arts Director's participation as lead trainer for a special joint project with the California Science Center to develop innovative methods of linking art and science instruction.

Project Description: The development of the landmark Mercado La Paloma project is an essential element in Esperanza's strategy to revitalize our neighborhood, bringing together new economic, health, social and cultural resources under one roof. Located at 37th Street and Grand Avenue (near Exposition Park and USC), the project involves the redevelopment of a vacant, deteriorated 34,000 square foot, two-story warehouse and adjacent 1/2-acre parking area into a premier neighborhood-gathering place. The ground floor public market will offer a supportive venue for emerging entrepreneurs, health educators, and artists to sell or share their homemade/handmade goods and services. The second floor will house local non-profit organizations dedicated to ensuring access to health and social services for low-income families.

Esperanza Community Housing serves a population of approximately 132,000 people, residing in our four square mile service area. Over the past decade, the population has grown 22%. Seventy percent of local residents are Latino; the remaining cultures represented are African American (21%), Asian (4%) and white (5%). Over 31% of residents in our community live in poverty, compared to the County average of 12.5%. An alarming 60% of children and youth under 18 live below the poverty line. The per capita income is only $5,836. Government assistance rates are extremely high with 48% of the population in our area receiving some form of public assistance (cash aid, food stamps, and/or Medicaid). Developed from ideas and needs presented by community residents, the *Mercado* helps to address the distress among families in the neighborhood by building on the assets of local community residents.

The ground floor public market will provide the following community benefits: 80 employment and business ownership opportunities for low-income residents; training for low-income entrepreneurs; assistance to help very small businesses buy and install essential equipment (commercial stoves & hoods, shelving...); support for local artists and artisans to display and sell their work; arts workshops and festivals; permanent murals and mosaics; health information and assistance in accessing health care for low-income families; nutrition and healthy cooking programs; a weekly farmers' market offering access to fresh produce; and festivals of all kinds (music, animation, folk art, dance, international books, plants...).

With the W.M. Keck Foundation's support, Esperanza seeks to create 16,000 square feet of office, training and meeting space for the following non-profit organizations, which have committed to locating on the second floor of the *Mercado*:

1. 1736 Family Crisis Center: provides comprehensive services for battered women and their children, as well as homeless and runaway youth.
2. The Children's Collective: provides educational and counseling services to at-risk children and their families.
3. Community Clinic Association of Los Angeles County: provides technical assistance, education and support to 37 member non-profit community clinics.
4. Health Care Consortium of Central Los Angeles: coordinates activities among hospitals, clinics and community-based organizations to improve health services and access for low-income residents.
5. Health Access: works with a coalition of more than 200 members to increase access to quality, affordable health care services.

By bringing a rich mix of direct service, technical assistance, education and advocacy organizations together under one roof, the proposed "W.M. Keck Non-Profit Floor" of the *Mercado* will offer a unique opportunity for groups to exchange ideas and information, share planning efforts and resources and stay in constant contact with neighborhood residents and other community-based organizations. These groups will also coordinate with the direct health education and access activities taking place in the permanent Health Promotion stall on the first floor of the *Mercado*.

The *Mercado* is designed to become the heart of the community, creating a focal point and central gathering place for residents. The *Mercado* will provide access to new resources, rebuild our community networks, stabilize the neighborhood, nurture community residents' creativity and reinforce positive social values. The *Mercado* will also begin to change attitudes of people who work, but do not live, in the neighborhood, providing them an inviting facility in which to experience the talents of the local community.

Evaluation: Esperanza, the participating non-profits and outside evaluators will conduct regular reviews and make modifications accordingly based on criteria including: benefits to community residents (accessibility, quality of services, outreach to families in need), extent and effects of inter-organizational communication, and the self-sufficiency of the *Mercado*'s operations. While the development of the *Mercado* project is complex, one principal measure of its success will be relatively straightforward to evaluate. Because of its very public nature, even a casual observer will have a fairly easy time determining if there is substantial activity in the *Mercado*, if the building is inviting and clean, and if the people who visit the *Mercado* are pleased with the goods, services and environment.

The *Mercado*'s on-site full-time manager will assist the micro-businesses to access all of the information and expertise they need to continuously improve their operations; monitor their progress (through observation of stall operations and analysis of direct financial data); and anticipate and help micro-businesses prevent or solve problems through one-on-one discussions and regular meetings. Esperanza has also engaged Mark Wall and Marion Kalb, experienced market developers currently working with Esperanza as consultants, to do short and long interviews with vendors and visitors. These interviews will provide them with the insight to make recommendations to Esperanza's staff and market management for improving the *Mercado* operations.

Esperanza has devised several mechanisms to gauge the extent to which the "W.M. Keck Non-Profit Floor" successfully enables groups to exchange ideas and information, share planning efforts and resources, and stay in constant contact with neighborhood residents and other community-based organizations. Esperanza's Director of Community Development will meet quarterly with representatives from the 5 non-profits to find out about: new partnerships or joint activities among the groups based at the *Mercado*; information or insights gleaned from other groups that have helped individual organizations plan or implement their activities more successfully; level and usefulness of interface with Health Promotion stall or other 1st floor activities or facilities; input from participants, clients, staff, Board members and visitors about the space; and level and significance of networking and planning activities facilitated by the conference room use.

Timetable for Implementation: The *Mercado* is currently under construction and is scheduled to open in August, 200. In order to facilitate the timely completion of this complex project with its many interdependent parts, Esperanza is proceeding utilizing a combination of grant funds and short-term loans while we continue our Mercado Campaign. Our goal is to complete the Mercado Campaign by March, 2001. Because of the nature of the project, there will be a number of opportunities to celebrate and dedicate various parts of the project. If the W.M. Keck Foundation were to fund the Non-Profit floor, a special celebration would be planned involving all the participating non-profit organizations, elected representatives and community residents to dedicate the floor.

Summary of Fundraising Plans: Through the Mercado Campaign, Esperanza has raised $3,677,155 for the Mercado to date. In order to complete the Mercado's funding and make the project fully self-sustaining after the first two years of operation, Esperanza needs to raise an additional $2,467,845. We currently have a large number of requests being considered, including a proposal to the Kresge Foundation for a Challenge Grant of $500,000, which will be decided in June.

Justification: We are requesting a $387,500 grant from the W.M. Keck Foundation because of this project's tremendous potential to weave together organizational and sectoral resources to create a larger, stronger, and more integrated safety net for poor children and their families living in South Central Los Angeles. We thank you for your consideration of our request and would welcome the opportunity to provide you with greater detail about this landmark new project.

Sincerely,

Sr. Diane Donoghue   Melanie Stephens
Executive Director   Director of Community Development

Mercado La Paloma -- Project Budget

Capital Expenses		
Acquisition	2,000,000	
Predevelopment Expenses		
Architecture & Engineering	170,000	
Environmental Assessment/Abatement	30,000	
Construction - Basic infrastructure	1,943,079	
Tenant improvements for vendor stalls (1)	375,000	
Tenant improvements for offices (2)	387,500	
Construction Contingency (3)	194,421	
SUBTOTAL		5,100,000
Project Development Expenses		
Consulting Services	45,000	
Holding Costs (4)	242,000	
Insurance	5,000	
Fire/Security Alarm	4,800	
Trash Disposal	1,050	
Utilities	14,500	
Title & Recording	1,250	
Project Management	120,000	
SUBTOTAL		433,600
Program Development Expenses		
Project Management	60,000	
Entrepreneur Outreach & Training	107,900	
Arts Projects	100,000	
Health Program Development	343,500	
SUBTOTAL		611,400
Total Uses	.	**6,145,000**

BUDGET NOTES

Tenant improvements for vendor stalls (1)
> *for vendors who have received training and passed the*
> *financial review, ECHC is offering 0% interest loans*
> *for tenant improvements, not to exceed $15,000 per business*
> Cost estimated at $15,000 x 25 businesses   375,000

Tenant improvements for offices (2)
> Cost estimated at $25/sq. ft x 15,500   387,500

Construction Contingency
> computer wiring/equipment, telephone box, security system,   194,421
> arts installations, landscaping

Holding Costs
> Rent on Mercado from June, 1999-March, 2001   242,000

United Cerebral Palsy Association of Santa Clara/ San Mateo Counties
Mountain View, California

To

Peninsula Community Foundation
San Mateo, California

Requested amount: $20,000; **Amount received:** $20,000

Funder's comments:

"United Cerebral Palsy's (UCP) letter of inquiry was clear and complete, containing all of the elements we request that grant applications include. I was able to learn a great deal about the proposed project, the need for the project, and community support for the project within the brief three-page format. After reading this letter of inquiry, I had a clear understanding of the many steps that UCP had taken to ensure that the project would be successful.

"The application was concise and yet specific in detailing the need for and the benefits of the proposed project. Each paragraph contained useful and relevant information that I could use to form a funding recommendation. I appreciated the attention to both the big picture—e.g., national statistics regarding playground injuries—and specific program facts—e.g., how UCP had engaged children, the local medical community, and other partners in putting the project together. The need statement was compelling on both a factual and emotional level. It painted a picture of the benefits of a successful project for children with physical disabilities, their siblings, parents, and the community at large.

"The budget was clear and well-presented, listing all of the other sources of support for the project, as well as the different categories of expenses. While not necessary, it would have been helpful to include a projection of the number of children who would benefit from the project, as one other way to describe the impact the project would have. The writing style struck a good balance of clarity, detail, and brevity."

Srija Srinivasan, Program Officer, Peninsula Community Foundation

Notes:
The letter of inquiry included the following attachments: project budget, playground design and list of items to be purchased, and IRS tax-exempt letter.
Letter of inquiry written and submitted to the funder by Jane A. Lefferdink, Executive Director.

Understanding Disabilities
Creating Opportunities

United Cerebral Palsy Association of
Santa Clara/San Mateo Counties, Inc.
480 San Antonio Road, Suite 215
Mountain View, CA 94040-1218
(408) 279-8987 (650) 917-6900
(650)878-8272 FAX (650)948-8503
WEB http://www.ucpscsm.org

December 15, 2000

Srija Srinivasan
Program Officer
Peninsula Community Foundation
1700 S. El Camino Real, Suite 300
San Mateo, CA 94402-3049

Dear Srija:

Thank you for talking with me about the accessible community
build playground which UCP, the San Mateo County
Department of Parks & Recreation, KABOOM and the
American Academy of Orthopaedic Surgeons plan to build
on February 27, 2001, come rain or shine. This is an exciting
project, one which will benefit all children age 2-12. It will be
built at San Mateo County's well utilized and highly visible
Coyote Point Park.

I will be out of the State for the holidays, but will be pleased
to talk with you on my return on January 2nd.

Best wishes for the Holidays and in the New Year!

Sincerely,

Jane A. Lefferdink
Executive Director

MOLLY KENNEDY
President

JEFF LEWIS
Vice-President of Program

SILVIA MARTINELLI
Vice-President of Finance

AUDREY HERMANSON
Secretary

GORDON GOTTSCHE
Treasurer

Directors:

DEBORAH DRANE
ERIN FASO
GINA HARRINGTON
HYLAND HEBERT, M.D.
JAMES KENEFICK
LARRY PETILLO, D.D.S.
JUDITH PIFER, MSW
JANE A. RICHARDS, FNP

JANE A. LEFFERDINK
Executive Director

LETTER OF INQUIRY

United Cerebral Palsy Association of San Mateo/Santa Clara Counties, Inc. (UCP),
Established in 1953 and 1956 respectively, is one of 130 affiliates of the National
Corporation. UCP is a not-for-profit public benefit corporation governed by a volunteer
Board of Directors comprised of Parents of Children with Disabilities, Adults with
Disabilities and Members of the General Public.

The Mission of UCP is: *To advance the independence, productivity and full citizenship
of people with cerebral palsy and those with other disabilities.*

UCP is asking the Community Foundation for support in the amount of $20,000 of the
$218,800 required to build an accessible Community Build Playground at San Mateo
County's Coyote Point Park. The Playground will be designed to serve children with
disabilities, their non-disabled siblings, cousins and friends aged 2-12 residing throughout
San Mateo County.

All children need to play in order to develop fully. They also need to play in safe
environments on a safe playground. According to the National Program for Playground
Safely, 1999, "every 2-1/2 minutes a child goes to an emergency room because of a
playground-related injury." Well designed playgrounds offer opportunities for healthy
physical, social and creative development. The playground we intend to build will be
state of the art in safety and accessibility. It will include ramps to access elevated play
areas and a new poured in place Fibar and rubberized surface which will also insure
wheelchair access to ground level play structures and activities. It will be fenced to
insure that children do not run into adjacent parking areas or "escape" from supervisors.

A playground safety audit was completed in February 2000 for the Parks Division of the
San Mateo County Department of Parks and Recreation by a certified Playground Safety
Inspector. That audit showed that many of the Parks' playgrounds required total
upgrading or removal to be compliant with new safety requirements. The Eucalyptus
Playground site, where the new playground will be built, was one of the sites identified
for either removal or total renovation. Funds to build a new playground were not
Budgeted.

UCP has formed a coalition with the San Mateo County Department of Parks &
Recreation, the American Academy of Orthopaedic Surgeons and KaBOOM a national
non-profit organization created to help design and develop safe and much needed
playgrounds across the Country.

UCP has held meetings on 3 separate occasions with parents of children with disabilities
and their children, both disabled and non-disabled, to receive their input on the design for
a new playground which would be accessible for all children. Input was also solicited
from occupational and physical therapists who work with children with disabilities. They
noted that a child with a disability gains significantly from play and will frequently gain
benefits beyond what can be done in therapy. An additional meeting co-sponsored by
The American Academy of Orthopaedic Surgeons, KaBoom, the County Department of
Parks and Recreation and UCP was held with 80 plus 4th and 5th grade students without
disabilities to receive their input on their ideal playground. They were asked to keep in
mind how individuals with disabilities could be included. Input from children at the near

Letter of Inquiry
UCP
Page 2

by San Mateo Boys and Girls Club was also received in the form of drawings of their ideal playground. The attached playground design and equipment list is a direct result of those conversations.

To our knowledge, no other playground in the San Mateo County area is as fully accessible as the one to be built at Coyote Point Park. The newest playground in the area is at Flood Park in Menlo Park. It is somewhat accessible and meets all safety requirements. However, it is not fully accessible.

Key personnel involved in this Project include those with experience working with individuals with disabilities. Those who have degrees in Recreation. Those with special certifications in playground safety. San Mateo County Council and members of the Board of Supervisors have also been involved in the process.

This Playground creates a win-win situation for all involved. 1) All children, those with disabilities and those without, between the ages of 2 and 12 will be able to play together in the same environment. 2) Children with physical limitations will be motivated to do beneficial developmental activities through play which is a greater motivational force than therapy. 3) Parents and extended families will benefit psychologically and emotionally by having a place where their children, those with and those without disabilities can play together in an integrated environment. 4) Children will play in a safer environment, thus fewer will sustain playground injuries.

The San Mateo County Department of Parks and recreation has committed the land, has removed the equipment on the site and has committed staff resources in excess of $25,000. UCP has committed staff time valued at $15,000. KaBOOM has committed $27,000 to the Project Budget in personnel and other resources. The American Academy of Orthopaedic Surgeons has committed $73,225 to the Project for equipment purchase as well as personnel valued at $10,000. An estimated 300 individuals will donate their time and skill to build the Playground on February 27th, 2001 ($36,000). The total Project cost, including removal of the old playground equipment and surface, pre-Build Work/Site Preparation, Playground equipment for about 23 play events, surfacing equipment and personnel is estimate to be $218,800. The Community Foundation is being asked to provide $20,000 or approximately 9% of the cost, not including the land value.

Thank you for your consideration of this request.

Sincerely,

Jane A. Lefferdink
Executive Director

PROJECT BUDGET
COYOTE POINT PARK PLAYGROUND

EXPENSES

PERSONNEL(including benefits)

American Academy of Orthopaedic Surgeons	$10,000
KaBOOM (Designer/ Coordinator/Consultants)	26,775
County Parks & Recreation Department (Includes Directors time, Harbor Master as County Project Coordinator, Park Rangers and other maintenance workers)	35,000
UCP (Coalition Lead staff)	15,000
Volunteers for Community Build Day (300 at $XXXXX hour x XXXXX hours per) (most are orthopedic surgeons)	36,000

TOTAL PERSONNEL   **$122,775**

PLAYGROUND PREPARATION/EQUIPMENT & BUILD

Pre-Build Work/Site Preparation	20,000
Playground Equipment & Tools	29,000
Beautification Projects (plants, mural, etc.)	2,000
Playground Signage (Rules, Thanks, Braille)	1,425
Surfacing Containment System	2,000
Surfacing (poured rubber)	30,000
Shipping	1,800
Fencing	4,000
Equipment for accessible Bathroom up grades	4,300
Food for 300 Volunteers on Build Day	1,500

TOTAL PLAYGROUND PREPARATION/EQUIPMENT   **$ 96,025**

TOTAL ALL EXPENSES   **$218,800**

INCOME

PERSONNEL (ALL PERSONNEL IS IN-KIND BY THE COALTION PARTNERS & VOLUNTEERS	**$122,775**
AMERICAN ACADEMY OF ORTHOPEDICA SURGEONS	73,225
SAN MATEO COUNTY PARKS & RECREATION DEPT	2,800

TOTAL INCOME   **$198,800**

INCOME OVER EXPENSES   **($ 20,000)**

REQUEST FROM PENINSULA COMMUNITY FOUNDATION   **$20,000**

A Letter of Inquiry From
Volunteer Legal Services Program of the Bar Association of San Francisco
San Francisco, California

To
Lisa and Douglas Goldman Fund
San Francisco, California

Requested amount: $5,000; **Amount received**: $5,000

Funder's comments:

"This letter of inquiry is concise, clear, and informative. It is well organized and free of jargon. Because it provides pertinent information about the organization and the project for which funding is needed, including background and budget, I was able to determine the project's appropriateness for possible funding without requesting additional materials. A well-written, concise letter of inquiry such as this one makes the funding process much more efficient for both grantors and grantees."

Nancy Kami, Executive Director, Lisa and Douglas Goldman Fund

Notes:

The letter of inquiry was accompanied by the project budget.

Letter of inquiry written and submitted to the funder by Wayne Salazar, then Institutional Gifts Director, on behalf of the Volunteer Legal Services Program.

THE BAR ASSOCIATION OF SAN FRANCISCO

VOLUNTEER LEGAL SERVICES PROGRAM

February 19, 1999

Ms. Nancy S. Kami, Executive Director
Lisa and Douglas Goldman Fund
One Daniel Burnham Court, Suite 330C
San Francisco, CA 94109-5460

Dear Ms. Kami:

I am writing to inquire about the suitability of submitting a full proposal to request a grant of $5,000 to support the Volunteer Legal Services Program's SSI for Children Project.

Supplemental Security Income helps families to afford special care for children with disabilities, but stringent new regulations make SSI harder to obtain. In many cases these benefits provide disabled children with access to health care and medical services which were previously unavailable to them. Parents of children with disabilities rely on SSI benefits to enable their children to grow up to be productive, employable adults.

With this proposal, the Volunteer Legal Services Program (VLSP) aims, through its SSI for Children Project, to increase the number of children with disabilities from low-income families who receive SSI benefits in San Francisco. VLSP is the largest and only fully comprehensive legal services program in San Francisco, available to help in virtually all areas of civil law. In 1998, VLSP volunteer attorneys, paralegals and social service professionals provided more than 110,000 hours of free legal and social services to nearly 30,000 individuals and families. These services address a wide array of issues, including eviction prevention, immigration documentation, domestic violence, public benefits advocacy, disability rights and job readiness. VLSP operates on an annual budget of $2.9 million, and is supported by the legal community, as well as government, foundation and corporate grants. The SSI for Children Project is budgeted at $63,019.

I would welcome the opportunity to submit a proposal that describes our work in more detail. Should you have any questions or concerns regarding this request, please contact me at 415-782-8974, or wsalazar@sfbar.org. Thank you in advance for your consideration.

Sincerely,

Wayne Salazar
Institutional Gifts Director

VOLUNTEER LEGAL SERVICES PROGRAM
465 California Street, Suite 1100
San Francisco, CA 94104-1826
(415) 982-1600 • TDD (415) 782-8985 • Facsimile (415) 477-2390

HOMELESS ADVOCACY PROJECT
995 Market Street, Suite 915
San Francisco, CA 94103
(415) 974-6541 • Facsimile (415) 512-7334

ws 2/10/99
VOLUNTEER LEGAL SERVICES PROGRAM
SSI FOR CHILDREN PROJECT BUDGET 1999

Personnel		**Committed Funds**	
Staff Attorney @ 50%		David & Lucille Packard Foundation	$14,500
Intake Worker @ 40%		Crescent Porter Hale Foundation	$1,600
Clerical Support @ 20%		Morris Stulsaft Foundation	$2,500
Fringe Benefits @ 25%		True North Foundation	$6,600
Total Personnel	**$45,800**	**Total Committed Funds**	**$25,200**

Nonpersonnel		**Pending Funds**	
Rent	$5,245	Dresdner RCM Global Investors	$10,000
Office Supplies and Expenses	$2,389	Macy's West	$5,000
Computer Maintenance & Supplies	$350	Lisa and Douglas Goldman Fund	$5,000
MIS Support	$551		
Postage	$1,076		
Printing & Copying	$1,377		
Telephone	$1,350		
Audit	$445		
Insurance	$817		
Volunteer Training	$807		
Clinics	$691		
Library and Resource Material	$173		
Litigation	$100		
Travel & Training	$730		
Public Relations	$77		
Temporary Help	$595		
Depreciation	$292		
Miscellaneous	$154		
Total Nonpersonnel	**$17,219**		

TOTAL PROJECT BUDGET   **$63,019**

A Letter of Inquiry From
Westside Children's Center
Culver City, California

To
W. M. Keck Foundation
Los Angeles, California

Requested amount: $500,000; **Amount received:** Invited to submit a full proposal and subsequently awarded $500,000

Funder's comments:

"It should be noted that we strongly encourage applicants to contact the foundation prior to submitting a letter of inquiry and we often schedule a telephone or face-to-face consultation in advance of a formal submission. This is Phase I, the first step in our process.

"The foundation's Statement of Policy and Procedures asks for a narrative on letterhead, not to exceed three pages, signed by the applicant's chief executive, and a one-page budget. We also request a full, certified audit and copies of the organization's determination letters from the Internal Revenue Service and the California Franchise Tax Board stating that it is tax exempt. We indicate eight topics to be covered in the letter—the amount requested from the foundation; the institution's background; a project description; if a capital project, information on the permit status, the facility to be constructed, and programs to be offered; need statement; timetable for implementation; amount raised and fundraising plans; and justification for why this request is submitted to this foundation as opposed to other private or public funding sources. This is the first step in our process, and we look for strong organizations, substantiated need for the project, evidence of thorough planning, demonstrated capacity for implementation, impact, and justification for philanthropic support. A full proposal is required if the applicant is invited to Phase II. The review process also includes a site visit and input from experts. The foundation's board of directors is involved in both Phase I and Phase II decisions.

"The letter of inquiry submitted by the Westside Children's Center used subheadings that mirrored our guidelines and addressed the required points to be covered. It contained a strong need statement—information on demand (number of families turned away); explanation of why current space is inadequate (too small for expansion; city requiring trailers to be replaced).

"The project description gave a relatively clear presentation of the new facility (square footage), population to be served (ages, characteristics, numbers), and a sense of the program (caregiver-to-child ratio; assessment of children for developmental delays and behavior problems; access to family support services). This agency has a track record of providing early childhood education and care, and the project is a good fit with the foundation's interests.

"The timeline provided in the letter demonstrated that the construction plan fit with the foundation's grant cycle. The letter clearly showed evidence of successful fundraising by citing dollars raised to date and public funding received. The attached budget gave us the appropriate level of detail for this stage of the process.

"The letter might have been improved by including a more detailed description of the program, including staff qualifications, and data, if available, on program impact."

Dorothy Fleisher, Program Director, W.M. Keck Foundation

Notes:
The complete proposal included the following attachments: audited financial statement, organization's brochure, IRS tax-exempt letter, California Franchise tax board letter, list of board members, three expert references, fundraising history, and curriculum vitæ of three key personnel.
Letter of inquiry written by Diane Netzel, Netzel & Associates; Gloria Waldinger, Board Secretary; and Linda Thieben, Director, Fund Development; submitted to the funder by Linda Thieben.

WESTSIDE CHILDREN'S CENTER

November 13, 2000

Dr. Dorothy Fleisher
Program Director
W.M. Keck Foundation
550 South Hope Street, Suite 2500
Los Angeles, CA 90071

Dear Dr. Fleisher:

Following our recent meeting regarding Westside Children's Center, I am pleased to submit this Phase I inquiry letter for the W.M. Keck Foundation's Early Learning Program. We are respectfully requesting $500,000 toward our $13.4 million capital project goal, which includes funds needed to build a new 18,600 square foot Child Development Center at our Lindblade Center in west Los Angeles, adjacent to Culver City and Mar Vista.

WCC's Background

Since 1987, Westside Children's Center (WCC) has been committed to providing an array of services to address the problems of families with younger children, living in poverty-stricken pockets of west Los Angeles County.

The Center was launched by Lezlie Johnson in the mid-80's to recruit caring families to foster drug-exposed babies that had nowhere to go. Today, WCC provides a continuum of integrated services tailored to the needs of low-income parents and their young children. In addition to foster care services, programs include: adoption services, subsidized day care, family support services such as counseling, health consultations and parent education, collaboration on community-wide health fairs, and referrals to other community agencies. WCC is accredited by the California Alliance of Child and Family Services.

For many children, the need for WCC services is immediate. The number of families with critical needs far exceeds WCC's existing resources and the Westside Children's Center has launched a major capital project to build a new Child Development Center and Community Services Building to enable us to expand urgently needed services.

Project Description

To address the need for a new Child Development Center and a Community Services Building, we will construct 32,000 square feet of carefully designed space at our Lindblade Street site in west Los Angeles.

We are grateful to our friends and supporters who contributed $1,554,000 toward our Phase Ia goal, enabling us to purchase the three-acre Lindblade site. The Phase Ib goal ($7,746,000) will allow us to replace the double-sized trailer that serves as our on-site child care unit. Phase II ($4,125,000) will enable us to replace our aging two-story community services building and the single trailer that provides office space, consulting and therapy rooms for our family support services.

Dr. Dorothy Fleisher
November 13, 2000
Page 2

Facility Being Constructed

The cornerstone of our capital project is construction of the new Child Development Center to better serve the area's low-income parents who are seeking to improve their economic position through education or employment. The complex will have a new infant center to serve babies three to 18 months, a toddler unit for children 18 months to three years, and a pre-school unit for children ages three to five. There will also be a child care reception area, a large community meeting space, and a kitchen for preparing nutritious meals. Each of our child development units will provide an age-appropriate curriculum, taught by caring teachers who are trained in early childhood education. The necessary permits have been obtained to enable construction to begin.

These thoughtfully-designed buildings will enable Westside Children's Center to provide subsidized day-care services for many more children, 100 in total, who are in need of a stimulating and nurturing environment. WCC's caregiver to child ratio will be maintained at a minimum of 1:4 for infants and toddlers and 1:7 for preschoolers.

Summary of Need

There are many families in crisis in the poverty-stricken pockets of the west Los Angeles area. Here, as in other urban settings, disintegration of extended family networks and neighborhoods has increasingly isolated parents and families. Violence between rival Venice and Mar Vista street gangs further divides the community and isolates residents. Many parents are being forced to return to work by welfare reform, yet, are unable to find affordable child care.

WCC is putting the 'care' back into child care. Our service population includes parenting adolescents, children exposed to domestic violence, children with serious emotional problems, and children with fetal alcohol and drug exposure. Eighty per cent of parents receiving WCC child care services are single parents and all enrolled families have incomes below 75 per cent of the state median income level. Eighty-three per cent are from ethnic minority backgrounds. Of the 400 children we current serve, 57 are cared for on-site at our Lindblade and Mar Vista locations. The remaining children are cared for in licensed, private, family child care homes. WCC's two center-based child development programs provide child care for children ages three to five years in a nurturing and stimulating environment. The licensed family child care homes accommodate children ages three months to seven years.

All of our caring staff are well trained in early childhood education. Because so many of our children come from troubled homes, each child is assessed for developmental delays and behavioral problems. We provide special play therapy, the opportunity to explore various kinds of play equipment, work puzzles, sort shapes and colors, and begin to read as they develop fine and gross motor skills, hand-eye coordination and cognitive abilities.

Currently, WCC must turn away more than 30 low-income families each month, or almost 400 each year—all of them in urgent need of affordable child care to enable them to improve their economic situation and reduce family stress. Additional space for on-site child development is desperately needed to keep pace with the growing demand. Construction is required because the trailers for our child care facility and family support staff have outlived their usefulness and we have already over-extended the time permitted by the City to replace them.

Dr. Dorothy Fleisher
November 13, 2000
Page 3

Timetable for Implementation

The fund raising and construction timelines have been developed in parallel to ensure that the funds will be secured in a timely way to support the building project. Construction is expected to begin this winter and to be completed by summer 2001.

The professional fund raising firm of NETZEL ASSOCIATES, INC. was hired on July 1, 2000 to provide counsel during Phase Ib and II of the capital project. We are currently completing the leadership gifts phase of our fund raising campaign to secure commitments from the board, senior staff and campaign leadership. The process of securing founders and major gifts will follow this phase and continue through summer 2002, at which point mail and community gifts will be solicited.

Fund Raising Plan Summary

A gift chart has been developed that indicates the target number of gifts at each gift level to accomplish the overall fund raising goal of $13,425,000. This Phase I and II goal includes the $1,425,000 (Phase Ia) already raised toward the purchase of the Lindblade site. The fund raising plan calls for 67 per cent ($9,000,000) to be from gifts of $100,000 or more (called 'Founders Gifts'), 29.7 percent ($3,980,000) to be from gifts $10,000 to $999,999 ('Major Gifts'), and the remaining 3.3 percent ($445,000) to be from mail and community gifts. As of September 15 2000, a total of 25.3 percent ($3,389,975) had been received or pledged. Leadership gifts, which may be of any gift size, currently comprise nine percent of the overall fund raising goal. . The City of Los Angeles has awarded WCC $900,000 Proposition K funds toward the Child Development Center.

Justification

WCC considers that the W.M. Keck Foundation's Early Learning Program is an excellent match for the organization. By building a new child care center on its west Los Angeles site, WCC will increase the community's access to therapeutic learning opportunities.

Summary

The capital project will enable WCC to secure 100 places for children aged three months through five years in the Child Development Center. *This high quality program will provide therapeutic learning opportunities and increase the social and cognitive abilities of the young participants.*

At this time, the Westside Children's Center is reaching out to its friends and community and asking for generous support of these plans. Pledges are payable over a period of up to five years. Many opportunities are available to recognize the names of major contributors.

Children grow up fast and cannot wait for services. The experiences that a child under three is having today will influence how that child will function from the preschool years all the way through adolescence into adulthood. Your help is critical. All children deserve to be protected and set upon a path to a positive future filled with hope and promise.

Thank you for your consideration of this request. If you have any questions, or require additional materials, please contact me or Linda Thieben, Director of Development.

Sincerely,

David Emenhiser, ED.D.
Chief Executive Officer

Westside Children's Center

Attachments

A. One-Page Project Budget

B. Three Expert References

C. Fund Raising History:
- Foundation & Corporation Five-Year History
- Five Largest Gifts in Past Five Years

D. Audited Financial Statements

E. 501(c)(3) Tax Determination Letter

F. California Franchise Tax Board Letter

G. Optional Background:
- Fact Sheet/Brochure
- Curriculum Vitae of One to Three Key Personnel

DRAFT as of 10/3/00

Westside Children's Center
Preliminary Capital Project Budget

		PHASE-Ia	PHASE-Ib	PHASE II		
		Land Acq. and Master Site Planning	Child Dev. Center 18,600 sq. ft.	Community Services Bldg. 13,400 sq. ft.	PROJECT TOTAL	NOTES
DIRECT PROJECT COSTS —						
1	Cost of Construction	$0	$2,703,000	$2,900,000	$5,603,000	Total project 32,000 sq. ft.
2	Site Preparation	82,932	398,000	0	480,932	
3	Fixtures, Furnishings & Equipment	0	210,000	295,000	505,000	
4	Landscaping, Fencing, Paving/Parking	0	0	115,000	115,000	Phase-Ib in line #1
5	Architect, Engineering, Permits, etc.	562,358	280,000	385,700	1,228,058	includes project management
6	Contingencies	0	260,000	204,300	464,300	
7	Escalation Factor	0	210,000	0	210,000	
8	SUB-TOTALS:	$645,290	$4,061,000	$3,900,000	$8,606,290	
INDIRECT PROJECT COSTS —						
9	Acquisition of Land	$1,087,000	$0	$0	$1,087,000	
10	Start-up Costs	0	450,000	0	450,000	2 yrs. Child Development Ctr.
11	Program Support (Represents only partial annual requirements)	0	1,100,000	0	1,100,000	3 yrs. Program Support
12	Development / Fund Raising Costs Materials, supplies, counsel, secretarial support	38,058	389,000	0	427,058	
13	Pledge-Construction Financing [NET]*	(216,348)	1,440,000	0	1,223,652	Credits from interest and investments on early pledge payments; PHASE II cost TBD
14	Contingencies	0	166,000	225,000	391,000	
15	Allowance for Pledge Shrinkage	0	140,000	0	140,000	
16	SUB-TOTALS:	$908,710	$3,685,000	$225,000	$4,818,710	
17	*Preliminary CAPITAL PROJECT GOAL:*	$1,554,000	$7,746,000	$4,125,000	$13,425,000	
18	PHASE-I:	$9,300,000				
19				PHASE-III:	$5,000,000	Endowment
20					$18,425,000	

NOTE: These projections should be used only as a guide in developing future project budgets.
Construction estimates by architect or builder are required to determine scope of project.
* Assumes Phase-Ib construction begins in September 2000

9

Cover Letter

First impressions are important. In the arena of proposal writing, the cover letter is one of the components that conveys a first impression. So it is vital to make sure that it portrays the organization, the project, and the people appropriately.

The cover letter is formatted as a standard business letter, and its contents do not vary very much. It lays out the basics of the appeal: the amount requested, abbreviated description of the project, brief background about the organization and its expertise, explanation of why this foundation is being approached, and reference to any prior contact between the grantseeker and the funder. It usually offers to answer questions or to meet with the funder.

Since the cover letter is typically one page in length, using succinct and clear language is essential. The amount of the request should be very apparent. You'll notice that most of the letters included here state the amount requested in the first paragraph.

The cover letter is usually signed by the nonprofit's chief executive officer or even the chairman of the board. This indicates the highest level of organizational support for the request.

Six of the eight cover letters included in this chapter also appear with the full proposals in their respective chapters elsewhere in the book.

The cover letter from Central Arizona Shelter Services, Inc. in Phoenix accompanied a full proposal to the Flinn Foundation that requested funds for staff salaries in order to provide dental services to the homeless. This was prepared by Maggie Martin, who was the Development Director.

CompuMentor in San Francisco used a cover letter to introduce its proposal to the Peninsula Community Foundation. In commentary on this proposal, the funder cited the excellent synopsis of the amount requested, impact, and project description in this cover letter.

Nashville Ballet in Nashville, Tennessee, provided a cover letter with its proposal to the Frist Foundation requesting funds to upgrade computer equipment. Since the proposal provided three options for possible support, the letter does not specify one single request amount.

Nashville CARES in Nashville, Tennessee, provided a cover letter with its proposal to the Gill Foundation. Its very succinct language lays out the broad outlines of the request, states the organization's mission, and refers the funder to its record of accomplishment in an efficient and effective manner.

New York Hall of Science in Queens, New York, prefaced its full proposal to the Altman Foundation with a cover letter introducing the Early Childhood Science Inititiative. The funder praised the effective brevity and specificity of the language of the letter.

NPower Michigan in Detroit initiated a full proposal to the Charles Stewart Mott Foundation with a cover letter requesting a leadership gift covering two years. The funder noted that vision, mission, and energy were all well articulated in this document.

The Rhode Island Youth Guidance Center in Pawtucket, Rhode Island, sent a cover letter with its full proposal to the William Bingham Foundation. The letter makes note of the proposal contents and in a compelling manner begins to build the case for funding.

The Virginia Museum of Fine Arts Foundation in Richmond, Virginia, provided a cover letter to accompany its endowment request to the Lettie Pate Evans Foundation. The letter makes reference to earlier contacts and prior funding, and it indicates precisely the nature and amount of the request.

A Cover Letter From
Central Arizona Shelter Services, Inc.

To
The Flinn Foundation

United Way
*A United Way
Partner Agency*

December 21, 2000

Ms. JoAnn Fazio
Grants Manager
The Flinn Foundation
1802 North Central Avenue
Phoenix, AZ 85004-1506

Dear Ms. Fazio:

Thank you for allowing Central Arizona Shelter Services (CASS) to submit this proposal to the Flinn Foundation. Our request is for $46,000 to support salaries and employee related expenses of the Valley's *only dental program for homeless people*. As Arizona's largest emergency homeless shelter, CASS is addressing the unmet needs of our clients by creating the **CASS Dental Clinic (CDC)**. CDC will vastly increase the accessibility of dental care for homeless individuals and families by providing an on-site dental clinic to serve at least 1,200 people yearly.

The **CASS Dental Clinic** not only improves access to health care, but also improves the quality of dental care that our clients may receive. Through CDC, all clients will receive emergency care to alleviate pain and infection. Case managers may refer selected clients for restorative treatment such as crowns, bridges, and dentures. The outcomes include better health and new smiles for improved self-esteem. Both conditions will contribute to more fruitful job searches.

CASS has served the Valley of the Sun since 1984. Our agency's reputation for innovative and effective programs for this vulnerable population is unmatched in our community. The Maricopa County Health Department and the Arizona State Department of Health Services endorse the **CASS Dental Clinic** and are contributing financially and in-kind to the program. The program has garnered enthusiastic community support from volunteer dentists, hygienists, and local businesses that pledge in-kind donations of service, equipment, and supplies. Funding from the Flinn Foundation will help CASS launch CDC to begin helping patients as soon as possible.

Thank you for considering our request. For further information or to arrange a site visit, please contact Kris Volcheck, DDS, at (602) 256-6945, ext. 3041.

Sincerely,

Mark Holleran
Chief Executive Officer
Enclosures

1209 WEST MADISON ▪ PHOENIX, ARIZONA 85007-9974 ▪ (602) 256-6945 ▪ FAX (602) 256-6401
Central Arizona Shelter Services, Inc. is a 501(c)(3) non-profit charitable organization.
For more information, visit us at www.cass-az.org

CASS. THE CAUSE THAT HAS AN EFFECT.

A Cover Letter From
CompuMentor

To
Peninsula Community Foundation

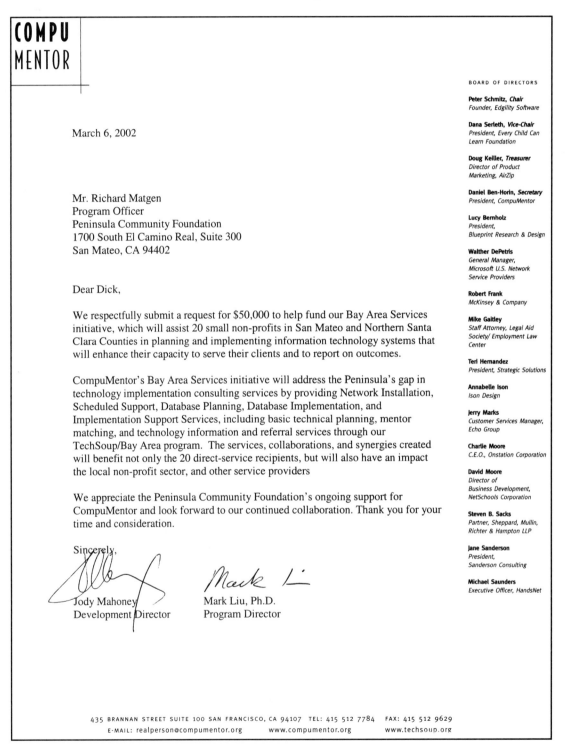

COMPU MENTOR

March 6, 2002

Mr. Richard Matgen
Program Officer
Peninsula Community Foundation
1700 South El Camino Real, Suite 300
San Mateo, CA 94402

Dear Dick,

We respectfully submit a request for $50,000 to help fund our Bay Area Services initiative, which will assist 20 small non-profits in San Mateo and Northern Santa Clara Counties in planning and implementing information technology systems that will enhance their capacity to serve their clients and to report on outcomes.

CompuMentor's Bay Area Services initiative will address the Peninsula's gap in technology implementation consulting services by providing Network Installation, Scheduled Support, Database Planning, Database Implementation, and Implementation Support Services, including basic technical planning, mentor matching, and technology information and referral services through our TechSoup/Bay Area program. The services, collaborations, and synergies created will benefit not only the 20 direct-service recipients, but will also have an impact the local non-profit sector, and other service providers

We appreciate the Peninsula Community Foundation's ongoing support for CompuMentor and look forward to our continued collaboration. Thank you for your time and consideration.

Sincerely,

Jody Mahoney
Development Director

Mark Liu, Ph.D.
Program Director

435 BRANNAN STREET SUITE 100 SAN FRANCISCO, CA 94107   TEL: 415 512 7784   FAX: 415 512 9629
E-MAIL: realperson@compumentor.org   www.compumentor.org   www.techsoup.org

A Cover Letter From
Nashville Ballet

To
The Frist Foundation

NashvilleBallet
Paul Vasterling ∎ Artistic Director

February 5, 2002

Ms. Lani Wilkeson
The Frist Foundation
3319 West End Avenue
Nashville, TN 37203

Dear Lani,

Thank you for taking time out of your busy schedule last Thursday to meet with us regarding Nashville Ballet's growing technology needs. It was a pleasure to finally meet you.

Please refer to the enclosed revised request that outlines our most pressing technology needs as well as our overall technology picture. As we have demonstrated, Nashville Ballet is in dire need of reliable computer equipment for the development office and community relations office. Several unsuccessful attempts have been made to add additional memory to these existing systems. New fundraising software and a data import facility have been donated by Nashville Ballet board members. Conversion was graciously donated as well. Unfortunately, the existing computer software cannot handle this large of a program. In addition, there is not a computer in the executive director's office. The computer in the community relations office is also inadequate for daily use. In addition, the Ballet's computers are not networked nor do they have the ability to add Internet access. Therefore, Nashville Ballet is seeking an emergency grant from the Frist Foundation to update our current technology that is no longer adequate for our growing needs.

We thank you for your kind consideration of this request. Nashville Ballet is indeed fortunate to have the continued support and friendship of the Frist Foundation. If you have any questions, feel free to call our development office at 297-2966, ext. 15.

Sincerely,

Paul Kaine
Executive Director

Robin Dillon
Director of Development

Eugene Lotochinski
Technology Committee

3630 redmon street ∎ nashville, tn 37209-4827
t.615.297.2966 f.615.297.9972
http://www.nashvilleballet.com

A Cover Letter From
Nashville CARES

To
Gill Foundation

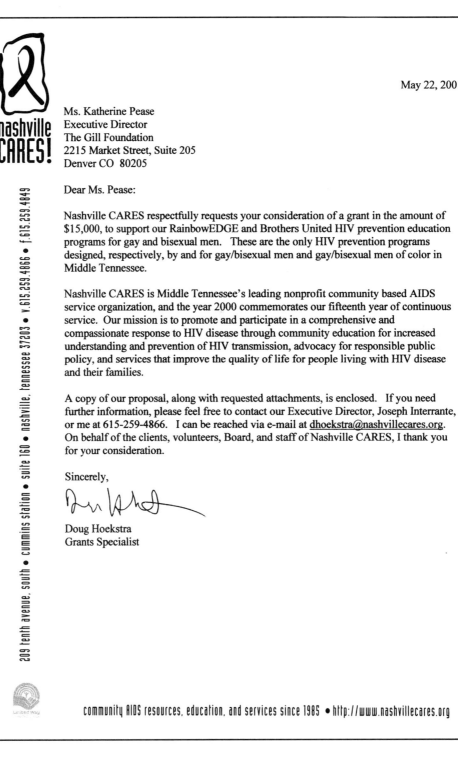

May 22, 2001

Ms. Katherine Pease
Executive Director
The Gill Foundation
2215 Market Street, Suite 205
Denver CO 80205

Dear Ms. Pease:

Nashville CARES respectfully requests your consideration of a grant in the amount of $15,000, to support our RainbowEDGE and Brothers United HIV prevention education programs for gay and bisexual men.   These are the only HIV prevention programs designed, respectively, by and for gay/bisexual men and gay/bisexual men of color in Middle Tennessee.

Nashville CARES is Middle Tennessee's leading nonprofit community based AIDS service organization, and the year 2000 commemorates our fifteenth year of continuous service. Our mission is to promote and participate in a comprehensive and compassionate response to HIV disease through community education for increased understanding and prevention of HIV transmission, advocacy for responsible public policy, and services that improve the quality of life for people living with HIV disease and their families.

A copy of our proposal, along with requested attachments, is enclosed. If you need further information, please feel free to contact our Executive Director, Joseph Interrante, or me at 615-259-4866. I can be reached via e-mail at dhoekstra@nashvillecares.org. On behalf of the clients, volunteers, Board, and staff of Nashville CARES, I thank you for your consideration.

Sincerely,

Doug Hoekstra
Grants Specialist

209 tenth avenue, south ● cummins station ● suite 160 ● nashville, tennessee 37203 ● v.615.259.4866 ● f.615.259.4849

community AIDS resources, education, and services since 1985 ● http://www.nashvillecares.org

A Cover Letter From
New York Hall of Science

To
Altman Foundation

Alan J. Friedman, Ph.D.
Director

3 January, 2002

Ms. Jane B. O'Connell
President
Altman Foundation
521 Fifth Avenue, 35th Floor
New York, NY 10017

Dear Ms. O'Connell:

On behalf of the Board of Trustees of the New York Hall of Science, we are writing to request a grant of $125,000 from the Altman Foundation. We are requesting support from the Altman Foundation toward the **Early Childhood Science Initiative**; specifically, we are requesting funding to prototype and test new programs for our youngest visitors, and to begin an exchange of expertise with the Brooklyn Children's Museum. Together, these will improve our ability to serve the fastest growing segment of our constituency, family audiences with young children.

The Hall is located in what the New York Times called the "epicenter of immigration" to the region and to the country. In our closest school district, District 24, over 100 languages are spoken in the students' homes. It is our mission to assure that *all* the young people, families, and teachers of this region have access to high-quality science learning experiences. Therefore we are working to engage culturally diverse communities with a wide range of educational backgrounds.

We are grateful for your consideration of this proposal, and for the initiative that your staff has taken to foster new collaborations. You and Nina will be glad to hear that the planning for this collaborative program has already led to joint activities between the Hall and the Brooklyn Children's Museum.

Have a wonderful new year, and please do feel free to call me (718) 699-0005 x 316 or Eric Siegel at x 317 if we can provide further information.

Sincerely,

Alan J. Friedman

New York Hall of Science 47-01 111th Street, Queens, NY 11368-2950 ✱ 718.699.0005 ✱ Fax 718.699.1341 ✱ www.nyscience.org

A Cover Letter From
NPower Michigan

To
Charles Stewart Mott Foundation

9 April 2002

Mr. Elan Garonzik
Charles Stewart Mott Foundation
Mott Foundation Building
503 S. Saginaw St., Suite 1200
Flint, MI 48502

Dear Mr. Garonzik:

Attached please find our proposal for a C.S. Mott Foundation grant, the purpose of which is to establish NPower Michigan's technology training and consulting services for Michigan nonprofits. We are asking the C.S. Mott Foundation to make a leadership gift of $160,000 each year for the first two years of NPower Michigan's operation, with plans to consider extending the support for an additional two years at the end of the initial granting period.

Your support during the planning stages of NPower Michigan demonstrates your awareness of the need for increasing the technology skills of the many people in the Michigan nonprofit community who work so very hard, but have so few resources. NPower Michigan is now poised to help these people stretch their organizations' resources by training them to use technology effectively and imaginatively. If agencies can streamline their paper work, automate their mailings or budget processes, set up interactive Web sites, or provide self-help opportunities for clients, they will be able to greatly expand their services without a significant expansion of personnel or other resources.

Many people in these agencies already know how they would like to use technology to achieve or extend their missions, but they lack the necessary skills and the funds needed to acquire the skills. Thus, the non-profit community tends to lag behind business and government in its use of technology. NPower Michigan can them help bridge that digital divide.

NPower Michigan's technology assistance is focused on and priced for non-profits. We envision a community of non-profits using technology with a resourcefulness and effectiveness equal (or superior) to the most technology-enabled businesses. That is the vision we are asking you to help us realize.

Thank you for considering our proposal. Please let me know if I can provide any further information that may assist you in your decision.

Yours truly,

Kathleen F. Teodoro,
Executive Director
NPower Michigan
Enclosure

A Cover Letter From
Rhode Island Youth Guidance Center

To
The William Bingham Foundation

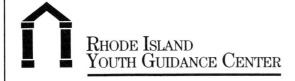

RHODE ISLAND
YOUTH GUIDANCE CENTER

A Gateway Healthcare Provider

82 Pond Street
Pawtucket, RI 02860
Telephone: (401) 725-0450
Facsimile: (401) 725-0452
TT/TTY Relay Service
(800) 745-5555

March 15, 2001

Laura H. Gilbertson, Director
The William Bingham Foundation
20325 Center Ridge Rd.   Suite 629
Rocky River, OH 44116

Dear Laura:

On behalf of the Board of Directors of the Rhode Island Youth Guidance Center and the staff of the agency's growing Mediation program, I am pleased to have the opportunity to submit the enclosed proposal for consideration by The William Bingham Foundation for a grant in the amount of $25,000. With this grant, Rhode Island Youth Guidance will be able to expand its current pilot venture in Family Mediation to serve more families in Rhode Island in the upcoming 2001-02 program year. The lessons which have been learned from our experience thus far shows us that mediation is a refreshing and productive alternative for parents and their adolescent children because it is rooted in the present, focused on the future, concrete, and user-friendly. Given the project's careful development during the past year by our excellent co-coordinators, Becky Minard and Kim White, the foundation has been laid for expanded activity as we take the project to scale in the Providence metro area, encompassing the cities of Providence, Pawtucket, and Central Falls.

In addition to the requested twelve copies of the proposal, budget, and program information, we include our IRS determination letter, FY2000 audited financial statements, FY2002 projected budget, agency strategic plan, and Board of Directors list. Please feel free to contact me at (401) 725-0450 ext. 127 with any questions you may have during the review process. Thank you for your time and consideration. I look forward to speaking with you in the near future.

Sincerely,

Robert F. Wooler
Executive Director

Enclosures

A UNITED WAY AGENCY

A Cover Letter From
Virginia Museum of Fine Arts Foundation

To
Lettie Pate Evans Foundation, Inc.

VIRGINIA MUSEUM OF FINE ARTS FOUNDATION

2800 GROVE AVENUE/RICHMOND, VIRGINIA 23221-2466/804-367-0805

August 30, 2000

Mr. Charles H. McTier
President
The Lettie Pate Evans Foundation, Inc.
50 Hurt Plaza, Suite 1200
Atlanta, GA 30303

Dear Pete,

You may remember that we spoke earlier about the possibility of the Lettie Pate Evans Foundation supporting the Virginia Museum of Fine Arts' capital campaign, which has yet to be publicly announced.

As a Director of the Virginia Museum of Fine Arts Foundation, I am writing with a special request. In December 1992, The Lettie Pate Evans Foundation gave a generous $500,000 gift to the museum for the purpose of creating the Evans Exhibition Fund. As of December 31, 1999, the market value of this fund had grown to $1,096,000. As we approach the eighth anniversary of the establishment of this endowment, I am writing to ask the Foundation to consider augmenting the corpus of the fund with a gift of $500,000.

Your gift would increase the value of the Evans endowment to $1.5 million. Moreover, in recognition of the immense support that the Evans Foundation has given the museum through the years, we propose to match that endowment. A match of $1.5 million, made from institutional reserves, would raise the value of the Evans Exhibition Fund to more than $3 million. At that level, the Fund would not only enable the museum to compete nationally and internationally for special loan exhibitions of the highest quality, but also to recognize the Evans Foundation on a regular basis as the generous sponsor.

We hope you will find this suggestion as appealing and exciting as we do. We have enclosed a 1993-1999 stewardship report of special exhibitions over seven years that have been made possible by the Evans Exhibition Fund. The report reflects the museum's original proposal to use the endowment to underwrite exhibitions of European, British, and American art, as well as Ancient Eastern and Western art, in deference to Mrs. Evans' personal taste.

We are also enclosing our campaign brochure, which presents an overview of the museum's future plans. If I can provide any further information, please do not hesitate to contact me. I look forward to hearing of the Foundation's decision. Thank you for considering our request.

Sincerely yours,

Herbert A. Claiborne, Jr.
Director, Virginia Museum of Fine Arts Foundation

10

Budget

The budget is a critical component of the overall proposal. Surprisingly, in our work with grantmakers over the years, we have learned that many of them turn first to the budget before delving into the narrative of the grant proposal. It often is an opportunity, therefore, to make a strong first impression. The budget presents the financial picture of what the organization intends to do during the grant period, enumerating with some degree of specificity what resources will be required. A complete understanding of the project is a necessary ingredient to preparing a good budget.

Like the proposal itself, there are standard elements that grantmakers expect to find in proposal budgets. And so, although each budget included here may look different, they all share common features. They are all for a set time frame. Most include detailed lists of expenses arranged in two categories: personnel and non-personnel. Some include support to be received or revenue to be earned, as well. As you will see by the examples in this chapter, there are a variety of ways to format a budget. Nonetheless, keeping it clear and simple for the proposal reviewer should be a primary objective of any budget design. Some funders have specific forms or formats to follow, and in that case, it is important to adhere to those specifications.

Some budgets, especially for multiphase projects or complex organizations, are enhanced by a brief accompanying budget narrative. This helps to explain any large or unusual items and also serves to respond to potential questions a grantmaker may have. Additional or explanatory information, if needed, can be added in the form of footnotes or in brief text at the end of the budget.

The budgets in this chapter represent grant requests ranging from $1,500 to more than $1,300,000. Three of them also appear with the complete proposals in their respective chapters.

The budget prepared by American Social History Productions in New York is for a one-year project request to the J. P. Morgan Chase Foundation. Personnel expenses are segregated and explained here in some detail. Note that this budget also includes an income section, which itemizes various sources of funding. The budget is part of a complete proposal that was prepared by consultant Caroline Harris.

The budget that accompanied a Bresee Foundation of Los Angeles letter of inquiry to the W.M. Keck Foundation includes four years of operating expenses and a separate section on program expansion costs.

The Phoenix-based Central Arizona Shelter Services, Inc. budget is for a multiple-year project. This was prepared by Maggie Martin, who was the Development Director. This budget includes a revenue section, with both funding and service fees. It incorporates in-kind revenue and expenses. This document also provides an example of budget footnotes with explanatory information, as does the following budget prepared by the Council on Library and Information Resources for the Digital Leadership Institute. The Digital Leadership Institute budget is also multiyear and includes a line for amounts contributed from other sources and a specific request to the grantmaker.

The budget for New Settlement Apartments project is for a two-year period, with a separate column specifically identifying what is requested of the New York Foundation. The budget is divided into several categories of direct expenses, including personnel, equipment, and other costs, and separately, indirect expenses. Some foundations will cover an organization's indirect or overhead costs on a project. If that is the case, it is appropriate to include these costs, usually based on a formula, often supplied or approved in advance by the funder.

The next budget, prepared by San Francisco Reclaim May Day for a proposal to the Agape Foundation, is quite simple since it is for a one-time event. Note that it includes both event expenses and income from the event. It was prepared by Jen Collins.

The last budget is a preliminary capital project budget sent with a letter of inquiry by Westside Children's Center. The notes indicate it is a guide for future budgeting, but it is included to demonstrate the multiphase structure of a very large project budget. The budget includes not only the construction contemplated but also an endowment component.

A Budget From
American Social History Productions, Inc.

To
J.P. Morgan Chase Foundation

PROJECT BUDGET SEPTEMBER 1, 2001 - AUGUST 31, 2002

EXPENSES

<u>Staff</u>

Co-Director of Education @ 15%		XXXXX
Historian and Multimedia Producer 10%		XXXXX
Program Coordinator @ 50% time		XXXXX
(Coordinate summer institute, follow-up workshops, and evaluations; maintain on-line forum.)		
	Subtotal	$30,750
Benefits @ 30%		$9,225
1 City University of New York Faculty Fellow 15%		XXXXX
2 Experienced Teachers/Seminar Leaders 15% each		XXXXX
	Subtotal Personnel	<u>$63,225</u>

<u>Summer Institute</u>

Stipend for 30 teachers (XXXXX days x $XXXXX/day		$11,250
Xeroxing of workshop materials and readings		$1,900
Catering/Coffee		$3,000
Professional lectures		$1,200
Curriculum resources (textbooks, videos)		$6,000
Postage		$400
Stationery and supplies		$450
Misc. for messengers, FedEx, etc.		$225
Local Transportation		$150
	Subtotal Summer Institute	<u>$24,575</u>

<u>4 Workshops</u>

Stipend for 30 teachers (XXXXX days x $XXXXX/day		$9,000
Xeroxing of workshop materials		$1,700
Catering/Refreshments		$2,400
Professional lectures		$600
Curriculum resources (teacher handbooks, CD-ROMs)		$4,500
Venue - security for Saturdays and computer lab tech (1 day)		$690
Postage		$300
	Subtotal Workshops	<u>$19,190</u>

<u>Evaluations</u>

Development of evaluations, mailings to participating teachers, school visits for case schools, data entry, assessment of data collected, report to funder		$5,800
	Subtotal Evaluations	<u>$5,800</u>
TOTAL PROGRAM COSTS		<u>**$112,790**</u>

INCOME

Government Agencies

NYC Board of Education	$14,000
City University of New York	$29,000

Private Foundations

Bodman Foundation	$20,000

Corporate Foundations:

JPMorgan Chase	$20,000
Joseph Seagram & Sons	$20,000
Citigroup	$10,000

TOTAL INCOME	<u>**$113,000**</u>

A Budget From
Bresee Foundation

To
W.M. Keck Foundation

BRESEE FOUNDATION PROJECTED EXPENSES

Youth Dev. Operating Costs	2000	2001	2002	2003
Salaries*	331,851	430,031	463,982	477,902
	10.5 FTE	13 FTE	14 FTE	14 FTE
Benefits and Taxes	71,395	94,585	106,577	115,819
Contract Labor	25,500	28,500	31,452	32,000
Drug and Alcohol Testing	840	1,350	1,500	1,600
Insurance (Vehicle and Liability)	9,552	9,839	10,134	10,438
Supplies	24,716	30,210	32,180	33,598
Telephone and Internet	9,334	18,500	19,000	20,357
Postage and Shipping	4,162	4,352	4,838	4,983
Building Maintenace, Utilities, etc.	42,590	43,590	43,590	44,000
Equipment and Maintenance	11,366	19,776	23,500	25,000
Printing and Publications	7,670	9,895	10,200	11,120
Travel	7,320	11,825	13,580	14,856
Youth Activities and Summer Camps	18,755	23,525	24,685	25,418
Meetings, Conferences, Staff Training	4,341	8,206	8,721	9,125
Fundraising Costs	15,185	17,669	18,375	19,584
TOTAL	584,577	751,853	812,314	845,800

Program Expansion Costs		2001	2002	2003
Salaries		98,180	132,131	146,051
		2.5 FTE	3.5 FTE	
Benefits and Taxes		23,190	35,183	44,424
Contract Labor		3,000	5,952	6,500
Drug and Alcohol Testing		510	660	760
Insurance (Vehicle and Liability)		287	582	886
Supplies		5,494	7,464	8,882
Telephone and Internet		9,166	9,666	11,023
Postage and Shipping		190	676	821
Building Maintenace, Utilities, etc.		1,000	1,000	1,410
Equipment and Maintenance		8,410	12,134	13,634
Printing and Publications		2,225	2,530	3,450
Travel		4,505	6,260	7,536
Youth Activities and Summer Camps		4,770	5,930	6,663
Meetings, Conferences, Staff Training		3,865	4,380	4,784
Fundraising Costs		2,484	3,190	4,399
TOTAL		167,276	227,738	261,223

Keck Foundation Request				
Salaries		50,000	50,000	30,000
Other Operating Expenses		25,000	25,000	20,000
Equipment - computers, pool tables, refrigerator, video projector, office furniture (desks, chairs, etc.), Youth Center furniture (couches, tables, chairs, cubicles)		75,000	0	0
TOTAL REQUEST		150,000	75,000	50,000

A Budget From
Central Arizona Shelter Services, Inc.

To
The Flinn Foundation

Central Arizona Shelter Services, Inc.
Dental Services
Proforma Budget

	Year 1	Year 2	Year 3	Year 4
Revenue				
PacifiCare Foundation - proposal	10,000	-	-	-
St. Luke's Health Initiatives - pledged	59,000	-	-	-
Maricopa County dental service fees	50,000	52,000	54,100	56,300
CASS support from general operating funds	-	20,000	35,000	50,000
Foundation/corporate support	85,200	137,200	125,100	113,300
	204,200	209,200	214,200	219,600
In-Kind Revenue				
Dental professional services (a)	76,500	76,500	76,500	76,500
Lab services - crowns, bridges, dentures (b)	63,000	63,000	63,000	63,000
Total Revenue	**343,700**	**348,700**	**353,700**	**359,100**
Expenses				
Administrator salary	XXXXX	XXXXX	XXXXX	XXXXX
Assistant salary	XXXXX	XXXXX	XXXXX	XXXXX
Employee related expenses	21,000	21,900	22,700	23,700
Lab services	63,000	63,000	63,000	63,000
Supplies	24,000	24,500	25,000	25,500
Dental unit rental (c)	1,200	1,200	1,200	1,200
Utilities	6,000	6,100	6,200	6,300
Insurance	4,000	4,100	4,200	4,300
Licenses and fees	1,000	1,000	1,000	1,000
	204,200	209,200	214,200	219,600
In-Kind Expenses				
Dental professional services (a)	76,500	76,500	76,500	76,500
Lab services - crowns, bridges, dentures (b)	63,000	63,000	63,000	63,000
Total Expenses	**343,700**	**348,700**	**353,700**	**359,100**

(a) *$51/hr. average for combined hygienists + dentists at 125 hours per month*

(b) *20 labs donating $500/mo.each x 12 months*

(c) All costs associated with maintenance of the dental unit are the reponsibility of the
Arizona State Department of Health Services (DHS). CASS will be assessed a nominal monthly rental
of $100 by DHA, although they have estimated the monthly fair market rental of the dental unit to be $2,500.

12/21/00

A Budget From
Council on Library and Information Resources

To
Robert W. Woodruff Foundation, Inc.

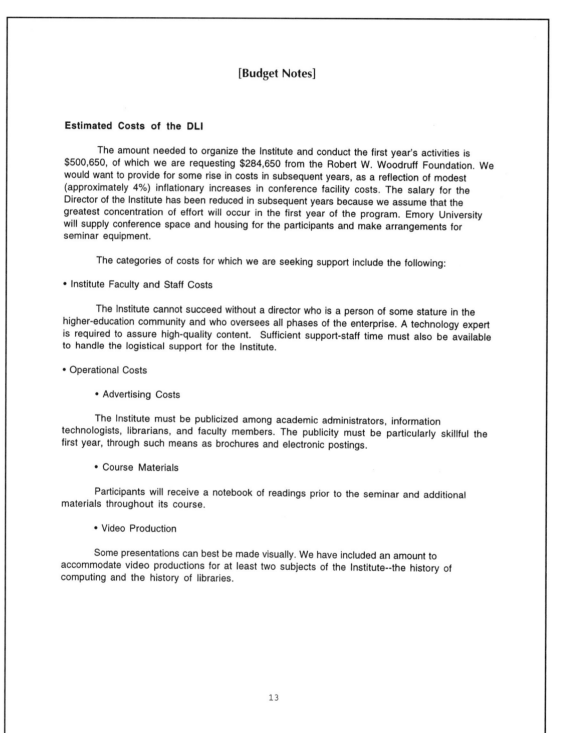

[Budget Notes]

Estimated Costs of the DLI

The amount needed to organize the Institute and conduct the first year's activities is $500,650, of which we are requesting $284,650 from the Robert W. Woodruff Foundation. We would want to provide for some rise in costs in subsequent years, as a reflection of modest (approximately 4%) inflationary increases in conference facility costs. The salary for the Director of the Institute has been reduced in subsequent years because we assume that the greatest concentration of effort will occur in the first year of the program. Emory University will supply conference space and housing for the participants and make arrangements for seminar equipment.

The categories of costs for which we are seeking support include the following:

• Institute Faculty and Staff Costs

The Institute cannot succeed without a director who is a person of some stature in the higher-education community and who oversees all phases of the enterprise. A technology expert is required to assure high-quality content. Sufficient support-staff time must also be available to handle the logistical support for the Institute.

• Operational Costs

    • Advertising Costs

The Institute must be publicized among academic administrators, information technologists, librarians, and faculty members. The publicity must be particularly skillful the first year, through such means as brochures and electronic postings.

    • Course Materials

Participants will receive a notebook of readings prior to the seminar and additional materials throughout its course.

    • Video Production

Some presentations can best be made visually. We have included an amount to accommodate video productions for at least two subjects of the Institute--the history of computing and the history of libraries.

13

Digital Leadership Institute
Five Year Budget

	Year 1	Year 2	Year 3	Year 4	Year 5	5-Year Total
Institute Faculty & Staff						
Director						
Salary	XXXXX	XXXXX	XXXXX	XXXXX	XXXXX	XXXXX
Benefits @ 25%	XXXXX	XXXXX	XXXXX	XXXXX	XXXXX	XXXXX
Support Staff						
Salary	XXXXX	XXXXX	XXXXX	XXXXX	XXXXX	XXXXX
Benefits @ 25%	XXXXX	XXXXX	XXXXX	XXXXX	XXXXX	XXXXX
Technology Consultant (XXXXX days @ XXXXX/day)	$25,000	$26,000	$27,040	$28,122	$29,246	$135,408
On-site Coordinators (2 @ XXXXX/day, XXXXX days)	$13,000	$13,520	$14,061	$14,623	$15,208	$70,412
Travel to Emory (2 @ $1,000)	$2,000	$2,080	$2,163	$2,250	$2,340	$10,833
Lodging and meals (2 @ $200/day, 13 days)	$5,200	$5,408	$5,624	$5,849	$6,083	$28,165
Faculty Presenters (XXXXX @ XXXXX/day)	$14,400	$14,976	$15,575	$16,198	$16,846	$77,995
Travel to Emory	$12,000	$12,480	$12,979	$13,498	$14,038	$64,996
Lodging and meals	$28,800	$29,952	$31,150	$32,396	$33,692	$155,990
*Participants						
Lodging and Meals (60 @ $200/day, 13 days)	$156,000	$162,240	$168,730	$175,479	$182,498	$844,946
Travel	$60,000	$62,400	$64,896	$67,492	$70,192	$324,979
Operational Costs						
Advertising	$10,000	$10,400	$10,816	$11,249	$11,699	$54,163
Course Materials ($300 x 60 participants)	$18,000	$18,720	$19,469	$20,248	$21,057	$97,494
Video Production	$10,000	$10,400	$10,816	$11,249	$11,699	$54,163
Telephone, Fax, and Network Charges	$5,000	$5,200	$5,408	$5,624	$5,849	$27,082
Contingency	$10,000	$10,000	$10,000	$10,000	$10,000	$50,000
Total	$500,650	$504,276	$508,547	$513,489	$531,628	$2,558,590
Amount Contributed by Other Sources	$216,000	$224,640	$233,626	$242,971	$252,689	$1,169,926
Amount Requested from the Woodruff Foundation	$284,650	$279,636	$274,921	$270,518	$278,939	$1,388,665

> It should be noted that the annual costs shown above are not the full amount of what will be invested in the institute. The practicum will involve substantial costs for the home institutions.
> CLIR will contribute additional support staff, as needed, as well as administrative space and equipment.

* Institutions will be expected to cover the costs of their participants' travel to and from Atlanta. Other funders will provide the necessary dollars for participant lodging and meals.

A Budget From
New Settlement Apartments

To
New York Foundation

New Settlement Apartments
Parent Action Committee Community Organizing Project
Projected Expense Budget/Calender Years 2000 and 2001
(Jan. 1, 2000 - Dec. 3, 2001)

	2000 Budget	2001 Budget	Request to New York Foundation for 2000
Personnel			
Two Community Organizers (100 %)			
Program Assoc. for Community Dvlpmnt. (33 %)			
Three Parent Organizers/Part Time (75%)			
Administrative Asst./Part Time (75%)			
Benefits			
Subtotal Personnel	$ 179,554	$ 184,942	$ 39,670
Other than Personnel Services			
Equipment & Supplies			
Office Equipment	$ 750	-	-
Simultaneous Translation Equipment	$ 900	-	-
Computers & Peripherals	$ 1,500	-	-
Portable P.A. Systems	$ 800	-	-
Subtotal Equipment	$ 3,950	0	0
Meetings & Conference			
Space Rental	$ 400	$ 400	-
Meals	$ 7,000	$ 9,500	$ 750
Travel	$ 1,600	$ 2,400	$ 600
Child Care	$ 6,600	$ 9,000	$ 1,000
Guest Trainers	$ 500	$ 500	-
Conference/Retreats	$ 3,500	$ 5,500	$ 715
Other Meeting Expenses	$ 400	$ 800	-
Subtotal Mtgs. & Conf.	$ 20,000	$ 28,100	$ 3,065
Publications, Printing & Duplication	$ 4,800	$ 6,200	-
Translation to Spanish	-	-	-
Monthly Newsletter			-
Meeting Agendas & training materials	-	-	-
Fliers and information materials	-	-	-
Subtotal Publications, Printing & Dup.	$ 4,800	6200	0
Other Supplies & Expenses			
Telephone & Internet Services	$ 1,250	$ 1,250	-
Postage and office supplies	$ 1,000	$ 1,400	-
Arts supplies for placards; film; etc.	$ 400	$ 600	-
Publications	$ 200	$ 200	-
Advertising	$ 450	$ 900	-
Miscellaneous expenses	$ 1,000	$ 1,000	-
Subtotal Other Supplies & Expenses	$ 4,300	$ 5,350	0
Total Direct Expenses	$ 212,604	$ 224,592	$ 42,735
Indirect Expenses	$ 36,143	$ 38,181	$ 7,265
Grand Total Expenses	$ 248,747	$ 262,773	$ 50,000

A Budget From
San Francisco Reclaim May Day

To
Agape Foundation

Expenses

Mayday 2001 Budget			
Expenses			
Operating			
Office Supplies		$	50.00
Merchandise: T-shirts		$	300.00
Phone		$	20.00
Photocopying		$	240.00
Postcards (Outreach)		$	500.00
Event Expenses			
Food		$	950.00
Truck Parking		$	100.00
Sound System Rental		$	500.00
Permit Fee		$	72.00
Paint/Markers (Grafitti Wall)		$	100.00
Puppet and Prop Supplies		$	200.00
Port-a-Potties		$	405.00
Nextel Rental		$	240.00
Garbage/Recycling		$	120.00
Transportation		$	100.00
Total Expenses		$	3,897.00

Income

Mayday 2001 Budget		
Income		
Contributed Income		
Rainbow Grocery Donation	$	950.00
Agape Foundation Grant	$	1,500.00
Festival Donations	$	647.00
In-Kind Donations	$	200.00
Vehicle Donations	$	100.00
Earned Income		
T-shirt sales	$	500.00
Total Income		$ 3,897.00

A Budget From
Westside Children's Center

To
W.M. Keck Foundation

Westside Children's Center
Preliminary Capital Project Budget

		PHASE-Ia	PHASE-Ib	PHASE II		
		Land Acq. and Master Site Planning	Child Dev. Center 18,600 sq. ft.	Community Services Bldg. 13,400 sq. ft.	PROJECT TOTAL	NOTES
DIRECT PROJECT COSTS —						
1	Cost of Construction	$0	$2,703,000	$2,900,000	$5,603,000	Total project 32,000 sq. ft.
2	Site Preparation	82,932	398,000	0	480,932	
3	Fixtures, Furnishings & Equipment	0	210,000	295,000	505,000	
4	Landscaping, Fencing, Paving/Parking	0	0	115,000	115,000	Phase-Ib in line #1
5	Architect, Engineering, Permits, etc.	562,358	280,000	385,700	1,228,058	includes project management
6	Contingencies	0	260,000	204,300	464,300	
7	Escalation Factor	0	210,000	0	210,000	
8	SUB-TOTALS:	$645,290	$4,061,000	$3,900,000	$8,606,290	
INDIRECT PROJECT COSTS —						
9	Acquisition of Land	$1,087,000	$0	$0	$1,087,000	
10	Start-up Costs	0	450,000	0	450,000	2 yrs. Child Development Ctr.
11	Program Support (Represents only partial annual requirements)	0	1,100,000	0	1,100,000	3 yrs. Program Support
12	Development / Fund Raising Costs Materials, supplies, counsel, secretarial support	38,058	389,000	0	427,058	
13	Pledge-Construction Financing [NET]*	(216,348)	1,440,000	0	1,223,652	Credits from interest and investments on early pledge payments; PHASE II cost TBD
14	Contingencies	0	166,000	225,000	391,000	
15	Allowance for Pledge Shrinkage	0	140,000	0	140,000	
16	SUB-TOTALS:	$908,710	$3,685,000	$225,000	$4,818,710	
17	*Preliminary CAPITAL PROJECT GOAL:*	$1,554,000	$7,746,000	$4,125,000	$13,425,000	
18		PHASE-I: $9,300,000				
19				PHASE-III:	$5,000,000	Endowment
20					$18,425,000	

NOTE: These projections should be used only as a guide in developing future project budgets.
Construction estimates by architect or builder are required to determine scope of project.
* Assumes Phase-Ib construction begins in September 2000

Appendix A

Glossary of Terms Related to Proposal Writing

Attachments: Documents appended to the proposal narrative that complete the proposal package. Most grantmakers will expect to find the IRS tax-exempt letter of determination, list of board members, brief staff profiles, current operating budget, and audited financial statements among the attachments.

Budget narrative: An optional section of a proposal's project budget used to explain unusual line items in the budget or to provide more detail.

Capital support: Funds provided for endowment purposes, buildings, construction, or equipment.

Challenge grant: A grant that is paid only if the donee organization is able to raise specified additional funds from other sources. Challenge grants are often used to stimulate giving from other donors.

Common Grant Application Form: A format adopted by groups of grantmakers to allow applicants to produce a single proposal for a specific community of funders, thereby ensuring consistency and thoroughness, and saving time.

Community foundation: An organization that makes grants for charitable purposes in a specific community or region. The funds available to a community foundation are usually derived from many donors and held in an endowment that is independently administered; income earned by the endowment is then used to make grants, some at the explicit instruction of the donor (alive or deceased) and some at the discretion of the community foundation's board. Most community foundations are 501(c)(3) public charities and are thus eligible for maximum tax-deductible contributions from the general public.

Company-sponsored foundation (also referred to as a corporate foundation): A private foundation whose assets are derived primarily from the contributions of a for-profit business. While a company-sponsored foundation may maintain close ties with its parent company, it is an independent organization, often with its own endowment, and as such is subject to the same rules and regulations as other private foundations. *See also* Private foundation.

Conclusion: The final section of a proposal narrative, summarizing the main points. Usually no more than two paragraphs in length, the conclusion offers the grantseeker a final opportunity to make the case for support, and to portray the benefits and the beneficiaries of the project.

Corporate giving program: A grantmaking program established and administered within a for-profit corporation. Because corporate giving programs do not have separate endowments, their annual grant totals generally are directly related to company profits. Corporate giving programs are not subject to the same reporting requirements as corporate foundations.

Cover letter: The first page in a proposal package. The letter is usually one page in length, and contains the funding request, reason for approaching the funder, reference to any previous contact, description of the application contents, a brief project description, and an offer to provide additional information. The letter is usually signed by the organization's chief operating officer.

Donee: The recipient of a grant. Also known as the grantee or the beneficiary.

Donor: An individual or organization that makes a grant or contribution to a (usually nonprofit) donee. Also known as the grantor.

Endowment: Funds intended to be invested in perpetuity to provide income for continued support of a nonprofit organization.

Evaluation plan: A proposal component that describes how the project's impact will be measured to determine how well its objectives have been achieved. This can be done by informal monitoring reports or by a formal plan to measure the product or analyze the process, depending on the nature of the project.

Executive summary: A proposal component that provides the abstract of a grantseeker's case for a project or organization and a summary of the key information in the proposal that follows.

Family foundation: An independent private foundation whose funds are derived from a member or members of a single family. Family members often serve as officers or board members of family foundations and have a significant role in grantmaking decisions.

Fiscal sponsorship: An individual grantseeker's affiliation with an existing nonprofit organization for the purpose of seeking, receiving, and administering grants. The fiscal sponsor may charge a small fee for this service.

501(c)(3): The section of the U.S. tax code that defines nonprofit, charitable, tax-exempt organizations; 501(c)(3) organizations are further defined as public charities, private operating foundations, and private non-operating foundations.

Form 990: The information return that public charities file annually with the Internal Revenue Service.

Form 990-PF: The information return that all private foundations are required by law to submit annually to the Internal Revenue Service, and that are part of the public record.

General/operating support: A grant for the day-to-day operating costs of an existing program or organization. Also called an unrestricted grant or basic support.

Grantmaker: A foundation, corporate giving program, or public charity that awards grants to nonprofit organizations and in some instances to individual grantseekers. Also known as funder.

Grantseeker: A nonprofit organization or individual seeking to obtain foundation, government, or other grant support for a project or programs.

Guidelines: Procedures set forth by a funder that grantseekers must follow when applying to that grantmaker for funding.

Independent foundation: A grantmaking organization usually classified by the IRS as a private foundation. Independent foundations may also be called family foundations, general purpose foundations, special purpose foundations, or private non-operating foundations. *See also* Private foundation.

Letter of inquiry/Letter of intent: A brief letter outlining an organization's activities and its request for funding that is sent to a prospective donor in order to determine whether it would be appropriate to submit a full grant proposal. Many grantmakers prefer to be contacted in this way before receiving a full proposal; some rely on this letter to make a decision instead of a full proposal. Also called a Letter proposal, and sometimes referred to as LOI.

Matching grant: A grant that is made to match funds provided by another donor.

Mission statement: A concise statement in which a nonprofit organization describes its identity, purpose, and the beneficiaries of its work.

Need statement: A proposal component that explains why the grantseeker's project is necessary by succinctly and persuasively describing the problem that exists. The need statement often includes relevant supporting data and statistics. Also called the Statement of Need.

Operating foundation: A 501(c)(3) organization classified by the IRS as a private foundation whose primary purpose is to conduct research, social welfare, or other programs determined by its governing body or establishment charter. An operating foundation may make grants, but the amount of grants awarded generally is small relative to the funds used for the foundation's own programs.

Operating support: *See* General/operating support.

Organization information: The section of a proposal that describes the mission, history and governing structure of the nonprofit grantseeker, its primary activities, audiences, and services.

Overhead: A proportion of ongoing expenses such as rent, utilities, certain administrative salaries, and other costs that some funders will support as part of a project budget.

Planning grant: Support for such efforts as goal-setting, information gathering, needs assessment, consensus or coalition building, or planning for a larger grant.

Private foundation: A nongovernmental, nonprofit organization with funds (usually from a single source, such as an individual, family, or corporation) and program managed by its own trustees or directors. Private foundations are established to maintain or aid social, educational, religious, or other charitable activities serving the common welfare, primarily through the making of grants.

Program officer: A staff member of a foundation who reviews grant proposals and processes applications for the board of trustees. Only a small percentage of foundations have program officers, or indeed any staff at all.

Project budget: The document created for a proposal that outlines the anticipated costs of personnel, non-personnel, and overhead expenses, as well as revenue.

Project description: The component of a proposal that provides details about the goals, objectives, and methods related to a proposed project. Typically this section also includes details about staffing and administration, a timeline, a description of project evaluation, and sustainability.

Proposal: A written application, accompanied by supporting documents, submitted to a foundation, corporate giving program, or government agency in requesting a grant. Most foundations and corporations do not use printed application forms but instead require written proposals; others prefer preliminary letters of inquiry prior to a formal proposal. Grantseekers should consult published guidelines.

Seed money: A grant or contribution used to start a new project or organization. Seed money grants may cover salaries and other operating expenses of a new project.

Tax-exempt: Refers to organizations that do not have to pay taxes, such as federal or state corporate tax or state sales tax. Individuals who make donations to such organizations may be able to deduct these contributions from their income tax.

Timetable or Timeline: A graphic representation of the sequence of steps needed to complete a project, sometimes included in the project description section of a grant proposal.

Trustee: A foundation board member or officer who helps make decisions about how grant monies are spent. Depending on whether the foundation has paid staff, trustees may take a more or less active role in running its affairs.

Appendix B

Selected Resources on
Proposal Development

by Sarah Collins

Anderson, Cynthia. *Write Grants, Get Money*. Worthington, OH: Linworth
Publishing, 2001.
    This is a proposal writing guidebook for school media specialists and other
    K-12 librarians who wish to improve library programs and facilities.
    Written for novice as well as veteran proposal writers, the book covers all
    stages of the grantwriting process. Appendix includes samples and a
    glossary.

Barbato, Joseph and Danielle S. Furlich. *Writing for a Good Cause: The Complete Guide to
Crafting Proposals and Other Persuasive Pieces for Nonprofits*. New York, NY: Simon &
Schuster, 2000.
    The authors share practical instructions about the art and craft of writing
    related to fundraising proposals, as well as case statements, newsletters,
    and other communications devices used by a typical development office.
    Includes glossary.

Barber, Daniel M. *Finding Funding: The Comprehensive Guide to Grant Writing*. 2nd ed.
Long Beach, CA: Bond Street Publishers, 2002.
    This handbook provides advice for writers of proposals to government
    agencies, foundations, and corporations. The book includes a section on
    responding to a request for proposal and also instructions for creating a
    letter proposal. Includes glossary.

Brewer, Ernest W., Charles M. Achilles, Jay R. Fuhriman, and Connie Hollingsworth. *Finding Funding: Grantwriting From Start to Finish, Including Project Management and Internet Use.* 4th ed. Thousand Oaks, CA: Corwin Press, 2001.

> The book is targeted to the education field and specifically to those submitting proposals to agencies of the federal government. Part 1 explores the research process and how to use the *Catalog of Federal Domestic Assistance* and other resources. Part 2 covers the elements of a standard proposal to a government agency or foundation, a sample proposal (funded by the U.S. Department of Education), and a discussion of how proposals are handled once received by funders. Part 3 relates to project management, explaining how to execute a project once it is funded.

Burke, Jim and Carol Ann Prater. *I'll Grant You That: A Step-by-Step Guide to Finding Funds, Designing Winning Projects, and Writing Powerful Grant Proposals.* Portsmouth, NH: Heinemann, 2000.

> The main part of the book is organized according to the sections of a proposal, and covers project planning as well as proposal development. Also explains how to write a letter of inquiry. Each chapter concludes with a checklist. The appendices contain a glossary and sample proposals.

Burke, Mary Ann. *Simplified Grantwriting.* Thousand Oaks, CA: Corwin Press, Inc., 2002.

> Directed primarily to schools and educators, the book offers templates and worksheets for planning programs, managing fund development work, and crafting proposals that succeed with grantmakers. With bibliographic references and an index.

Carlson, Mim. *Winning Grants Step by Step: The Complete Workbook for Planning, Developing and Writing Successful Proposals.* 2nd ed. San Francisco, CA: Jossey-Bass Publishers, 2002.

> This workbook contains instructions and exercises designed to help with proposal planning and writing, and to meet the requirements of both government agencies and private funders. Provides a special resource section that includes how to research funders, how to evaluate a proposal through the funder's eyes, and a bibliography.

Clarke, Cheryl A. *Storytelling for Grantseekers: The Guide to Creative Nonprofit Fundraising.* San Francisco, CA: Jossey-Bass Publishers, 2001.

> Clarke puts forward the notion that proposals share much with great stories: characters, setting, and plot. She shows proposal writers how to craft documents that include elements of drama. The book also covers the research process and cultivation. Includes a sample letter of inquiry and sample budgets, as well as information on packaging the proposal.

Geever, Jane C. *The Foundation Center's Guide to Proposal Writing.* 3rd ed. New York, NY: The Foundation Center, 2001.

> Geever guides the proposal writer from pre-proposal planning to post-grant follow up. The book incorporates excerpts from actual grant proposals and interviews with foundation and corporate grantmakers about what they look for in a proposal. Includes chapters on researching, contacting and cultivating potential funders, as well as a sample proposal and a selected bibliography on proposal development.

Geever, Jane C., Liliana Castro Trujillo (trans.), and Marco A. Mojica (trans.). *Guía para escribir propuestas* [in Spanish]. 3rd ed., New York, NY: The Foundation Center, 2003.

> Geever guides the proposal writer from pre-proposal planning to post-grant follow up. The book incorporates excerpts from actual grant proposals and interviews with foundation and corporate grantmakers about what they look for in a proposal. Includes chapters on researching, contacting and cultivating potential funders, as well as a sample proposal and a selected bibliography on proposal development. In Spanish.

Hall, Mary Stewart and Susan Howlett. *Getting Funded: The Complete Guide to Writing Grant Proposals.* 4th ed. Portland, OR: Portland State University, 2003.

> Hall explains the components of a standard proposal, with advice about project development and researching funders. This edition includes a recommended syllabus for those who teach proposal writing.

Knowles, Cynthia. *The First-Time Grantwriter's Guide to Success.* Thousand Oaks, CA: Corwin Press Inc., 2002.

> This toolkit covers the elements of the proposal package, writing style, budget development, and other aspects of completing the application for grants from government and private sources. Includes glossary and bibliographic resources.

Kosztolanyi, Istvan. *Proposal Writing.* Baltimore, MD: Johns Hopkins University Institute for Policy Studies, 1997.

> This short book outlines the standard elements of a grantseeking proposal and includes a handy checklist. The pamphlet was specifically developed for nonprofit managers in Central and Eastern Europe and is available in Bulgarian, Czech, English, Hungarian, Polish, Russian, Slovak, and Slovene languages.

Miller, Patrick W. *Grant Writing: Strategies for Developing Winning Proposals,* 2nd ed. Munster, IN: Patrick W. Miller and Associates, 2003.

> A manual for creating proposals to the federal government, specifically in response to requests for proposals (RFPs). Begins with the activities that

should precede the RFP and continues through post-submission efforts. Accompanied by numerous worksheets, charts, exercises, and exhibits. Provides suggestions for the narrative as well as the numerical aspects of the proposal. Includes glossary.

New, Cheryl Carter and James Aaron Quick. *How to Write a Grant Proposal*. Hoboken, NJ: John Wiley & Sons, 2003.

The authors include the key elements of standard proposal formats, including the executive summary, need statement, project description, evaluation, and budget. Each chapter contains examples and checklists.

Nugent, Carol and Tom Ezell. *The Grantwriter's Start-Up Kit: A Beginner's Guide to Grant Proposals*. San Francisco, CA: Jossey-Bass Publishers, 2000.

This 30-minute videotape discusses the basic elements of grant proposals and is accompanied by a workbook.

Orlich, Donald C. *Designing Successful Grant Proposals*. Alexandria, VA: Association for Supervision and Curriculum Development, 1996.

The author presents the standard elements of grant writing, with checklists at the end of each section. Includes a copy of a funded proposal and a reading list.

Quick, James Aaron and Cheryl Carter New. *Grant Seeker's Budget Toolkit*. Hoboken, NJ: John Wiley & Sons, 2001.

In this guidebook on project budgets, the authors explain the calculation of direct costs, with chapters specifically describing personnel and travel costs. Also discusses the estimation of overhead and indirect costs. Elaborates on the entire budgeting process, including writing the budget narrative. Sample budget worksheets are included.

Robinson, Andy. *Grassroots Grants: An Activist's Guide to Proposal Writing*. Berkeley, CA: Chardon Press, 1997.

The writer provides step-by-step guidance on how to create successful proposals, design projects, and manage grants. Four sample proposals are included.

Appendix C

About the Editor

Sarah Collins has been manager of bibliographic services for the Foundation Center since 1998. In this role, she creates and maintains the *Literature of the Nonprofit Sector Online* (lnps.fdncenter.org), the Center's unique database of print and electronic materials on the subject of philanthropy. She is also responsible for collection development, acquisitions, and original cataloging for the Center's five libraries.

Ms. Collins joined the Foundation Center in 1989 as director of its New York Library. During her tenure, she has been co-editor of *The Foundation Center's User-Friendly Guide: A Grantseeker's Guide to Resources*, revised edition, (1996), and author of the *Orientation to Grantseeking*, an online tutorial. Ms. Collins is the book review editor of *Philanthropy News Digest* and creates Topical Resource Lists on a variety of subjects for the Learning Lab at the Center's Web site.

Ms. Collins holds a Bachelor's Degree from Grinnell College and a Master's Degree in Library Service from Columbia University. Prior to joining the Center, she held administrative positions in special and public libraries.